BRITISH OPINION AND IRISH SELF-GOVERNMENT, 1865–1925

British opinion and Irish self-government, 1865–1925

From Unionism to Liberal Commonwealth

G.K. PEATLING

IRISH ACADEMIC PRESS
DUBLIN • PORTLAND, OR

First published in 2001 by
IRISH ACADEMIC PRESS
44, Northumberland Road, Dublin 4, Ireland
and in the United States of America by
IRISH ACADEMIC PRESS
c/o ISBS, 5824 NE Hassalo Street,
Portland, OR 97213-3644.

website: www.iap.ie

British Library Cataloguing in Publication Data
Peatling, Gary
British opinion and Irish self-government, 1865–1925, from unionism to liberal Commonwealth
1. Public opinion – Great Britain. 2. Ireland – Politics and government – 19th century – Public opinion. 3. Ireland – Politics and government – 20th century – Public opinion.
4. Ireland – Foreign public opinion, British
I. Title
320.9'415
ISBN 0-7165-2661-1

Library of Congress Cataloging-in-Publication Data
Peatling, Gary, 1970–
British opinion and Irish self-government, 1865–1925, from unionism to liberal commonwealth / Gary Peatling.
p. cm.
Includes bibliographical references and index.
ISBN 0-7165-2661-1
1. Ireland—Politics and governemnt—1837–1901. 2. Public opinion—Great Britain—History—19th century. 3. Public opinion—Great Britain—History—20th century.
4. Ireland—Politics and government—1901–1910. 5. Ireland—Politics and government—1910–1921. 6. Ireland—Foreign public opinion, British. 7. Home rule—Ireland. 8. Irish question. I. Title.

DA957.P53 2001
320.1'5'09415—dc21 00-058072

Typeset in 11.5 pt on 13.5 pt Dante by
Carrigboy Typesetting Services, County Cork
Printed by Creative Print and Design (Wales) Ebbw Vale

Contents

IMPERIALISM

List of Illustrations

The caption of the cover illustration reads as follows:

WELSH WIZARD 'I now proceed to cut this map into two parts and place them in the hat. After a suitable interval they will be found to have come together of their own accord – (aside) – at least let's hope so; I've never done this trick before.'

Abbreviations

AGGP	Alfred George Gardiner papers (British Library of Political and Economic Science, London School of Economics and Political Science)
AMP	Alfred, Lord Milner papers (Bodleian Library, Oxford)
CPSP	Charles Prestwich Scott papers (microfilm copies, Bodleian Library)
CR	The *Contemporary Review*
DH	The *Daily Herald*
DN	The *Daily News*
DNB	The *Dictionary of National Biography*
EPC	The English Positivist Committee
ESBP	Edward Spencer Beesly papers (University College London Library)
FHP	Frederic Harrison papers (British Library of Political and Economic Science)
FR	The *Fortnightly Review*
FSMP	Francis Sydney Marvin papers (Bodleian Library)
HLRO	House of Lords Record Office, London
HWNP	Henry Woodd Nevinson papers (Bodleian Library)
JKIP	John Kells Ingram papers (Public Record Office of Northern Ireland, Belfast)
LM	Lothian Muniments; the papers of the eleventh Marquess of Lothian (Philip Kerr) (National Archives of Scotland, Edinburgh)
LPS	The London Positivist Society
MG	The *Manchester Guardian*
MP	The *Morning Post*
NC	The *Nineteenth Century (and After)*
NR	The *National Review*
NS	The *New Statesman*

NYN	The *New York Nation*
PMG	The *Pall Mall Gazette*
PP	Positivist papers (British Library, London)
PR	The *Positivist Review*
QR	The *Quarterly Review*
RCP	Richard Congreve papers (Bodleian Library)
RO	*Revue Occidentale: Philosophique, Sociale et Politique*
RT	The *Round Table*
RTP	The Round Table papers of Lionel Curtis (Bodleian Library)
Scott diary	T. Wilson (ed.), *The political diaries of C.P. Scott, 1911–1928* (London, 1970)
SR	The *Sociological Review*
WASHP	William Albert Samuel Hewins papers (Sheffield University Library)
WG	The *Westminster Gazette*
WHLP	Walter Hume Long, Viscount Long of Wraxall papers (Wiltshire Record Office, Trowbridge)

Definitions

Conservative, Conservatism: of or pertaining to the British Conservative party.

conservative, conservatism: of or pertaining to the belief that the maintenance of established political and social institutions is a fundamental condition of a stable and successful society.

Imperialist, Imperialism: of or pertaining to the belief in the necessity of closer relations between the states of the British Empire (especially between the self-governing colonies and the United Kingdom) – see below, pp. 112–14.

imperialist, imperialism: of or pertaining to pride in or the necessity of the defence of an empire (the British Empire unless otherwise stated).

Liberal, Liberalism: of or pertaining to the British Liberal party.

liberal, liberalism: of or pertaining to the belief that individual political and social liberty is a fundamental condition of a stable and successful society.

Nationalist, Nationalism: of or pertaining to the Irish parliamentary or Nationalist party, (i.e., the party led by Charles Stewart Parnell from 1880–1890, by John Redmond from 1900–1918, and by John Dillon thereafter).

nationalist, nationalism: of or pertaining to the belief that national identity can be treated as a fundamental unit of social and political analysis, a belief which is usually associated with the assumption that such national units can be regarded as internally homogeneous and externally distinct, and with the belief that the assertion and retention of political sovereignty by a particular national entity is one of the most important political aims (see below, pp. 179–80).

Positivist, Positivism: of or pertaining to the philosophical, religious, social and political beliefs of Auguste Comte, and the avowed adherents of that system.

positivist, positivism: of or pertaining to the belief that the methods associated with the natural sciences (particularly inductive methods) can and should be extended to the study of human society. There is no necessary correlation between this and Positivism with a capital 'P' (see M. Pickering, *Auguste Comte: an intellectual biography*. Vol. 1 (Cambridge, 1993), pp.3–4, 694–8.).

Unionist, Unionism: of or pertaining to Unionist parties (i.e., parties favouring the retention of the Union between Britain and Ireland, or between Britain and Northern Ireland). Unless otherwise indicated, the terms when used here in the context of periods before (and including) 1921, will refer to Unionist parties in Britain *and* Ireland. When the terms are used here in the context of periods *after* 1921, they will refer to Unionist parties in Ulster.

unionist, unionism: of or pertaining to the belief that the Union between Britain and Ireland before (and including) 1921 should be maintained, or to the belief after 1921 that the Union between Britain and Northern Ireland should be maintained.

Acknowledgements

THIS BOOK IS BASED on a doctoral thesis completed at the University of Oxford in 1997 entitled 'British ideological movements and Irish politics, 1865–1925'. I am grateful to the British Academy for its financial assistance, without which the completion of that thesis would have been impossible.

The title of this book is influenced by the title of Deborah Lavin's excellent *From empire to international commonwealth: a biography of Lionel Curtis* (Oxford, 1995). Curtis was involved in the negotiation of the Anglo-Irish Treaty of 1921, and thus features prominently in the final stages of this book. The evolution of Curtis' thought about the British Empire/ Commonwealth, and the associated development of his ideas about Anglo-Irish relations, were not in detail representative of the evolution of British public opinion towards Irish self-government in the years 1865–1925. Nonetheless, Curtis was representative, I contend, in that throughout many vicissitudes, his interpretation of Anglo-Irish relations was consistently actuated by a fundamentally ideological view of Britain's role in the world and relations with other states. Deborah Lavin's work assisted me greatly in interpreting Curtis' thought and significance.

A small portion of the arguments and material in this book have previously appeared in three articles: 'The last defence of the Union? The Round Table and Ireland, 1910–1925' in *The Round Table, the British empire/ commonwealth and British foreign policy*, edited by Andrea Bosco and Alex May (London, 1997), pp. 283–303, published by the Lothian Foundation Press; 'Who fears to speak of politics? John Kells Ingram and hypothetical nationalism', *Irish Historical Studies*, xxxi (1998), 202–21; 'New Liberalism, J.L. Hammond and the Irish problem, 1897–1949', *Historical Research*, lxxiii (2000), 48–65. I would like to thank the editors and publishers of these journals and collections for agreeing to this small amount of overlap.

I would like to thank the staff and administrators of the following manuscript libraries, record offices and archive centres for their assistance: Birmingham University Library: The Bodleian Library (Oxford): The British

Library (London): The British Library of Political and Economic Science at the London School of Economics and Political Science: The Harry Ransome Humanities Research Center (the University of Texas at Austin): The House of Lords Record Office (London): Jesus College Library (Oxford): The National Archives of Scotland (Edinburgh): The National Library of Ireland (Dublin): The National Library of Scotland (Edinburgh): The Plunkett Foundation Library (Long Hanborough near Oxford): The Public Record Office of Northern Ireland (Belfast): Reading University Library: The Rhodes House Library (Oxford): The University of Sheffield Library: Trinity College Dublin Library: University College Dublin Library: University College London Library: The Wiltshire Record Office (Trowbridge). I would also like to thank the staff of the Bodleian Library, of the British Library, and of the British Newspaper Library at Colindale.

I owe, in fact, an unusual double debt to the librarians of Oxford University as a whole. Not only have they greatly assisted me with numerous complicated book, thesis and manuscript queries over the six years which this book has taken me to produce, but I fear that they had to cope with my being rather distracted in the fulfilment of my duties with Oxford University Libraries Automation Service during the period of this book's completion. I am also greatly indebted to Everard Robinson and colleagues for doing their best to make up for my resulting deficiencies.

I would like to thank the following in connection with the reproduction of copyrighted material: Mr. John Grigg (for his generosity in allowing me to quote from unpublished manuscripts written by Baron Altrincham, Sir Edward Grigg): Mr. Leo Amery (Leopold Amery, 1873–1955): Hon. David Astor (Lord and Lady Astor papers): Sir Edward Ford (Lord and Lady Astor papers and Robert, Baron Brand papers): Corbett Macadam (Lionel Curtis): Professor John Ledingham (James Louis Garvin): Professor Nicholas Hammond (John Lawrence Le Breton Hammond): Martin, King, French & Ingram, solicitors, Limavady, County Londonderry (John Kells Ingram): The Marquess of Lothian (Lord Lothian, Philip Kerr): Mrs. Penelope Massingham (Henry William Massingham): The Warden and Fellows of New College, Oxford (Alfred, Lord Milner): Mr. Alexander Murray (Gilbert Murray): Mr. Robin Farquhar-Oliver (Frederick Scott Oliver): Lord Dunsany (Sir Horace Plunkett): The Round Table (the Round Table papers of Lionel Curtis): The Scott Trust (C.P. Scott): The Earl of Selborne (Maud, Countess of Selborne papers): Christie, Viscountess Simon (Lord Simon papers). I would also like to thank the Bodleian Library, University of Oxford (for permission to quote from and access to the Baron Brand papers, Richard Congreve papers, Lionel Curtis papers,

Geoffrey Dawson papers, Herbert Fisher papers, Hammond papers, Gilbert Murray papers, Henry Woodd Nevinson papers, the Round Table papers of Lionel Curtis, John Satterfield Sandars papers, Countess Selborne papers, John, Viscount Simon papers, and Sir Alfred Zimmern papers): The Council of Trustees of the National Library of Ireland (George Fitz-Hardinge Berkeley papers): The Deputy Keeper of the Records, Public Record Office of Northern Ireland (Lord Carson of Duncairn papers, and John Kells Ingram papers): The Churchill Archives Centre, Churchill College, Cambridge (Chartwell trust papers): University College Dublin Library (Constantine Curran collection): The British Library of Political and Economic Science (Alfred George Gardiner papers, Frederic Harrison papers, and the London Positivist Society papers): The Harry Ransome Humanities Research Center, the University of Texas at Austin (James Louis Garvin papers): The House of Lords Record Office (David Lloyd George papers): The National Archives of Scotland (the Lothian Muniments): The Trustees of the National Library of Scotland (F.S. Oliver papers): The Plunkett Foundation (Sir Horace Plunkett papers). Quotations from the William Albert Samuel Hewins papers are reproduced by kind permission of the University Librarian, University of Sheffield. I would like to thank the Board of Trinity College Dublin for access to the Robert Erskine Childers and John Dillon papers, and to thank the copyright owners of those collections. Being unable to trace a living copyright owner for William Edward Hartpole Lecky, I would also like to thank the Board of Trinity College Dublin for raising no objection to my reproducing an extract from Lecky's unpublished writings. I have been unable to trace copyright owners for Edward Spencer Beesly, Richard Congreve, Leonard Trelawny Hobhouse, John Morley (Viscount Morley of Blackburn), H.W. Nevinson, Thomas Power O'Connor, or Shapland Hugh Swinny. I would like to thank Reading University Library for allowing me access to the Astor papers, the University of Birmingham Library for access to the Chamberlain papers, and the British Library for access to the Lord Northcliffe papers and to the Positivist papers.

Two illustrations, 'The perplexed elector' (by E.T. Reed) and 'The kindest cut of all' (by Sir Bernard Partridge), have been reproduced with permission of Punch Ltd. I would also like to thank the Bodleian Library, University of Oxford, for permission to reproduce the illustration 'The perplexed elector' and an illustration from the *Covenanter*, and Dr Patricia Kelvin for 'The perplexed elector'. I have been unable to trace the artist of the illustration from the *Covenanter*, nor a successor body to the publishers of that journal, Jordan-Gaskell Ltd. of London.

I would like to thank Dr. Paul Adelman, Dr. Geoff Bell, Professor Tom Dunne, Mrs. S.D. Ellins (for Dr. R.E. Ellins), Mr. Neill Hamilton, Dr. Michael Hart, Professor Tony Hepburn, Dr. Steve Inwood, Dr. Patricia Kelvin, Dr. Alex May, and Professor John Stubbs for generously allowing me to cite their unpublished dissertations.

I would like to acknowledge the comments, advice and assistance of the following, which materially assisted the completion of this book; the late Baron Amery of Lustleigh, Mr. Mark Barrington-Ward, Professor Andrea Bosco, Professor George Boyce, Professor Peter Clarke, Stefan Collini, Dr. John Davis, Mr. Robin Farquhar-Oliver, Mr. John Grigg, Dr. Jose Harris, Professor Christopher Harvie, Dr. Clive Holmes, Dr. Alvin Jackson, Professor Angela John, Dr. Roy Johnston, Professor Greta Jones, Deborah Lavin, Emmanuel Lazinier, Professor John Ledingham, Dr. Donal Lowry, Dr. Alex May, Dr. Ben Novick, Professor Margaret O'Callaghan, Mr. Michael Pollard, Dr. Benedikt Stuchtey, Mrs. Kate Targett of the Plunkett Foundation, and Dr. Nicholas Whyte.

I am grateful to the late Professor Colin Matthew and to Professor Theo Hoppen who were not only extremely sympathetic examiners of my D.Phil. thesis, but who also offered several useful suggestions which I have incorporated in this book. I am similarly grateful to the editors of this series for their many helpful suggestions. Unfortunately I am unable to thank by name the critics, who responded either to articles which I have submitted to academic journals over the years, or to papers I have presented to academic seminars. But their comments have also proved very useful.

I am particularly indebted to Professor Roy Foster, who supervised my thesis, and whose patience, wisdom and quiet encouragement have, I am sure, inspired whatever is of value in the following. Whatever is weak or remiss in this book, on the other hand, is entirely due to the failings of its author.

Miss Rosie Bagshaw and Mr. Phil Russell assisted me in many ways, not least in drawing my attention to the cartoon which forms the cover illustration for this book, and I would like to thank them. I would also like to thank Mr. Rodney Bagshaw.

Finally, I would like to acknowledge a debt of gratitude to my family and friends. Without the tolerance and sympathy of these individuals this book would never have appeared.

This book is dedicated to my grandmothers, Mrs. Lucy Peatling and Mrs. Queenie Wingate.

Ideology, Intellectuals and Ireland, 1865–1925

IN MODERN PARLANCE, 'ideology' is a word with sinister connotations. Both non-Marxist and Marxist philosophers have tended to agree that it is a cloak for vested interests and an obstruction to the true methods of science.[1] If such assumptions are applied to the analysis of politics, political conflict appears to be merely a competition for power between rival groups. Political ideology, which is generally defined as a system of belief avowing internal consistency and delineating political goals to be attained and methods of attaining them,[2] seems irrelevant to this political process. According to such assumptions, ideology is not an interesting subject of historical analysis which can only be concerned with uncovering the strategies used by competing interests.

For the historian of late nineteenth-century British politics, such assumptions suggest the paramount virtues of the study of 'high politics'. High and low politics, an influential pair of historians have argued, are 'simply not in close connection': 'the politicians' world of the time was a closed one'. The public 'understood very little of Westminster, and Westminster felt itself remote from the public. Explanations of Westminster should centre not on its being at the top of a coherently organised pyramid of power whose bottom layer was the people, but on its character as a highly specialised community, like the City or Whitehall, whose primary interest was inevitably its own very private institutional life'[3].

If political events are indeed dictated within a very narrow 'specialised community', it would appear that 'intelligentsia politics', publicists, journalists and low politics in general may safely be consigned to the political historian's wastepaper basket. Those who take a systematic ideological stance, the intellectuals, or 'chattering classes', are a sinister group who cloak personal ambition behind a pretentious and sanctimonious display.[4] They represent nobody, and their political activities merely threaten a pre-existing 'necessary moral cohesion'.[5]

Many nineteenth- and twentieth-century political crises have given rise to high political commentaries which at once describe and prescribe the nature of the political process.[6] But consideration of British attitudes to Irish politics in the nineteenth and twentieth centuries (and in particular, consideration of the first home rule crisis) seems especially to necessitate assessment of the role of ideology in politics.[7] The events of 1885–6 formed the subject matter of Cooke and Vincent's *The governing passion*, perhaps the archetypal expression of the view that it is both dangerous and naive to suggest that ideology is relevant to the political process. This 'high political' interpretation, as most commentators now realise, is deficient as an explanation of the role of ideology in British attitudes to Irish politics, but it remains a thought-provoking standard against which to develop more subtle heuristic concepts. Such an exercise can also suggest new lines of enquiry about the politics of Anglo-Irish relations.

Historians of 'high politics', it has been argued, adopt the naive assumption that politicians' behaviour is determined by a particularly narrow form of self-interested rationality. In *The governing passion*, politicians not only seek merely what is consistent with their personal self-interested ambitions, but they apparently only ever adopt the right strategy to obtain it. The hypothesis that Gladstone sought only the leadership of the Liberal party in taking up home rule in 1885–6 (or any alternative hypothesis) is, other historians have suggested, pure speculation, impossible to prove on the basis of the limited surviving records.[8] Ostensibly, it appears reductive and simplistic; the personal ambitions of politicians (which undoubtedly do exist) are not necessarily inimical to the existence of ideological dimensions in politics.[9] The assumption that rational group- or self-interest and ideological conviction can be analytically demarcated is naive. The motivation of historical individuals remains inscrutable, barely matter for the historian at all, but, in Louis MacNeice's phrase, 'matter for the analyst'.

More particularly, Cooke and Vincent's account is informed by the assumption that every aspect of Gladstone's behaviour during 1885–6 must have been logically consistent with some grand strategy. 'As Gladstone's conduct when forming his 1886 ministry showed', they argue, 'no one could hope to pass a home rule measure unless they could depict their ministry as representing the silent majority of the country and its conventional prudence'. Thus, 'Gladstone's sudden decision to revert to radical rhetoric after the Easter recess showed his immediate object by then was control of the party, and not a marathon constitutional contest'.[10] These authors find it difficult to grasp the idea that politicians might behave illogically, mistakenly or inconsistently in pursuit of their goal. This is a considerable weakness of their model of political behaviour, since psychologists agree that even highly educated people are prone to defective preferences for illogical strategies.[11] Not surprisingly therefore, many historians think it much more plausible to suggest that Gladstone did not solely have a narrow self-interested goal in 1886, but rather made some serious political mistakes.[12]

One of the reasons historians of high politics find the possibility of strategic errors by politicians so hard to grasp is their assumption that politicians had only to deal with an isolated political world, at Westminster, which was relatively easy to control. This also is debatable. The levels of the political pyramid often do seem remote and it is tempting indeed to assume that they are totally disconnected; but without some common thread of belief, that cooperative action which is the essence of collective political association would be impossible. In other words, political parties could not exist without some ideological links between high and low politics; modern political parties can only otherwise be explained in terms of mass false-consciousness, mass psychosis, or some form of crude economic materialism. It has been persuasively argued that there was an ideological consistency in Victorian Liberalism across time and space; Gladstone was certainly not felt to be 'remote from the public'.[13]

High political writers overlook the significance to the political process of the way in which every public political act is interpreted as possessing symbolic ideological importance. Cooke and Vincent, as Margaret O'Callaghan points out, tend to argue that

> Public language . . . is barren and meaningless, essentially a lie, and history, the search for 'truth', is concerned with what *really* happened behind the scenes. Not merely is that view philosophically naive, in that it posits a recoverable 'truth' behind a smokescreen, but it also involves a fundamental failure to recognise the salient and essential characteristic of the political: the degree to which its meaning is defined only when it becomes a public act through language. By definition the focus of such analysis is microscopic and necessarily static. Process or change cannot be accommodated by an analysis that is exclusively concerned with unravelling private motivations, one that considers 'real' politics to be over at the moment that its labyrinthine hinterland gives way to public language or public action . . . [in fact] Public political language is not

> a redeemable temporary expedient – it is an irrevocable political act that changes the nature of political reality.[14]

For Cooke, Vincent and Maurice Cowling' politicians are coolly in control of the symbolic political consequences of their actions, and intellectuals and journalists have almost no influence on political decision-making. Politicians are also 'paramount' in 'calling up' political belief.[15] For instance, Salisbury's speech of 15 May 1886, in which he presented Conservative policy for Ireland as 'twenty years' resolute government', is depicted in *The governing passion* as a clever move in the political game, designed to rally Liberals behind a home rule policy which was bound to fail.[16] Yet, what became most significant about this speech was the extent to which the political *and ideological* symbolism of its language committed Conservatives (at least) to a confrontational attitude to Nationalist politicians for over a generation. Cooke argues that this consequence was due to clever and misleading Nationalist propaganda (a rather tired claim which Unionists have often made when their aims have been frustrated in Ireland). Nevertheless, this misses the point that Salisbury's speech had served to limit the political options open to himself and his associates.[17]

Since public opinion is influenced by ideological values, almost any public action by a politician is effectively a form of ideological commitment – a fact which Cooke and Vincent do not deny, but bemoan. They argue that public opinion judges politicians by impossibly high standards which would make political and party life impossible; ideological consistency ought not to be expected from politicians.[18] Yet, this shows the problems historians run into when they confuse prescription and description of the political process. Instead of bemoaning the existence of these standards, the political historian needs to develop a hypothesis which enables him/her to interpret their significance.

It can also be argued that the conception of politics articulated by historians such as Cowling, Cooke and Vincent is anachronistic, grounded in late twentieth-century scepticism about 'boffins' and cynicism regarding 'Victorian values' and about the public spirit of politicians to an extent which is inappropriate for a historian of this period.[19] The argument that political life was conducted in a 'highly specialised community' in late nineteenth-century Britain can certainly be overstated.[20] Intellectual change influenced the shared 'fabric or texture of arguments, assumptions, values, ideas [and] associations' underlying political debate during this period; intellectual life affected the structures of politics.[21] That there were appreciable links between intellectual and political life was shown in 1886, when rival politicians competed keenly to find notes of approval for their policies in the writings of influential jurists and historians, such as the Irish historian W.E.H. Lecky (biographical notes on historical personalities who appear in the text several times [excepting the most well-known such personalities] may be found on pp. 289–98.).[22] In fact, one of Gladstone's first reactions to the defeat of his home rule policy in the general election of 1886 was to commission a series of writings offering an intellectual justification of the policy.[23] It is hard to see how such incidents can be explained with the rather naive assumption of a crude division between the worlds of politics and intellect suggested by some historians of the period.

Dichotomies between politics and intellect are not merely anachronistic, however, but would distort analysis of practically any historical period.[24] One would expect a politician of the kind high political writers depict to be contemptuous of intellectuals, and happy to leave the interpretation of history to the irrelevant, reclusive academic. This is far from being the case. In fact, 'history is often seen as far too important a matter to be left to historians'.[25] More broadly, politicians are aware that ideas are weapons which can be used politically.[26]

It appears then that a narrowly focused high political interpretation, when applied to the politics of Anglo-Irish relations, is most open to criticism on the grounds that it trivialises the ideological significance of the public aspects of politics, particularly of political rhetoric. The aim of political rhetoric has been defined by Michael Bentley as 'the cultivation of a satisfactory language in which enlightened pragmatism might find a home'.[27] In other words, the most successful politician is likely to be the one who most manages to avoid being committed to specific policies or ideas through his/her rhetoric. Bentley introduces the notion of 'doctrine', the 'formulaic, non-reflective' part of politics, to describe the limits on political pragmatism. Party doctrine influences both the way in which 'the political world' is conceived by the politician, and the way the words and actions of politicians are received by the electorate: 'Successful politicians are seen to be successful, not because they apply doctrine to their politics, but because they recognise that their politics will produce as a necessary consequence doctrine which will need to be controlled and manipulated'.[28]

Although Bentley's model of the political significance of ideology is considerably more sophisticated than that of writers such as Cooke and Vincent, the implication that this significance is limited to a 'predictable' consequence of political action which can be manipulated is not quite appropriate.[29] As O'Callaghan shows, political language is a public act from which the politician can retreat only with some difficulty. This is the case because the language of the politician is received at a multiplicity of levels and is thus subject to innumerable interpretations, reinterpretations and criticisms. Moreover, the interpreters are heavily influenced by ideological and moral values. Politicians who misjudge the ideological environment find themselves stigmatised for being inconsistent and/or for violating political taboos – as indeed, Gladstone was in 1885–6.

It is not only extremely difficult for politicians to avoid ideological commitment – it is questionable whether they actually wish to avoid it. A successful political party is one which *most* effectively deploys political symbols and rhetoric in order to associate itself exclusively with goals which are recognised to be desirable by as many people as possible. During the last hundred years, the British Conservative party has successfully employed strategies which have enabled it to appropriate symbols which have a patriotic significance at the expense of its competitors. Arguably, it was the political crisis of 1885–6 which allowed Conservatives to initiate this process.[30] The Conservative party has, in other words, profited from depicting itself and its opponents as ideologically committed in particular directions, and the effort by some of its sympathisers to deny the role of ideology in politics constitutes an effort to perpetuate this myth of a primal association between Conservatism and patriotism. The argument that ideology is a side-show in politics *is* an ideological position.

This analysis suggests that the political significance of ideology, particularly in relation to British interpretations of late nineteenth- and early twentieth-century Irish political developments, is threefold. First of all, ideology is a distorting glass through which politicians view the world. Secondly, it is a consequence of the actions and words of politicians which is hard to control and almost impossible to retract: moreover it is a consequence which skilful politicians, far from avoiding, will endeavour to deploy as broadly and consistently as possible. Thirdly, it is a factor which is inherent in the nature of political language, even apart from its reception. As Gareth Stedman Jones has maintained: 'We cannot . . . decode political language to reach a primal and material expression of interest since it is the discursive structure of political language which conceives and defines interest in the first place'. It is necessary 'to study the production of interest, identification, grievance and aspiration within political languages themselves. We need to map out these successive languages of radicalism, liberalism, socialism etc. both in relation to the political languages they replace and laterally in relation to rival political languages with which they are in conflict. Only then can we begin to assess their reasons for success or failure at specific points in time'. If one attempts 'to peer straight through these languages into the structural changes to which they may be notionally referred', one is likely to gain a distorted image of political and social developments.[31]

Political ideology is therefore worthy of study for its own sake, and particularly for its influence on politics through the popular opinion of the day, and through its effect on the language and assumptions of politicians and populace alike. Individuals and institutions which disseminated ideology are thus likely to form a useful context for the study of political change in a particular period.

In the early twentieth century, the political press was a substantial influence on the British population in a number of ways. Newspapers had a 'monopoly on the commodity of propaganda'. Newspapers were still political institutions. The commercial imperative in newspaper editing was coming to predominate over the political, but this transition was hardly complete by the first two decades of the twentieth century, the 'golden age of great editors', which 'owed its lustre . . . to the recognised status of its representatives as party or factional spokesmen'.[32] Although the 'new journalism' of the late nineteenth century gave a higher profile to sport and sensation at the expense of politics, many newspapers still had an avowed political identity. And editors such as J.A. Spender, C.P. Scott and J.L. Garvin were highly placed in the counsels of national political leaders. Newspaper editors were perceived as influential by many politicians and were courted accordingly. Politics and the press were intimately connected during this period.[33]

Of course, large claims cannot be made for newspapers' ability to persuade or cause dramatic political 'conversions' amongst readers, precisely because so many of them had a clear political identity. Newspapers were read as much because they 'confirmed existing prejudices and provided rationalisations for established loyalties' as for any other reason.[34] But this is not to suggest that newspapers had no political influence. Like almost any other political declaration or publication of the day, newspapers added to and shared in the corpus of political arguments which could be used in a favoured cause; people derived their language, including their political language, from newspapers.[35] It is not really important that there is only scanty evidence that the newspaper and periodical press faithfully represented the view of the British majority about Irish politics, since there is equally scanty evidence that political decision makers reflected that view, which only found sporadic (if any) expression during elections. What matters is that writers in the periodical and newspaper press expressed political opinions publicly, prominently, persistently and often coherently, outside of the political decision-making process. By definition therefore, such writers must be considered an important aspect of any study of British public opinion about Irish politics. And significantly, in the columns of newspapers and journals, particularly in their editorial columns, rival political ideas were expressed in an undiluted form before a mass audience: 'less inclined to compromise with practicality, publicists demanded fidelity to doctrine': 'Unlike politicians, who might retire into a guarded silence, newspapermen were required to address their publics at appointed intervals . . . There was no time for their passions to cool'. The press was alike an important vehicle of public opinion and of political ideology in the early twentieth century.[36]

Cooke and Vincent express a rather self-conscious worldly-wise scepticism about the nature of British politics which is particularly relevant to the subject of Anglo-Irish relations, which many adjudge to be 'infinitely depressing'.[37] Historians have tended to assume that British politicians' interest in Ireland was a purely Victorian (if not purely Gladstonian) phenomenon which quickly faded.[38] Political ideology is rarely regarded as having much relevance to contemporary British political debate on Northern Ireland, partly because (excluding a few fringe elements) British politicians regularly unite in support of major British policy initiatives in Northern Ireland,[39] and partly because as little thought as possible has historically been given in Britain to the politics of Northern Ireland. As Cooke and Vincent contend: '"English opinion about Ireland" was manufactured in England for home consumption, had nothing to do with Ireland, and everything to do with England'.[40]

This sense of despair is certainly exacerbated by the lack of systematic consideration which historians have given to the long-term acceptance in Britain of *separate* self-government in Ireland. This constituted, by any standard, a significant political development. In the 1860s and 1870s, any type of measure designed to satisfy the desire expressed by political representatives of nationalist Ireland (and by the majority of nationalist Ireland's political representatives between 1865 and 1921) for a legislature or parliament to represent and govern solely that country[41] was beyond consideration for all but the most radical and eccentric of educated Britons. Yet in December 1921, the concession of a large degree of self-government to twenty-six counties of Ireland was greeted with almost euphoric relief in Britain. This was a development which laid the foundations for the modern pattern of Anglo-Irish relations, and its significance for historical investigation of Anglo-Irish relations is hard to overstate. If such a large movement in 'British opinion about Ireland' was brought about only by the self-interested political calculations of individuals, and by weak and distracted responses to political violence in Ireland, all appeals in this period for understanding between the peoples of Britain and Ireland were either disguises for dark designs, or doomed to be totally ineffective. On such assumptions, while moral exhortation may have had some effect in counteracting the influence of military force and nationalistic prejudice, rational argument can have had very little. Probability alone therefore suggests that greater mutual amity would have been unlikely to develop (and presumably is still unlikely ever to develop) between the peoples of the Atlantic archipelago to any systematic or significant degree.

However, although historians have only schematically contested these 'depressing' assumptions, there does appear to be scope for a more nuanced interpretation. The high political model of Anglo-Irish relations is not theoretically satisfying.[42] It also seems to have been refuted by recent events. All recent British governments have, with some success, pursued the goal of better relations with the Irish Republic[43] – meanwhile, within the Irish Republic, political attitudes to Britain have changed significantly in the last generation, a change which it would be hard to contend had nothing to do with ideological factors.[44] Cynicism about Ireland, the wish that the island would just disappear, however prevalent in British politicians' private moments,[45] is hardly a fitting tone for their public statements. Historically, British politicians have frequently partaken of the practice of 'talking up the Irish problem' (i.e., displaying optimism about the possibility of a diminution of political violence in the country), rather as sitting governments are accustomed to 'talk up the economy'.[46] The generally up-beat initial responses in the British media to the Provisional IRA ceasefire of September 1994, and to the Good Friday Agreement of 10 April 1998, reveal the limits of attitudes of cynicism and indifference in Britain to Northern Irish politics. Neither John Major nor Tony Blair have said that it was their 'mission to pacify Ireland'; nonetheless, the Northern

Ireland policy of each is popularly perceived as among their greatest successes. It can thus be suggested that public debate in Britain about Irish politics has retained an ideological element. There were and are aims of British policy in Ireland which were and are perceived as desirable and attainable; thus ideologies, whether manifested in word, deed or symbol, were and are tested by their capacity in theory and practice to bring such goals nearer.

One would thus expect ideological movements to play a role in large changes in 'British opinion about Ireland' such as that between 1865 and 1925. A narrow focus on the reactions of individual politicians during short political crises may make for interesting speculation, but it runs the risk of obscuring the significance of ideological elements. British opinion, and changes therein, made a large contribution to the process which led to the creation of the Irish Free State.[47] This book will thus investigate ideological manifestations of this change in 'British opinion about Ireland'. This will involve an assessment of attitudes to Irish political developments in educated British circles throughout this period. It is divided into three parts, each of which focuses on a phase of change in British opinion towards the Irish national question, or on a group of political activists who played a significant role in the movement in British opinion towards Irish home rule.

The first part is an analysis from an unusual perspective of the assumptions and language of the discussion of Irish politics in Britain before, during and after the first home rule crisis. It focuses on the followers of the Positivism of Auguste Comte. The British Positivists were a small group who adopted a self-consciously peripheral posture to conventional politics, and who cannot be said to have exerted a significant influence on Anglo-Irish relations. Their importance in this context lies in the fact that they were the first articulate group of Britons after the famine to advocate the concession of self-government to Ireland. It cannot and will not be suggested that the Positivists initiated a process of mass national conversion to Irish self-government. However, a comparison between an ideology uniquely conducive in Britain to support of Irish home rule on the one hand, and the assumptions implicit in more mainstream ideological influences on British policy in Ireland on the other, does furnish valuable insights into the bases of British resistance to the idea of Irish self-government before 1885, and into those elements of belief important to Britons' ultimate acceptance of Irish self-government.

The second part of this book will deal with the new Liberals, particularly with new Liberal journalism, in the period 1910–22. Historians have usually suggested that the new Liberals were largely concerned with fashionable issues of social reform and were indifferent to Irish politics. However, it will be argued that the new Liberals have been convicted of indifference only because historians have concentrated on prominent 'new Liberal' Cabinet members such as Winston Churchill and David Lloyd George. New Liberalism, as an ideological movement of social reform and anti-imperialism expressed by intellectuals and journalists, was startlingly consistent in its support of Gladstonian home rule. In fact, this persistence led the radical press to criticise government policy in Ireland during the years 1919–21 – criticism which helped to bring about the Anglo-Irish truce of July 1921, and the Anglo-Irish Treaty five months later.

The final part will describe and explain the influence of Imperialism[48] on British policy in Ireland during the years 1910–25. A group of publicists, journalists and politicians, including the Round Table, James Louis Garvin and W.A.S. Hewins, are taken as being representative of early twentieth-century Imperialism. This part, unlike the previous two, will deal with men such as Lionel Curtis and Philip Kerr who, through official positions, had a direct influence on government policy in this period. But like the previous part, it will also deal extensively with the daily press in the early twentieth century. It will be shown that the ideological assumptions of the most liberal variants of this kind of Imperialism came to inform British policy in Ireland in the 1920s and, arguably, long after.

This book will conclude by assessing the relationship between these three movements and the wider environment of British interpretations of Irish politics. Continuities and discontinuities in the discourse and assumptions of educated British commentators on Ireland in the years 1865 to 1925 are assessed, and the role of Britons' self-image and of interpretations of Britain's role in the world are highlighted.

G.K. PEATLING
University of Wales Aberystwyth,
July 2000.

POSITIVISM AND THE FIRST TWO HOME RULE CRISES

CHAPTER ONE

'The Business of the Theorist'

BEFORE GLADSTONE'S conversion in 1885, the numbers of British home rulers are generally recognised to have been infinitesimal. As one historian has observed: 'In the 1870s even the sympathetic Bright and Bradlaugh had thought any kind of separatism too much to countenance'.[1] The most extreme and self-conscious exceptions were the small group of avowed adherents to the Positivism of Auguste Comte.[2] The Positivists, writes Royden Harrison, 'were always staunch friends of justice for Ireland and were the first influential body of Englishmen to concede that she had a right, not only to home rule, but to complete independence'.[3] The Positivists were peripheral to British politics, and it cannot be suggested that they played a material part in the growth of the acceptance of Irish self-government in Britain. Nonetheless, comparison between Comtean Positivism and more mainstream expressions of ideological influence on British political debate around the time of the first two home rule crises is highly instructive. Precisely because they were the first to accept the possibility of Irish self-government, the Positivists, interpreted in the context of their thought and action in nineteenth- and twentieth-century British society, shed light on how Britons first began to regard the suggestion as plausible. Even features of British Positivism in decline and obscurity can yield observations about the politics of the Irish question, and ultimately about the process by which the idea of Irish self-government achieved an unlikely predominance in Britain.

The Positivism of the French philosopher Auguste Comte (1798–1857) was one of the most audacious intellectual systems of the nineteenth century, a rival to the synthesis of Karl Marx in its breadth if not in its twentieth-century appeal. Comte attempted to delineate a law of intellectual and social development, advocate a new political system, and initiate the religion of the future. Comte anticipated the emergence of a global spiritual organisation in control of this religion of humanity, and he felt it essential that this body should not be endowed with temporal powers of government: the temporal and spiritual powers would finally be distinct in society.[4] Under the guidance of this global spiritual authority, Comte expected the nations politically to develop peacefully, harmoniously and interdependently. The later years of Comte's life were spent in anticipating the forms and rituals of the new religion in great detail.[5]

The response to Comte in Victorian Britain was a paradoxical one. Comte's projected religion of humanity was widely ridiculed and gained at most two hundred full adherents in the United Kingdom. The most important of these adherents included Richard Congreve, a Fellow of Wadham College, Oxford in the mid-nineteenth century, and three of his pupils, Frederic Harrison, Edward Spencer Beesly, and John Henry Bridges.[6] Yet Comte's philosophical method, his suggestive critique of orthodox religions, and his 'sociology' (a word Comte invented)[7] provoked widespread attention. Indeed most of the major personalities of Victorian culture felt it necessary to comment on Comte's system, whether for the purpose of refutation, assessment or proselytisation.[8] Frederic Harrison, the most prominent British Positivist, himself became a major cultural figure, an author of over fifty books, and a regular contributor to the Victorian periodical press.[9] Other British and Irish Positivists, while not quite so renowned, were also active on a variety of platforms. Comtean Positivism shared many of the anxieties, political and cultural, of the mid-Victorian intelligentsia,[10] and can be and has been used as a measuring stick of cultural, social, political and religious tendencies in Victorian Britain.[11]

'THE TRUE IDEAL'

Positivists were far from seeing their function as narrowly political. They were contemptuous of the institutions of contemporary British politics. Comte distrusted parliamentary government and told Positivists to avoid political and literary activity until public opinion was sufficiently educated in Positivist principles. In the interim, the preservation of order by conservative rulers would be in the interest of Positivists, providing the appropriate peaceful atmosphere for the propagation of a new religion. This heavily circumscribed what the Positivists could do as a vocation and by way of educating public opinion.[12] Ultimately several Positivists did stand for election at local or national level, while many Positivists contributed to periodicals and newspapers, and a *Positivist Review* was established in 1893. Positivists also tried to influence opinion through official declarations of principle, frequently articulated via the London Positivist Society (established by Congreve in 1867), on topical political matters.[13]

Positivists' two main theatres of political activity were labour and imperial questions. Regarding the former, Henry Crompton, Frederic Harrison and E.S. Beesly made important contributions to the reform of labour law in the years 1867–76, and were eloquent supporters of trades union rights.[14] Positivists believed that the social and political instincts of the working class were superior to those of other social classes, and associated with working-class movements on several political causes.[15]

But anti-imperialism was the more constant theme of Positivist activity. Indeed, the two issues were very closely connected in the Comtean system; international peace was supposedly in accordance with the interest and the social and moral ideals of the working class.[16] According to Comte, different countries were, in any case, freely developing to a harmonious and peaceful unity: 'the action of one nation upon another, whether by conquest or otherwise, though the most intense of all social forces, can effect merely such modifications as are in accordance with . . . existing tendencies'.[17] The era of conquest was a temporary phase, associated with the absence of international spiritual authority. With such an authority created, states could revert to their normal, small size: 'No combination of men can be more durable if it is not really voluntary'.[18] The presumption of Positivism was thus heavily in favour of permitting a subject people to work out their own 'natural course of development'; attempts forcibly to adjust this development could only produce friction and inefficiency in both societies.[19]

Positivists believed that politics should be subordinated to morality and adopted a passionate anti-imperialist rhetoric, arguing that imperialism was 'a deplorable, though no doubt temporary, reversion to bygone ideals and anti-social aims'.[20] They particularly feared the effects of imperialism on the politics and people of England.[21] Positivists supported extensions of international arbitration, 'a real step forward in the civilisation of humanity and towards an era of peace'. They wanted to see a cooperative system of relations, particularly between the countries of western Europe.[22] Their critique of imperialism was also associated with a relativistic defence of non-Christian cultures. Bridges contended that 'the theory of the intrinsic superiority of the Anglo-Saxon race and of Anglo-Saxon civilisation to all other civilisations and races must be uprooted and abandoned', and he criticised Britain's adoption of a 'forward' policy in

China.[23] Meanwhile, Sir Henry Cotton (a Positivist and briefly a Liberal MP) and Hugh Swinny had many Indian nationalist friends and were frequent critics of British policy in India. Swinny argued that 'the West, in the midst of its revolutionary transition, affords no model for the re-organisation of the East'.[24] As early as 1857, Congreve had rather ambitiously urged that Britain evacuate India as well as Gibraltar.[25]

As Christopher Kent has contended, such sentiments 'coincided with the widespread opposition to colonialism of the 1850s and 1860s' and constituted 'an aspect of Comtism which was quite palatable to English tastes'. Willing cooperators with the Positivists were not wanting among radical critics of the British Empire. In fact, in the 1860s Harrison and Beesly projected the formation of a broad anti-imperialist lobby including Richard Cobden and Goldwin Smith.[26] In denouncing British policy in Ireland, too, the Positivists were assisted by those on the radical fringe of liberalism; in 1867, when Positivists presented a petition to the House of Commons urging clemency for captured Fenians, John Bright and J.S. Mill supported them.[27] In 1866, Beesly rejected the plea of one fellow contributor to the *Commonwealth* for Irish national independence, calling instead for the Fenians to give up the 'hopeless path of secret conspiracy' and 'join with us in building up a freer and happier society for these islands where industry shall reign supreme and the blight of privilege be known no more'.[28] The concept of 'Irish self-government' was particularly problematic at this time – the Union, of course, in a sense, included self-government for Ireland (though not separate self-government) since Ireland was represented at Westminster,[29] and British observers therefore found it hard to think in terms of any alternative to the Union besides full independence for Ireland. Harrison and Beesly's wish for cooperation between British and Irish reformers in improving the British polity as a whole was thus common to many contemporary radicals.[30] Although in 1866 Harrison anticipated the *eventual* creation of an independent Irish state, he expressed the belief of many of his associates that 'at the moment the Irish question is not international but social'.[31]

However, Postivists' hostility to British rule in Ireland was inspired by an unusual dogmatism and passion. Late in 1867, when Bridges published a series of letters on Ireland in the *Bradford Review*, he thus adopted a far less fashionable position on the 'Irish question'. Bridges defended those who were awaiting execution for the Fenian Manchester 'outrage'; these were patriots, like Garibaldi and other continental revolutionaries, who acted for 'no selfish purpose'.[32] Bridges declared:

> The true policy for Ireland appears to me to be . . . union under the same executive authority, with separate and independent legislatures. Complete separation in the present inflamed state of parties in Ireland involves the immediate risk of civil war; agrarian war between landlord and tenant; religious war between Protestant and Catholic.[33]

Bridges argued that the same policy that had been adopted towards Canada would make the British Isles more united:

> It is fairly open to consideration whether the same remedy is not applicable here that we applied five-and-twenty years ago to our own disaffected colonies; disaffected then, but our most assured supporters now that they are knit to us by ties which, though politically slender, are woven of the far surer bonds of interest and friendship.[34]

As a Positivist, Bridges wished relations between nations to be harmonious and cooperative. He therefore had little sympathy with the argument that a self-governing Ireland might pose a strategic threat to Britain: 'It is Ireland discontented and rebellious, not Ireland self-governing and satisfied, that is ever likely to be dangerous to England. Ireland occupied by a hundred thousand French troops could hardly be more dangerous'.[35]

In his suggestion that Ireland be given a separate legislature and treated in a similar way to the colonies of the white empire, Bridges, even at this early stage, was describing a policy close to that which would ultimately be advocated by British and Irish supporters of home rule.[36] Harrison was at first sceptical, describing Bridges' sentiments as 'far too national', but in a paper (or self-styled 'sermon') read in 1868, Congreve echoed Bridges conclusions.[37] Congreve called for 'the reconstruction of Ireland, as a self-existent state'. He advocated the 'peaceful dismemberment' of the British Empire: 'It is a dream to think of incorporating Ireland with England'.[38] Like Bridges, Congreve did not hope or anticipate that a total separation of Ireland from England would result from the independence of the former; he hoped instead for a truer and closer 'union of hearts'. At this stage Congreve's views on Ireland were, in the words of one historian, 'as radical as could be', and in subsequent years Harrison and Beesly called for the creation of an independent Irish state in an equally unequivocal fashion.[39] It is these assumptions which underlay the Positivists' discussion of Irish politics for the next twenty years.

The origins of Positivists' support for an independent Ireland can be traced to Comte. Comte had argued that the aggregation of states into larger political units was not a normal tendency, but a historically specific phase. During the Reformation the decline of the Catholic Church had meant that larger states had been the only means of bonding peoples together. The establishment of a true universal Positivist church would not only make possible the emergence of a cooperative and interdependent system of relations between nations (firstly in 'the West' – France, Italy, Spain, England and Germany – and finally over the whole world),[40] but would also 'enable the gradual reduction of these huge and temporary agglomerations of men to that natural limit, where the State can exist without tyranny'.[41] Thus, the break-up of empires and 'peace in the West' would make possible the reversion of states to their optimum small size, wherein the individual was more likely to feel 'a real sense of the relations of citizenship'. Comte even expected that 'by the end of the nineteenth century, the French republic will of its own free will be divided into seventeen independent republics', and had no doubt as to 'the approaching separation of Ireland', and indeed, Scotland and Wales, from 'l'Angleterre proprement dite'.[42] Congreve agreed that the disintegration of larger states, 'oppressive and factitious unities called into existence to meet certain evils', was inevitable:

> In a state of the size of Ireland, or even in a much smaller one, such as Holland, all rightly directed energies might find a legitimate sphere, and by the co-operation of all its citizens the stable welfare of such a whole might be indefinitely promoted.[43]

Positivists' vision of a future of free and interdependent small nations was therefore fundamental to their relatively early support of home rule. The Union of Britain and Ireland not only resulted in the misgovernment of Ireland, but also hampered the progress of British society. Internationally, the Irish question weakened Britain's moral influence and her strength; it deprived her of the assistance of the Irish people and of the good opinion of the civilised world.[44] Congreve observed: 'The whole human family has become more organic, so that each part's suffering is more instantly felt by the other parts'; it was thus forlorn to hope that foreign condemnation of British rule in Ireland would cease.[45] As Bridges suggested, the assumption that Ireland had to be held down against her will was based on the erroneous tenet that antagonism was the normal state of relations between neighbouring countries, such as Britain and France.[46]

In domestic terms, Positivists believed the government of Ireland by Britain to be no less disastrous for the latter. As Congreve implied, home rule in Ireland would assist the efficient direction of 'energies' in England and home rule for Ireland also meant home rule for England.[47] The Positivists also regarded the organisation of the Irish peasantry for land reform to be exactly on a par with the efforts of trade unions to secure better working conditions for the British working classes. As Henry Crompton later explained, the Positivists had endeavoured in the 1860s and 1870s to 'secure complete legal independence for workmen and their legitimate combinations . . . to make them more respected and more conscious of their own work; to lift them to a higher moral level', and in the 1880s they tried to perform the same service for the Irish peasantry.[48] Positivists therefore believed that the coercive legislation enacted by British governments in the 1880s against the Irish Land and National Leagues was an immense social evil. Crompton warned the British working class that the Irish question materially affected themselves and their liberties; the type of coercion used in Ireland could equally be inflicted on British trade unions. The Land League was 'neither more nor less than a Trades Union'.[49] Beesly argued that the possession of Ireland by England only benefited the 'wealthy class',[50] and that the working class had 'no interest in refusing to the Irish people the fullest measure of Home Rule that they could get, and they had no interest in refusing them even complete independence'.[51] As Positivists generally followed what they perceived to be the political interest of the working class on the questions of the day, they aligned themselves more and more with Irish nationalist and agrarian movements. Late in 1881, Congreve could thus cite Crompton and Beesly as evidence of a determined British body of opinion desiring a 'deliberate and well-matured concession of full independence to Ireland',[52] and when the Irish national leader Charles Stewart Parnell was threatened with prosecution in 1880, Congreve offered a contribution to his defence fund.[53]

Of course, many contemporary British observers felt that coercive legislation in Ireland was necessary in view of the forms of political and social agitation utilised by Irish nationalists. Agrarian outrage and boycotting were hardening many hearts against any possible Irish parliament.[54] Many Britons suspected that intimidation rather than conviction underlay the growth of the movement for Irish home rule.[55] But British Positivists were far more concerned by the coercion of Irish nationalist opinion by British governments than by the coercion of landlords by Irish nationalists. In fact, because of the distinction they drew between spiritual and temporal factors, many Positivists felt there was a lot to be said in favour of the practice of boycotting. Comte valued freedom of opinion but he interpreted this freedom in a particular way. He felt that the legislative or forcible coercion of opinion by temporal government was a great evil, but expected that those who refused to cooperate in the final harmonious order would be subject to moral coercion, or a form of 'social excommunication'.[56] This was closely analogous to practices not only of the Roman Catholic Church, including the political practices of groups of Irish Catholics, but the picketing and strikes of English trade unions, and the boycotting of Irish agrarian movements. According to the Positivists, these were manifestations of public opinion or spiritual influences which were entitled to absolute freedom; interference in these by temporal governments was wrong.[57]

The British Positivists also regarded themselves as a spiritual influence and recalled that Comte had instructed them to leave temporal matters well alone for the time being. Beesly thus avowed no desire to usurp the function of the statesman:

> Let England . . . by all means continue to be governed by practical men. But it is essential to good government that these men should understand and recognise the true ideal. To ascertain *that* is the business of the theorist. It is for the practical statesman to apply the principles which theory has established; to decide the how, the when and the how far.[58]

In so far as theory had established principles such as the dissolution of the British Empire and the separation of Ireland from the United Kingdom, Positivists recognised that it was unlikely that these would be adopted for some time. In 1881, Beesly acknowledged that:

> the English people [are] not yet educated to the point of being willing to let Ireland go. And here, as elsewhere in Europe, it is desirable that the *status quo* should not be utterly disturbed . . . Especially is this desirable in Ireland, where theologism is so strong and sectarian animosity is bitter.

Beesly added however that 'those who think that Ireland will settle down into permanent acquiescence in the effacement of her nationality do but deceive themselves'.[59] Positivists saw nothing irresponsible or inconsistent in acting as pioneers of visionary political schemes, because they self-consciously adopted a curiously casual relationship to the practical politics of their day.

In the intervening period, while the 'practical statesman' determined 'the how, the when, and the how far' 'the approaching separation of Ireland' from England could be applied, Positivists were prepared to advocate some policies which seem in retrospect very different from self-government. They had no scruples about suggesting that parliamentary systems were unsuited to Ireland and called for dictatorial government of the country.[60] This was consistent with some authoritarian tendencies in Comte's philosophy and with his ultimate plans for the temporal organisation of humanity; he had anticipated the replacement of parliaments by authoritarian governments.[61] Bridges had suggested in 1868 that a strong (British) executive might be necessary in the early years of Irish self-government. He believed that 'few Irishmen would complain of an exercise of dictatorial power which placed in clearer light than ever their distinctness from England', if this 'dictatorial power' were 'wisely exercised' and 'avowedly temporary'.[62]

Although Positivists had already advocated Irish self-government and an improved 'understanding between the English and the Irish people' for twenty years, Gladstone's decision to attempt to effect a 'union of hearts' between the British and Irish peoples through home rule legislation was not necessarily assured of their blessing.[63] Indeed, Positivists' varied reactions to the first home rule crisis shed light on many disagreements within Positivism, as well as on many differences between the bases of Gladstonian Liberals' decisions to support Irish self-government and the inspirations of the Positivists. The British Positivist movement had split during 1877–8 as a result of a complicated series of disputes arising from questions of strategy, personality, temperament and belief among the leaders of the Positivist movements in Britain and France. As a result of the schism, those Positivists who continued to associate with Richard Congreve (including the Crompton brothers Henry and Albert) retained control of the movement's British headquarters in Chapel Street, London. However, they lost more than half of the Positivist Society, including many of its most prominent members, such as Harrison, Beesly and Bridges. The remaining majority of Positivists set up their base in Newton Hall in Fetter Lane, London.[64]

One of the most important differences between the two groups of Positivists was their interpretations of Comte's instruction to avoid direct involvement in the politics and journalism of their day. Henry Hutton, an Irish sympathiser with Congreve, argued that Harrison and his supporters had sought 'immediate popularity' with 'controversy, journalism and general exposition – methods condemned by our Founder, who, apart from his own works, mainly counselled example, and propaganda and opportune publications [on] questions of special importance'.[65] Harrison meanwhile felt Congreve's somewhat sparser publications were unnecessarily provocative and dogmatic, likening his argumentative technique to that of an orator mounting a 'post [to] say, "Gentlemen! I am an atheist, and strongly advise you to cut your throats"'. Harrison particularly believed that Congreve was guilty of over-dogmatic anti-imperialism.[66]

By the exacting tests imposed by Congreve and like-minded Positivists, the imperial policy of the Gladstone ministry of 1880–5 was certainly a disappointment. Gladstone's decision to accept Irish home rule in 1885–6 did nothing to alleviate their suspicion of him.[67] Congreve had argued that once an independent Ireland was made the avowed aim of British policy, 'temperate discussion of the best form of outward union, or of the best mode of effecting separation, becomes possible'.[68] The fact that Gladstone advocated a significantly more limited measure of autonomy for Ireland than Congreve suggested led Congreve and Albert Crompton to become highly suspicious of Gladstone's motives.[69] Congreve wanted 'Justice to Ireland, rejecting [Gladstone's] qualifications, which deprive it of reality'. He wanted an Irish policy untainted by the precondition that Ireland must remain in the Empire:

> It is to separation that I adhere as to the only satisfying issue of the great controversy . . . I would have this complete and final independence to be the clearly designed and openly avowed aim of all English policy in reference to Ireland, an ultimate aim to be gradually and peacefully attained by such wise preparatory measures as it ought to be within the competence of the statesmen of both countries to devise. I deprecate consequently the unsatisfactory transition which the Home Ruler accepts.[70]

Congreve believed that British opinion was 'ripening' to this 'larger conclusion than any [Gladstone] is willing to accept', i.e., 'the orderly development of separation'.[71] While this larger movement of opinion took effect, Congreve was prepared to accept Unionist interpretations of Irish politics and Unionist government of Ireland. Doubtless Congreve believed that Unionist government was the temporary dictatorship (although not 'admittedly' temporary) which Positivists had long suggested would be the best interim government of Ireland, and that Unionist reforms constituted, albeit unintentionally, the 'wise preparatory measures' which were likely to make an independent Ireland a more stable country.[72] Yet it would be inaccurate to describe Chapel Street Positivists as Unionists; they were in fact probably the only British observers of Irish politics in 1885–6 consciously to reject Gladstonian home rule because it did not go far enough.[73]

Newton Hall Positivists also had doubts about the limited autonomy offered to Ireland in Gladstone's first Home Rule Bill. Some (noticeably Benjamin Fossett Lock, the secretary of the English Positivist Committee) became outright opponents of Gladstonian home rule.[74] James Cotter Morison would have preferred 'free and unconditional separation': 'self-inflicted ruin' would bring Ireland 'to her senses': 'Experience alone can be her teacher'.[75] As Beesly later told the Irish Positivist John Kells Ingram, he had long believed that the best policy in relation to Ireland would be 'to give her complete independence: and then, if she desired it, as I think she would, to negotiate new terms of alliance, as between independent states'.[76]

Yet, although Beesly had suggested in 1881 that Irish independence was some years distant, and although Gladstonian home rule was not the Irish policy he would ideally have liked, he joined the most prominent of British Positivists in public support of the measure.[77] The great attraction of Gladstonian home rule was Gladstone himself. Gladstone's campaign was, Bridges felt, 'an education of public opinion',[78] and so he believed that 'the time has come when Home Rule should be tried'.[79] Positivists had said that the decision as to 'when and how far' their principles were to be applied had to be left to the 'practical statesman'[80]; and in Harrison's view, Gladstone was just the 'great Popular Chief' who could galvanise popular enthusiasm behind a measure which embodied a great principle.[81] Beesly agreed that in 1886 it was better to trust Gladstone than Parliament.[82]

Beesly and Harrison's commitment to the cause of home rule led them to stand as home rule candidates in London in the 1886 General Election.[83] Meanwhile, Bridges, convinced that the 'chief obstacle' to the success of home rule was Englishmen's ignorance of Irish history,[84] contributed to *Two centuries of Irish history*, a volume commissioned as part of Gladstone's intellectual propaganda campaign in favour of home rule.[85] Congreve believed that Harrison and Beesly had erred in opportunistically associating themselves with a political party which had imperialistic tendencies. By 'attaching what is essentially a spiritual movement to the temporal power, compromising our just independence', Congreve felt they had also failed to adhere to Comte's doctrine of the division of powers.[86] Such considerations inspired even Harrison and Beesly to keep their distance from Gladstonian Liberalism; the Positivists' parliamentary candidatures (particularly Harrison's) were hardly energetic.[87] Yet, this same notion of the distinction between the temporal and the spiritual aspects of human existence had helped to inspire the Comtean Positivists' relatively early advocacy of Irish self-government.

HYPOTHETICAL NATIONALISM

A further important factor in Positivists' acceptance of Irish independence was their peculiarly essentialist view of Irish nationality. Positivists felt that nations had a definitive geographical basis marked by 'compactness and due limitation of territory'. Thus, the island of Ireland was a distinct and unitary nation: 'Nature meant [England and Ireland] to be inhabited by independent nations'.[88] Significantly, the ideal of 'compactness and due limitation of territory' affected English Positivists' own sense of national identity, which was distinctly English rather than British. Beesly regarded his 'own country' as 'England, little England . . . I cannot extend my affection to a land and a people of aliens'.[89]

Interpretations of history also contributed to Positivists' support of Irish self-government. Swinny believed that the past had consolidated a remarkably distinct national identity in Ireland.[90] Ireland, declared Harrison was 'as distinct and organic a nation as any in Europe', and 'has felt herself a nation'.[91] 'Union in political action', declared Bridges in the second of his four letters of 1867–8, 'is the essential characteristic of a nation'. And where, as in Ireland, such a collective identity had withstood great misfortunes – oppression, civil conflict and famine – 'in such a case it is very certain that forces are at work by which a nation, in the true sense of the word, is, sooner or later, to be brought to birth'.[92] Swinny agreed that the Irish people had shown themselves beyond doubt a nation by their consistent 'self-sacrificing' defence of their national idea in difficult circumstances. He was particularly impressed by the example of the last two decades of the eighteenth century and believed that this was a spirit felt by both Protestants and Catholics:

> the Irish Protestant may feel a pride in his country when he remembers how, in the hour of temptation, the Catholics of Ireland declared their trust in their Protestant fellow-countrymen . . . The Irish Catholic may remember with thankfulness how, when the Protestants of Ireland were alone in a position to defend her, they were found true to the cause of their country . . . It is such memories as this that make a nation.[93]

The Positivists' key 'tests' of aspirant nationalities were thus far more favourable to the idea of 'Ireland a nation' than those tests they regarded as merely subsidiary, such as race, religion, language, culture and material interest. On the other hand, Positivists had little sympathy for any claim that Ulster was a nation. The boundary between what was a nation and what was not was hard to draw, but the fact that Ulster's claim to be distinct from southern Ireland rested on differences in orthodox religion was hardly likely to make the Positivists sympathetic. Swinny sought to emphasise the potential for a 'third religion' (Positivism) to unite Catholic and Protestant in Ireland,[94] and disarmingly declared: 'I cannot help thinking that Protestants would be in a far stronger position if they were more Nationalist'.[95]

Swinny felt that Ulster's historic destiny lay in a nationalist Ireland, a legacy bequeathed to them especially by 'the part their fathers played in '98'.[96] In 1868, Bridges recognised that:

> [the] belief that friendly cooperation between Ulster and Connaught, between Protestant and Catholic, is impossible [renders] thousands of Englishmen, who would otherwise be eager to satisfy Irish sympathies, acquiescent in the suppression of Irish self-government, which, as they imagine, must inevitably result in a miserable and endless series of internal quarrels.

His antidote to these 'erroneous' English fears was to recount the history of late eighteenth-century Ireland, because he believed it confirmed the possibility of that same 'friendly cooperation'.[97] 1798 in particular was the seminal moment of Irish history for the Positivists. Swinny admitted that as a nationalist schooled in the traditions of 1798 and 1848, the Gaelic revival movement of the early twentieth century puzzled him. 1798 made 'sad reading for a Nationalist – not because the men of that age failed, but because their sons have turned away from the glorious path their fathers trod'.[98] Harrison meanwhile believed that his maternal grandfather (Alexander Brice, a Belfast Protestant) had participated in the rebellion of 1798.[99] The Positivists found Ulster Unionists' failure to absorb this vision lamentable and incomprehensible, and opposed pleas for the partition of Ireland.[100] Harrison argued that 'Ireland, in fact, is one of the most homogeneous' of modern nations and that her divisions were 'child's play compared to some internal struggles': 'Each crag and sod, each blade of grass, on the sacred soil of Erin, from sea to sea, from shore to mountain top, belongs by indefeasible inheritance to the Irish nation, and to no one else on earth'.[101] He declared later, even when relatively disenchanted with Irish nationalism: 'Ireland is *one* – must be *one* – can only live as one nation'.[102]

From afar, it might be possible to regard the divisions in Ireland as 'child's play'. To Positivists resident in Ireland, it was hardly possible to be so dismissive. The three noteworthy Positivists in Ireland, George Allman, John Kells Ingram and Henry Dix Hutton, were lifelong adherents of Comte and among his earliest disciples. All three were highly educated men of Protestant (Anglican or Unitarian) background.[103] They were mainly interested in the religious aspect of Comtean Positivism and in cultivating moral and religious change in their country. The sectarian bitterness of Irish politics, and particularly of Parnellite Nationalism, disillusioned them, as it did many contemporary educated southern Irish Protestants. Consequently, these three Irish Positivists aligned with Congreve in the schism of 1877–8.

These Irish Positivists, however, were undoubtedly Irish patriots. This is most clearly revealed in the lines of 'The memory of the dead', a poem written by Ingram in 1843 when he was only nineteen years old. After its anonymous publication in the Irish newspaper the *Nation*, it became widely known by its first line, 'Who fears to speak of '98', and was adopted into a song very popular with Nationalists. Ingram, however, did not openly acknowledge its authorship until 1900.[104] Yet, although it became a nationalist anthem with a party political significance, 'Who fears to speak of '98?' did not overtly advocate the struggle (whether armed or peaceful) for the political independence of Ireland from Britain – it was instead a call for unity and moral regeneration within Ireland. Throughout his life Ingram was convinced that moral change was the precondition of independence in Ireland. After encountering Comte he identified conversion to the religion of humanity to be the social transition that was required in Ireland as elsewhere. Positivism helped Ingram and the other Irish

Positivists to reconcile their awareness of the severe divisions in Ireland with their fierce pride in their country. Through Comte, their aspiration that Ireland develop a national existence distinct from that of Britain could be safely deflected to a hypothetical undivided Positivist Ireland of the future.[105] Positivism seemed to assure Ingram's fellow Irishmen and women of a destiny, 'they know not what – but surely something great'.[106] Like the British Positivists, Ingram desired the political independence of an Ireland he could not really know.

Significantly, the qualified nature of the patriotism of the Positivists resident in Ireland was a source of disappointment, not just to Comte,[107] but to those Positivists of Irish or part-Irish descent resident in Britain (such as Beesly, Harrison, Swinny[108] and the Newcastle Positivist Malcolm Quin).[109] Ingram felt such Positivists were too obsessed with the English failure in Ireland, 'if it be a failure'.[110] Not only was it much easier for a Positivist to be an Irish nationalist from afar; Positivism in fact rendered its followers far better hypothetical nationalists than actual nationalists. According to Positivist ethics, '*nul n'a droit qu'a faire son devoir*'; political duties were more important than political rights, a principle on all fours with the Positivist motto, 'live for others'.[111] As Comte recognised the historical importance of nationalities, this doctrine was collective as well as personal: 'Nations, like individuals, are more profitably occupied in recognising and correcting their own faults than in crying out against those of their neighbours'.[112] Thus, several English Positivists considered themselves keener Indian nationalists than Indian students of Positivism.[113] Predictably, therefore, one of the few Positivists of an Ulster Presbyterian background, J. Carey Hall, stated in 1916 that 'the Presbyterian Church in Ireland' was responsible for the sorry state of Irish politics, and looked to his fellow Ulstermen to become Irish nationalists, 'showing themselves worthy successors of the Presbyterians of 1782'.[114]

Ironically, the Positivists claimed their faith would ultimately eradicate such spurious 'imagined' nationalism; the disaggregation of large states was supposed to create small states restricted in size to 'the limits [of] constant social intercourse'.[115] Yet, Frederic Harrison, who consistently claimed to be an Irish 'Nationalist',[116] never visited Ireland, in spite of his Irish ancestry.[117] At times, the ferocity of Harrison's Irish 'Nationalism' exceeded even that of Irish nationalist leaders themselves.[118] In 1886, the Irish historian W.E.H. Lecky attributed this to Harrison's ignorance of the true nature of Irish nationalist political culture: 'I wish you would read enough of what is written in Ireland to convince yourself of the simple truth, that your policy means separation and [the] confiscation of a great mass of property'.[119]

Lecky's warning proved highly pertinent. Like Ingram's, Harrison's hypothetical nationalism was insufficient to prevent his disenchantment with Irish nationalism in the face of subsequent developments in Irish politics. This began with the Parnell affair of 1890–1.[120] The Nationalist leader's behaviour at this time in publicly vilifying his former political ally William Gladstone for withdrawing his support for Parnell drove Harrison to immediate despair of Irish politics: 'Englishmen and Scotchmen can do nothing until Irishmen have another policy, and a leader whose hand a decent man can touch'.[121] In 1911, Harrison wrote:

> I find deep-seated in the Irish mind two perversities which distort every opinion and bring cankers into every attempt at conciliation between the two races. They are these:
>
> > First, the Irish thirst for revenge and retaliation outweighs and paralyses efforts for improvement.
> > Secondly, the Irish mind attributes every form of suffering, famine, poverty, improvidence, to external oppression – never to nature, circumstances, or themselves.[122]

Just before the First World War, Harrison's growing misgivings about Irish nationalism led him to express a sympathy for the temporary partition of the country which contrasted rather dramatically with his earlier writings.[123] During that war, Harrison believed that Britain was entitled to expect full support for its war effort from all over the United Kingdom. He therefore perceived Irish nationalist dissent as a treachery to the Allied cause which he was prepared to offer very short shrift indeed.[124] In 1919, Harrison wrote of Ireland to Lord Rosebery: 'the only thing left is to clear out – let the natives murder each other – and if they then touch British interests, conquer the island over again – and start fresh – if it cannot be sunk in the Atlantic'.[125]

There were significant differences of temperament and belief within British Positivism.[126] There were certainly subtle (and occasionally unsubtle) differences of opinion about Ireland. Few Positivists reacted to the Parnell split in the same way as Harrison,[127] and none subsequently became quite so disillusioned with Irish nationalism as he did.[128] But the reality of developments in Irish politics after 1890 still severely challenged the hypothetical nationalism of the Positivists. Positivists, like many of their liberal-minded contemporaries, professed a philosophy dominated by a spirit of optimistic rationalism; they assumed that human nature was essentially reasonable, and thus that it should not ultimately be difficult even for nations divergent in interest to cooperate.[129] Consequetly, they assumed that the nationalisms of the future would be harmonious. The true spirit of patriotism, Positivists believed, was that expressed in Ingram's 'The memory of the dead'; a simple reverence for one's own nation and its leaders, uncomplicated by xenophobia, hostility or vengeful antipathy to other peoples.[130]

Therefore, under Comte's inspiration, Positivists assumed that the Irish people would be able to unite internally and would independently gravitate to a harmonious relationship with England; Bridges hoped that the Irish would thus share a pride in being British.[131] The Positivists had focused disproportionately on periods of Irish history which provided evidence of the potential for such developments. In reality, political divisions in Ireland were being consolidated and the growing antipathy of Irish nationalists to all things British eventually placed Sinn Féin in the ascendant in southern Ireland. Both developments disappointed Swinny and other Positivists.[132] After 1921 Ireland gained self-government as Positivists had predicted, but in some respects at least, self-governing Ireland did not live up to their expectations. The established creeds on the island did not immediately weaken,[133] and the 'thirst for revenge' continued for many years to have a hold over Irish minds.[134] Positivists' faith in Irish self-government, based as it was on an 'imagined' non-sectarian Ireland of the future, an Ireland peopled by United Irishmen tutored in Comte, was much more convincing to young Positivists than to their disillusioned, more mature incarnations.

The British Positivists were the first prominent group of Britons openly to advocate separate self-government for Ireland. Their unusual attitude to Irish politics is to be explained on four grounds. First of all, Comte's vision of the future of international relations, one of independent but harmonious small states, provided a conceptual framework highly compatible with Irish home rule. Secondly, the Positivists believed that Irish independence was in the interest of the British people, in the sense that it would give Britain freer domestic government and better relations with other states. Thirdly, Positivists subscribed to the view that matters intellectual and matters political should be kept as distinct as possible. This not only gave them freedom to advocate visionary political principles, but also made them highly sympathetic to features of Irish nationalist political culture which repelled most contemporaries. Finally, Positivists' 'hypothetical nationalism' enabled them to develop an essentialist view of Irish nationality which, although somewhat naive and prone to eventual disillusionment, insulated them against several possible sources of doubt about Irish nationalism before and during the early days of the Irish home rule movement.

It cannot be contended that Positivists brought much (if any) direct influence to bear on British political decision-making about Ireland. Evidently many of the themes in Positivists' advocacy of Irish self-government bore little relation to the more historically significant Gladstonian Liberal campaigns for home rule in the 1880s and 1890s. There was however an affinity between some intellectual inspirations and arguments in both. A comparison between Positivist attitudes to 'the Irish question' and those featuring in more mainstream ideological debate can therefore enlighten several features of the growth of, and the limits of, British support for Irish self-government during these two decades.

CHAPTER TWO

'Practical Politics'

'In some cases, the world has frankly accepted the ideals we have so long preached . . . in none is the tide running against us as it did so short a time ago . . . Ireland may well give us new confidence in the future of mankind.'

Shapland Hugh Swinny, 1922[1]

THE FOCUS OF MUCH of what historiography there is of the acceptance of the idea of Irish self-government in Britain on the first home rule crisis can create a misleading impression that the idea had made no progress before Gladstone's conversion. The examples of the Positivists, and of a handful of others on the fringe of Liberal politics, show that a few Britons had already accepted the policy before Gladstone's 'Hawarden Kite' of December 1885.[2] The importance of such individuals is hard to gauge with precision. It is of course not appropriate naively to suggest that all political pronouncements by 'intellectuals' had a significant direct influence on the political process, especially those emanating from a group of intellectuals who spurned that same process as ostentatiously as did most Positivists. Indeed, the Positivists were not very successful in their efforts directly to mobilise a British working-class movement in support of Irish home rule.[3] However, it is equally implausible to assume that a crude division existed between 'the world of politics' and 'the world of thought'.[4] The Positivists did have an influence on the same milieu of radical working-class opinion in the 1860s and 1870s which was to produce pockets of passionate Gladstonians. Gladstone's critique of Disraelian expansion (and ultimately of the Anglo-Irish Union) appealed to the same constituency as the anti-imperialist rhetoric of the Positivists.[5] Even here, however, it must be conceded that the Positivists played a relatively minor role.

However, if, as the most convincing historiography of the first home rule crisis suggests, ideological factors *did* play a role in the division of mainstream intellectual and political opinion on the question of Irish self-government,[6] the primary historical significance of Positivism in this context is comparative. Consideration of more influential ideological expressions of opinion about Ireland reveals much that was exceptional in Positivists' interpretations of the Irish question, and thus helps to clarify why the acceptance of Irish self-government made only limited progress in late nineteenth-century Britain. However, such a comparison also reveals an affinity (if a largely incidental affinity) between some of the roots of visionary Positivist advocacy of Irish independence and the emergence of the convictions among more politically active liberal intellectuals which would make home rule a realistic political gambit in the Palace of Westminster. An analysis of the attitudes to Irish politics of influential British liberal intellectuals in the light of Positivists' more esoteric views therefore proves enlightening.

IDEOLOGY AND THE EMERGENCE AND DEFEAT OF GLADSTONIAN HOME RULE

John Stuart Mill articulated one prominent liberal interpretation of Irish politics at the time that the Positivists were beginning to advocate self-government for Ireland. Mill was, incidentally, also one of the most influential mediators between Comtean thought and British culture. In fact, Comte proudly declared in his *Discours sur l'esprit positif* (translated by Beesly) that Mill 'is henceforth fully associated with me in the direct foundation of the new philosophy'. Mill used Comte's *Cours de philosophie positive* extensively in his own *System of logic.*[7] He largely accepted Comte's historical analysis, his philosophy of science, and the separation of the temporal and spiritual powers. As is well known, however, Mill dissented from Comte's views on psychology, political economy and female emancipation. He also rejected the utopian model of Comte's later *Système de politique positive.*[8] Comte's intellectual development was, in Mill's view, 'a monumental warning to thinkers on society and politics, of what happens when once men lose sight in their speculations of the value of Liberty and Individuality'. Mill was suspicious of the effect that the *organised* spiritual power advocated by Comte would have on freedom of opinion.[9]

Mill's views about Ireland have been the subject of a good deal of dispute among historians.[10] Mill certainly expressed a concern about coercive government in Ireland analogous to that of Positivists. A belligerent opponent of Governor Eyre's repression in Jamaica in the 1860s, Mill feared the occurrence of 'Jamaican horrors' in Ireland.[11] Mill consequently supported reforms in Ireland which were radical in contemporary terms, such as peasant proprietorship. Yet in the late 1860s, when Positivists were beginning to voice their support for Irish home rule, Mill's discourse was unionist. He doubted that an independent and largely Catholic Ireland would be well governed and feared it would ally with France or the Papacy and promote reactionary causes in foreign affairs.[12] But Mill's 'Unionism' was conditional:

> If . . . we attempt to hold Ireland by force, it will be at the expense of all the character we possess as lovers and maintainers of free government, or respecters of any rights except our own; it will most dangerously aggravate all our chances of misunderstandings with any of the great powers of the world, culminating in war; we shall be in a state of open revolt against the universal conscience of Europe and Christendom, and more and more against our own. And we shall in the end be shamed, or if not shamed, coerced, into releasing Ireland from the connection.[13]

The suppression of opinion in Ireland would have disastrous effects on Britain and could not be long maintained. At the very end of his life, therefore, Mill expressed the view that the full political separation of Ireland from Britain would ultimately be necessary.[14]

John Morley came to occupy a standing in the pantheon of intellectual liberalism almost as elevated as that of the younger Mill. Nevertheless in the 1860s, Morley was if anything more sympathetic to Positivism than Mill; at one time he seemed likely to profess Comte's religion of humanity.[15] But Morley refrained from adhering to an 'authoritative church', not wishing to give himself, as Harrison put it, 'entirely to Comte'.[16] This disagreement manifested publicly on the subject of Bismarck's *Kulturkampf* in 1874, when Morley inserted a critical footnote in one of his friend's regular *Fortnightly Review* articles.[17] However, Morley was still intellectually sympathetic to Harrison and remained a lifelong friend and correspondent. Yet, Morley's objections to Positivism were very similar to Mill's, and during the 1870s it was Mill and not Comte who became Morley's major intellectual mentor. Morley felt that Mill had been wise in refraining from any rash attempt, such as Comte's, to anticipate the final results of 'the much-needed extension' of positive modes of thought to religion, morals and politics.[18]

Distinctions between Morley and the Positivists were also evident in their interpretations of Anglo-Irish relations in the 1870s and 1880s. Morley became a leading advocate of home rule for Ireland and eventually Irish Chief Secretary in Gladstone's two home rule cabinets.[19] Peter Fraser has suggested that the grant to Ireland of a home rule parliament 'without cast-iron safeguards' was to Morley 'an adventure in statecraft, an exhilarating experiment in the force of just concession, trust and gratitude to overcome political difficulties . . . he regarded the Irish as a separate nation, and separation had no terrors for him'.[20] This perspective understates the pragmatic and qualified nature of Morley's approach to Irish home rule. His views on the Irish question, as befitted a more mainstream and politicised liberal, were considerably more nuanced than those of the 'formal' Positivists.[21] In the 1860s, Morley was merely sympathetic to the claims and ideas of Irish nationalists and Positivists.[22] In the early 1880s Morley was far from being a supporter of Irish separation;[23] in fact, in 1879 Morley had advocated 'an inquiry into the merits of home rule' because it 'might have one of two results. First, it might show that the idea is a fantastic and impossible craze and secondly, it might suggest certain improvements in the machinery of local government which, once applied, would go far to silence the Home Rule cry'.[24]

Local government was still regarded as a relatively radical proposal for Ireland in the 1880s. Irish 'home rule' or 'self-government' at this time was not clearly defined and an ambitious scheme of local government, such as those suggested by Joseph Chamberlain in 1885 or Morley in 1879, drew almost as much ire as the proposal of an Irish parliament. However, Morley and Chamberlain were not thinking at these times of a measure which would avow the aim of satisfying the demands of nationalist Ireland's political representatives for an Irish legislature.[25] Morley eventually accepted the latter type of measure, while Chamberlain did not. In the early 1880s, Morley became a prominent critic of the coercion policy of William Forster, the Liberal Chief Secretary for Ireland. As editor of the *Pall Mall Gazette* and the *Fortnightly Review*, Morley was in a good position to exert pressure on the British government at this time and his call for Forster's removal in 1882 was, as Forster's adopted daughter's diary of the period shows, deeply felt.[26] It can certainly be argued that Forster's hoisting 'by the earnest moral petard of John Morley's *Pall Mall Gazette*' marked a crucial stage in the development of Gladstonian Liberals' determination 'to enter into the conceptual framework of their opponents' the Parnellites, which would lead Liberals to take up home rule.[27] In 1885–6, as Fraser intimates, Morley was widely regarded in Britain as one of the few British advocates of Irish home rule from conviction (rather than from force of circumstances), a status which earned him his rapid political promotion.[28] But it was John Stuart Mill's *Considerations on representative government*, not Comte's work, that Morley eventually quoted in support of home rule. Morley's acceptance of home rule was far more reluctant, and far later, than that of the Positivists.[29]

The conventionality of Morley's attitudes to Anglo-Irish relations in 1872 was revealed when he defended the Younger Pitt's action in passing the Anglo-Irish Act of Union of 1800 from the criticisms of the Irish historian W.E.H. Lecky. For Morley, the Act of Union had at least alleviated the 'oppression and disorder' endemic in the government of Ireland through the parliament of a privileged 'Ascendancy': 'The suppression of their misused power, and the placing of the whole Irish nation in the healthier air of imperial government, were the only means then seen' for establishing 'a better state of things' in Ireland.[30] Yet ironically, the positions of Lecky and Morley were reversed in 1886; Lecky was then a committed Unionist. He was also one of the most frequently quoted authorities in the home rule debates, and therefore his thought on Irish history and politics is worthy of some detailed consideration. Lecky's early books, *The rise of rationalism* and *The history of European morals*, were concerned with long-term changes in intellectual and moral structures. Lecky argued that changes of belief and the success of any new proposition 'depended much less upon the force of its arguments, or upon the ability of its advocates, than upon the predisposition of society to receive it, and . . . that predisposition resulted from the intellectual type of the age'.[31] Irish history interested him by illustrating particularly 'the effects of political and social circumstances in forming national character'.[32] Like the Positivists, Lecky was influenced by a philosophy of history. Though the English writer H.T. Buckle had a greater influence on Lecky than Comte did, Lecky made a great impression on at least one Positivist (Swinny) during a formative phase.[33]

But Lecky's concept of progress was different from Positivists'. Lecky did not believe morality, religion and science to be easily reconcilable. It was an 'incontestable though mournful fact' that the discovery of scientific laws deprived 'phenomena of their moral significance, and nearly all the social and political spheres in which reverence was fostered have passed away'.[34] Lecky did not entirely regret this tendency; as the social virtues of morality and reverence declined, the individualist virtues of 'character', toleration, intellect and liberty emerged.[35] With a few reservations, Lecky believed this triumph of rationalism to be a 'brilliant picture'.[36] Those features of modern politics and thought which Lecky regarded as particularly retrograde were democracy, unpatriotic sectarianism, socialism and significantly, Catholic clericalism.[37]

Lecky believed that the merits of Catholicism were specific to a particular age, and that the period in which it had acted as a progressive influence was 'manifestly transitory'. Its social institutions were similarly chronologically specific in their virtues: 'It could only exist by the suppression of all critical spirit, by a complete paralysis of the speculative faculties'. The moral unanimity imposed by Catholicism was inimical to individual freedom.[38] Comte and the Positivists, on the other hand, had a keen sense of the value of the social institutions of Catholicism, its hierarchical structure and its independent spiritual power.[39] (Huxley, indeed, had famously described Positivism as 'Catholicism minus Christianity'.[40]) In 1911, Harrison declared: 'I am willing to believe that the good influence still surviving in Catholicism is more active and useful than that which survives in any non-Catholic Christianity'.[41] Congreve went so far as to argue that, 'were it not for the incurable weakness of the doctrine it teaches, the Roman hierarchy, concentrated as it now is, might well look for restoration of more than its medieval supremacy'.[42] The Positivists felt Protestantism was inferior. It lacked Catholicism's independent spiritual force, its tradition and its aspiration to universality. Swinny argued in 1917 that Protestantism, though more progressive than Catholicism, might prove an obstacle to the 'final emancipation':

> Comte spoke of the southern nations as having been 'saved from Protestantism', and no words of his were received with more indignant strictures in this country; but many will now be inclined to agree that the survival in some countries of the Catholic tradition had its advantages.[43]

Lecky believed that states were tending to, and would continue to, unite to form large 'heterogeneous empires'. He admitted that 'there is much that is melancholy in this revolution'. Small states were often superior in financial prosperity, political liberty, and intellectual progress, 'and their security is in every age one of the least equivocal measures of international morality'.[44] However, Lecky was convinced that the British Empire at least was a benign influence on the world at large. His hopes for the future incorporated neither the global spiritual unity nor the disaggregation of large states envisaged by Positivists.[45]

These elements of Lecky's philosophy were closely related to his interpretation of Irish history and politics. Lecky was an Irish patriot, and supported 'the greatest amount of self-government that is compatible with the unity and security of the Empire' – though he always felt that the 'unity and security of the Empire' were paramount.[46] Lecky did not feel that Ireland was congenitally prevented from becoming a successful self-governing country due to race or religion; he sought to refute J.A. Froude's suggestion that 'Irish ideas' were compounded of various forms of disorder. British misgovernment, particularly the penal laws of the eighteenth century, had helped to make the country disorderly. Irish history provided evidence 'of the moral effects of bad laws and of a vicious social condition'. The circumstances in which Irish national character was formed accounted for its faults, and thus demonstrated 'how superficial are those theories which attribute them wholly to race or to religion'.[47] But as early as 1866, just as the Positivists were starting to articulate their support for the idea of an independent Ireland, Lecky sensed that the predominant political culture of Ireland had rendered the country, for the moment at least, 'absolutely incapable of any vestige of self-government'.[48] This 'vicious social condition' under which Ireland laboured, which made her liable to demoralisation when subject to 'bad laws', was exacerbated by the religion of the majority of her people. 'Catholicism', said Lecky, articulating a view not uncommon among his contemporaries, 'is on the whole a lower type of religion than Protestantism': and in Ireland as elsewhere it had operated to the detriment of 'political freedom' and of the 'first conditions of national progress', 'independence of intellect and . . . of character'.[49]

Like Ingram (and other Irish Positivists resident in Ireland),[50] Lecky was connected all his life with the Protestant educational establishments of ascendancy Ireland. In their youth, all therefore sympathised with predominantly Protestant mid-century nationalist movements and hypothetically would have liked to see their country independent. But during the seventies and eighties, Lecky, Hutton and Ingram became increasingly hostile to a Nationalist movement dominated by Catholics and by agrarian aims of which they disapproved.[51] The consequence was that like Ingram, Lecky had to endure the distressing experience of seeing his own youthful work, infused as it was with a sense of patriotic optimism, used in favour of Gladstonian home rule.[52] Lecky mourned the loss of Grattan's parliament precisely for the same reasons that he opposed

Parnellite home rule. In the years after 1886, Lecky was to repeat *ad nauseam* his contention that the best and most loyal elements in Ireland, the very elements which had been represented in Grattan's parliament, opposed home rule. Whereas Grattan's parliament, properly handled, might therefore have been a source of strength to the British Empire, home rule would be fatal to it.[53] Consequently, there was no analogy between Grattan's parliament and 'modern schemes for reconstructing the government of Ireland on a revolutionary and Jacobin basis, entrusting the protection of property and the maintenance of law to some democratic assembly consisting mainly of Fenians and Land-Leaguers, of paid agitators and penniless adventurers'.[54]

This reasoning was too subtle for many. Ingram's British co-religionists, for instance, believed that the Catholic tradition was better qualified than the Protestant to provide moral and spiritual leadership for the Irish people.[55] In the eighteenth century, wrote Swinny, it had been 'the one example of a Church like that of the middle ages – the protector of the oppressed and the friend of the people'.[56] The Positivists believed the Protestant minority in Ireland, not the Irish Catholics, were guilty of anti-national sectarianism.[57] The growing domination of the Irish nationalist movement by Catholic, anti-landlord and anti-English elements, which began in the 1870s, thus had no negative effect on Positivists' sympathy for Irish nationalism. And although the same development was fatal to Lecky's personal support for Irish self-government, Positivists continued to regard Lecky's works as a source of arguments in favour of home rule.[58]

During the first two home rule crises, Goldwin Smith joined Lecky in acting as an outspoken defender of the Union. Yet in the 1850s and 1860s, his radical criticism of British imperial and Irish policy had put him in close sympathy with the Positvists.[59] He also shared Morley's dislike of the Anglican ascendancy in Ireland; Morley preferred Smith's 'democratic or cosmopolitan or philosophic' interpretation of Irish history (as expressed in his *Irish history and Irish character*, published in 1861) to Lecky's defence of the government of Ireland by the Anglo-Irish.[60] Thus, Smith's sympathies overlapped with those of Positivists on a great many questions. He lived in Canada for most of the second half of his life and expected Canada eventually to secede from the British Empire, probably to join the United States.[61] But in spite of the similarity of their opinions on imperial questions, Harrison and Smith fell out in the 1880s, over Positivism and Ireland. There followed a long gap in their correspondence until the Boer War.[62] Smith regarded the Union as a truly national institution, the maintenance of which should be held immune from involvement in the kind of party conflict which resulted from Gladstone's taking up home rule. Early in 1885, he declared: 'If morality requires it, I can bear to see England reduced to the dimensions of Kent; but I cannot bear to see her wrecked by faction, poltroonery, and scoundrelism'.[63] Smith argued that the endeavour to preserve England as a 'great moral power' was not imperialistic.[64] It was only late in life that Smith revised his attitude to home rule, principally because he feared that Irish nationalism had been given renewed strength by the analogous anti-imperial struggle of the Boers.[65]

Smith's Unionism was undoubtedly influenced by ideas about the national character of the Irish.[66] Smith believed that the Celtic, Catholic and clannish elements in Irish national character meant that parliamentary government could not yet be successfully applied to the country: 'till the savage clansman is worked out of the Irishman's character, and he is politically abreast of the Englishman, force will sometimes be requisite, as it is now, to uphold the reign of law'.[67] Like Lecky, Smith believed that the influence of the Catholic priest and the vitriolic nationalist press in Irish politics had further demoralised the Irish people. But contrary to some cruder arguments about 'Irish national character' which were popularised in the 1880s, Smith did not believe that this demoralisation was necessarily permanent in its effects.[68] Smith's views on this point were essentially consistent over the course of his life,[69] though in the 1880s he emphasised the demoralised state of contemporary Irish national character to an extent which dismayed Irish nationalists and their sympathisers.[70]

James Bryce was among Morley's ministerial colleagues in Gladstone's home rule governments. Bryce was a respected and moderate liberal and his approach to home rule was even more uncertain than Morley's.[71] In 1884, in a paper presented to a Liberal committee established to investigate the Irish question, Bryce had posited the notion that the violence of Irish political life was due to the fact that the Irish people lacked:

> some of the qualities which have made the English and the Americans succeed in working free institutions – self-restraint, moderation, a sense of the relative importance of different aims, a willingness to see what can be said on the other side, a preference of solid men and solid objects to brilliant disclaimers and seductive visions. It is no reproach to them to be in these respects deficient, for few races have possessed these gifts, and even in England and America it is by long

> experience of freedom that they have been developed and nurtured . . . as the mass of the [Irish] people have had no training in self-government, so the leaders have had nothing to do but criticise, and have given little or no help to the English Government by any practical suggestions.[72]

This suggestion was a commonplace of political discourse at the time, and could be made just as easily by Unionists.[73] To stand a good chance of gaining a hearing on Ireland, any politician had to imply that there was some way in which the country was capable of political and social improvement, even if merely that after being governed 'resolutely' for 'twenty years', 'you will find that Ireland will be fit to accept any gifts in the way of local government or repeal of coercion laws that you may wish to give her'.[74]

The attraction of such language from the point of view of British observers was that it placed Britain in the flattering position of 'teacher', implying that she was in a sufficiently advanced position to guide the wayward Irish into political maturity. This perspective was hardly a faithful reflection of the political life of Ireland, and such distorted metropolitan perceptions of Ireland certainly helped to disturb Anglo-Irish relations in this period.[75] Only a philosophy as exotic as Comte's could inspire a British commentator to claim that the Irish were as civilised as the British, 'not a whit behind [England] in political knowledge, public spirit, or morality'.[76] This is a reminder of the intrinsic similarities of the assumptions of British home rulers and Unionists. Both groups, of course, emerged from the same political culture, and so shared many ideals, aims and points of reference, imperial and domestic. Even British home rulers such as Morley presupposed the superiority of Anglo-Saxon Protestant institutions.[77] These similarities enabled home rulers to claim that Unionist arguments (particularly Lecky's arguments) were in fact home rule arguments, a common feature of these discussions. In 1888–9, when Harrison became involved in a *Contemporary Review* controversy with the Duke of Argyll, he answered Argyll 'mainly by citing a few passages about history from Lecky, G. Smith and Dicey and etc'.[78] As Argyll observed, 'the pleasure of quoting a unionist against himself seems to have been an insuperable temptation'.[79]

After taking up home rule with Gladstone and Morley in 1885–6, Bryce's language about Ireland changed little. He contended that the Irish people required political education before they would be in any position to approach Anglo-Saxon levels of attainment; but practical experience only could provide the Irish people with this 'training in self-government'.[80] Bryce described faith in home rule as 'the belief in the power of freedom and self-government to cure the faults of nations, in the tendency of responsibility to teach wisdom'.[81] In 1882, Gladstone had told Forster, 'it is liberty alone which fits men for liberty. This proposition, like every other in politics, has its bounds; but it is far safer than the counter doctrine, wait till they are fit'.[82] To many Britons, however, the relevance of this doctrine of political learning by doing to the Irish context was distinctly questionable.[83] Irish Nationalists' threatening attitudes to political opponents (such as the majority of Irish Protestants) did not suggest even to many liberal British observers that the risks involved in sending nationalist Ireland to the school of self-government were worth taking – at least for the time being.[84] Different methods of political education were preferred. Goldwin Smith, like Salisbury, advocated an attempt to work 'the savage clansman' out of the Irishman by coercion.[85] Others wished to try to educate the Irish electors through land or local government reform.[86] The Positivists' notion of the division between the spiritual and the temporal led them to believe that the formation and activity of organisations such as the Land and National Leagues was an exercise of liberty of opinion, and any limitation on it was a simple act of oppression.[87] But for the majority of their British contemporaries, the choice between coercing the Irish nationalists and allowing the nationalists to coerce their fellow Irish people, and perhaps harm the interests of Britain, was by no means as easy.

The early Liberal supporters of home rule, though largely free from the influence of Comtean dogmatism, articulated arguments similar to those used by the Positivists. Liberals also argued that the concession of self-government to Ireland would remove an obstacle to the right ordering of British (and Irish) society and politics. During the 1880s Morley gradually became convinced that home rule was the only alternative to coercion in Ireland. Morley argued, as had Mill, that coercion was not a price worth paying for the maintenance of the Union: 'constant resort to [coercion] blinds us to the desirableness of so adjusting our system of government in Ireland as to rest on the public opinion in Ireland'.[88] Coercion could also only be enacted to the detriment of British politics (especially of British Liberalism), and was unlikely to be sustainable in an era of democratisation: 'English opinion is not the most constant force in the world'.[89] Liberal home rulers, especially Gladstone, also contended that

Ireland had to be treated as a nation. It was as a nation that Ireland had been misgoverned in the past and as a nation that Ireland had to be given reparation in the present. The reparation to be given was that demanded by the vast majority of her representatives as returned at the 1885 General Election – home rule.[90] The adoption of Irish self-government by politically mainstream Liberals also meant that the advocacy of the principle in Britain no longer depended on self-conscious visionary postulation by groups such as the Positivists.

Morley's acceptance of home rule was far more hesitant than the Positivists', and he was far from always seeing eye to eye with them on every issue. But even in their disagreements, such as over Bismarck's treatment of the Roman Catholic Church in 1873–4, Morley and Harrison shared Comtean assumptions about the desirability of liberty in 'spiritual' matters; any 'opinion', such as that expressed by the Irish home rule movement, should not be casually suppressed.[91] Comte had inspired his British followers' early belief that British government of Ireland would be unsustainable in the face of public opinion and would complicate Britain's relations with other countries.[92] To a lesser extent, the shadow of Comte also hovered over Morley's relatively early commitment to Irish home rule. Yet more moderate liberals, uninfluenced by Comte, were drawn at least a little by similar considerations. Even the eminent academic Unionist Albert Venn Dicey echoed John Stuart Mill in his influential *England's case against home rule*, in speculating on a hypothetical future when the burdens necessary to maintain the Union with Ireland might be too great for British power or for:

> the humanity or the justice or the democratic principles of the English people . . . then it will be clear that the Union must for the sake of England, no less than that of Ireland, come to an end. The alternative policy will then be not Home Rule but Separation.[93]

It is significant that this negative consideration should have been so prominent as British advocacy of Irish home rule moved into the sphere of practical politics. Morley's principal argument for home rule was that it was not the existing Union: 'who supports things as they are? Things as they are have become unsupportable'.[94] Bryce ultimately agreed; the British system of party politics was ill-designed for coercive government in Ireland, and ultimately home rule was inevitable.[95] To those who accepted the inevitability of the Comtean millennium, there were compelling constructive arguments in favour of home rule. Home rule fitted neatly into an ideological framework in which small nations and the disintegration of empires were valued for their own sake.[96] To those uninfluenced by this esoteric philosophy, however, this element was lacking, and the most powerful arguments in favour of home rule carried a pessimistic air.[97] Gladstone could contend that 'to make ample provision for local independence, subject to Imperial unity' was true to British traditions – his Home Rule Bill was adapted to parts of British imperial practice.[98] But in 1886 this seemed a weak argument,[99] especially in the face of recent Irish Nationalist disloyalty.

Unionist arguments, on the other hand, were compatible with an ideological framework and an interpretation of the national mission of the United Kingdom which *were* widely accepted outside of the Comtean milieu. Liberal Unionists were generally convinced that only powerful, large and united sovereign states would prosper in the contemporary world.[100] Irish home rule would plant an impetus towards disintegration at the heart of the British Empire and place that tendency (as Lecky frequently emphasised) in the power of untrustworthy men, liable to oppress loyal fellow Irishmen and women.[101] Accordingly, such Unionists cherished the belief that the political and moral unity of the United Kingdom was highly potent.[102] Unionists were more confident than home rulers that loyal and patriotic British electors would act with sufficient coherence to defeat the secessionist threat from Irish nationalism. Dicey's greater confidence in such united action from British voters and politicians distinguished his 1880s writings in the *New York Nation* from those of his friend Bryce.[103] Salisbury thus declared that a government of Ireland that would not 'alter in its resolutions or its temperature' in response to changes in the balance of parties at Westminster was crucial to the implementation of Unionist policy in Ireland.[104] Even Unionists who had been sympathetic to continental nationalist movements of the 1860s could consistently regard Irish nationalism as disintegrative and destructive.[105] Even outspoken anti-imperialists such as Goldwin Smith could also be Unionists, if they accepted the view that the maintenance of the Union was essential to England's moral standing in the world.[106]

There were many factors involved in determining individuals' party commitment in the first home rule crisis. The role of self-interested political calculation, of personal attachment and of reactions to political violence in Ireland cannot be denied. But ideology *was* significant. At the very least, the range of possible political manoeuvres was limited to those that could be justified in the light of existing structures of political belief. Contrary to the intimations of some historians, there were respectable ideological justifications for liberal British politicians accepting a home rule policy in 1885–6. However, the role of these justifications was largely negative and therefore the attraction was limited. This is an indication as to why British political observers continued to prefer the maintenance of the Union, and as to why that policy prevailed in 1886, and, with a short and ineffective intermission, for twenty years afterwards.

POSITIVISM IN DECLINE

The disintegration of large states and empires anticipated by Positivists did not materialise in the years immediately following the first home rule crisis. Imperialism, that 'reversion' to the morals of an earlier age, did not seem in the 1890s to be as 'temporary' as they suggested.[107] The failure of the Liberal government of 1892–5 to evacuate Egypt led Beesly to suggest (without success) that the Irish home rulers should withhold support from Gladstone's government until it reversed its Egyptian policy.[108] Harrison's advice to his friend Morley on how to advance his political career seems in retrospect particularly sound: 'Don't go mixing yourself up with us about Empire etc. I am not in practical politics thank my stars and can say what I like'.[109]

Positivists' criticisms of contemporary trends in British foreign policy in the 1890s only served to distinguish them further from their fellow Britons at a time when the movement was clearly in decline. Its most active representatives in London, Swinny, F.S. Marvin and Philip Thomas, though persistent, were hardly as well-known to contemporaries as Harrison, Beesly and Congreve had been in the first generation.[110] Active provincial leaders of Positivism, such as Malcolm Quin in Newcastle,[111] Frederick Gould in Leicester,[112] and a succession in Liverpool,[113] also failed to win much attention for Comte's doctrines. As the twentieth century began, Positivism was a dying movement without much influence.

Yet, Positivists continued to find cooperators in activities on the fringes of conventional politics. In 1899–1902, Positivists aligned on the South Africa Conciliation Committee with Liberal critics of the Unionist government's policy during the Boer War.[114] Swinny's characteristically Positivist anti-imperialism also gained a hearing at gatherings such as the 1907 Subject Races Congress.[115] Further interaction took place on the Sociological Society (founded in 1903).[116] Leonard Hobhouse, a radical

Liberal, the joint first holder of a British university Chair of Sociology and first editor of the *Sociological Review* (1908–11), was sympathetic to Positivists' philosophy and critiques of imperialism, and his interest was reciprocated.[117] Hobhouse was also related by marriage to Bridges, and felt a particular affinity with Bridges' interpretation of Comte's doctrines.[118]

Such intellectual and political societies did not exercise perceptible influence on the making of British policy, nor did they bring closer the global model of small, independent, but associated states articulated by Comte. However, within the context of the British Empire, developments did occur towards the end of the lives of Beesly, Harrison and Swinny which such followers of Comte could commend. The creation of the self-governing Union of South Africa in 1909–10 seemed to be a practical and successful application of the principles advocated by 'pro-Boers' like the Positivists during the Boer War. It also constituted, felt Swinny, 'a practical demonstration of the advantages of Home Rule' which could also be applied to Ireland.[119] British policy in Europe also found increasing favour among Positivists in the early years of the twentieth century. Positivists such as Harrison had long wished for more amicable relations between Britain and France (the land of Comte's birth and the country Comte had anticipated would initiate the global Positivist transformation), and were very suspicious of Bismarckian and Wilhelmine Germany.[120] Therefore, they could wholeheartedly support Britain's alliance with France before and during the First World War. Harrison shocked liberals such as Morley, who had grown accustomed to looking upon him as a powerless but politically agreeable eccentric, by the extent to which he was prepared to advocate rearmament before 1914 and a single-minded prosecution of the war under authoritarian leadership thereafter, in a manner which aligned him more closely with the political Right in Britain.[121]

The Positivists' patriotic support of the war certainly brought them closer to the political mainstream than they had previously been.[122] This was partly due to the fact that changes in the structure of the British Empire led them to perceive it as an approximation to that community or 'commonwealth' of nations which they had anticipated.[123] Swinny was particularly impressed by the efforts of the Liberal governments of 1905–1915 to concede varying degrees of self-government to South Africa, India and of course, Ireland. He perceived the Empire's development 'into a free commonwealth of nations', 'the protector, and not the oppressor, of the weak', as a vindication of Britain's 'noble tradition': 'The German method was quite different'.[124] Although this 'commonwealth' was restricted to parts of the world under the Union Jack, it at least constituted progress towards that 'union of the nations which should be our ideal in peace'.[125] The emergence of the League of Nations also found favour with Positivists.[126]

After the war Positivists continued to express satisfaction with the Empire's new aspect.[127] Swinny lived just long enough to see self-government in Ireland, if a divided Ireland.[128] Meanwhile the Positivist historian Francis Sydney Marvin, a close friend of Gilbert Murray,[129] edited the 'Unity History Series', collections of essays emanating from a series of summer schools held during and after the Great War. Marvin perceived one of the volumes at least to be an updated version of the Positivists' *International policy* of 1866.[130] Several contributions to the series, including essays by mainstream liberal intellectuals, argued that political, social, cultural and economic movements increasingly took place in international rather than national contexts. They also suggested that British traditions, including the British Empire, had played a prominent role in this development. Marvin believed that Britain's concession of self-government to Ireland demonstrated an awareness that:

> the safety and progress of humanity demanded the cooperation of free and strongly organised national units, that the promotion of this ideal has been England's historic mission in the world even when she was least conscious of it, and that her worst lapse was in the case which lay nearest to her doors.

Due to the flexibility shown by some Positivists in the light of Comte's declining influence and changes in Britain's 'international policy', the movement had been transformed from a group of radical cranks without realistic hope of gaining the ear of their contemporaries, into a movement which apparently professed mainstream patriotic sensibilities and conventional ideals.[131]

Positivism had very little direct influence on British politics, or on the politics of Anglo-Irish relations. Some factors in Positivists' unique attitudes to 'the Irish question' in the years before 1885 were consequently peripheral to conventional political debate. By 1923, it had been a waning movement for some years.[132] But ironically, in the throes of this decline, supporters could observe that, against the odds, in some respects, the world had turned its way. In 1923, the English Positivist Committee's annual report claimed that there was a:

> steady world progression towards a humane, scientific and therefore Positivist attitude to domestic, national and world-wide problems and aspirations. Whilst therefore, there may be no great noticeable recognition of Comte's inspiration and genius, the gradual and often unconscious permeation of his spirit gives us cause for satisfaction and encouragement.[133]

In particular, Comte's initially apparently implausible prediction of the 'separation' of Ireland from Britain had been vindicated.

Although their influence was minimal, in some respects, Positivists' concerns about British policies in Ireland were highly apposite to the dilemmas of their liberal-minded contemporaries. Positivist ideas on the Irish national question, visionary as they had seemed in the late 1860s, had become the conventional wisdom by 1923. Assessment of other, more influential political ideologies sheds further light on this startling development.

NEW LIBERALISM

Ireland in New Liberal Theory

Home Rule and other good causes will be damaged when Liberalism ceases to be true to itself . . .

Charles Prestwich Scott, 1914[1]

THE DECLINE OF THE British Liberal party has posed many questions for historians. Some have argued that Liberalism was a vibrant ideology up to the start of the First World War, capable of winning three elections in 1906–10 and of inspiring constructive programmes of social reform which attracted working-class support more effectively than the Edwardian Labour party. Were it not for the accident of war and the questions of personality and principle which arose therein, there would have been no reason for Labour to replace the Liberals as the focal point of 'progressive' politics in Britain. Some writers have argued that this Liberal revival can be related to the influence of new Liberalism, an 'ideology of social reform' inspired in particular by the writings of John Hobson and L.T. Hobhouse.[2] This has been contested in a variety of ways. Some historians have argued that progressivism was a minority and contradictory creed within Liberalism, and that long-term social and economic forces made the decline of Liberalism hard to avert,[3] or that Liberalism owed its Edwardian revival to the limitations of the contemporary franchise and never really had a mass appeal; the revival was a shallow and localised phenomenon.[4] Other historians have contended that the nature of politics precludes the initiation of a programme of reform by any theory, Liberal or otherwise; the social reforms of 1906–14 were a piecemeal response by ministers unaffected by 'new Liberal ideology'.[5]

The assumption that new Liberalism, whether represented by its intellectual originators or by the most sympathetic Cabinet ministers, David Lloyd George and Winston Churchill, was principally an ideology of social reform has, however, not been much disputed. It has been intimated that 'new' Liberals were economic radicals, 'predictably and significantly bland' on 'old Liberal issues' such as foreign policy and home rule for Ireland.[6] Patricia Jalland's book *The Liberals and Ireland* offers a forceful assessment of the significance of Ireland for the new Liberals. Jalland accepts that Irish home rule was part of the heritage of Edwardian Liberalism, but she associates enthusiasm for the project specifically with the 'old' Liberal element of Asquith's government of 1908–14. The 'new' Liberals, 'the more creative and dynamic elements in contemporary liberalism, wanted the traditional pledges discharged as rapidly as possible, to allow the social reforming impulses of New Liberalism to resume their progress . . . for many Liberal and Labour members, Home Rule blocked the way for all the other measures about which they cared more deeply . . . The Liberal weekly, the *Nation*, expressed these sentiments fairly accurately, regretting in December 1911 that "we are to look at questions which were ripe for settlement twenty years ago". The Liberal party had more to gain from continued emphasis on socio-economic reform'.[7]

This meant that speedy acceptance of compromises which were likely to disarm detailed and protracted criticisms of the Liberal home rule plans of 1911–2 was in the interest of the new Liberals. The symbol of this difference in perspective between 'old' and 'new' Liberals was the rejection by the rest of the Cabinet of a proposal by Lloyd George and Churchill in February 1912 to exclude Unionist Ulster from the 1912 Home Rule Bill. Jalland regards this rejection as a 'tragic omission'.[8] Before this decision was made, 'the Liberal party, in some regions at least, was proving its ability to accommodate and appeal to the growing working-class electorate. The party appeared to be in no danger of extinction'.[9] After such an 'omission' the downward trend was largely set:

> the Irish problem of 1911–4 demoralised the Liberal party at a critical time and contributed significantly to the party's decline . . . Home Rule highlighted Liberalism's difficulty in reconciling the 'progressive' demands of the twentieth-century electorate with the traditional commitments of Gladstonian Liberalism . . . The war gave the *coup de grâce* to the Liberal party, but the inability to meet the challenge posed by the Ulster problem was itself a symptom of chronic debility. The Liberal party was already being consumed by the Orange cancer before it was run over by the 'rampant omnibus' of war.[10]

Thus, the Liberal party's decline is related specifically to its failure to pay closer attention to the new Liberal line, instead of trying to fulfil a 'Gladstonian Liberal dream' in Ireland.[11]

Jalland's hypothesis is substantially accurate. It is not proposed in this part to dispute the contention that the course of action Jalland suggests in the circumstances of 1912 *could* have been wiser.[12] However, it will be argued that underestimation of the ideological dimension to new Liberal attitudes to Irish policy can lead to serious distortion. It also leaves at least two important questions unanswered.

First of all, if Lloyd George can be taken as representative of new Liberal thinking about Ireland, it is curious that progressive Liberals were among the leading critics of his coalition government's Irish policy in the years 1918–21. An explanation of this curiosity may be sought in a proper appreciation of the relationship between 'new' Liberalism and the Gladstonian Liberal tradition of 1868–94 with its emphasis on Ireland as a distinct 'mission' of Liberalism. Secondly, if the 'successes' of Asquith's government's social reform policies are to be ascribed to an intellectual milieu influenced by the writings of Liberal theorists,[13] it would seem unlikely that the failures of Liberal policy in Ireland during the same period could be explained solely as the outcome of a period of political confusion (the ambiguous results of the 1910 General Elections) and the defective vision of individual statesmen. Connections can usefully be sought between the evolution of new Liberal thought in relation to Ireland particularly as articulated in the radical press,[14] and the calculations and policies of contemporary British governments. The place of Ireland in the 'Liberal mind', from the moment in 1886, when the efforts of Gladstone, Morley and the Positivists (among others) had combined to make home rule a viable political alternative,[15] until after the Treaty of 1921, is a subject worthy of historical attention.[16]

AN OBSTRUCTION TO HEALTHY METABOLISM

The term 'new Liberalism' is in fact almost as old as the Liberal party itself, and has been used by supporters of a new departure in Liberal politics on successive occasions when the party ran into electoral difficulty.[17] But historiographically, 'new Liberalism' has become associated with the only such movement to produce a fruitful legislative yield, that of the Edwardian period. Hobson argued that with the Liberal party's legislation of 1906–9, a 'new conception' of liberalism based on a 'fuller appreciation and realisation of individual liberty' and 'equal opportunities of self-development' had emerged.[18]

Liberal theory had traditionally always involved a delicate symbiosis between unity and diversity. John Stuart Mill, for instance, had attempted to combine the description of those principles which were morally and scientifically true of human nature in any context, with an assertion of the vital importance of differences between individuals and of the collision of opinions between individuals.[19] New Liberalism, as expressed in the writings of Hobson, Hobhouse, other theorists and in the Liberal press, shared this quest for balance but articulated it in a new language.

Under the influence of Idealism and evolutionary biology, new Liberals adopted the metaphor of society as a self-conscious organism with interdependent parts or organs.[20] 'Economically', said Hobson, 'no man liveth to himself': 'the struggle for existence', said H.W. Massingham, was 'continually modified as man discovers he cannot save himself alone'.[21] This discourse involved the possibility of the central direction of society by a 'cerebral centre' (in Hobson's phrase),[22] through the development of societal forms of conscious cooperation, or 'mind'.[23] Such language intimated the need of an active interventionist state, and could be used in support of Edwardian measures of social reform.

'In a healthy organism', due to the interdependence of its parts, every organ had to be supplied and replenished by a 'just circulation' of resources. Hence Hobson suggested society be ordered according to the 'full organic formula', 'from each according to his powers, to each according to his needs'. But given that these writers were Liberals, the just needs of each 'cell' in the social organism included its liberty, its right to 'veto' oppressive central direction.[24] The *Progressive Review* expressed this subtle balance in defining its faith:

> If it shall still be considered the chief business of the State to secure liberty, this term must carry an enlarged and enlightened conception of the functions of the State which shall be limited only by the power of the conscious organisation of society to assist in securing for its members the fullest opportunities of life.[25]

The problem of protecting the individual from himself or herself and others while preserving individuality was tackled in different ways by Hobson and Hobhouse. Hobson emphasised the need of uniformity, while Hobhouse relied on 'harmony', notionally to ensure that the freedoms of heterogeneous individuals did not infringe the freedoms of others and the needs of the community.[26]

Progressive Liberals also explored the delicate balance between individual nations and the wider international community. Unlike some contemporary 'organic' thinkers, new Liberals believed that there was also a potent system of organic relations between societies; nations were also 'moral beings'.[27] Like the Positivists, new Liberal writers such as J.L. Hammond anticipated the evolution of an interdependent and cooperative community between peoples;[28] just as 'economically' no man was an island, 'states can no more live without association than without liberty': 'The absolute independence of a country has no more basis in . . . equity than that of an individual'.[29]

Hobhouse, the brother-in-law of the Positivist John Henry Bridges, articulated a notion of the unity of 'the West' similar to that of the Positivists, and contended that 'the concept of a common humanity' was ceasing to be just 'the dream of a philosopher' and becoming 'a popular emotion'.[30] In international relations between states, as in economic relations between individuals, Hobson, therefore, did not believe that freedom consisted in the removal of all hindrances, but that it required institutional support. Thus, there was both the need and the potential for the development of an international cerebral centre, some system of 'international government'.[31] In such a community, national governments would have to surrender some sovereign powers, namely their right of 'assailing the rights of all others'.[32] And the reality of the international community was growing stronger:

> The whole progress of humanity . . . is the story of this enlargement of the human horizon. But in that enlargement there is no loss of individuality. It is only the extension of the self to the community of ever widening circles, until the world itself is one society.[33]

Therefore, national individuality would be preserved in the germinating international community. As Charles Masterman declared, it would be no 'world state established by one or two great Empires . . . issuing fiats which others are compelled to obey from fear of force only'.[34] Such a mechanical unity would be counterproductive, since each people had some sort of distinct contribution to make to humanity: 'True patriotism is the corner-stone of true internationalism'.[35] Hobhouse thus regarded the white commonwealth before 1914 as a model of the ultimate world state.[36] New Liberalism contained 'a recognition that it belongs to the common good of nations to leave each nation liberty to govern itself in all matters where such liberty does not directly and clearly contravene the common good'.[37]

Consequently, limited autonomy and home rule were in theory desirable solutions, applicable to a range of political circumstances.[38] Local self-government, Positivists and new Liberals agreed, was highly preferable to the imperial tutelage of a subject people. New Liberals saw in imperialism 'the reverse of liberalism':[39] 'democratic Imperialism is a contradiction'.[40] Projects of imperial adventure competed with social reform for government money, parliamentary time (a serious consideration in this period)[41] and popular attention;[42] it was possible for political reactionaries to use imperial and foreign policy issues to avert domestic reforms.[43]

New Liberals argued that imperialism was not just practically inconsistent with liberalism, but also morally incompatible. A nation could not act in an illiberal manner regarding its foreign policy while sustaining a liberal domestic polity; the reactionary spirit of jingoism would infect home politics. As Hobhouse wrote in the 1920s, 'every failure of the ideal [of self-government] is a danger to such success as it has won':

> Political principles, like other things, succeed by success and fail by failure. The triumphs of Bolshevism and fascism alike are infectious, and those who justify the indiscriminate shooting of an Indian mob have at the back of their mind the Freudian wish that they might see the same treatment meted out to Welsh miners. Conversely, the success of responsible government in South Africa conduced to the settlement of the Irish Free State.[44]

In the language of progressive Liberalism, a subject nation incorporated arbitrarily in the body politic, such as Ireland was in the United Kingdom, was a 'foreign body', an 'obstruction to the healthy metabolism' of the entire society, since ultimately its incorporation could only be maintained by the creation of reactionary illiberal institutions. No nation, no empire, could be at once half-slave and half-free.[45]

New Liberals were thus disposed to urge the concession of political autonomy to any community of feeling which constituted a nation. Like his brother-in-law Bridges, Hobhouse believed:

> the test of nationality lies in history. If the life of one people can be absorbed into that of another so that free Government can proceed unimpeded, not violated by the habitual resort to 'exceptional

> legislation', the union is justified by the event. If on the other hand the demand for autonomy remains clear and persistent, through evil report and good report, through coercion and concession . . . there is the proof that nationality is a vital principle, and a permanent force with which liberty must make its account.[46]

To Liberals of the generation of Goldwin Smith, it was not clear that Ireland had passed such a 'test'.[47] To new Liberals, particularly in the early twentieth century, the persistence of Ireland's demand for autonomy made it seem clear that the Anglo-Irish Union was not 'justified by the event'. By this time, even Liberals who were something less than 'ardent' about home rule saw it as an axiomatic necessity.[48] Like the Positivists, the new Liberals had decided that Ireland was a nation and they had become convinced that resistance to that nation's demand for separate political representation could only harm Britain.[49] The need of a 'quasi-Federal' arrangement for the oppressed Irish nationality had become a central element of Liberalism, and the advocacy of Gladstone and Morley seemed prophetic.[50]

YEARS IN 'THE WILDERNESS',[51] 1886–1907

For some Edwardian progressive Liberal intellectuals the first home rule crisis was a formative political experience. L.T. Hobhouse and Gilbert Murray (an Australian of 'Irish Rebel background')[52] were active in support of Gladstonian home rule whilst Oxford undergraduates.[53] H.W. Massingham began his journalistic career at the London *Star* in 1888 under the editorship of the Irish Nationalist MP T.P. O'Connor, and his first pamphlet was strongly in favour of home rule. Therefore, when Massingham, as editor of the *Nation* in 1911, had his journal declare that home rule should have been granted twenty years earlier, he was not expressing impatience with the issue, but justifying his youth.[54] Home rule was one of Massingham's most prominent political goals throughout his active life.[55]

But one very important new Liberal journalist was an established part of the political landscape by 1886. C.P. Scott had begun his remarkable editorship of the *Manchester Guardian* in 1872. It lasted for over fifty years, a period which transformed the *Guardian* from a provincial daily to the key organ of the Liberal conscience.[56] The *Guardian*'s support of home rule in 1886 was a crucial phase in this transformation; its local Liberal rival, the *Manchester Examiner*, rejected Gladstonian home rule and subsequently went out of business. As a result, the *Guardian* was presented with a secure local base from which to expand.[57]

Before 1886, the editorial policy of the *Guardian* had been Whiggish, though W.T. Arnold, the paper's occasional Irish correspondent, had established it as sympathetic to the grievances of the Irish Land League.[58] The *Guardian* swallowed rather hard in accepting Gladstonian home rule;[59] but it quickly warmed to the new policy. Scott stood as a Gladstonian candidate in the 1886 General Election and the issue subsequently lay close to his heart.[60] The *Guardian*'s rhetoric in 1886 had much in common with the later new Liberal justification of home rule. It argued that 'so long as Ireland is subject to repressive laws and denied the means of effective self-government, so long also England will be subject to Tory domination and denied the path of progress'.[61] Like Gladstone and J.H. Bridges, it drew a parallel with the history of colonial Canada, where a concession of self-government had apparently strengthened the moral bonds of the Empire.[62] Like Morley, Mill and the Positivists, the *Guardian* was convinced that it was not 'safe' 'to crush out the national life and hope of a people . . . nor, indeed, possible – to do so when once the conscience of the stronger people has become convinced that it is not honourable'.[63] In March 1886, the *Guardian* had suggested that Gladstone's Land Bill was the most advantageous feature of his Irish policy.[64] Within the year, the paper and Gladstone had divorced themselves from this unpopular Bill.[65] But the paper's attachment to home rule had been established; and with Scott's son-in-law, the Irish-born C.E. Montague as assistant-editor, it was unlikely to go back.[66]

Together, the *Guardian* and Gladstone had learnt much in 1886 that would later be of use to the new Liberals. In particular, they had learnt to be flexible about the details of their home rule policy.[67] The alliance between radical Liberals and home rulers was further consummated by the Newcastle programme of 1891 – though there was still area for debate and disagreement, for instance between Massingham and O'Connor.[68] The Liberal government of 1892–5 achieved little, but Scott was convinced that a change of strategy over home rule was not necessary. In 1894 he pressed the Prime Minister Lord Rosebery to challenge the House of Lords' rejection of home rule, rather than to disown the policy, 'for which we have sacrificed everything'.[69] A few months later, Scott, seconded by David Lloyd George, proposed a resolution that home rule held 'the foremost place in the policy and programme of the Liberal Party' at a National Liberal Federation conference.[70]

After 1895, Liberal journalists and intellectuals, amidst much soul-searching, saw their party deprived of power for ten years – and the Liberal commitment to home rule was certainly among the causes of their unpopularity. But there was continuity in radical Liberal attitudes to Ireland throughout these difficult years. Indeed, in many ways Liberals' commitment to home rule was strengthened when they viewed Ireland through the prism of the Boer War.

New Liberals opposed the Boer War and supported the early grant of self-government to the Boer provinces conquered therein. Massingham resigned from the *Daily Chronicle* in 1899 rather than accept an imposed policy of editorial silence on the war.[71] Many progressive Liberals wrote for the *Speaker*, which was fiercely hostile to imperialism, under the editorship of J.L. Hammond between 1899 and 1907. Here, for instance, Hobhouse attacked the Fabian Socialists George Bernard Shaw and Sidney Webb, whom he regarded (a little unfairly) as fellow-travellers of imperialism. This 'socialistic development of Liberalism', Hobhouse maintained elsewhere, had diminished 'the credit of the school which had stood most strictly for the doctrines of liberty, fair dealing, and forbearance in international affairs'.[72] The Boer War also put new Liberals further out of sympathy with Liberal imperialism.[73]

Although a subsidiary issue to this split,[74] support for home rule for Ireland was to emerge as one of the distinct tests of radical liberalism. The *Speaker* defended the policy at the 1900 Election; when Rosebery offered his 'clean slate' on Ireland, this radical weekly declared that this was not 'the spirit in which the great liberals of history . . . carried great reforms'.[75] The *Daily News* agreed that the 'best' Liberals always stayed loyal to the Gladstonian 'standard' of home rule.[76] In 1901, Massingham rejected any suggestion that nationalist Ireland's demand for separate self-government was diminishing in intensity.[77] Scott always found it difficult to forgive Asquith his association at this time with Rosebery and with Rosebery's highly suspect commitment to this traditional Irish policy of Gladstonian Liberalism.[78]

Ireland, like South Africa, was politically (if not legally or constitutionally) an imperial issue. Though it was certainly possible for avowed imperialists to support home rule in the 1880s and 1890s, it was politically difficult because the Unionist party had managed to cultivate a public image as the imperial party, emphasising the supposed imperial necessity of resisting home rule.[79] The defence of self-government as a policy in South Africa and in Ireland tended to become associated; radical liberals criticised Milnerite policy in South Africa for tending to create another Ireland.[80]

This analogy also appeared in reverse. The *Speaker* declared during the South African War: 'Home Rule for Ireland would be an incalculable benefit to the Empire . . . every material boon is the merest dross in comparison with the supreme moral ideal which inspires and sustains the cause of national freedom'.[81] Most new liberals were also advocates of colonial self-government in South Africa. They regarded the results of Campbell-Bannerman's administration's adoption of this policy after 1906 as an outstanding success, a confirmation of mid-nineteenth-century experience in Canada, and of home rule in general.[82] Thus, the 'healing power of self-government in South Africa' indicated the likely fruits of the implementation of Gladstonian home rule in Ireland.[83] Progressive Liberals believed that the strength of the Empire lay not in its territorial magnitude but in its liberalism, its moral greatness. As Masterman appreciated, this was not a distinctively 'new' Liberal principle, but this did not diminish the enthusiasm with which he and his colleagues articulated the idea that the survival of the Empire depended on the mutual good will of its member states. In recognising this principle, Liberals felt they revealed themselves to be 'the true party of Empire'.[84] Analogies with South African experience subsequently featured heavily in new Liberal political discourse, particularly in connection with Ireland.[85]

Events in South Africa also strengthened the political status of Liberalism as the ideology of social reform. Through the home rule crisis and the Boer War, Unionists had stigmatised the Liberals as an anti-imperial party, and depicted themselves as the party of a coherent, organised and well-defended empire. But imperial defence, as the Boer War showed, was costly, and the preferred means of financing social reform for adherents to this ideology was tariff reform, which fell disproportionately on the working class. Liberals' alternative vision was of an empire in which the colonies were self-governing and therefore self-sufficient in terms of defence. This was cheaper and ideologically consistent with social reform financed by a more politically palatable means, direct taxation. 'Nothing is so expensive', claimed the *Speaker*, 'as the government of a disaffected nation. Self-government spells economy, as Imperialism spells extravagance'.[86] In this indirect way, Gladstonian home rule had politically strengthened the hands of radical social reformers within the Liberal party.[87]

The Boer War cost the new Liberals some progressive allies. But on organisations such as the South Africa Conciliation Committee, Hobhouse, Scott and others were assisted by 'old' Liberal anti-imperialists such as F.W. Hirst, Leonard Courtney, James Bryce and John Morley, as well as by the Positivists. They were far more in sympathy with the moderate progressive Liberals Murray and Hammond and their *Liberalism and the empire* than with Bernard Shaw's *Fabianism and empire.*[88] J.A. Hobson was sent to South Africa as *Guardian* correspondent at the time of the Boer War, and as a result wrote, with Murray's approval, the new Liberal classic, *Imperialism: a study.*[89] New Liberals became re-initiated in the appreciation of the timeless liberal values of international peace, self-government and liberty. 'Foreign policy is the touchstone of all policy', noted Scott at this time.[90] It is in this context that Liberals' later persistent criticism, even of the foreign and Irish policies of governments led by the Liberals Asquith and Lloyd George, should be set.[91]

The success of Unionist reforms in Ireland in the years 1895–1903 further tested the new Liberal faith in home rule. The contemporary trials of the Irish nationalist movement led many to believe that home rule was dying. The Unionist Land Act of 1903 was expected to take further wind from its sails.[92] New Liberals normally preferred measures of tenurial reform to peasant proprietorship.[93] But home rulers could profit from the measure by arguing that it would improve Ireland's social stability: 'Every thoughtful Liberal mind sees Home Rule at the end of the long and turbulent transaction which the Wyndham Bill [i.e., the Land Act of 1903] invites', wrote Massingham.[94] The 1903 Act required a local authority as an intermediary: thus, the *Speaker* contended that the Act brought home rule nearer by treating Ireland differently from the rest of the United Kingdom, 'an admission that after all Mr Gladstone and Mr Morley were right'.[95] Radical Liberals were still arguing for home rule. In the tortuous debates and divisions within the Liberal leadership in the years 1903–5, Campbell-Bannerman's fidelity to the Gladstonian idea of home rule seemed to new Liberals 'a great credit'.[96]

In 1907, the *Speaker* was converted to the *Nation* and placed under the editorship of Massingham.[97] With Scott at the *Guardian*, and A.G. Gardiner editor of the *Daily News* under the proprietorship of the Cadburys, the cast of radical Liberal editors for these crucial years in the history of the party was established. These were the three journals most often cited as representative organs of radical Liberalism; other Liberal newspapers, such as the *Westminster Gazette* and the *Daily Chronicle*, were in this period at least intermittently regarded as relatively moderate.[98]

These three radical journals had wide pretensions and gave coverage to academic writings by Liberal intellectuals such as Hammond and Hobhouse.[99] It is therefore not surprising to find that editorials in these publications were informed by the concepts and values of new Liberal theory. Much of what follows will draw on the editorial policy of these three journals as indicative of new Liberal views of political crises in Ireland during the years 1910–25.

These publications used both native Irish correspondents and British reporters especially sent to the country, in their coverage of Irish politics. Both could influence editorial policy and both frequently established long-term links with specific political and social networks in Ireland. Alice Green, the Irish-born widow of the English historian John Richard Green, became an important intermediary between nationalist Ireland and British radical Liberalism. Though she was regarded with distrust by contemporary fellow historians of Ireland (who, unlike Mrs Green herself, were generally Unionists) and hardly had a contemporary repute for impartiality,[100] her opinions on Ireland were respected by radicals. She wrote for the *Guardian* in 1888, advised Scott on the employment of John Francis Taylor (a close personal friend of Green) in the early twentieth century, and was later a contact for the *Guardian* with Sinn Féin.[101] Green and an associated circle of Anglicised and largely Protestant, largely moderate nationalists (including Horace Plunkett, Stephen Gwynn, Roger Casement,[102] George Russell – better known as Æ – and Constantine Curran, Irish correspondent of the *Nation* from 1916–24) were an early port of call for visiting Liberal journalists like H.W. Nevinson and J.L. Hammond.[103] Many of these Irishmen and women were involved in the Irish literary revival of the early twentieth century, a movement admired by Liberals.[104]

Generally, Liberal editors liked to employ Irish nationalists with an independent cast of mind for comment on Irish affairs. Scott listened to, but did not always heed, the advice and complaints of the Nationalist leader John Dillon (a close friend for over fifty years) about *Guardian* Irish correspondents.[105] The columns of the *Daily News* were frequently open to the views of Irish nationalists such as Gwynn, J.G. Swift MacNeill,[106] and the Ulster-born nationalist Robert Lynd.[107] Articles in the *Nation* were more frequently anonymous (on Massingham's insistence),[108] but signed articles from Nevinson and Hammond featured, and the editorial policy of the weekly was closely under Massingham's control and frequently echoed his own regular pseudonymous column, 'A London diary'.[109]

In 1907, the Liberal government attempted a 'step-by step' approach to home rule in an effort to reconcile the aspirations of Irish Nationalism with those of a Unionist-dominated House of Lords. But its measure, the Irish Council Bill, petered out. The *Nation* felt this devolution scheme was weak, amounting merely to 'crumbs from the table of freedom', a poor dish to offer an Irish nation starved of liberty in comparison to the hearty helping of self-government recently served up to conquered South Africa. It called it a 'patched-up compromise' based on 'what the House of Lords would pass'.[110] Radical journalists regarded the Nationalist rejection of the Bill as a tactical error, but the *Manchester Guardian* greeted this rejection with good humour: 'no serious Liberal is disturbed at the prospect of having his faith in Home Rule tried by Mr Redmond's standard; on the contrary, good Liberals will rather rejoice in it'.[111] The Council Bill was not 'the justice which [English Liberals] will one day seek once more to do to Ireland'. It followed that the 'real struggle for Ireland', as for the whole 'progressive' movement, was to confront the Lords with the land question. This was the 'only way', because on this popular issue it would prove possible to defeat the Lords and prepare the way for great Liberal measures such as home rule.[112] The Liberal press had already anticipated the party's procedure in the years 1909–14; it did not reopen the home rule issue with its eyes closed.

Coping with Resistance, 1910–14

> There is no more vindictive spirit than your 'pacifist' when he is not allowed to get his own way.
>
> James Louis Garvin, 1912[1]

IT WAS NOT MERELY the dependence of the Liberal government of 1910 on the Irish parliamentary party for a parliamentary majority which caused Liberals to reopen the home rule issue.[2] Liberal politicians, such as Campbell-Bannerman and Winston Churchill, notwithstanding the failure of the Council Bill of 1907, had declared themselves committed to an attempt on the larger policy after the election due in 1913.[3] The ambiguous result of the first Election of 1910, and the associated constitutional crisis, merely hastened consideration of the question. Though their conviction that home rule was necessary was earnest, new Liberals were still in some ways not fully equipped for their party's third home rule campaign. Once the Liberals were dependent on the support of the Irish and Labour parties, Hobhouse realised that he knew none of the Nationalist MPs – something which had apparently not bothered him before.[4]

The association of new Liberals and Irish Nationalists was, indeed, not always easy. The two groups did not always find each other congenial company. Some Irish Nationalist leaders, such as John Redmond, were politically sympathetic to Conservatives on some issues, and to the chagrin of Liberals such as Gardiner's proprietor George Cadbury, were occasionally prepared to support Conservative or Unionist governments enacting specific reforms in Ireland.[5] On the other hand, Irish nationalists were hostile to some new Liberal reforms, including the old age pensions legislation of 1908 and the Liberal Budget of 1909, particularly the whisky duties proposed in the latter. When it was clear the Irish Nationalists could help to inflict parliamentary defeat on this Budget after the Election of January 1910, there was discussion of the possibility of some amendment of these clauses. Ultimately the Redmondite Nationalists did not insist on such changes. They did not prove as hostile to the Budget as did the Independent Nationalists, led by William O'Brien and Tim Healy.[6] Other Nationalist leaders were in closer sympathy with new Liberal social reform than was Redmond. These included Dillon, T.P. O'Connor and Joseph Devlin.[7] Dillon's views on foreign policy were particularly close to those of the radical critics of the Liberal Foreign Secretary Sir Edward Grey. Scott confided to his diary: 'Dillon, as I have long felt, is the last of the great Liberals of the last century – of the tradition of Gladstone and C[ampbell-]B[annerman] – and I told him so. He seemed rather to like the accusation'.[8]

The political crisis arising from the Budget of 1909 illustrated that the new Liberals had to face the House of Lords question. Hobhouse observed: 'the last twenty years have been overshadowed by the Lords, and nothing can be done till they are done with'.[9] The reform of the composition of the House of Lords was one possible solution. But such proposals lacked the simplicity of the Campbell-Bannerman resolutions of 1907, which suggested restrictions on the Lords' powers of veto. This latter policy was more in tune with radical Liberals' fighting spirit.[10]

A third solution, and in some ways the preferred option for radical Liberals, was the calling of a referendum in the event of disagreements between the two Houses. This was favourably discussed by Hobhouse, Scott, Massingham and Hobson during the years 1907–10. Its democratic virtues were obvious to radical Liberals.[11] But progressive Liberals were less certain about its practical benefits. The crucial question was whether the electorate, given the chance, would actually endorse specific progressive proposals. Many Unionists especially felt that home rule did not have popular approval in the Edwardian period. It is unclear if this is true. What is clear, however, is that Liberals were much more circumspect than Unionists in placing their Irish proposals before the Edwardian electorate.[12] In 1910 for instance, Scott pragmatically tried to persuade George Kemp to remain as sitting 'Liberal' member for north-west Manchester. In spite of Kemp's ambivalent attitude to home rule, Scott believed no-one more Liberal would be able to hold the seat. Both Scott and Dillon were keen to avoid a referendum on home rule.[13]

Liberals were democrats, and thus had to assume that a policy with genuine popular approval had intrinsic value. Political activists who did not submit their case to the electorate did 'not believe in their own cause. They don't think that they have the nation with them'.[14] When Liberal policies like home rule lacked popular approval, Liberals struggled to reconcile their principles. But one aspect of Gladstonian Liberal heritage could be employed in 1910 to escape this dilemma and rebuff calls for a referendum on home rule. This was the rhetoric of the 'union of hearts', according to which the alliance between the Irish Nationalist party and the radical 'mass of the Liberal party' to assail the Lords' powers of veto symbolised a 'union' between 'the democracies of England and Ireland' which needed no electoral test:

> The firm and consistent attitude of Mr Redmond and his party, by enforcing the demand of the more courageous Liberal for a simple and immediate anti-veto policy, bringing the matter to an issue without delay, has rendered to British democracy a distinguished service. Among conservative mischief-makers it is common to represent the democracies of England and Ireland as hostile in sentiment, in interests and in policy. This is a libel upon both nations . . . the Irish people and their representatives have always shown keen sympathy for the noblest and best aspirations of English liberalism.[15]

The policy of the Parliament Act passed in August 1911, which elaborated the Campbell-Bannerman resolutions and reduced the Lords' veto on legislation to a two years' delay, held none of the terrors for Liberal journalists that it held for Liberal Cabinet ministers. It rather promised a Liberal utopia: 'The party has renewed its youth', claimed the *Daily News*, 'by returning to the fountain-head of its principles, to Home Rule, Democracy and Social Reform. Any repetition of the movement towards reaction, any paltering with Imperialism and Unionism would be the death of Liberalism's soul'.[16]

HOME RULE PROBLEMS, 1911–12

As the Parliament Act became law, home rule had been on the Liberal mind for twenty-five years. But during this time the details of the measure had not been considered much by Liberals. Much of the home rule case was based on general principle. The necessity of designing another home rule measure from 1911–12 caused debate and disquiet in Liberal circles.[17]

The most prominent point of debate was on the relative merits of 'federal' and 'colonial' measures of home rule. 'Federal home rule' would have involved the creation of regional parliaments with limited authority in Ireland and elsewhere in the United Kingdom. A federal settlement was suggested by many (including some Unionists) around this time.[18] A 'colonial' settlement would have granted Ireland a larger degree of autonomy, more analogous to that possessed by the self-governing dominions. There were advantages to both kinds of measure. Scott advised Liberal politicians that a federal measure might offer a mechanism to resolve the dilemma of whether to retain Irish representation at Westminster after home rule, an issue which had caused Gladstone a great deal of difficulty.[19] An additional advantage of a federal measure was that, unlike a more extensive concession of fiscal autonomy to Ireland, it would not have deprived the country of 'the benefits of recent British social legislation, and [of] the Imperial credit which can alone render possible the completion of land purchase'.[20]

However, a 'colonial' settlement offered one major argumentative advantage. For Liberals, the Campbell-Bannerman government's policy of conferring self-government on the conquered Boer provinces of South Africa had been a spectacular success in healing antagonism between Boer and Briton in the aftermath of the Boer War. It could thus be argued that the 'South African precedent' was a 'thing to imitate' in Ireland:[21] home rule in Ireland would make for a similar state of peace, while a Unionist policy of coercion would prove just as unsustainable as it had in South Africa.[22] Liberals also noted that opinion in the white self-governing colonies was strongly in favour of home rule.[23] The South African analogy dominated Liberal discourse on home rule in this period, and this argument was obviously more apposite if the Liberal home rule scheme was close to the kind of self-government enjoyed by the white dominions.

This debate took place during the winter of 1911–12 in several publications (notably a collection called *Home rule problems* produced by a Liberal committee) and in the Liberal press.[24] Perhaps the most important Liberal partisans of the federal and colonial approaches were respectively J.H. Morgan and Erskine Childers.[25] Morgan's views were endorsed by a group of Liberal MPs with Scottish connections including J. Murray MacDonald, J. Cathcart Wason, J.M. Robertson and Arthur Ponsonby.[26] Childers, prospective Liberal candidate for the seat of Devonport, was supported by Basil Williams, a historian who had fought with Childers and the Imperial forces in the Boer War, and who had later been a member of Lord Milner's 'Kindergarten'.[27] Childers declared: 'If we really believe in the Colonial analogy, we lose its whole value in laying stress on Federalism, which is irrelevant'.[28] Williams believed that Ireland should be given home rule 'as complete as we have given to the Dominions. In South Africa we have a notable example of the ready response given to ungrudging confidence hampered by no timorous shackles'.[29]

Not surprisingly, the eventual measure of home rule presented by the Prime Minister Asquith to the House of Commons on 11 April 1912 constituted an attempt to combine these advantages. It promised the later development of a federal system for the United Kingdom, though Liberals argued that the Irish problem had to be treated first, as 'ripe for treatment . . . the most urgent and practical problem of Imperial politics', as even Morgan agreed.[30] But the measure also contained colonial characteristics, including, to Unionists' dismay, the power for the proposed Irish parliament to enact import tariffs for Ireland slightly different from any enacted at Westminster for Britain.[31] Liberals such as Childers who were very much committed to either type of home rule measure were not too satisfied with this compromise.[32] However, a hybrid Bill was the easiest kind for progressive Liberal scribes to defend; they could use both the arguments articulated by proponents of a federal measure and those voiced by advocates of a 'colonial' scheme, in support of the Bill at different times. The potential contradictions in a hybrid scheme troubled the new Liberals little, as their ideas about constitutional problems had never been very precise. The *Nation* had declared its support for 'Devolution, Home Rule, Federation or whatever the plan may be'. The *Daily News* claimed that 'no matter what is the form ultimately adopted, every Home Ruler will accept it as a great boon, even though he may retain his view that a form different in this or that particular would have been a still greater boon'.[33] The use of the colonial analogy by most Liberals in 1912 was not meant to imply that they contemplated the creation of an Irish dominion. South African experience merely illustrated a law of human nature, that such a political concession tended to produce good will and efficient regional government. Therefore, Liberals at least affected to believe that any opponents of Irish home rule were professing 'extravagant theories of Irish depravity'.[34]

The only possible details of home rule which radical Liberals discussed with much relish were proportional representation and women's suffrage. These policies did not just find their favour in the Irish context but they were also democratic measures which men like Scott had long supported.[35]

Proportional representation promised to break up the sectarian 'watertight compartments' of Irish politics, and thus promised to satisfy parties who felt aggrieved about home rule.[36] The question of women's suffrage, however, was far more of a threat to the cordial relations which had developed between the Irish Nationalists and the radicals. While practically all new Liberals supported women's suffrage keenly out of principle, Irish Nationalists felt obliged to oppose the policy throughout the years 1910–13 for the sake of the parliamentary balance. The Irish Nationalist leaders were also personally unsympathetic to the measure. Dillon felt 'a very large proportion of the political catastrophes in the history of the human race were brought about by women'.[37] Liberals argued that women's suffrage was just as much a measure of political liberation as Irish home rule and therefore felt the Nationalists were being hypocritical.[38] Some liberal journalists felt so passionately about women's suffrage that they sympathised with the militant suffragettes. Two important examples of this were Henry Brailsford and Henry Nevinson, who both resigned from the *Daily News* in 1909 in protest at its relatively moderate attitude to women's suffrage.[39]

Though a somewhat heterodox Liberal, Nevinson was of great importance in the relations of nationalist Ireland and the new Liberals. Of all radical journalists, he perhaps spent the most time in Ireland and felt most passionately about the country, regarding it as 'my adopted mother'.[40] Nevinson, a remarkable character, had many nationalist friends in Ireland, male and female, including Alice Green, Maud Gonne, W.B. Yeats, Roger Casement and Casement's cousin Gertrude Bannister, with whom he enjoyed a passionate if chaste relationship around the time of Casement's execution.[41] But women's suffrage was Nevinson's greatest crusade. Both of his wives were suffragettes. His second wife Evelyn Sharp (who also worked as a correspondent in Ireland) was twice imprisoned before the Great War as a result of her 'militancy'.[42] Scott and Brailsford both threatened in 1913 that if Irish Nationalists did not adopt a more sympathetic attitude to women's suffrage, Liberal 'keenness for Home Rule will be blunted'.[43] But most new Liberals did nothing to actualise such threats. Nevinson rejected his colleagues' fear that his ire at the Nationalist party and its obstruction of women's suffrage would turn him against home rule: 'however much I hate the Gov[ernmen]t and Parliamentarian Irish, I love the Irish people'.[44]

The unprogressive and sectarian nature of Irish nationalist political culture thus caused new Liberals no little discomfort on several occasions. Liberals saw that Irish politics were dominated by the division of Ireland into Protestants and Catholics.[45] Individuals on both sides of this sectarian divide were obliged to preserve an unreal unanimity in order to avoid giving anything away to the other on the all-pervasive constitutional issue. Consequently, Unionists and Nationalists each had a relatively safe regional hegemony, respectively in the north and the south of the island. Irish politics were untouched by that 'collision of opinion' which J.S. Mill had felt so necessary – 'they are scarcely called upon to argue . . . in a contested election'.[46] There was, as a result, little place in Irish politics for the discussion of social issues. The Liberal press believed that this lamentable state of affairs led Irish Nationalist leaders not only to adopt unenlightened attitudes towards women's suffrage, but to respond in a hostile or apathetic manner to labour questions and social reform, as was revealed during the Dublin transport strikes of 1913 and in the city's social conditions at this time.[47]

But it was possible for progressive Liberals in 1912–13 to argue that the creation of an Irish parliament would effect a modernisation of Irish politics and of Irish nationalist political culture. Home rule would enhance the importance of social issues in Ireland and promote a healthy debate and a healthier division of parties based on such questions. In imaginative moments, the Liberal press speculated on a future Dublin parliament in which Irish political divisions would be 'like the differences of English politics':

> A Home Rule party is impossible in a Home Rule Ireland. There might be a moderate Conservative party, led, let us say, by Mr Redmond, or a Clerical Party, relying on Mr Healy, or a moderate Liberal party, looking chiefly to Mr Dillon, or a more advanced Radical party, in which Mr O'Connor and Mr Devlin would be leading figures. There would be a natural gravitation of interest of capitalist Dublin to capitalist Belfast, a natural sympathy on the other hand, between the urban democracies of North and South.[48]

This development, perhaps further enhanced by the emergence of an Irish labour party under the direction of James Larkin,[49] and by proportional representation, would show that the sectarian fears of the Ulster Unionists were without basis. Therefore, the *Nation* urged Ulster to drop its forlorn battle for the preservation of the Union, forget the past and concentrate on the 'urgent questions of work and wages' that were sure to dominate the political firmament in the new Ireland.[50]

THE ULSTER DIMENSION, 1912–14

Before April 1912, the federal-colonial issue, not Ulster, dominated Liberal debate about home rule. The beginnings of the Ulster campaign to resist home rule at this time were treated dismissively in the Liberal press. In new Liberal discourse, Ireland was a 'living body', an 'organism',[51] and partition would be 'vivisection'.[52] Progressive Liberals therefore usually regarded Ulster Protestant Unionism as a parasitic, 'anti-National' movement,[53] conspiring with upper-class British Unionists and manipulating popular sectarianism in order to maintain a position of 'unqualified dominion'.[54] New Liberals did not distinguish the cause of Ulster from the Anglo-Irish minority's traditional pursuit of ascendancy in Ireland. In 1918, Nevinson was to cite and approve a statement of Charles Gavan Duffy from 1842, that there were only two parties in Ireland, that which gained from her national degradation and that which suffered from it.[55] Ulster Protestants were the 'men who for centuries have served as the British garrison in Ireland, a dominant minority accustomed to power and intolerant of association on equal terms with the rest of their fellow-countrymen'.[56] In short, Protestant Ulster had no genuine grievance about home rule: 'It is no accident that Unionism has never produced a great democratic voice in Ulster; it cannot produce it, for great utterance can only come from the heart of a great and unselfish cause'.[57]

These errors of interpretation were in some ways understandable. Liberals noted the support of the wealthy, educated and privileged in Britain and Ireland for the Ulster resistance.[58] As MPs discussed the Agar-Robartes amendment to exclude four counties of Ulster from home rule (June 1912), the Liberal press inferred that Unionists were not out for special treatment for Ulster, but would like to defeat home rule altogether. The exclusion of Ulster, said the *Daily News*, was 'an English expedient . . . There has been no real support for it from anyone who can be said to think in Irish terms or to represent Irish interests'.[59] Before 1914, few clear political differences between Ulster and southern Irish Unionism were apparent to British observers.[60] British Unionists occasionally almost admitted that Ulster was merely 'a tool with which to attack the Parliament Act' and defeat the government and its social reform proposals.[61] Liberals could thus argue that what they were faced with was an anti-social conspiracy, a class war declared by the rich and privileged,[62] which bore no relation to the rights and wrongs of the Irish question.

Liberals had little understanding of Unionist Ulster, which they regarded as reactionary in politics, intolerant in religion and backward in economics. 'All here are in economic theory like England of 1860', noted Nevinson in Belfast in March 1914.[63] The whole Ulster movement was therefore opposed to the new Liberal line of progress. Into the 1920s, new Liberals continued to hope that the rise of labour in Ireland would transcend the sectional divide; the Ulster working class would surely see through its false consciousness, once home rule was in place.[64] Ulster was perceived as a crucial test of the nerve of Liberalism: 'If the government held firmly by Home Rule, if with equal zeal they pursued the principles of true Liberalism and democracy at home and abroad, and if they could inspire again in this country that personal and moral enthusiasm such as a few of our past statesmen have inspired', Nevinson confidently predicted, 'then within a few weeks or months of the Royal Sanction to the Bill, we should hear no more of Ulster fighting and being right'.[65]

The irony of course was that this vision was not itself without prejudice. Liberals believed that Unionist Ulster's opposition to home rule was 'sincere, though stupid', the product of 'a state of hallucination' about home rule[66]:

> 'for the . . . simple-minded Orangeman of the Cromwellian type', commented the *Nation*, 'one has a very considerable respect . . . His political creed, to be sure, ought rather to be called a political cult, a compound of fears, instincts, hatreds, and traditions in which facts are metamorphised out of all semblance to reality. But he is a fine fellow, and he will be quite honestly the most surprised man in the world when he finds that Home Rule has not taken his farm from him, or closed his workshop, or forced him to attend Mass, or dissolved his marriage by Papal decree'.[67]

The Liberal press thus claimed to be confident that Ulster was given to 'bluster' and 'threats', and that its resistance to home rule would melt away: 'In ten years half the Ulster firebrands will probably be Home Rule ministers or ex-ministers'.[68] This was extremely patronising and probably inflamed Ulster Unionists further against the Liberal government. In February 1912, when Ulster Unionists protested at the plans of Winston Churchill to speak in Belfast in favour of home rule, the *Guardian* declared that these were 'Hottentots . . . incapable of self-government'.[69] Ulstermen were the 'spoilt children' of the Empire, without genuine grievance, but used to getting their own way.[70] New Liberal language about Ulster at this time was therefore in many ways (sometimes deliberately) reminiscent of Unionist rhetoric about Irish nationalists years earlier.[71]

Liberals were hardly likely to consent to the partition of Ireland on the whim of this anti-social and obsolete Ulster Unionist movement. They were almost as attached as Irish Nationalists were to the ideal of Irish unity. Unionists, especially Ulster Unionists, asserted that if the case for home rule were based on the claim that the government of Ireland should have the consent of the governed, the corollary was that the government of Ulster should also have the consent of *its* majority community, and that a separate measure for Ulster ought to be considered.[72] The new Liberals could use their favourite colonial analogy against this; dominion 'Irelands have been given Home Rule with the best results. Their own "Ulsters" have loyally acquiesced'.[73] In an important (and much praised)[74] essay of 1912, L.T. Hobhouse argued that Ireland was a nation, and that her demand for self-government was based on a national self-consciousness which had survived centuries of oppression:

> Does Belfast . . . call itself a nation? Not if its desire is, what we have always understood it to be, to remain directly subject to the British Parliament. It is in fact, the focus of an old but decayed Ascendancy caste . . . If such a demand is put forward not merely in order to wreck Home Rule, but as a substantive proposal seriously intended, it will constitute a new fact . . . At present it can only be regarded as highly improbable that such a claim should be maintained or even put forward except in a fighting mood. That Belfast should sustain her opposition to the whole Bill is perfectly natural, but given that there is to be Home Rule as one of the fixed conditions of a settlement, her natural position is that of a centre and rallying point for the dispersed forces of Irish Protestantism.[75]

This suggestion that the Ulster movement should be ignored as it was not a nationalism was much respected by new Liberals.[76] Hobhouse contended elsewhere that movements such as that in Protestant Ulster claiming special treatment required the test of:

> practical experience. If it turns out possible to maintain the undesired union without special restriction on the political and personal rights

> of the recalcitrant people, well and good. But the stronger the national feeling, the less likely is this to be the case and the further are governments driven along the road of coercion and into the forbidden ground of the modern spirit . . . if the best-ordered society is that which makes room for the self-development of many different types . . . there [is] room . . . for those groupings of individuals which spontaneously form and stubbornly maintain themselves against legal pressure.[77]

This of course was dangerously close to the argument that 'legal pressure' had to be applied against Protestant Ulster to see if resistance were 'stubbornly' maintained. In a sense, the years 1912–14 constituted this test.

If it were indeed legitimate for Liberals to heap on Unionist Ulster the kind of obloquy which the most partisan Unionists had expressed towards nationalist Ireland in the 1880s, the corollary might have seemed to be that the coercion of Ulster, like that of Irish Nationalism under Unionist governments, was justified. But new Liberals were self-confessed inept coercionists, preferring 'even a partial or a maimed settlement rather than a strong settlement soiled by blood'.[78] The Irish question and the tortuous nature of their ideology, thus imposed some difficult decisions on Liberals in these years; how were they to deal with this wrong but stubborn Ulster movement? If new Liberals really believed that the Ulster resistance would just go away, the Derry by-election of February 1913, as well as the opinion of a few unrepresentative Ulster Protestant home rulers, could be cited as evidence.[79] But as autumn 1914 neared, and the Lords' two-year veto on home rule began to expire, such hopes ceased to reassure even the most blinkered new Liberals, and it became clear that Liberal journalists would need to suggest an Ulster policy for the government.[80]

J.A. Hobson had no doubts that the Ulster resistance was not bluff, but sedition, and should therefore be put down with all the resources of civilisation.[81] Hobson was largely uninterested in the rights and wrongs of home rule; the well-to-do sponsors of the Ulster movement in Britain were merely out to frustrate democracy and social reform. The Liberal government's home rule policy was merely the occasion for this conflict, but as that government had been democratically elected, the measure had to be pushed through; all talk of concession jeopardised liberty and order throughout the Empire.[82] Hobson felt the kind of resentment for Asquithian concessions to 'Ulster' which was articulated by Liberal activists all over Britain. In September 1913, for instance, the *Daily News* claimed to be overwhelmed by correspondence from Liberals opposed to Lord Loreburn's famous letter to the *Times* calling for a bipartisan conference to settle the home rule controversy.[83] Hobson had never thought very much specifically about Ireland, and the extent of his commitment to home rule may be questioned. In this, as in his proposals for Irish policy in the years 1912–14, he was out on a limb among new Liberals.[84]

Henry Massingham's *Nation*, and his occasional *Daily News* articles, in the years 1912–14, articulated views that were more nuanced and more typical. Massingham accepted in part the Unionist argument that the home rule issue had not been the most prominent at the December 1910 Election.[85] He also realised that many Liberals, and most English people, would dislike the coercion of Unionist Ulster.[86] Early in 1912, the *Nation* suggested that the leaders of the Ulster Unionist agitation against home rule ought to be prosecuted.[87] However, it also insinuated that the Protestant population of Ulster were merely 'the blind and witless dupes of their own prejudice' and of these leaders. The Unionists of Ulster were not exactly bluffing – at least not consciously – but in the long-term, they could and would be peacefully won over to an acceptance of home rule.[88]

Massingham and his colleagues advocated a limited concession to Protestant Ulster on the grounds of policy and of justice. His *Nation* professed its preparedness to have the Ulster issue thrashed out at length in Parliament, even at the 'sacrifice of other parts of the Ministerial programme'. It contended that this approach would be consistent with the spirit of a 'measure of appeasement' such as home rule.[89] It would serve notice to the British and Ulster electorates that the Liberal government had gone out of its way to conciliate Ulster. C.P. Scott was similarly prepared to see much parliamentary time used to investigate the possibility of compromise settlement: 'Nothing is more desirable', Scott's *Guardian* declared, 'than that the contrast between the Government's tenderness for all reasonable expectations and the Opposition's self-abandonment to methods of obstruction in Parliament and anarchy in parts of Ireland should be heightened to the utmost'.[90]

Patricia Jalland has argued that Massingham's *Nation:*

> faithfully expressed the views of the radical wing of the Liberal party . . . The Government's Home Rule policy was loyally supported as the fulfilment of an obligation to 'old Liberalism', which should be settled as rapidly as possible to make way for the social reforms of the New Liberalism.[91]

It is true that new Liberals broadly preferred discussing social issues to any other, and were more moderate about Ulster than many Liberals 'in the country'. However, Massingham's conciliatory interludes cannot be regarded as 'faithfully expressing' the views of radical Liberal journalism on this point. As he noted: 'I never say a conciliatory word . . . without feeling that most of my fellow-Liberals disagree'.[92] New Liberals professed periodic impatience with the 'wait and see' Ulster policy of Asquith, and in 1913–14 they often regretted the 'restraint . . . perilously like weakness' shown to the Ulster rebels earlier in the crisis,[93] especially when Unionists and Ulster leaders appeared to have taken actions which were seditious. After the 'Curragh mutiny',[94] Massingham wrote: 'Ulster has sickened [English Liberals]. Her arrogance, her ignorance, her uncivilised and irreligious hatred, do not appeal to modern minds . . . we can afford to be quite calm about the "coercion" of Ulster . . . we have done her justice';[95] and after the Ulster Unionists landed a shipment of weapons at Larne in April 1914, Massingham's *Nation* struck an equally determined note.[96] For his part, Scott assented to many of Hobson's reactions to the Ulster crisis, particularly those espoused in his pamphlet *Traffic in Treason*.[97] Liberal editors were generally long-time home rulers and were genuinely concerned about avoiding inflicting an intractable Ulster problem on Ireland at the start of her career as a self-governing nation.[98] Thus, throughout the years 1913–14, they were prepared to adopt whatever means were necessary to remove Ulster's objections to home rule; their organs fluctuated between coercion and conciliation in a manner which Jalland has aptly described as 'schizophrenic'.[99]

Massingham hardly advocated the exclusion of Ulster from Irish home rule as willingly as the Labour weekly, the *New Statesman*.[100] The new Liberals preferred the plan of 'Home Rule within Home Rule' for Ulster (which Scott was advocating as late as June 1914).[101] Massingham's attitude was close to that of William O'Brien of the Independent Nationalist movement, who was prepared to offer Unionist Ulster great concessions in terms of governmental machinery to ensure Irish unity, yet was not prepared to admit that Protestant Ulster could not be won over to home rule (i.e., that its Unionism was elemental).[102] Noticeably, O'Brien, Massingham and Scott all praised Loreburn's call for a compromise settlement which would maintain the unity of Ireland.[103] In other words, Massingham was not aggressive in his tone towards Ulster Unionism, but in so far as he suggested to Protestant Ulster that its Unionism was not a matter of robust conviction, his statements were provocative in a far more subtle way.

Fundamentally, the new Liberals were emotionally and ideologically committed to home rule for a united Ireland on Gladstonian lines. This was a long promised Liberal project, and its attainment would symbolise the full victory of Liberalism over all its political foes in the United Kingdom. They were also out of sympathy with the tone, aims and character of Unionist Ulster, and they saw that the British allies of Ulster Unionism were those who always sought to frustrate political 'progress'. Thus 'if there had been no Ulster question the issue would have been raised on something else', and yielding to the Ulster resistance would have meant 'an end to peace in Ireland, or for that matter England'.[104] New Liberals were also advised by Nationalist friends that the unity of Ireland had to be upheld. T.P. O'Connor told Gardiner that 'no change of conditions and no pressure can make Ireland take any other view. She would regard herself as asked to surrender the unity of her Nationhood, and she would throw aside a dozen Home Rule Bills rather than accept that principle'.[105] Meanwhile, Dillon counselled Scott against both the coercion of and concession to Unionist Ulster; the movement was just not to be taken seriously.[106] This counsel, and new Liberal journalists' own predilections, left them criticising the Asquith ministry for being at once too conciliatory to Unionist Ulster and not conciliatory enough.

In March 1914, Asquith announced the terms of his government's proposal to deal with the Ulster controversy, an Amending Bill eventually introduced into the House of Commons in May 1914. Under this measure, each county of Ulster in which a majority voted against their initial inclusion in the Home Rule Bill would be excluded from its operation, in the first instance for a maximum of six years. Presently, fear of violence in Ireland drove some Liberals to consider further concessions to their Unionist opponents.[107] The new Liberals began to feel demoralised by their government's handling of Ulster. Scott wrote: 'I am beginning to feel . . . that the existing Liberal party is played out and that if it is to count for anything in the future it must be reconstructed largely on a labour basis'.[108] Hobhouse also despaired: 'Better far, to my mind, to lose Home Rule than to accept a compromise based on the dictation of Carson with the backing of the army and society . . . Even if the HR Bill is passed it must under these circumstances remain a dead letter'. A measure such as the Amending Bill, he maintained, 'should have been carried through earlier, not under coercion'.[109] But such suggestions were made with the benefit of hindsight. Hobhouse's own essay in *The new Irish constitution* of 1912 had rejected exceptional treatment for Ulster, and the *Nation*, under

Massingham's editorship, had ridiculed the Ulster agitation at the same time.[110] The new Liberals were still home rulers, and Liberal journalists pressed for home rule to be placed on the statute book after the Great War began in August 1914.[111] If new Liberals had doubts in mid-1914 about the desirability of the kind of home rule then being negotiated, it was because their idea of what home rule ought to be was always unrealisable.

Jalland argues that by:

> introducing a Home Rule Bill for a united Ireland, the Government raised expectations which would not be fulfilled, so that any subsequent concessions were seen as treachery to the Nationalist cause. Meanwhile Ulster prepared for civil war and feelings on both sides hardened, as the influence of the extremists in Ireland increased.[112]
>
> At whatever time Asquith chose to agree that concessions for Ulster were required, he would be admitting that his original measure was far from perfect . . . The Prime Minister would have been the wiser to dictate his own terms for Ulster from the start and retain the initiative, instead of waiting for concessions to be forced upon him . . . The scheme known as 'Home Rule within Home Rule' had much to recommend it as a starting point . . . This would have been acceptable to most Liberals, and would have been far easier for the Nationalists to concede, since it did not violate the principle of a united Ireland . . . Moreover, 'Home Rule within Home Rule' did not exclude the possibility of further concessions if these proved necessary.[113]

Asquith's Irish policy from 1912–14 has not been defended, even by friendly critics.[114] The charge levelled against it by Jalland, that this policy made a series of dangerously cumulative concessions to political agitation unavoidable, has been one of the leading grounds of criticism. Yet, no realistic alternative policy can be suggested in retrospect which would not equally have involved 'the possibility of further concessions if these proved necessary' – unless it would have violated Irish unity, a most sacred maxim of Irish nationalism and Liberal ideology.

Historians have observed that from 1912–14, 'for the Liberals, the Ulster dimension remained in the background until a curiously late stage'.[115] An early commitment to the exclusion of the four predominantly Protestant counties of Ulster from home rule by the Liberal government might have helped to undermine the basis for Unionist opposition to the Home Rule Bill in the country at large. It might have produced a long-term settlement of the Irish question which, whether conducive to Irish unity or not, would have been more peaceable than the events of the next ten years. What is clear, however, is that new Liberals would have needed a lot of persuading before they could have found such a plan acceptable. Government proposals for the temporary exemption of parts of Protestant Ulster from home rule, even in the exceptionally tense circumstances of March 1914, caused considerable grumbling in the Liberal press and were regarded by the most moderate of new Liberal journalists as 'perilous'.[116] The progressive Liberal press would not have been satisfied with such a proposal in April 1912, whether sanctioned by the government or not. Far from the government 'raising expectations' for a unitarian home rule settlement, expectations already existed, in England as well as in Ireland.[117] In retrospect Liberals' 'curious' neglect of the Ulster dimension, and their equally 'curious' neglect of this kind of compromise, can be explained by a proper appreciation of the extent of Liberals' ideological commitment to a particular kind of Irish settlement. Asquith's partisan supporters would not even consider Ulster exclusion before it seemed absolutely obligatory. In these circumstances, a Liberal Prime Minister would have been remarkably imaginative to propound the policy before Asquith did.

CHAPTER FIVE

'Broken Hearts' and 'Decent Rage', 1916–21

THE CONDITIONS OF total war from 1914–18 stretched new Liberals' notional symbiosis between individuality and community to breaking point. Almost all had become opponents of a British government led by a radical Liberal by May 1921, a division fatal to the party.[1] The progressive Liberals entered the war with reluctance and regretted the methods used in fighting it.[2] This regret translated into outright opposition to the government at different times for different new Liberals: but this did not fundamentally divide new Liberals. Progressive Liberal supporters of the war praised those who opposed it, and those who took a stand against conscription in 1916 were admired by the less vocal. New Liberals' 'real anger' went elsewhere.[3]

But some ideas accepted by pro- and anti-war Liberals did make progress during the war. Liberal writers like Hobhouse were able to associate the fight against Germany with the rejection of the idea that the state was the 'supreme and final form of association' between human beings,[4] and thus with acceptance of the Liberal rationalist goal of a league of nations:

> a whole civilisation – which is at stake – is greater than a single nation . . . the chastening of adversity will shake the nonsense out of the world . . . We are fighting neither selfishly nor unselfishly, but for the whole of which we are members . . . here we may have the beginning of that true foundation in feeling which may be the basis of an international State.[5]

Like the Positivists, therefore, the new Liberals aspired to an ideal of global unity; and although both groups found themselves removed ever further from real influence over the seats of political power during the Great War, they could look on with some satisfaction as their pre-war schemes began to infiltrate the political language even of those who had been unsympathetic.[6]

RISING, CONVENTION AND CONSCRIPTION

Liberal consideration of Ireland was distinctly low-key between September 1914 and April 1916. In 1915, Hobhouse complacently argued that 'liberal measures', particularly the fact that home rule had been placed on the statute book in September 1914, had successfully 'incorporated' Ireland; this was supposed to illustrate the intrinsic superiority of British ideals and practice of liberty.[7] The Liberal press, like most of the British press, greeted the Easter Rising as a wicked minoritarian pro-German conspiracy. It did not detract from the loyalty to the Allied cause of Redmond's movement and of nationalist Ireland in general, and the need to punish the rebels was not questioned. The tone of Liberal editorial response to the Easter Rising only differed from that of Unionists in emphasising its Ulster roots. The Rising was regarded as the 'long-dreaded rebound from the Carson rebellion, the fatal crop that has grown from that sowing of dragon's teeth in a soil always fertile to such a growth'.[8] The Liberal press did not immediately regard April 1916 as an opportunity to reopen the home rule controversy; even in mid-May 1916, the *Daily News* preferred some form of executive reorganisation in Ireland to the immediate establishment of home rule.[9]

Doubts were soon expressed however about the actions of the executive in Ireland during the 1916 Rising. These initially concerned the killing of Francis Sheehy-Skeffington, who had acted as a *Guardian* Irish correspondent before the war, and who had been an ally of Nevinson in the cause of women's suffrage.[10] With the assistance of Nevinson and the British Liberal press, Sheehy-Skeffington's widow Hanna (herself an important Irish feminist) pressed successfully for an enquiry into her husband's death.[11] The protracted executions of the rebels in early May increased Liberal doubts. At the *Nation*, 'only Hobhouse as philosopher [held] out ag[ain]st his nature' for the executions.[12] Liberals soon realised the effect these were having in Ireland of putting the rebels into popular favour.[13] There were also objections on grounds of justice, given the lack of punishment meted out some years earlier to the 'Unionist rebel' Carson. Disturbing accounts of indiscriminate repression by the authorities were being circulated between Liberal journalists soon after Massingham made a brief trip to Ireland in May 1916.[14]

The final execution of 1916 became a *cause célèbre*. Roger Casement was greatly admired in radical circles before 1914. His work in exposing mistreatment of indigenous populations in colonial Africa brought him to the attention of the Liberal press, and into cooperation with E.D. Morel, Nevinson and others.[15] Casement was also an Ulster Protestant nationalist, and therefore a symbol of Liberals' hope that the Protestant and Catholic Irish would peacefully coexist under home rule. Nevinson regarded Casement as perhaps the 'wisest man I know'.[16]

Nevinson, Alice Green, George Bernard Shaw and others threw themselves into efforts to avert Casement's execution in mid-1916.[17] They were not supported by all new Liberals or by the whole resources of the progressive press. But the major radical Liberal editors (Massingham, Scott, Gardiner and G.P. Gooch of the *Contemporary Review*) all accepted that Casement's reprieve, whether just or not, was politic, and petitioned the authorities.[18] For Nevinson, Casement was an admirable and honourable friend, to whom he was prepared to give the benefit of some rather large doubts, and whose life was worth preserving for its own sake. R.B. Cunninghame Graham, a former ally of Casement and Nevinson in their colonial campaigns, disagreed publicly, and Nevinson gave him up as a friend for some twelve years.[19]

Events surrounding the failure of such efforts to save Casement have been the subject of much speculation and legend. It was common knowledge at the time that official efforts were made to discredit the campaign for clemency by the circulation of extracts from Casement's infamous 'Black diaries' which provided evidence relating to Casement's homosexuality (although these efforts were only officially acknowledged by a British government in 1994).[20] In Nevinson's view, these tactics were not entirely unsuccessful. Feelings of injustice among Casement's friends were increased by the fact that F.E. Smith, who acted as Casement's prosecutor on behalf of the Crown during Casement's trial for treason in June 1916, had associated prominently with Carson in the Unionist resistance to home rule during 1912–14. Nevinson believed Smith's past was no less treasonous than anything Casement had done, and Smith became an incarnation of all that Nevinson detested.[21]

Nevinson associated with Casement publicly and deliberately at a time when others saw good reasons for remaining relatively inactive.[22] Nevinson's emotion as he watched Casement being sentenced to death late in June 1916, as well as his increasing sympathy with Irish nationalism, are equally unquestionable: 'I wish I had shouted 'God save Ireland'. Not being Irish, I had no right, but I wish I had'.[23] Some time after Casement's execution for treason in August 1916, Nevinson complained that authorities had attempted to suppress his efforts to save Casement.[24] The lack of balance in some of Nevinson's writings on Ireland throughout the years 1919–21 is directly attributable to events in 1916.

In view of the discourse which Liberal supporters of the Allied cause in the war adopted, particularly after America began to participate in the war on the Allied side in 1917, Ireland was a distinct embarrassment, 'the one serious moral blemish' on the British record.[25] An Ireland denied self-government was a jarring contrast to the voluntarist rhetoric of Liberalism at war, and was a 'discredit' to British statesmanship.[26] At the very least, Liberals were determined to oppose the imposition of conscription on an Ireland in such a condition; such illiberal behaviour would have been befitting only of Prussia herself. The 'Dublin Executions', wrote Scott, 'gave an immense impetus to Sinn Féinism': 'the conscriptionists are trying to make Ireland pay for our blunder'.[27]

The immediate implementation of home rule was discussed in the weeks after the Easter Rising. But once again the problematic Ulster issue was the cause of frustration. New Liberals had little more sympathy with the character and claims of Ulster Unionism in 1916 than in 1912. Immediate home rule, which seemed probable in June 1916, was likely to embody some sort of Ulster exclusion, at best temporarily; and this was a policy which Liberals still regarded as an 'unworthy end'.[28] When the attempted Lloyd George compromise of July 1916 was aborted because it proved impossible to reconcile Ulster Unionism and Irish Nationalism on such a basis, Massingham criticised the government and defended the attitude of the Nationalist leader John Redmond.[29]

It is not surprising then to find the new Liberal press again adopting a rather threatening tone with Unionist Ulster on occasions during the war. Ulster could not stand in the way of the essential needs of the British Empire; she had too long been its 'spoilt child', and it was fair now to expect her to give as well as take.[30] New Liberals also thought it reasonable to expect some form of 'reparation' from Carson and the Ulster Unionists.[31] After all, as Alice Green was trenchantly to argue, Unionist Ulster's resistance to home rule from 1912–14 appeared to be responsible for reviving the idea of physical force in nationalist Ireland, leading to the Easter Rising and the rise of Irish separatism.[32] In wilder moments, the Liberal press suggested that Carson's 'little Prussian garrison in Ulster' had been 'one of the great factors in plunging the world into war'.[33] Partition was 'petty and pessimistic', based on 'obsolete pride and bigotry'.[34]

But once more the coercion of Ulster was hardly desirable or possible for Liberals. The best hope of escaping the Ulster tangle during the war seemed to be patience. New Liberals, and those Nationalist associates who contributed to the Liberal press, hoped that the association of Ulster and Nationalist Volunteers in the same wartime cause, alongside each other in the trenches of France, would tend to Irish unity.[35] This was a policy in all respects consistent with the rhetoric of wartime, and with Liberal tradition in colonial policy: 'Ulster is to be won to Ireland by the very same method by which Ireland is to be won to the United Kingdom, and that is by the same method by which South Africa and indeed all the Dominions have been won to the Empire', declared the *Manchester Guardian*. It understood that method to consist of 'abandoning the attempt to override the smaller people . . . whether by the force of arms or that of majority votes, and seeking to secure their willing assent to form a part of the larger union on condition that their internal liberties are respected'.[36] Massingham was similarly tempted to hope that the war might produce a united home rule Ireland as a *fait accompli*.[37]

But the Liberals recognised that there were also pressing reasons for doing something in Ireland immediately. The continued government of Ireland through the hated instrument of Dublin Castle was not just an embarrassment to British statesmanship; it also seemed likely to radicalise Irish nationalism and marginalise the Liberals' political allies in Ireland, Redmond's Nationalists.[38] Therefore, it was necessary to explore mechanisms which might hasten the implementation of self-government for a united Ireland. Liberal journalists identified two of these during the war. The first was associated with contemporary reconsideration of the constitutional relations between the states of the British Empire. It was anticipated that the dominions would have to have a greater say in the foreign policy of the Empire in future. Ireland, wrote Scott, ought to be considered in the light of 'the possibility of a general tightening up (not likely to go far, I fancy, but wh[ich] m[igh]t still be useful for easing the solution of the Irish problem) of the bond of Imperial unity'.[39] Massingham agreed:

> Our imperial constitution must assume Ireland to be a unit in the Empire, and give her both a local representation and a share in the imperial government. Her resulting liberties would then come, not as a gift from the nation that broke Ireland's Parliament, but from the union of states on which the stamp of her own exiled genius is visibly laid.[40]

The revision of imperial relations would mean some sort of constitutional conference, to which the Irish problem could be referred – if Ireland could wait that long.

A second possible mechanism for settlement was an Irish, rather than an imperial, Convention. The Lloyd George coalition government, which had been formed in December 1916, adopted this proposal in May 1917. The Prime Minister then had Scott help to draft a letter to Redmond offering the alternatives of immediate home rule with Ulster excluded, or an Irish Convention.[41] (Lloyd George later tried to use Scott's involvement in this project to suggest that Scott had a moral obligation to acquiesce in what Lloyd George depicted as similar coalition Irish policies).[42] Once the Irish Convention was called as a result, the Liberal press was broadly supportive, seeing it as offering the best chance of 'the only goal worth striving for, the goal of a united self-governing Ireland'.[43] After the Convention opened in July 1917, Massingham maintained an editorial silence on its proceedings in an effort to try to avoid prejudicing its success: 'It's the real way I am persuaded to an Irish Constitution that will last'.[44] But the *Nation* and other Liberal papers broke this silence early in 1918, attacking the 'selfish' resistance of Ulster to a unitarian settlement within Ireland.[45]

The Convention was a race against time.[46] Every delay in the implementation of home rule for a united Ireland compromised the position of the moderate Redmondite Nationalists in Ireland still further. During 1917, Sinn Féin began to constitute a viable political alternative to Redmond's party, as Massingham was informed by the *Nation's* Irish correspondent, Constantine P. Curran.[47] It was therefore becoming clear that Redmondite (and Gladstonian) home rule might no longer be enough for Ireland. In particular, the East Clare by-election of July 1917, which marked the birth of a new star in Irish politics, the Easter rebel, Eamon de Valera, led the *Nation* seriously to consider the merits of 'dominion Home Rule' for Ireland. Massingham wrote: 'Dominion Government will, I am assured, satisfy the country, while a substantially smaller plan is sure to be torn up by it'.[48] Other Liberal journals, though not quite so radical, would not be far behind.

The tortuous nature of the discussions at the Convention perturbed Liberals. By early 1918, new Liberals believed that agreement had been attained on many issues at the Convention, and that only details, and the stubborn and prehistoric attitudes of the Ulster Unionists stood in the way of settlement; southern Irish Unionism was no longer perceived as an obstacle. Nationalists who insisted on fiscal autonomy for a home rule

Ireland also tried Liberal patience. Scott commented: 'the whole Irish question looks pretty small. They are perhaps just now a good deal more comfortable than any other people in Europe'.[49]

But the focus of new Liberal sympathies in the sequel to the Irish Convention was in no doubt. In April 1918, the government announced proposals to introduce conscription into Ireland. The Liberals saw this as 'madness'. Scott warned Lloyd George: 'It is no part of statesmanship and must destroy all hope of a conciliatory policy in Ireland. It will double your cares and may even prove a disastrous turning point I believe in your career'.[50] Irish conscription, Liberals felt, would not strengthen Allied military resources, but would instead entail 'a net loss to our fighting strength, for it would not bring us anything like the numbers of soldiers' that would be required to enforce the policy. It would 'cause the shedding not of German but of Irish and maybe of British blood'.[51] The forces needed to defeat Germany's spring offensive of 1918 would come from the United States of America, so Irish conscription was not necessary. Moreover, the government had decided on Irish conscription before implementing home rule, and so without Irish consent.[52] This treatment of Ireland as a 'conquered province' would strengthen the separatist party in Ireland and make home rule unsafe and impossible. In Nevinson's words, it was 'the proposed murder of a nation'. The whole project threatened to 'discredit [British] objects in the war'.[53]

Irish conscription added to Gardiner's personal antipathy to the Prime Minister and forced the *Daily News* deeper into opposition.[54] Scott, meanwhile, was caught in an absurd position, between his two friends John Dillon (leader of the Nationalists since Redmond's death in March 1918) and Lloyd George, whose interpretations of events were radically different and who detested each other personally.[55] In June 1918, the government announced that it would not after all immediately implement conscription in Ireland. However, there was also no imminent prospect of home rule. A substantial rift had appeared between the radical press and its former icon, Lloyd George.

DOMINION HOME RULE, 1919–20

Even the Allied military victory on the Western Front in autumn 1918 did not heal this division in Liberal ranks. The Prime Minister's political strategy and language during the General Election of December 1918, which effectively strengthened the Unionist domination of his coalition and resulted in the decimation of Asquith's independent Liberal parliamentary group, did little to win back recalcitrant Liberals. Then, in June 1919, Lloyd George put his signature to the Treaty of Versailles. This post-war settlement consolidated radical disaffection with the government. Hammond recalled regretfully:

> At the beginning of the war, the British Empire, thanks mainly to two men, Gladstone and C[ampbell]-B[annerman], stood out in happy contrast to the illiberal traditions of Germany and Russia. Englishmen at home barely realise that today we are in danger of becoming in the eyes of the world the chief representative of reaction . . .
> the most glaring case of refusing the right of self-determination to a white people is to be found in our treatment of Ireland.[56]

To Liberals accustomed to basing their patriotic conception of England's greatness on her relatively liberal heritage in these very matters, this was too much to bear. Gardiner's personal attacks on Lloyd George rose to such a pitch that his proprietors the Cadburys not only found Gardiner's views politically uncongenial, but feared they were damaging the reputation of the *Daily News*.[57] In the light of this difference of opinion, Gardiner felt obliged to resign as editor of the *Daily News* in mid-1919, an event for which many of his admirers blamed the influence of Lloyd George. He continued to write for the paper regularly well into 1921 and his resignation did not materially alter the political commitment of the *Daily News*.[58]

New Liberals cast around for political alternatives to Lloyd George Liberalism. Asquithian Liberalism and Labour were both preferable to the coalition, but both had drawbacks.[59] The great pre-war Liberal party was in a sorry state, divided between a small faction in a government dominated by Unionists and a tiny independent remnant. It was tempting to attack Lloyd George for the post-war problems of Liberalism, and Ireland was one of the Prime Minister's vulnerable points.

But for new Liberals the death of home rule was not just an episode in their overall political strategy. An ideal with which they had kept faith for thirty years, against all the odds, and which had seemed so near attainment, had apparently been betrayed by Lloyd George. The new dominance of the separatist anti-English Sinn Féin party, which had usurped Dillon's party in nationalist Ireland, seemed to smash 'all the progress which has been made [in Ireland] since Mr Gladstone first undertook the work'.[60] New Liberalism still self-consciously maintained its traditional commitment to separate self-government for Ireland. 'Perhaps Liberals of the latest brand no longer concern themselves about Ireland, and are quite prepared to inaugurate another "twenty years of resolute government", the first twenty years having proved so gloriously successful', the *Manchester Guardian* declared sarcastically: 'If so, we shall confess ourselves of an older faith'.[61] Progressive Liberals had for years been fashioning a rhetoric and ideology for the problems of subject nationalities such as Ireland. Thus, unlike Labour journals (with the exception of the *New Statesman*), the new Liberal press paid persistent attention to criticising government policy in Ireland in the years 1919–21. Ireland had become 'an "acid test"' of Liberalism.[62]

After the end of the Great War, most new Liberals recognised that 'home rule all round' was of little relevance to the situation in Ireland.[63] The colonial analogy thus came into its own, and the Liberal press endorsed 'dominion home rule' as a policy for Ireland. This had the support of moderates in Ireland like Horace Plunkett, the influential Lord Justice James O'Connor and the Ulster nationalist Alec Wilson.[64] It entailed little change in Liberal rhetoric from pre-war days: 'The solution which saved Canada for the Empire nearly eighty years ago, and saved South Africa for the Empire scarcely more than ten years ago, is the only solution that can keep Ireland in any kind of sense within the Empire today'.[65] In the same spirit as Gladstonian home rule, it recognised the need for reparation for Ireland.

The Government of Ireland Act of 1920 was in part drafted by Herbert Fisher, Liberal intellectual, Cabinet minister and friend of many radical Liberals. Yet as even he recognised, it fell 'far short of the Liberal standard'.[66] The *Guardian* was initially far more restrained than the *Nation* about this measure;[67] but the Liberal press agreed that the deficiencies of this Act were the limited nature of the autonomy it gave to nationalist Ireland and its separate treatment of Unionist Ulster. The Act appeared to partition Ireland, establishing a separate parliament for the north of Ireland – not on the basis of temporary county by county exclusion, nor for all nine counties of Ulster (either of which might have been more acceptable to Liberals), but for a more solidly Protestant and Unionist six-county fragment of Ulster.[68] New Liberals felt this was 'a wrong principle'; Ireland was 'arbitrarily' divided by Ulster's 'poor and selfish solution'.[69] It also seemed hypocritical given the kind of settlement British politicians had impressed on central and eastern European states at Versailles: 'every new state has its Ulster . . . Why not a British Ulster in Ireland?' Liberals loathed the idea of the government of the new northern Irish statelet by an 'Anti-national ascendancy' and criticised the denial of self-determination to Northern nationalists.[70] In short, the Act seemed to be a device of the 'allied oligarchies of England and Belfast' for 'fostering the Orange ascendancy'.[71]

Nevinson recorded a conversation he had with an official of the new Northern Ireland Treasury in Belfast in 1921 in his diary: 'he pointed to a map and said you c[oul]d always tell the Cath[olic] and rebel populations by the bogs and mountains. I said quite naturally that of course the Engl[ish] and Scots had seized the richest parts and driven the Irish into the deserts. He didn't like that, having no official answer'.[72] Liberals still saw all non-nationalists in Ireland as foreign or deluded and were still hoping for an Irish labour party to effect unification in Ireland.[73]

ASHAMED TO BE BRITISH, 1920–1

New Liberal opposition to the actions of the executive in Ireland was focused by the treatment meted out to the hunger-striking Lord Mayor of Cork, Terence MacSwiney, in the summer of 1920. Liberals protested that political prisoners should not be subjected to the indignities awaiting 'the common thief'.[74] The government's policy of calling MacSwiney's bluff also seemed stupid and provocative. MacSwiney's fate was a powerful symbol of the frustrations of Irish nationalism and it caught the imagination of Liberal and Labour activists. Nevinson led protests outside Brixton Gaol and the *Daily Herald* kept a macabre vigil on MacSwiney's fast.[75]

This was the backcloth to the most gruesome of the 'unauthorised reprisals' of the Crown forces in Ireland. Much Liberal indignation was inspired by the attack on Balbriggan in September 1920.[76] Scott's *Guardian* employed what had become the common line of comparing British forces' behaviour in Ireland with that of German forces in Belgium during 1914–15. The latter had been publicised in the report of the famous Bryce Commission, and it is notable that the critics of executive actions in Ireland from 1920–1 eventually tried to organise a similar report and attempted to persuade Bryce to act as patron.[77] Balbriggan consequently became 'an Irish Louvain' in the Liberal press,[78] perpetrated in a spirit of 'Prussianism':

> while we have all been leading the world in talk about security for Armenians and freedom for little Belgium we have ourselves drifted into a position where our criminal failure to govern a conquered white people stinks in the nostrils of the world worse than any other contemporary scandal of misgovernment.[79]

The World War had irrevocably changed the discourse of radical critics of the government; the post-war settlement was 'Prussianistic', and Dublin Castle another 'old Prussian experiment'.[80] In a pamphlet issued in 1921, characteristically soaked in historical analogies, Hammond contrasted the wise and successful liberal policies of British history with the unwise and unsuccessful past policies of autocracies, including those of Prussia and Austro-Hungary in 1914. Contemporary British policy in Ireland was similarly dictated by 'Prussian minds': 'if it is a wise policy, then Prussia was wiser than England, Turkey was wiser than Prussia, and the Englishmen who died in Flanders or the East died, like Cavaliers, for a mistaken sentiment'.[81] Masterman agreed that British policy in Ireland was the 'denial . . . of the very principle for which five million men have died'.[82]

In October 1920, critics of government policy organised themselves in the Peace with Ireland Council. This was by no means restricted to progressive Liberals. It included churchmen, conservatives (including the Chairman, Lord Henry Cavendish Bentinck), Fabians, representatives of labour and some Irishmen and women. Nevertheless, Liberalism was well represented in the Council. Some of its methods of agitation were based on the Liberal home rule committee of 1911 (the group behind *Home rule problems*) and Basil Williams acted as its Treasurer. Hammond and Lynd wrote some of the Council's best pamphlets, while Nevinson, Hammond and Evelyn Sharp were among its speakers.[83] Liberals did express some reservations about some of the forces on their 'side' in this struggle for public opinion. Nevinson, who was hardly the most mainstream of the critics of the government, complained of popular apathy in relation to Ireland and eventually wrote off the Council, 'fast becoming useless: always "What will L[or]d Henry [Bentinck] think?"'. He began attending the meetings of the more radical Irish Self-Determination League. Williams fell out with his fellow organiser, the Irishman George Berkeley.[84]

The reaction of the Liberal press to reprisals had a pronounced ethical basis, as of course, did the whole of new Liberals' philosophy. They emphasised the 'Prussian' style of the repression in Ireland because they believed that such things were 'not the English way':[85] 'perhaps some . . .

Junker, loose from Potsdam,' mused the *Manchester Guardian* tongue-in-cheek, 'throws [the Englishman] into Holyhead Harbour, after stealing his clothes, and goes across the Irish Sea to make Zaberns, Louvains and Aerschotts in his name instead of the decent illogical workable compromises that he would have made'.[86] The Liberal critics of such policies were unashamed patriots – the patriotism of Hugh Martin, special correspondent in Ireland for the *Daily News*, was professed at least as earnestly as his impartiality by his apologists.[87] After a visit to America at this time, Nevinson wrote: 'It is a terrible thing to feel ashamed of the country one loves. It is like coming home and finding one's mother drunk upon the floor'. The *Guardian* agreed that Ireland made 'dismal reading' for 'patriotic English people'.[88]

It is significant that the patriotism of such Liberals was English and not British. Nevinson later edited a curious anthology entitled *England's voice of freedom* (curious not in the least because an extract from Nevinson's friend Casement's speech on being sentenced to death for treason was included as representative of a 'peculiarly English' heritage of liberty).[89] In 1916, Gardiner had noted how the advocates of a more determined prosecution of the war were generally not English at all – men like Lloyd George, Garvin, Carson and Northcliffe espoused a 'Celtic passion' for dictatorship.[90] There is a clue here as to why these critics were so much less concerned about criticising outrage on the *republican* side in Ireland, which seemed to them to be less of an anomaly because it was not perpetrated in the name of England. The fact that Lloyd Georgian methods in Ireland were a rejection of England's liberal heritage, in Clarke's words, 'put Lloyd George out of court for many Liberals'. In Hammond's words, Lloyd George had chosen 'to abolish liberty'.[91]

Government policy flew in the face of progress, a precious new Liberal assumption. The *Nation* bemoaned that 'some fatality seems to ordain that we should always relapse into the morals of an earlier age when we deal with a crisis in Ireland'.[92] As Barbara Hammond told Gilbert Murray after a trip to Ireland in March 1921, 'mankind has gone back to its caves but one side of the cavemen have got machine guns and searchlights and motors and the others nothing but revolvers'.[93] The *Guardian* echoed this tone of horror at the interruption to the advance of humanity:

> the nation that in the autumn of 1914 was alive with one of the few generous national passions of modern history has been dragged down to the level of the old Turkey and the old Prussia . . . Our

> Government has put us in the stocks . . . We may as well keep our tempers and take our pelting.[94]

New Liberals rejected the idea that the nationalist Irish had 'let England down' during the First World War by not recruiting in sufficient numbers and not consenting to conscription. Hammond instead focused on Redmondite Nationalists' support of the Allied cause in the early years of the Great War, and preferred to argue that the British government (and 'Ulster') had let 'Ireland' down.[95] As George Boyce has shown, critics of government policy in Ireland argued that 'outrage' was in some ways less acceptable from 'the forces of order' than from revolutionary nationalism (not least a revolutionary nationalism which in some ways did a rather better job of keeping order in these years than Dublin Castle did).[96] The Liberal critics admitted that 'there is terror on both sides', but argued that crime by a government assailed 'the very foundations of order'.[97]

Critics such as Amery suggested that Liberal editors and writers such as J.L. Hammond were the dupes of clever IRA propaganda.[98] It is true that the IRA won an outstanding propaganda success in the year before June 1921, though the errors of British policy made this rather easy for them.[99] Many Liberal critics of government policy had Irish friends, some of whom, like Erskine and Molly Childers or Alice Green, were republicans or Sinn Féin sympathisers. Erskine Childers wrote a series of articles for the *Daily News*, while his wife Molly saw that copies of Sinn Féin's *Bulletin* were forwarded to British sympathisers.[100] But the radical press did not ignore IRA 'outrages' such as the 'Bloody Sunday' murders of November 1920 and the attack on the Dublin Customs House of May 1921. Liberal journalists were also hardly likely to be guilty of innocent naïveté about a bloody conflict less than two years after a world war. If the new Liberals overstated atrocities by the Crown forces and understated republican outrage, it was deliberate.[101]

An important key to understanding the new Liberal position on Ireland in 1920–1 is their perception that they were fighting a losing battle for public opinion against overwhelming odds. Murray, for instance, felt that they were an indignant but 'small minority', just as when 'pro-Boer' from 1899–1901.[102] British Liberals had recently experienced the forceful state propaganda of the Great War. They had been unprepared in 1914 for the power and nature of this propaganda (or 'useful lying' as the *Guardian* termed it with evident distaste),[103] and attributed some of the defects of the Versailles settlement to it. The refutation of some of the most obvious

British propaganda excesses, especially after 1918, increased suspicion of the government in Liberal circles and also strengthened a reaction against wartime policies which assisted the inter-war movement for the appeasement of Germany.[104]

After the war, the new Liberals believed that the art of 'useful lying' was also being used by the British government and its supporters to justify their policies during the Anglo-Irish conflict.[105] Against such powerful agencies, Liberals feared they could do little; Nevinson believed all their protests could achieve was to 'show some decent rage and Irel[and] will hear of it'.[106] New Liberals, as always convinced that they had discovered the true lines of popular progress, felt that the internationalists, 'a few men, whose minds are filled with the sense of the world's needs',[107] held the key to the future, yet were regularly stigmatised as the 'friends of every country but their own'.[108] At the end of the Boer War, the *Speaker* had declared that:

> the great liberals of history . . . did not ask themselves whether they ran some risk of provoking odious epithets if they disagreed with every bawling and sprawling majority . . . it is the part of Liberalism not merely to carry certain reforms, but to keep alive in the nation certain sacred principles of freedom and justice. What is to become of the traditions of political sincerity, constancy, and courage, if the Liberal party forgets them?[109]

Once more, radical Liberals were convinced that they simply had to endure this odium in fighting against a dishonest and reactionary reversion to the 'methods of barbarism'.

Indeed, the efforts to suppress and evade reports from Ireland adopted by Lloyd George and his lieutenants during 1920–1 seemed not only disingenuous, but incredibly clumsy. They were obvious targets for editorial criticism. Nevinson and Martin had what they considered were perfectly good stories blankly contradicted by ministers. Nevinson's papers were confiscated by British soldiers and he feared that he might also lose his diary. Barbara Hammond's sister Katherine Bradby was imprisoned briefly in Ireland in 1921.[110] Most notable of all was the occasion when Martin was approached by members of the Royal Irish Constabulary in Tralee, in November 1920. He recounted to *Daily News* readers:

> I . . . gave my name when it was demanded as that of an English journalist associated with the Coalition.

> 'Is there a Hugh Martin among you?' was the next question, 'because if there is', the man added, 'we mean to do for him. It's him we want, and we're going to get him' . . . I handed him a cigarette. As I took the case from my pocket, I accidentally pulled out with it a letter which fell on the ground at my feet. By the light of the match I was able to read my own name. A constable stooped to pick it up politely, but I was too quick for him . . .[111]

Martin was the fairest and most widely-read of the critics of British policy in Ireland, and this incident gave the impression that the government were afraid of the truth.[112] Martin's former editor Gardiner was inspired by this report by Martin, the 'most formidable adversary of the Government', to write an indignant article: 'Let those of us who remember the wise things for which our country has stood in history,' he declared, 'who still cherish the idea we call England, . . . unite to redeem our name in the world . . . proclaim 'Peace with Ireland' as the single bond of our contract'.[113]

It is doubtful that the editorial policy of the *Daily News* or the *Nation*, or that of Labour publications such as the *Daily Herald* or the *New Statesman*, directly influenced Lloyd George, who had already written off such journals. But the *Guardian* was another matter.[114] As Stephen Koss explains, as 'the leader of a faction of the parliamentary Liberal Party, Lloyd George craved the benediction of at least one respected Liberal daily. The *Manchester Guardian*, which came closest to obliging him, held back partly out of principle and partly out of mistrust of the company he was keeping'.[115] Lloyd George undoubtedly respected Scott's opinions, and Scott was generally well-disposed to Lloyd George, but they had many disagreements on policy during these years. Ireland became the crux. A speech by the Prime Minister at Carnarvon in October 1920 which appeared to justify 'reprisals', seemed to Scott a 'turning-point in Mr Lloyd George's career'.[116] From then until July 1921 the two hardly spoke, Lloyd George later telling Scott: 'You and I have been so hopelessly at variance at late over Irish affairs that I was afraid it would be difficult for us to meet without coming to blows!'[117]

In May 1921, the *Guardian* celebrated its first centenary, and Scott his fiftieth year on the paper. Lloyd George wrote to congratulate him on this remarkable achievement. Scott wrote back:

> I wish events had not so utterly divided us. Your Irish policy breaks my heart, and what makes the thing worse is that I have the feeling

> all through that it isn't the real you that is finding expression either there or in the European policy, but that circumstances have laid a heavy hand on you. Forgive me for speaking so. I could not do it if I had not loved and admired you.[118]

Some months later Scott feared '"real war" with press censorship and everything [over Ireland] . . . In that case I shall certainly find myself in prison!'[119]

In the years immediately after the First World War, progressive Liberal writers and journalists exposed themselves to painful allegations, to the risk of imprisonment or even worse, in order to criticise the Irish policy of a radical Liberal Prime Minister. Their attitude, however, was so consistent with a long and powerful new Liberal tradition, that they can be dismissed neither as the dupes of republican propaganda nor merely as men and women with a chip on their shoulder.

'Vindication' and Retrospect

IN THE TWELVE MONTHS from July 1921 to June 1922, progressive Liberal discourse on Anglo-Irish relations markedly changed its emphases. This transition was initiated by the truce of July 1921 and Lloyd George's peace proposals of that month.[1] When these were published in mid-August, the *Daily News* declared that 'the opinion of the civilised world' on the question was now largely behind the coalition government.[2] Scott recalled his own role in drafting Lloyd George's earlier correspondence with John Redmond, and again felt that the Irish nationalists did not realise how much they were being offered.[3] Hammond agreed with Scott, feeling that if he 'were an Irishman', he would have accepted Lloyd George's terms, which offered nationalist Ireland as good a security against Britain as could be devised. He told Berkeley: 'England . . . only wants to get Ireland off its hands . . . I agree that England is to blame for the situation that exists today but there it is. How can we get out of it?'[4] His wife Barbara echoed these thoughts: 'Why oh why do they [Sinn Féin] make it so very hard for Lloyd George in his efforts to make peace which (for the moment from whatever motives) are sincere[?]'[5]

Several reasons for this shift can be suggested. The coalition government's change of policy enabled Liberals to be reconciled, at least tentatively, with former political allies and colleagues. Scott's close friendship with Lloyd George could resume,[6] and Herbert Fisher was especially relieved that his hitherto ineffective warnings within the Cabinet of the perils of a policy of military coercion at last seemed to have made some progress.[7] Radical Liberals found the government's Irish policy after June 1921 as congenial as such intercourse. They were impressed by the British government's willingness to discuss 'dominion home rule' for Ireland, given the policy's long association with liberal tradition. New Liberals had always felt that an Irish republic was impossible, and the *Nation* had been involved in the first of many arguments between British radicals and Erskine Childers on this issue.[8] The experiences of the previous seven years had, indeed, made new Liberal ideology even more antipathetic to the ideas of absolute independence which de Valera seemed to use in justifying a republican position, since the apparent failure of the Versailles settlement had consolidated pre-existing trends in new Liberalism: 'we do not wish to see Ireland an independent state. We were never in love with the politics of the Tower of Babel', said the *Nation*. 'We regard the balkanisation of Central and Eastern Europe as a world disaster and we should use every resource of statesmanship, persuasion and negotiation to prevent the Balkanisation of the British Isles'.[9] The *Guardian* called 'self-determination' a 'terrible phrase of . . . Muscovite origin': Ireland 'cannot for ever . . . cut herself off from the world . . . she will discover that it is a greater thing to be an independent member of a worldwide society of nations than a small and isolated unit'.[10] Self-determination, the *Daily News* agreed, 'is inevitably in a civilised world limited as individual liberty is limited'.[11] In August 1921, the *Nation* could legitimately contend that 'our general opinion that independence is commonly an illusion, and that a federal organisation is preferable to Balkanisation and multiplicity, is one which we formed and maintained in relation to Europe long before the Irish question reached its present phase'.[12]

The radical press advocated the creation of a united Ireland as a dominion, a settlement to which many of Lloyd George's negotiating tactics tended. 'Ireland is prepared to accept, in some form, the Imperial tie if Ulster will accept, in some form, the Irish tie', wrote Hugh Martin. Martin persistently argued in the second half of 1921 that difficulties in the negotiations were 'due solely to Orange Ulster'.[13] Hammond, writing under the pseudonym 'Politicus' in the *Guardian*, agreed:

> it has always been recognised that the minority must accept the principle on which public opinion has decided . . . Every sensible unionist must realise that this ought to have been done in 1914, and that we are now paying the penalty for the breach of that great, orderly, conservative tradition of our Constitution.[14]

New Liberals were tempted to suggest that moral pressure should be put on Ulster to join a united Ireland: 'The long and disastrous strife between England and Ireland . . . might be honourably closed tomorrow if some four hundred thousand Irishmen would agree to their inclusion in the Irish State' said the *Guardian*, and the *Nation* agreed that Ulster was the 'most selfish faction in Europe . . . in 1914, she cared little for the Empire . . . But she must now have a country, and learn to live with it'.[15]

Scott met de Valera for the first time in July 1921 and was not impressed, thinking him 'a closed mind and he had surprised me by the lengths to wh[ich] he was prepared to go', in justifying political violence by the IRA.[16] Nevinson's first impressions of de Valera were rather more favourable, but Nevinson, like Massingham and Brailsford, though republican in their private sympathies, judged that there was no point in arguing on these lines in the British press.[17] Even the *Daily Herald* and the *New Statesman* (along with the *Nation*) avoided arguing directly for a republic, preferring to take their stand on 'Ireland's right *to choose for itself what its status and its relations to this country should be*', and Nevinson believed that even this was 'promising beyond possible fulfilment'.[18] Noticeably, the *Herald* claimed that the eventual treaty embodied its long-term Irish policy; and some limitations on Irish independence were commonly proposed in the Labour press.[19] Martin argued that the result of the 1918 General Election in Ireland was misleading, and that Ireland was no more unanimously republican than Ulster was unanimously unionist.[20]

After five months of negotiation, during which a resumption of Anglo-Irish hostilities had frequently seemed likely, Liberal relief expressed itself in elaborate praise of the Anglo-Irish Treaty of 6 December 1921.[21] It seemed to embody advantages new Liberals had often claimed for the British Empire, its reconciliation of 'freedom with international duty and service. It has solved more satisfactorily than any other composite structure the problem of reconciling national patriotism with a wider international outlook'.[22] Hobhouse agreed: 'The British Commonwealth has solved several [racial and national] problems, but only, as now appears clearly enough, by divesting itself of the character of a unitary authoritarian state, and transforming itself into a voluntary union for certain purposes': 'This is made definite in the Irish Constitution'.[23] The patriotism of the new Liberals and the guilt many of them had felt at the policy of repression in Ireland, intensified their reaction when the Treaty relieved England 'of a crime she is too good to commit':[24] 'this chapter of our history' was 'closed' gleefully by the *Guardian*.[25] The 1921 Treaty was 'England's redemption'. Characteristically, Hammond attributed the achievement of the settlement specifically to the weight of *English* opinion against the coercion of nationalist Ireland, 'the growing English protest against injustice'.[26] Liberals hoped that the reunification of Ireland would result; in words which anticipated controversial clauses of the Irish constitution of 1937, the *Guardian* declared that it was 'certain' that the Free State 'will in due course include the whole of the Irish territory'.[27]

The contribution of new Liberals to the course of events leading up to the Anglo-Irish Treaty of 1921 was mostly indirect, through the medium of public opinion. The exception to this was C.P. Scott. Scott's was declared 'the most important part of all' by the *Nation*, an exaggerated but not insignificant claim.[28] Scott was undoubtedly influential with Lloyd George, and in the days before the 1921 Treaty he was a pacifier, urging against the resumption of hostilities in private and public. On the night that the tortuous negotiations ended, Lloyd George told Scott: '"we have succeeded at last in the task we have both worked at for more than thirty years"'. Not surprisingly, Scott agreed that with the signing of the Treaty, Liberals' aim from 'the long years during which [the party had] wandered in the wilderness' had been 'achieved in its fullest measure'.[29]

Basil Williams' wife Dorothy and George Berkeley of the Peace with Ireland Council congratulated Erskine Childers rather too hastily after the Treaty.[30] When Childers and de Valera declared their opposition to the agreement, many in Britain were dismayed. The resulting Treaty debates in the Dáil drove Hammond to despair.[31] New Liberals were unashamed supporters of the pro-Treaty faction in the Irish Free State when de Valera's anti-Treatyite faction emerged. This was reflected in their views of Ireland's political leaders. Arthur Griffith, for instance, according to the *Nation*, 'proved himself a statesman because he put Ireland above a doctrine. Mr de Valera put a doctrine above Ireland'.[32] Michael Collins' article in the *Guardian* the day after the Treaty was signed was much praised. Meanwhile, the *Guardian* called de Valera 'anti-social' and accused him of inciting violence between Irish people.[33] As an 'Englishman' interfering in Ireland, Erskine Childers was an even easier target. Fisher attributed Childers' apparently perverse suspicion of Britain to the influence of his American wife.[34] Years later Hammond still found it hard to forgive Childers and de Valera 'for all the lives that were lost because [they] preferred violence and plots to the Treaty',[35] and even Childers' biographer and friend Basil Williams felt that 'dear old Erskine' was 'living in a world of unreality' in his republicanism.[36] So far as new Liberals were concerned, the aspirations to absolute independence from Britain which de Valera and Childers seemed to be espousing were absurd – Ireland had to be associated with other states in one form or another, and the British Empire / Commonwealth was 'the most hopeful example of federation which has yet been tried' in the world.[37] In fact, by June 1922, Irish opponents of the Treaty had achieved the unlikely feat of drawing the radical press into praise of the Irish policy, not only of Lloyd George, but of Winston Churchill.[38]

When Collins and de Valera struck an electoral pact prior to the Free State elections of May 1922, radical Liberals felt that amicable relations between Britain and Ireland, and between North and South in Ireland, were being sacrificed to the intransigent and microscopic republican minority. New Liberals urged the Treatyites to desist from acting with such tenderness towards their former colleagues. 'Such political folly I have never seen', wrote Massingham. 'Is wisdom anywhere in Ireland?' asked the *Guardian* rhetorically.[39] The *Nation* complained that 'Ireland has her political verdict handed out to her in advance in the Bolshevist fashion'. New Liberals perceived Ireland to be lagging behind England on the path of political progress, lacking 'the habit of political tolerance that saw England finally through the turmoil of the seventeenth and eighteenth centuries'.[40] The *Guardian* complained that Ireland had learnt nothing since the days of 'Imperialism and Kaiserism, the political morality of the mailed fist and of the Jameson raid'.[41] Liberals also believed that Irish political leaders outdid 'even the most blind and stupid and insolent of all our rulers'.[42] When the Treatyite and anti-Treatyite factions finally did come to blows in the second half of 1922, 'English lovers of Ireland', in Evelyn Sharp's words, could do little; the Irish Civil War of 1922–3 'had at least this advantage over the "troubles", that it was Ireland's affair and not ours – except, of course, in the sense that it was one consequence of centuries of oppression for which England is responsible'.[43] Though the radical press tried to avoid 'Pharisaism' about the growing pains of the Irish Free State, this was transparently 'a terror o[f Ireland's] own'.[44]

In his first published book, Hobhouse had emphatically rejected political violence: 'we cannot allow people to discharge pistols in Piccadilly, or bombs at the base of our public buildings, however much they may be convinced that they are following their best impulses in so doing. We have to curtail the free play of their aspirations for the safety of ourselves and our fellow-citizens'.[45] Individuality and sociability had always been precariously balanced in new Liberal theory. Moral reform had always been as important in the improvement of society as social reform; social and political phenomena had individual as well as social levels of causation. The new Liberals decided that the 'anarchist' ultimately could not be excused by social or historical circumstances, and had to be restrained. 'Terrorist' violence (to use a largely anachronistic term) was distasteful to them, and Ireland quickly seemed to be acquiring a reputation for it; when friends of Hammond visited Newry in 1924, he expressed concern lest 'they . . . be picked off by gunmen'.[46] Nevinson also found the new Ireland a less congenial environment than he had anticipated. The use of the Irish language in the Dáil debates of August 1921 disconcerted him.[47] When Nevinson visited Dublin in July 1922 he found himself threatened at gunpoint by a nervous Irregular, nearly caught in a cross-fire, and having to read James Joyce's *Ulysses*. It is hard to detect which experience most distressed him.[48]

It is thus hard to avoid the impression that the first few months of Irish self-government in 1922 severely challenged radical Liberals' former illusions about Ireland, and that their views of the country were subtly changing. As Martin wrote in June 1922, 'decent Irishmen are blushing for the reputation of their country'.[49] One of their expectations had been that the partition of Ireland would not prove permanent. For over ten years Liberals had been saying that this was Ireland's own 'problem of appeasement' which would test her 'sense and decency'. 'The whole world is looking on now to see whether Ireland is politically capable': only 'if Ireland is foolish England can detach Ulster'.[50] The crucial issue after the Treaty certainly seemed to be the one within Ireland. Bolton Waller conducted the liquidation of the Peace with Ireland Council in 1922 and projected its replacement by a Peace *in* Ireland Council to deal with partition.[51] The strong all-Ireland Labour party which Liberals had long hoped for would, however, fail to emerge.[52] The 'competition in extremism' between North and South in Ireland after 1921 seemed to Liberals to be the 'clearest proof of Ireland's essential national unity'; both were equally uncivilised.[53] But it must have left Liberals feeling disappointed with the revealed level of political capacity in Ireland.

Proponents of home rule such as the new Liberals had also predicted that the concession of self-government would reconcile the Irish nationalists to the British people. In 1887, Morley had confidently assumed that nationalist suspicion of England was 'not one of those . . . animosities which blind men to their own interests . . . it will not survive the amendment of the system that has given it birth'. In 1918, the *Nation* had agreed: 'The hour of Ireland's full nationhood is the hour of her true union with Britain': 'When were Irishmen ungenerous?' it asked rhetorically.[54] In 1920, the same journal had based its opposition to coalition policy in Ireland on the assumption that a free Ireland would be a peaceful country with good and close relations with Britain:

> Ireland could do us no harm. The chances are that by the mere force of reaction she would become pro-English. We are certain that it would be our own fault if she did not. We fear the existence of a hostile Ireland on our flank. But . . . that is because we rule Ireland by

> force. Abandon it, and the general political cause of ill-will, and the continued friction . . . disappear together.[55]

New Liberal models of international relations were, like those of Positivists, teleological. Once sources of 'friction' were removed, different national individualities would be harmonious, not antipathetic. New Liberals thus struggled, rather as the Positivists did, to come to terms with instances of deep-seated social and ethnic hostility such as existed in Ireland.[56] One possible response was to indulge in that 'time-honoured recourse of blaming Irish ingratitude'. When C.P. Scott's sons visited Ireland in 1924, Hammond was particularly distressed by the lack of official recognition given by the Free State to the English newspaper run by their famous father: 'The *M[anchester] G[uardian]* was never mentioned and [Ted] and John [Scott] were introduced to all the big wigs without a word about it. I fancy it was a bit of a snub after all the *MG* has done for that ungrateful country'.[57]

Such disillusionment can be overstated however. New Liberals still professed confidence that Ireland was not going over to 'the devil and his angels',[58] and the moderate Irish nationalist associates of men like Hammond, Scott, Massingham and Nevinson continued to regard them as good friends to Ireland.[59] The *Manchester Guardian* and the *Daily News* maintained the liberal tradition of hoping for the unity of Ireland.[60] In 1924, the *Guardian* once more accused 'Ulster' of trying to dictate to a radical British government, when Ulster Unionists tried to resist the Labour government's efforts to summon the Boundary Commission promised in the Treaty. The people of the Protestant North, the paper suggested, should 'get the seventeenth century out of their politics'.[61] However, privately Scott perceived that the Treaty had been far from the guarantee of future Irish unity which the Liberal press had initially suggested. The Treaty had in fact helped to consolidate the parameters of the division of Irish territory drawn up in the 1920 Government of Ireland Act, and therefore entrenched a relatively robust Protestant hegemony in Northern Ireland. For this fact Scott continued to blame the hapless Fisher.[62] The Boundary Commission's deliberations thus ended in 1925 with no transfer of Northern territory to the Free State.[63] Well into the 1930s, Nevinson, as President of the Council of Civil Liberties, and the successors of Scott at the *Guardian*, criticised the Northern Irish administration for its treatment of the nationalist minority. The *Guardian* also continued to denounce partition.[64]

However, there was one prominent element of the tradition of new Liberal comment on Irish affairs for which there was very little scope after 1921. This was criticism of British government policy in Ireland. 'The obstacle to Irish unity is no longer England', but rather the refusal of Irishmen to face realities, suggested the *Guardian* in 1924. The appearances of Eamon de Valera on the stage of Irish politics were especially guaranteed to bring Liberal journals rallying to the side of British governments. 'Does he want a victory over Ulster or the hope of cooperation with Ulster?' the *Guardian* asked rhetorically in 1924. 'Does he want more miles of Free State territory or a good step forward to Irish unity?'[65] When C.P. Scott died early in 1932, a warm tribute was received from W.T. Cosgrave, Taoiseach and Cumann na nGaedhael leader.[66] But when Eamon de Valera's Fianna Fáil's victory in the Free State elections just a few weeks later heralded the start of a new Anglo-Irish quarrel, there was great distress at the offices of the newspaper synonymous with Scott. In May 1932, the *Guardian* had to point out again that 'Ireland . . . least of all European countries can afford to stand alone' and echo the plea of a British coalition government minister, this time J.H. Thomas, that the Free State in general (and de Valera in particular) 'look to the future and not to the unhappy past'. It all seemed ominously similar to the uncertain days immediately before the Treaty of 1921, and the paper feared that 'ghosts that we had all hoped had been laid may walk again'.[67] The *News Chronicle* (as the *Daily News* had become in 1930 after a merger with the *Daily Chronicle*), which was busy fighting a losing battle against import tariffs in Britain, was disappointed by the protectionist and parochial culture of de Valera's Ireland.[68] It also argued: 'The natural effect of de Valera's campaign – clear from the beginning to everyone except apparently Mr de Valera – is to drive Ulster away from the Free State and nearer to this country'.[69]

By this time, hopes of radical Liberalism reasserting itself, whether in defence of free trade or of anything else, were becoming forlorn. Although Hobhouse saw some good points to 'Labour in office', the 'sectarian' and class-based Labour party was uncongenial to many new Liberals.[70] The complexion of radical politics in Britain was in flux, and this transition contributed to the ebbing of the progressive Liberal tradition with its heritage of special sympathy for Irish nationalism. The disposition of Liberal and Labour MPs in the 1920s and 1930s largely complemented contemporary governments' 'ignorance and . . . abdication of responsibility' regarding the affairs of Northern Ireland.[71]

Indeed, by the mid-1930s, practically everything had gone wrong for new Liberalism; the political party, the international institutions and the dream for Anglo-Irish relations which it had cherished were all practically without force. For the latter at least Scott had blamed the generation of Tory domination of political power in the United Kingdom initiated by the British electorate's rejection of Gladstone's home rule policy of 1886. Scott believed that this more modest measure of self-government would have had greater potential to produce political unity in Ireland, and amity between Britain and Ireland, than the 1921 Treaty: 'What sane man will not now recognise that a smaller measure (with the element of growth) would have been infinitely better for Ireland and for us[?]'[72] Hammond believed that the disastrous consequences of the events of 1886 had yet wider significance for Britain's place in the world: 'If England had then followed Mr G[ladstone] and given Ireland Home Rule we sh[oul]d have averted the very grave consequences of being forced to violence in 1921. To the rest of the world we must seem to have given up Ireland, Egypt and India because we were too weak of will or otherwise to keep them'.[73] Hammond articulated this faith eruditely in his *Gladstone and the Irish nation*, a book published in 1938 which still merits attention among historians of the first two home rule crises. Hammond, inspired by a combination of deep historical learning and committed Liberal partisanship, contended that it had been in Britain's interest to pass home rule when Gladstone had first suggested it in 1886: 'In one hour of courage and generosity, England could gain strength at home, and shake the violent forces that were mastering the world'.[74] Hammond argued that home rule was a policy true to Gladstone's vision of Europe as a 'family of nations', a spirit which had been sadly lacking in British policy since 1886.[75]

When Hammond's book appeared, Anglo-Irish relations had taken another minor turn for the better, with the resolution of the trade and sovereignty controversies of 1932–8. In the spring of 1938, the *News Chronicle* looked forward with optimism to 'the final healing of the breach' between Britain and Ireland.[76] The *Manchester Guardian* was again thinking of Irish unity as a realistic (though not imminent) prospect.[77] But there would be few signs of progress in this direction over the next decade. On the contrary, Éire's neutrality during the Second World War, and her formal declaration of a Republic a few years later, further undermined the sympathy of the fast disappearing generation of new Liberals. To the distress of Murray and Hammond, Ireland after the grant of autonomy seemed to have fulfilled many Unionist predictions; it had insisted on full political separation, it had failed to act in cordial alliance with Britain in its international relations and it had become a country deeply and indefinitely politically divided on sectarian grounds, a state of affairs acknowledged by the British Labour government's Ireland Act of 1949.[78]

Such disappointments should not disguise the fact, however, that new Liberalism's mission to pacify Ireland had achieved a fair measure of success. It had contributed significantly to a process which had removed Ireland as a point of controversy from British politics. It had also helped to diminish the antipathy of nationalist Ireland to things British. It had however failed to avert the partition of Ireland. Inaccuracies in new Liberal presumptions about the nature of Irish politics had not only occasionally placed Ireland in peril, but had contributed to the decline of new Liberalism. Furthermore, its influence on British policy in Ireland had largely been indirect, limited to indignant newspaper columns. Although certainly more politically significant than the Positivists, and closer in terms of personal association and sympathy to the possessors of political power, the new Liberals were still largely critics of the official mind, only sporadically aware of the imperatives of the maintenance of the British Empire which so concerned British administrators in this period. Consequently, they were unable to exercise a consistent influence over the policy-making process. Ideological movements with a keener awareness of imperial necessities injected impulses towards the conciliation of nationalist Ireland more deeply into the heart of the British political establishment.

IMPERIALISM

Imperial Consolidation

EDWARDIAN IMPERIALISTS can be juxtaposed usefully with the new Liberals; they interpreted many of the problems of the contemporary British Empire, including the problems of British policy in Ireland, in a very different way. The Round Table movement, J.L. Garvin and W.A.S. Hewins had sympathies and associations with the Unionist party before 1914, and Imperialists such as Lord Milner, Garvin, Leopold Amery and Geoffrey Robinson (editor of the *Times* from 1912 to 1919) supported Unionist Ulster's resistance to Irish home rule.[1] But ultimately, such Imperialists could also be reconciled to the political autonomy of nationalist Ireland, and from 1910–14, Garvin, F.S. Oliver, Lionel Curtis, R.H. Brand, Edward Grigg and other Imperialists advocated a federal settlement in Ireland.[2] In 1920, Philip Kerr (later Lord Lothian) of the Round Table, whilst acting as Lloyd George's secretary, assisted in drafting the Government of Ireland Act of 1920, which also proposed self-government for Ireland.[3] In 1921, Hewins, Grigg and Curtis were all involved in efforts, official or unofficial, to negotiate an Irish settlement. The involvement of Curtis in Anglo-Irish relations continued after the Treaty, when he became an advisor to the Colonial Office on Irish affairs.[4] Partly through the influence of Curtis, his friend Richard Feetham was appointed Chair of the Irish Boundary Commission from 1924–5.[5] Meanwhile, Amery, as Secretary of State for Dominion Affairs from 1925, had responsibility for Anglo-Irish relations in subsequent years.[6]

In short, by December 1921, Imperialists and Liberals had come to a broad measure of agreement about the 'Irish problem', regarding the Treaty as a welcome and necessary solution. However, Imperialists had exercised the more important and direct influence in developing and implementing this policy. Changes in Imperialists' perceptions of Irish politics during the years 1910–1925 had therefore helped to shape the future of the Anglo-Irish relationship.

THE 'UNION OF ALL MANKIND'

It would be misleading to imply that Imperialism was a distinct and clearly defined political movement in Edwardian Britain. 'Imperialism' was a term elusive of precise meaning. Although radicals occasionally used it as a term of political abuse, few Britons in this period were totally without pride in the British Empire.[7] This was true of radical Liberals, who believed that the British Empire had made valuable and signal contributions to the political institutions of the world. The Empire's great achievement, they felt, consisted in the way that it had enabled autonomous states to associate together freely, equally and peacefully. Efforts to introduce greater centralisation into the Empire would not only sap the strength of the fragile moral bonds which held it together, but would also diminish the diversity and local freedoms which made the Empire great.[8] The Anglo-Irish Treaty of 1921 was commendable to many new Liberals because it seemed so highly compatible with this vision of empire.[9]

Avowed Imperialists shared many of these values and assumptions but came to a different conclusion. Tolerance, diversity and local self-government, they believed, were indeed distinctive characteristics of the British compared to other empires,[10] and Imperialists, like new Liberals, regarded these as both symptoms and causes of the Empire's success. One Imperialist thus argued: 'It is an immense step in the history of the world, the greatest ever made, that a quarter of its inhabitants, and that quarter an epitome of all stages of human development, should have been united into one international state, without that state abandoning, as did Rome, the principle of commonwealth for that of autocracy'.[11] The *Pall Mall Gazette*, under the editorship of J.L Garvin, declared in 1913: 'No political system which the world has known has ever carried such gifts abroad with less dependence upon might and menace'.[12] The Empire had brought 'order, security and peace' where previously there had been none, and therefore constituted a protection in many parts of the world against national and racial rivalries and disputes, class conflict and selfish individualism and materialism.[13]

Therefore, Leopold Amery wrote in 1912:

> The United Kingdom and the younger nations which have sprung from it represent the highest existing development of the ideal of the free self-governing national state . . . [for] unhappy features of the modern world the British Empire, within its confines, substitutes

> the rule of law, of conciliation and of mutual help . . . There is nothing, indeed, in Imperial Union, when we consider the diversity of race, civilisation and interest under the British flag, to differentiate it from that union of all mankind of which some idealists have dreamed, except just the comparatively unimportant difference of bulk.[14]

The British Empire thus constituted the most important and realistic form of free and peaceful international association. Other forms of internationalism were chiliastic and ineffective. Crucially therefore, Imperialists believed that the 'Imperial idea' was a greater force for good in the world than either Comte's vague notion of humanity, or liberal ideals, whether represented by mid-nineteenth-century Cobdenite non-interventionism or by the international institutions proposed by new Liberals such as Hobson in the early twentieth century.[15] Consequently, Hewins argued that the vague aspiration to 'international brotherhood' was without substance: 'the policy of internationalism is obviously quite impracticable in the real world . . . [its] practice of the nineteenth century has led to unsatisfying results'. The 'precedents of age' embodied in the Empire pointed the way to the creation of 'a real family of nations'.[16]

Imperialists therefore believed that their creed was far from simply being an instinct of British national self-interest. As Philip Kerr maintained, the vigorous defence of the Empire against 'particularist' sources of disruption and secession, such as Irish or Boer nationalism, was also a defence of the 'larger idea of a union of self-governing communities'.[17] Or, as Leopold Amery put it in *The 'Times' history of the war in South Africa*: 'Much sympathy has been wasted on small nations "rightly struggling to be free" . . . little sympathy is bestowed on the great nations rightly struggling for mastery, for supremacy of higher civilisation and higher political principles'.[18]

But Imperialists in the Edwardian period did not just feel that the Empire had to be forcefully defended in occasional crises as they arose. Imperialists believed in the necessity of Imperial 'consolidation', some form of 'closer union' between the states of the Empire (especially between the self-governing colonies and the United Kingdom).[19] They felt that the present system of cooperation between these states would prove insufficient to maintain the unity of the Empire in the perilous international environment of the early twentieth century.[20] As F.S. Oliver argued, stronger bonds of political union between the states of the Empire were 'not merely desirable [but] absolutely necessary, if these great national forces overseas, to which each year is now adding new strengths, are to be held together'.[21] It is this belief in the overriding necessity of closer imperial union which distinguished Imperialists in the Edwardian period. It lay at the heart of a series of projects for the future political, military and/or commercial organisation of the Empire floated by elements in or on the fringes of the Edwardian Unionist party.[22] That there were many divisions between Imperialists as to which of these schemes for imperial 'consolidation' should be effected is hardly surprising, for the imperial idea had an attractive power of a breadth almost to match the diverse elements of which the Empire was composed. As W.A.S. Hewins claimed in 1927:

> The man or woman belonging to the British Empire ought, from that very fact, to take a much larger and much more generous and a much more impartial view of the problems we have to consider than the Englishman or the Scotsman or the Welshman as such . . . nothing is so alien to the people of these islands as a narrow nationalism.[23]

For some Imperialists, as for many new Liberals,[24] the Boer War was crucial in moulding a vision of empire. During and immediately after the war, Sir Alfred Milner (later Lord Milner), acting as High Commissioner for South Africa from 1897 to 1905, recruited a group of young administrators, including R.H. Brand, Lionel Curtis, Richard Feetham, Philip Kerr, Geoffrey Robinson, Basil Williams and others. This set, and other associates such as Amery, became known as the 'Kindergarten' on account of their youth.[25] The group largely stayed in South Africa after Milner left office in 1905 and assisted, albeit indirectly, in the unification of the country after the South African Convention of 1909.[26] During this campaign for unity, as Curtis told Milner's successor Lord Selborne in 1907,[27] the Empire also began to appear to members of the Kindergarten to be in need of closer union, a rationalisation of its system of government and a reduction of the potential for friction implicit in its overlapping centres of sovereignty.[28] Thus, with the addition of F.S. Oliver, the Kindergarten reconstituted itself in 1910 as the Round Table, taking its name from its journal, which first appeared in November of that year. The group was soon joined by Edward Grigg, Alfred Zimmern and Reginald Coupland.[29]

But the Round Table was far from interpreting the form which the application of these principles to the Empire would take in a unanimous way. Curtis was the movement's dominant personality; but his passionate belief that the preservation of the Empire depended on the rapid implementation of a scheme of full imperial federation was far from representative of the group. Other members believed, or at any rate came to believe, that less formal cooperative links or systems of alliances between the different states of the Empire might have considerable utility.[30] The result was that two books published under Curtis' name in 1916, *The problem of the commonwealth* and *The commonwealth of nations, part I*, which cogently argued the necessity for full federation between the self-governing states of the white Empire, certainly did not receive the full endorsement of his Round Table colleagues. The effects of the Great War were in any case not conducive to Curtis' ambitious goal.[31] However, the movement's efforts to improve relations between the states of the Empire persisted during and after the war and its quarterly journal still survives.

Another controversial issue of imperial policy which troubled the Round Table was tariff reform. Its refusal to take up a definitive position on the question prevented the wholehearted cooperation of Unionist tariff reformers such as Amery, in spite of the fact that his ideas were in many ways similar to those of the Round Table.[32] A passionate Imperialist, though of part Hungarian-Jewish background, Amery believed tariff reform to be essential to the defence of the Edwardian Empire against emerging threats.[33] The economist W.A.S. Hewins was also drawn to the imperial idea expressed in tariff reform from ostensibly unlikely beginnings. In his youth Hewins had been disposed towards Liberalism, and while a student in Oxford had even been an organiser of the University Home Rule League.[34] But Hewins' subsequent experience as an academic economist[35] led him to question the internationalist assumptions of the discipline's free trade orthodoxy. As Hewins later recalled: 'In view of the actual developments of policy in Europe and the United States it seemed to me impossible to organise the British Empire unless the Free Trade policy of Great Britain was abandoned'. Modern mechanical methods had, as the free traders had predicted, increased the scale of production and trade; but this had not produced economic or political internationalism. Nationalist restrictions on trade, aggressive and defensive, were rather the norm. Thus, tariff reform and imperial preference were essential to the defence of the British Empire, economically and politically.[36] Consequently, in 1903 Hewins became a prominent proponent of Joseph Chamberlain's policy of tariff reform.[37]

Hewins' politics and religion have not been found so interesting by historians;[38] yet Hewins himself found them impossible to separate from his economics.[39] Hewins was highly sympathetic to the Roman Catholic Church and, after he formally entered that Church in September 1914,[40] became a close political advisor to Cardinal Francis Bourne, the effective head of the Roman Catholic Church in England.[41] Therefore, his diary for May 1919 reveals that he considered his 'war on the old economics' 'a preparation for the restoration of the Catholic faith in England and the British Empire'.[42] This was necessary for spiritual reasons, but Hewins also believed that on 'purely temporal grounds . . . the British Empire cannot last unless it becomes Catholic'. Only Catholicism could save the empire from social revolution by providing the necessary stability and social justice.[43] For Hewins, a true Catholic could not accept the materialistic assumptions of the free traders. The Empire's adoption of tariff reform would be a process closely akin to a religious salvation.[44]

Unfortunately, Hewins' political environment was not conducive to the practice of such a faith. Most of the political party for which Hewins was a Member of Parliament during the years 1912–18, the Unionist party, were non-Catholic, if not anti-Catholic.[45] On the other hand, Hewins frequently found that Catholics in the United Kingdom were unsympathetic to his imperial goals. This was particularly (although not exclusively) true of the largest united and distinctively Catholic grouping in Parliament, the Irish Nationalists. Their political activity on issues close to the heart of Hewins and his English conservative Catholic associates, such as Welsh disestablishment, was tainted by the heresy of liberalism.[46] The ensuing association between imperial loyalty and anti-Catholicism was a recurrent obstacle to Hewins' political aims. Indeed, the English conservative Catholic community as a whole, which included families such as Philip Kerr's and that of the prominent Unionist peers, the Duke of Norfolk and Viscount FitzAlan of Derwent (the last Irish Viceroy, in 1921–2), was certainly also troubled by this association.[47] In 1921 Charles Masterman described (somewhat unfairly) how the over-anxiety of this community to impress a suspicious country of their loyalty to the Empire drove them to outdo even the most rabid Orangemen in their 'contempt for the Irish people'.[48] Hewins was extremely sensitive to anti-Catholicism. In May 1915, for instance, he carefully noted that the new coalition Cabinet contained not a single Catholic minister.[49] His passionate Imperialism in the face of these obstacles is certainly testament to the potential breadth of the attraction of the imperial idea.

James Louis Garvin's journey to the harbour of the imperial idea is perhaps yet more arresting evidence of this breadth. For Garvin was of

Irish descent and began his journalistic life as an Irish nationalist and an admirer of Parnell.[50] The split in the Irish parliamentary party of 1890–1, and the deposition of Parnell as the party's leader, began Garvin's disaffection with Irish politics. For Garvin, 'Parnell was more important than Home Rule'.[51] As he later explained to Milner, political divisions in Ireland, the 'utter want of a common conception of patriotism', disgusted Garvin.[52] The parochialism of Irish politics in both the Nationalist and the Unionist communities had driven Garvin to seek a more satisfying faith on a wider stage.[53]

At the start of the twentieth century, just as the Kindergarten in South Africa was becoming conscious of the dangers of an ethnic and sectarian Boer nationalism which seemed to be pushing South Africa out of the Empire,[54] Garvin was in search of an alternative to the sectarian vision of politics common in nationalist Ireland. And like the Round Table and Hewins, Garvin found this alternative in the larger idea of imperial unity.[55] Garvin's experience and background, though different from that of many other Imperialists, inclined him to aim for the largest degree of political unity possible in the Empire and in the United Kingdom. Nevertheless, in spite of the similarity of Garvin's ideas to those of the Round Table the tariff issue became a fundamental difference in his case as well.[56] Garvin became an enthusiastic supporter of Joseph Chamberlain's policy of tariff reform after 1903 (ultimately he completed the first half of a six-volume biography of Chamberlain).[57] Garvin's passionate Imperialism and undoubted talent as a political journalist soon attracted attention. After editing the weekly *Outlook* (with Grigg's assistance) during the years 1905–6, Garvin was made editor of the *Observer* in 1908 (replacing Frederic Harrison's son Austin),[58] by the proprietor Lord Northcliffe. Although Northcliffe and Garvin fell out in 1911 over tariff reform,[59] it was the proprietor who left the newspaper. Garvin also edited a daily, the *Pall Mall Gazette*, from 1912–15.

The rare combination of influences on Garvin and his tendency to float many, varied, and apparently contradictory schemes at once, made him a misunderstood figure.[60] This was illustrated in the autumn of 1910 when Garvin attacked the Irish Nationalist leader John Redmond as 'the Dollar Dictator' for accepting funding for his party from Irish-American sources for the second Election of that year,[61] only a couple of weeks after Garvin had been advocating a moderate measure of Irish home rule.[62] Liberal journalists, who pretended to assume that Garvin 'dictate[d] Tory policy',[63] ridiculed Garvin for this supposedly characteristic piece of inconsistency.[64] But Garvin in fact evades easy political categorisation, and never ceased to be an Irish patriot. In 1910 he told Balfour's secretary that an Ireland united and loyal to the Empire remained his 'dearest wish'.[65] Garvin was constantly on the alert for ways to reconcile his Imperialism with his Irish patriotism,[66] a goal which did not altogether fit in with the priorities of his fellow Unionists. However, the delicate balance between Garvin's sympathies inspired him to interpret Anglo-Irish relations with a persistence and perception rare among his contemporaries – even if his perception was sometimes obscured amidst the immensity of his journalistic output over the years.

'NARROW NATIONALISM'

Garvin was by no means alone among Imperialists in his ambiguous relationship to Unionism. Historians have shown that the Edwardian Unionist party was often tempted to claim for itself the status of 'the Imperial' or 'the patriotic party'.[67] Imperialists such as Garvin certainly also had their moments of partisanship, claiming that the 'strength of the Unionist Party' was essential to 'the ultimate safety of the State'.[68] Yet the relationship between the interests of party, country and empire was not always harmonious, and the group here under consideration deliberately made imperial consolidation, not the position of the Conservative or Unionist parties in domestic politics, their highest priority.

According to Garvin, the coalescence of Liberal and Conservative Unionism had the long-term effect of infusing a new element of creative thought about the Empire into Conservative counsels.[69] Milner and Chamberlain, the major influences on Edwardian movements of closer imperial union, had both been Liberals before 1886, and Garvin and Hewins both stayed outside the pale of Unionist politics for longer. Perhaps Leopold Amery of all these individuals had the most harmonious relationship with the Unionist party, which he described as 'an instrument – a pretty poor one, the Lord knows, at times – for carrying out the ideas I care for'. Milner described himself as 'a political Ishmaelite who has found hospitality in the Unionist camp'.[70]

The Round Table movement tried particularly hard to project itself as a movement without domestic party affiliation, partly in an effort to assuage the suspicions of elements in the dominions.[71] Certainly the aims and sympathies of the Round Table movement gravitated in the direction of the Unionist party in domestic politics – Curtis found the strength of sympathy with the British Liberal party in the self-governing white dominions 'unpalatable'.[72] But the movement retained a certain freedom and flexibility, which eventually developed in some surprising directions. Not only did several of the most active members of the Round Table become supporters of Lloyd George Liberalism, but it has been contended that the 'larger idea' espoused by Lord Lothian (Kerr) in particular, helped to inspire:

> the rebirth of federalism on the continent of Europe after the Second World War. Lothian is considered a pioneer by continental scholars and federalists because he understood better and before anyone else that pacifism and patriotism are necessary but not sufficient foundations on which to build peace . . . he was able to move beyond the idea of Imperial Federation, and anticipate world federation.

This can be presented as the 'logically extreme' conclusion of Round Table Imperialism.[73] Ultimately, the advocates of closer imperial union cannot be associated in any narrow sense with Unionism, Conservatism or the defence of the Anglo-Irish Union. Their proximity to Unionism rather meant that a greater flexibility was applied by the party to several imperial problems, including Ireland, than Unionism could of itself generate.

Yet there were limits to the flexibility and inclusivity of this vision of empire. Milner suggested that the 'only real and permanent tie' of the Empire was race: 'I am a British (indeed primarily an English) Nationalist'.[74] Imperialists did not frequently express a 'Nationalism' as forthright as this. However, there was a feeling, as Hewins put it, that the 'ideal of groups of nations as families bound together . . . into a higher community' was an 'English creation. It is not Irish or Scotch [sic] or Welsh – it is English pure and simple'.[75] The imperialist 'larger idea', in other words, constituted the core values of English history projected onto a grander world stage. This is what Oliver meant when he said that 'England' 'is a far dearer word to me, a Scotsman, than the British Empire'. It is also why Curtis felt unable to 'tell the world the truth about England. I love her too much to see it. The best I can offer the world is the tale of a lover'.[76] Garvin was (at least when he wanted to be) Irish; but after 1910, he expressed antipathy to those non-English sections of the

United Kingdom whose votes maintained the Liberal government in power. His *Pall Mall Gazette* complained:

> The 'predominant partner' is [too] prepared to merge himself in the united nation – to let himself be led by the nose by the Celtic fringe . . . England, after all, if the least articulate, is the most solid and stable element in the sisterhood of nations. British thought and British civilisation is, and must be, in the main English.[77]

Given the origins of this type of Imperialism in the secession from Liberalism over home rule from 1886, none of this is surprising. Unionism had seized on the symbols and discourse of English nationalism in those years as among its most powerful weapons.[78]

Imperialists were unashamed (and at times politically naive)[79] admirers of these English values because they believed that it was beyond contention that the Empire with England at its heart had been able to secure the adhesion of other peoples and races by the wise creation of institutions of popular government, and largely without the use of aggression.[80] As even Milner suggested, the successes and value of the Empire rested in its 'broad inclusiveness': 'the power of incorporating alien races, without trying to rob them of their individuality, was characteristic of the British system', 'distinctively British'. Thus, this feature of the Empire had to be cherished and protected. Milner contended that this 'principle of boundless tolerance has like everything human, "the defects of its qualities". It may become a source of weakness by being carried too far'.[81] Force as well as fine ideals was sometimes necessary to defend characteristically British or English virtues.[82] All of this was a cliché of the Edwardian political landscape – many Liberals would have heartily agreed. The problem was that 'Imperialism' was therefore increasingly defined by its relative readiness to use force to defend this vision[83] – and here the Imperialists were on particularly shaky ground. Whenever Imperialists suggested that the Empire had to steel itself to prepare for a conflict of self-defence, critics could insinuate that Imperialists were expressing a lack of courage in what they themselves had claimed to be the attractive power of characteristically British ideals.[84]

Anglo-Irish relations thus placed Imperialists in a position of some delicacy. Their relative willingness to advocate forcible methods in defence of the finer ideals of empire, their intolerance of secessionist movements,[85] and the tendency of their idealisation of supposedly distinctively English values to become exclusive, combined occasionally to lead Imperialists to endorse the coercion of nationalist Ireland. However, the pressure on Imperialists to live up to their idealisation of the Empire was great. Nationalist Ireland experienced manifestations of British imperialism which seemed very different from its most liberal professions: far from being alone in this it could be argued that nationalist Ireland got off lightly.[86] But ultimately these liberal professions were of some significance for the course of Anglo-Irish relations. The process by which they took effect, however, was a tortuous and difficult one for all those involved.

Nevertheless, in spite of the difficulties it was a process throughout which the anonymous editorials and articles in the *Round Table*, the *Observer*, the *Times* and the *Pall Mall Gazette* displayed an underlying ideological consistency. There is no guarantee that any specific editorial in newspapers edited by Garvin or Robinson was written by those editors.[87] Ireland was, naturally enough, however, a specific concern of Garvin's, and he was particularly determined in his efforts to control editorial policy at the *Observer*. Both Garvin and Robinson (at the *Times*) fell out with the proprietor Lord Northcliffe, respectively in 1911 and 1918–19, on the issue of editorial control.[88] In spite of the force of Northcliffe's interventions at the *Times*, its policy on Irish and imperial problems while under Robinson's editorship was heavily influenced by his friends in the 'moot' (the London centre of the Round Table).[89] Taken together therefore, in spite of all the differences of personality and influence within Imperialism, these journals propagated an interpretation of Anglo-Irish issues from the years 1910 to 1925 which was reconcilable with Imperialists' private sentiments, surprisingly coherent and often influential.

Federalism and Resistance, 1910–14

> I certainly don't know what you are going to call the new country across St. George's Channel, with part of it taken out . . . It cannot be called Ireland at any rate.
>
> William Albert Samuel Hewins, 1914[1]

THE PROPONENTS OF imperial consolidation, even the Irishman Garvin, had spent little time in Ireland. Curtis appears to have only visited Ireland once (briefly, to attend an Irish Agricultural Organisation Society meeting in 1912) before a rather more important trip in 1921.[2] Before 1917, the *Round Table* covered Ireland sporadically, often with transparent unease,[3] and often with reluctant pieces by Oliver.[4] In December 1913, Edward Grigg wrote an important article in the journal on Ireland, apparently without specifically visiting the country.[5] In fact, Round Table attitudes to and experiences in South Africa were probably as influential as they were on their attitudes to Ireland as they had spent so much longer there. To Philip Kerr, the parallel was apparent even in 1905. He told Herbert Fisher at that time that South Africa was 'going to be as difficult a country to govern as is Ireland. People are just as irresponsible and politically are just as immoral'.[6]

Imperialists generally distrusted Irish sources of information, particularly Irish nationalist sources of information. They tended to dismiss 'official' Irish Nationalist interpretations of Irish political and social life, believing that Irish Nationalists had a tendency to overlook unwelcome facts.[7] Among the Redmondite Nationalists only one, Stephen Gwynn, was a regular source of counsel for the Imperialists on Irish politics. Gwynn, who was seen by Imperialists as a relative moderate, was a friend of F.S. Oliver, and after the First World War was an occasional advisor to Philip Kerr and a correspondent for Garvin's *Observer*.[8] One important native commentator on matters Irish whom Imperialists did deem particularly trustworthy was Sir Horace Plunkett.[9] Plunkett was seen as an impartial non-sectarian figure in Irish politics and so was admired by the Round Table.[10] But before the First World War, journals more closely associated with the Unionist party such as the *Times* could contend that his methods of agrarian and economic cooperation had demonstrated a line of progress in Ireland in which self-government was no necessary feature.[11] Milner, Hewins and Oliver also spoke admiringly of Plunkett's work,[12] and Garvin's *Outlook* argued that Plunkett had shown that fundamentally 'the Irish question is an economic question'.[13]

THE PRINCIPLE OF UNION

Some historians have pointed out that various Unionists had an instinct that Irish self-government would ultimately prove impossible to avert. The policies of Unionist governments during the years 1886–1905 should thus be regarded not as an attempt to 'kill home rule with kindness', but as an attempt to apply reforms to set the country on a peaceable basis, whatever political system finally emerged. Balfour, for instance, seems intermittently to have felt that home rule was inevitable: 'After all', he told Wilfrid Blunt, 'when it comes I shall not be sorry. Only let us have separation as well as Home Rule'.[14] In October 1886, Milner had told Goschen:

> by the goodness of Providence and your influence, I was saved from taking the Gladstonian side in the late struggle. All my natural leanings were to Home Rule, and, in the far future, I still think it may be the best, or the only, Constitution for Ireland. But, under present circumstances, I am sure it would have meant a most fearful disaster.[15]

Other Unionists argued that by 1910–11, 'circumstances [had] entirely changed since '86', and an entirely negative attitude of opposition to home rule was no longer tenable.[16] Garvin argued that wise legislation, particularly land reforms, enacted by Unionists, had created a 'new and quieter Ireland' a country with a propertied majority, a 'nation of Haves'. In this context, Garvin contended that the 'old Unionist position' no longer applied in quite the same form to Irish politics, and the concession of a limited measure of self-government could be safely considered.[17]

But such claims of consistency can be pushed too far. Early in 1905, George Wyndham had been forced to leave his office in Balfour's Unionist government as Irish Chief Secretary, having been associated with the devolutionary schemes of Sir Anthony MacDonnell. The *Outlook* under Garvin's editorship had suggested that such plans were 'premature'; changes in Irish politics, which would necessarily be a 'slow product' of 'education and social well-being', had to precede changes in the 'machinery' of the government of Ireland. Due to Unionist policies of the previous twenty years, the journal contended, Ireland's 'malady of centuries' was 'yielding'; but Garvin clearly expected the continuation of similar policies for some years to come.[18] The dangers to Britain's place in the world implicit in home rule had not diminished, but increased.[19] Therefore, in 1910, an awareness of political necessity played a large role in Garvin's partial acceptance of Irish self-government – as in 1906, Unionists found themselves out of office, forced against their better judgement to accommodate, at least partially, a Liberal government's plan to grant self-government to a recently disaffected region.[20]

Unionists, of course, preferred the Union on a point of principle; and even Imperialists who were not party Unionists agreed with them in large measure. As advocates of imperial consolidation, they felt there was a deep issue at stake. The Union, after all, was a wider form of association and thus embodied the 'larger idea' of a 'higher civilisation' – the same principle which underlay the union of states in the British Empire – whereas home rule was parochial and stood for lesser ideals. Imperialists needed a lot of persuading before they could see any virtues in home rule. Amery was disappointed with his fellow Unionists during the home rule debates of 1912–14 for failing to articulate a sense of United Kingdom nationalism; privately, he wished that the word 'Ireland' had been abolished in 1800.[21] During the Great War, Oliver wished that a tunnel could be built under the Irish Sea to ensure the closer political unity of the United Kingdom.[22]

Ian Colvin suggested that the Round Table's interest in United Kingdom federation was born of a naive love of federal systems.[23] But late in 1910, Curtis recognised that the existing Union was more consistent with the spirit of Imperial consolidation: 'Is it not wiser for us as Imperialists to accept the units as we now find them, including the United Kingdom, and to accept all the logical consequences of treating them as National units[?]'[24] If the states of the white Empire were gravitating to a closer relationship, as Imperialists wished, such a division of one of those states as home rulers suggested would be 'a step back'.[25] Curtis also believed that the incorporation of Ireland into the United Kingdom by Pitt's Act of Union of 1800 had been a crucial precondition of the Empire's development, as he told listeners in South Africa in 1906:

> There was as you know, a time when England, Wales, Scotland and Ireland each had separate governments. In result the British people were unable to control their major interests and remained unable to control them, until they merged those four governments into one. This one government, at Westminster, has given to England the name and place that she holds today, the freest and strongest country in the world.[26]

Irish self-government was thus a distinctly second-best solution. Unlike home rulers, Imperialists tended to believe that Ireland was not a nation, but a deeply divided region. They felt some affinity to the Ulster Unionist community, because its acceptance of the symbols of British patriotism and its vigorous qualities of self-help seemed such a welcome contrast to the nationalist Irish; in the *Times* in 1918, Oliver articulated the Ulster Unionist assumption that the Celtic Irish were a race of economic failures.[27] Sources of the Imperialist idea that there were in fact 'two Irish nations' included the Ulster Liberal Unionist, Thomas Sinclair,[28] and W.F. Monypenny, whose book *The two Irish nations* was published posthumously in 1913. Monypenny was also a Protestant Ulsterman and a colleague of Robinson on the *Times.*[29] Robinson read this 'admirable little Essay . . . in the train' to Ireland in January 1914,[30] and Monypenny's ideas influenced *Times* leaders at that time with the idea that the contemporary political conflict in Ireland bore 'no resemblance to the conditions of a normal party struggle'.[31] But it would be incorrect to deduce from this language that Monypenny (or the Imperialists) expected or wanted these two separate nations to proceed in entirely different political directions. On the contrary, Monypenny held that Irish unity, to 'bridge the gulf that separates these two sectarian nations and combine them into one', was a 'noble ideal' which was 'by no means unattainable': both 'nations' were 'essentially Irish'. But the condition of this unity was the British connection: 'The Union is indeed the only hope of unity': 'The Union stands for equality . . . Home Rule for ascendancy'.[32] Imperialists such as Garvin agreed: 'religious divisions . . . still cleave Ireland asunder and make Home Rule an impossibility': only the 'impartial strength and authority of the Union' maintained peace in Ireland.[33] Significantly, an academic justification of the Union penned by Walter Alison Phillips after the Anglo-Irish Treaty of 1921 used the same language: 'the Union . . . alone stood between Ireland and a sea of troubles . . . it was only the fact that Ireland was embraced in a wider unity that kept her united'.[34]

Of the two Irish nations, Imperialists most doubted the cohesion and determination of the south. Imperialists retained a strong conviction that home rule was unnecessary because the Irish parliamentary party was in fact a decaying husk, undermined by successful Unionist administration and sustained only by a despotic political machine, party discipline at Westminster and Liberal promises and weakness towards nationalist Ireland: 'Many who know Ireland maintain that, if the issue had been left in abeyance, the desire for Home Rule would have entirely disappeared within another decade. The Nationalists were steadily losing influence'. With continued Unionist government, Nationalism would have disintegrated.[35] Whether Unionists had tried to 'kill home rule by kindness' in the twenty years following 1886 or not, after 1910 they certainly talked as if they had tried, and still intended to try.[36]

FEDERATION OR DOMINION? 1910–12

From 1910, when political circumstances brought the maintenance of the existing Union into jeopardy, many tactical divisions started to emerge within Unionism.[37] Some Imperialists, notably Oliver and Garvin, began to advocate a federal form of constitution for the entire United Kingdom. They saw this as the best way of resolving the difficulties of their party and the Empire.

Oliver wrote a series of letters to the *Times*, under the pseudonym 'Pacificus', around the time of the cross-party negotiations on the House of Lords crisis of 1910.[38] He hoped for a settlement by agreement of this question. He believed the Constitution should be 'safeguarded against light and hasty' changes made in a party spirit: 'Have we lost our political instinct for settling things – that genius for popular government which has saved us time and again from revolution – about which we are never tired of boasting[?]'[39] United Kingdom federation might form the basis of such a necessary and patriotic compromise and might secure other desirable objectives. Matters of domestic policy would be removed from Westminster, where imperial issues could be discussed at leisure without the intrusion of party. The unnecessary antagonism of social reform and empire, produced by the want of parliamentary time under the present system, would therefore be eradicated. In Ireland, Oliver associated federalism with the loyal imperialism of Isaac Butt, as opposed to the separatist nationalism of Parnell and Redmond. He believed a businesslike conference of the political leaders held behind closed doors would distinguish sane federalism from the empty rhetoric of Gladstonian home rule. Oliver also hoped to remove the threat posed to the Empire by the direction of its affairs by Asquith and his 'Whiggish' supporters.[40]

Though his writings were not coordinated with Oliver's,[41] Garvin agreed that decentralising local affairs to regional assemblies might enable more systematic attention to be given to national and imperial issues. Federalism might give some local power to the Irish nationalists, but these were at least saner than 'our own anti-naval, anti-militarist and socialist factions'. Through a bipartisan settlement of outstanding issues, Garvin thus hoped to serve some of his highest priorities. He told Balfour that with the national issue settled, Ireland might return 'a solid majority of Conservatives to help defend in the Imperial Parliament nearly all we care for'.[42] Therefore, a federal compromise would undermine the Liberals' attack on the House of Lords, strengthening its position as an Imperialist rearguard to resist socialism and the 'suicides club' (Garvin's favoured epithet for the radical opponents of an increase in the size of the navy).[43] In view of the global balance of power and the state of opinion in America and in the dominions about Anglo-Irish relations, Garvin was indeed particularly anxious to 'place the navy once for all upon an unassailable footing', and thus sought to impress federal ideas on his readers and on leading Unionist statesmen.[44]

This proposal, embodying as it did the idea of a Dublin legislature for Irish affairs, seemed to many Liberals no different from their own home rule schemes; the fact that Garvin and Oliver could subsequently act as opponents of the 1912 Home Rule Bill seemed to expose their intentions as purely destructive.[45] To an extent, Imperialists admitted that the differences between their own 'federalism' and Liberals' 'Home Rule' were exaggerated by the use of a distinct nomenclature: 'federalism' was 'respectable and may be stretched sufficiently to cover what is meant'.[46] However, in Garvin's words, federalism still was 'quite another proposition'; there were real differences between ideas of federal and Gladstonian home rule.[47] Oliver aimed to direct Unionist comment 'on to arguments which are only destructive of the separatist measure', leaving the way free for his party to take up federalism. Federalism was anti-separatist precisely because it involved the grant of subordinate legislatures 'all round'.

Unionist federalists insisted that the degree of autonomy accorded to the units of a United Kingdom federation had to be in 'substantial uniformity'.[48] In 1913, Milner told Oliver he:

> would not give anything to Ireland, or parts of Ireland, that could not be equally given to other sub-divisions of the U[nited] K[ingdom] . . . a really sub-ordinate 'parliament' or 'legislature' . . . for Celtic and Catholic Ireland, and 'wait and see' for the rest of the UK, would be the best solution.[49]

As Amery later pointed out: 'A dual system inevitably tends towards separation, and rejects restrictions by one partner on the other. A federal system is naturally stable and tends towards greater unity'.[50] Indeed, these Unionists advocated a United Kingdom 'federation' so centralised and with such weak regional parliaments, that they were probably thinking in terms merely of devolution, rather than true federation.[51]

On the assumption that the 'old Unionist system' was 'dead',[52] and that the object was merely to limit the degree of autonomy conceded to Ireland, there was a movement in Ireland which gave Imperialists ground for hope. William O'Brien's Independent Nationalists had no great love for the Liberal party.[53] They also seemed to transcend the 'narrow bigotry' of the Redmondite 'Molly Maguires',[54] and were prepared to consider concessions to Protestant interests to try to win over Ulster and avert any partition of Ireland.[55] O'Brien's movement was perceived by Imperialists as a 'sign of altered times' in Ireland, of a people 'sick of a wasting strife [, who] want prosperity', the product of Unionist legislation. Garvin declared that in Cork O'Brien was establishing a 'second Ulster'.[56]

As negotiations between Unionists and Liberals on the constitutional question collapsed in the autumn of 1910, Garvin urged his fellow Unionists to capitalise on this 'coming cause' in Ireland: 'If Mr Redmond were to repudiate [a moderate] form of settlement', the *Observer* had commented, 'we are tolerably confident that the new Ireland would repudiate him' for O'Brien.[57] O'Brien had reciprocated the endorsement, commending the *Observer*'s advocacy of United Kingdom federation in October 1910.[58] In 1905, Garvin's *Outlook* had rejected devolution until 'the Irish attitude towards the Empire shows a fundamental change'. Five years later, ever anxious to reconcile his two deeply held creeds, he regarded O'Brien's movement as evidence of such a change in the Irish mind.[59] 'The Irish question after fifteen years is taking a slow seizure of me again and at last', he had told Plunkett: 'I always knew it would'.[60]

Consequently, the Unionists needed to give O'Brien moral support, and Garvin hoped to give him even more practical assistance. He had told Balfour's secretary after the first Election of 1910 in January: 'we must give O'Brien and Healy some chance of coming back for another struggle with half the Nationalist representation'.[61] With the aid of Moreton Frewen, an Irish-American (soon to be an Independent Nationalist MP), Garvin helped to raise funds for O'Brien's campaign in the second Election of 1910 in December, securing him one donation of £5,000. But O'Brien would not accept 'Tory money'. There were limits to the extent to which any Irish nationalist could associate with British Unionism, though Garvin felt that this might have been different had the Unionists a 'proper sense of the wise and inevitable about federalism';[62] Unionist leaders had rejected Garvin's arguments for federalism.[63]

However, as the cross-party conference was breaking down in October 1910 Garvin had come up with a further suggestion. He felt that the failure of the official Nationalists to adopt a conciliatory attitude had created the risk that Unionist Ulster may not wish to be part of an all-Ireland assembly, and he believed that it would not be desirable to coerce Ulster into joining such a body. Though Garvin 'profoundly' regretted it, he feared 'a distinct Belfast Assembly for the great Northern Conclave' may therefore be necessary. Nevertheless, this need not mean the 'permanent vivisection' of Ireland: 'Why should there not be an Irish Upper House or National Council for the whole country, elected under conditions ensuring the preponderance of moderate opinion . . . coordinating the work of the separate Lower Chambers?' He suggested that this common body could deal with matters of concern relating to all parts of Ireland, such as railways and marketing. He suggested that after some years of such an arrangement, Ulster might be given the opportunity to vote on whether to 'throw in its lot completely with the common Irish system'. The Dublin Parliament would thus 'have to subordinate everything' to the goal of winning Ulster over, which would have 'an admirable restraining effect' on the Redmondite Nationalists and would promote 'the definite reconciliation of sects and classes North and South, and the solution of the Irish problem as a whole'. The possibility of partition in Ireland had been aired previously and Garvin advanced this particular suggestion tentatively. However, the fact that he had recognised the division in Ireland, and advanced an arrangement involving self-government for the 'two Irish nations' in such detail, would be of some significance in subsequent years.[64]

Oliver was also having trouble with those who lacked a 'proper sense . . . about federalism' – in his case the moot.[65] Twenty years earlier, another supporter of imperial federation, Cecil Rhodes, had viewed Ireland as a possible self-governing unit in an Imperial federation and assisted the Irish parliamentary party financially.[66] In an important letter to Curtis in September 1910, Kerr considered what impact United Kingdom federation would have on the prospects for imperial federation. If home rule embodied a limited measure of autonomy for Ireland, with Britain and Ireland remaining 'a single nation in fundamentals though allowing a large measure of liberty in administration and administrative law to local groups', Kerr realised that federation in the United Kingdom would only impact on the larger imperial stage 'indirectly',[67] by demonstrating the workability of federal constitutions. However, if Britain and Ireland were to remain 'united for purposes of defence only . . . and in other respects pursue their careers as independent nations', progress would have been made towards the creation of an imperial parliament with strictly 'Imperial functions', 'a preliminary step towards Imperial Unity before the Dominions are ready to be represented in a true Imperial assembly'.[68] Nevertheless, Kerr recognised that the British people were generally not 'prepared to see the destruction of the unity of the United Kingdom' to the extent of this latter 'improbable revolution':

> the difficulties in the way of achieving any sort of federation for the UK, and especially the only one which can effect Imperial Union, are so immense . . . that to take up federation is to go out of our way to become encumbered with a movement which will arouse a vast amount of opposition e.g., to Irish Home Rule, . . . which would not maintain itself at all to the separation of Imperial and national affairs which we chiefly desire.[69]

Kerr rightly predicted that the Asquith government would eventually introduce a scheme of autonomy for Ireland more limited than that enjoyed by the dominions, and saw that 'imperial Unity has no essential connection with the movement for federation for the UK, for it can be achieved without it'. Therefore, in spite of their personal interest in the idea, Kerr and Curtis put little effort into persuading the moot to support Garvin and Oliver's 1910 campaign for United Kingdom federation.[70]

Kerr thus believed that schemes to grant a wide-ranging measure of home rule to Ireland had dubious connotations, and decided that for the moot to associate itself with any such plan in the hope of persuading the dominions to align themselves in a similar relationship with Great Britain, would be unwise. Instead, Kerr believed that once the advocates of United Kingdom federation had broken up the ground for federal ideas, public opinion would be receptive to closer imperial union. With the benefit of hindsight, it could be argued that this was a mistake. Kerr's more painstaking approach presupposed (wrongly)[71] that time was on the side of the proponents of imperial consolidation. Associating the Round Table with a grant of extensive home rule to Ireland would instead have rapidly changed its public image; it would have appeared as a democratic liberalising movement, instead of the militaristic centralising one radicals saw. Given the difficulties Kerr highlighted, 'the strongly Home Rule sympathies of the Dominions' and 'the fact that the [British] Liberals are somewhat careless of Imperial problems', a different image would have been to the advantage of the Round Table.[72] Consenting to a wide-ranging 'Dominion' version of home rule would also have put the Round Table in touch with a constituency in nationalist Ireland. In 1917, Æ reported to Oliver that Curtis' recently published *Problem of the commonwealth* had struck a chord in Ireland. It seemed to many nationalists that Curtis' model of the relationship which would eventually operate between the independent constituent states of an Imperial federation was immediately applicable to the Anglo-Irish connection.[73] An echo of this was discovered by Curtis and John Dove in Ireland in 1921 when they tracked down a Sinn Féiner on the run in Dublin, and saw '*The Commonwealth of Nations* peeping out of the shelf behind his bed'.[74] By then, however, it was too late for Ireland, the Empire, and for the Round Table.

Analogies between Ireland and the white self-governing dominions, of course, featured heavily in Liberal justifications of home rule, whereas Unionists denied that they were applicable. Kerr and Curtis, eager as ever to include the Liberals in their plans for the reform of the Empire, had considered this analogy a good deal more closely than party Unionists. Nonetheless, it could be argued that the moot had missed an opportunity because it fell on the Unionist side of this, the clearest political fault-line of the day on the Irish question. Imperialists argued that Ireland and Britain had too many 'common interests' to be perceived as separate nations, as each of the dominions were.[75] Imperialists believed that the fiscal independence given to the dominions was inapplicable to Ireland; indeed, they were to contend that the Asquith government tacitly conceded this point by withholding some such powers from the Irish

Parliament proposed in the 1912 Home Rule Bill.[76] But dominion home rule was not just irrelevant to Irish circumstances – it was a step in the wrong direction for the entire Empire. Imperialists believed that 'Dominion home rule' could not settle 'the problem of the relations between the different sections of the Empire';[77] closer union or independence would be the permanent arrangement. There was no 'half-way house', as Kerr maintained, between limiting Irish self-government within the bounds of a federal settlement for the United Kingdom on the one hand, and the practical separation of Ireland from Britain on the other.[78]

As Hewins stated, Liberals had tried to enlist 'appreciation of the good achievements of self-government in the British Empire' in defence of their Home Rule Bill.[79] But Imperialists interpreted the political evolution of Canada and South Africa to yield two rather different lessons – that full political union (possibly with some system of provincial devolution) was the natural arrangement for regions situated as were the constituent parts of South Africa, Canada or the British Isles, and that once the imperial links of a country such as Ireland had been settled (as they were in South Africa by war), local unity was only a matter of time.[80] Amery contended that 'Unionists and Imperialists can choose no better ground for their resistance to Home Rule than the wide and varied field of colonial experience'.[81] On the contrary, however, ultimately the distinctions which Unionists tried to draw in order to refute the colonial analogy were too subtle. Liberals' assumption that the characteristically British institution of self-government had benefited the Empire in South Africa was reassuringly familiar to British political observers as it complemented their conventional sense of patriotism (a form of patriotism to which Imperialists often appealed). And by spending so much time trying to refute the colonial analogy, such Unionists tacitly admitted that 'nothing [had] done more' to strengthen the case for home rule.[82]

Imperialists resisted the idea of breaking up the United Kingdom by creating an Irish dominion because they perceived that states simply did not commit suicide in such a way. Home rule, a concession to a secessionist movement at the very centre of the Empire, might provide encouragement to the demands of other discontented minorities. By resisting home rule, Unionist Ulster thus held the pass for the Empire.[83] In the House of Commons in 1912, Amery drew an analogy with the position during the American Civil War: 'One or [the] other has got to surrender, and surrender finally, and certainly we do not mean to surrender lightly. Did the United States surrender on these terms when the Southern States demanded separation?'[84] 'For this reason', Milner explained to Oliver in 1911, 'I should be careful to leave the door open to ultimate support of a reasonable revolt of Ulster'; such a revolt could be perceived as a defence of the idea of a common United Kingdom citizenship.[85] In the British Isles, as in South Africa and in the United States of America, the Imperialist felt that the rights of the wider political community embodied the higher ideal.

UNION OR PARTITION? 1912–14

The Parliament Act of August 1911, reducing the House of Lords' power to veto home rule merely to a prerogative to delay the measure for two years, made the introduction of a Gladstonian Home Rule Bill inevitable. It was perceived as a 'moral disaster' for Unionism and left many Unionists feeling frustrated.[86] Garvin's attitude rapidly became one of 'fight, fight, fight'; his die-hard resistance to the Parliament Act merged with his resistance to home rule.[87]

But Garvin's strategy in the years 1912–14 was in fact highly complex. He hoped that the threat of violent resistance in Ulster to home rule would force the Liberal government to consent either to a general election on home rule, or to a bipartisan compromise settlement. In the latter eventuality, Garvin's columns presented a federal settlement as 'the better choice among alternative evils'; though sometimes they again suggested that 'in many ways the best settlement' would be the scheme he had briefly hinted at in October 1910, the establishment of two parliaments in Ireland (one in Ulster) to send equal-sized delegations to meet to discuss problems of common concern.[88] However, in essentials, Garvin was still upholding 'the policy of the Union':

> The case for the Union was never so strong as it is today . . . If the present Bill could be submitted to a vote of the whole people and rejected . . . the sequel would undoubtedly be beneficent. The centralised administration from Dublin Castle would be thoroughly reformed; the economic welfare of the country would be more powerfully prosecuted; a better system of subordinate self-government would be gradually built up than ever can be created by any British Government dependent on the Nationalist vote . . . That is our policy . . .[89]

Garvin's *Observer* continued to sponsor federalism in 1912; but because the Liberal Home Rule Bill of that year was not strictly federal, and because the Liberals seemed to be behaving in a partisan fashion, Unionists such as Garvin and Amery focused on 'the destruction of the present Bill' and the removal of the Liberals from office as 'the indispensable preliminary' to any peaceful settlement in Ireland.[90] It was the 'duty of Unionists at Westminster . . . to force at all costs an appeal to the country'.[91] During the following two years, Garvin therefore saw no contradiction in suggesting a variety of political schemes for Ireland in rapid succession. Garvin was hedging his bets; and as home rule neared the parliamentary finishing post, Ulster exclusion, against his will, would come through as his strongest horse.[92]

Garvin's columns in the years 1912–14 perplexed Liberals. The *Manchester Guardian* described the *Observer* as 'a good Home Rule paper sometimes, although Carsonian just now'.[93] In fact, Garvin was in a sense a 'home ruler' and a 'Carsonian' simultaneously. Henry Nevinson later described Garvin's behaviour during the signing of the Ulster Covenant in Belfast in September 1912:

> All the time during that solemn ceremony, while Carson was bowing over the fateful document as at an altar of religion, Mr Garvin, in subdued tones, kept assuring me of his profound affection for Charles Stewart Parnell. He loved Carson and he loved Parnell. He had been the first to stand publicly at Parnell's side after his 'fall'. He had revered him to the last and he reverenced his memory. It was all perfectly true and sincere, but a little difficult for a foreigner to understand when he was listening to quill pens scratching the signatures of Ulster Covenanters on the parchment, and knew that in England Mr Garvin supplied the Unionist party with brains.[94]

Hewins told a Dublin audience in 1913 that he was 'in favour of using every possible means short of compromise to prevent so great a disaster as the destruction of the unity of the United Kingdom'.[95] But in his case also, pugnacious rhetoric concealed a complex analysis. Hewins saw 'the Irish question' largely as an economic question. Garvin agreed that finance was the 'crux' of the home rule issue; and, as Patricia Jalland has noted, it was a problematic dimension for home rulers.[96] Early in the twentieth century, reforms passed by Liberal and Unionist governments, particularly pensions and land reform legislation, had meant that Ireland

'Now who will stand on either hand. And keep the bridge with me?'

Fig. 1: The *Covenanter*, no. 1, (20 May 1914), p. 5.

was 'costing' more than she was 'contributing' to the finances of the Union.[97] As a result, home rule would either deprive Ireland of some financial benefits to which the Union had accustomed her, or necessitate continued financial support for Ireland from the imperial exchequer. The Liberals decided that the latter option was the most politically palatable, and their Home Rule Bill of 1912 proposed that an annual subsidy to the Irish exchequer would prolong the effects of the recent legislation. As Amery, Hewins and Oliver pointed out, this seemed unfair to the rest of the United Kingdom. A further clause of the Bill suggested that if the Imperial Parliament introduced any import tariffs for the United Kingdom in the future, the Irish Parliament would have had the power to adjust them for Ireland by a rate of up to ten per cent. This concession to Irish separatist sentiment was of little significance to those Liberal free traders who thought import tariffs were unlikely to be a future feature of British commercial policy; but for Hewins and Amery (for whom tariff reform was an imminent proposition),[98] the measure appeared nonsensical and created the prospect of an Anglo-Irish tariff barrier. The anomalies of the Bill's proposed financial settlement, Unionists contended forcefully, illuminated the impossibility of its proposed compromise between separatist Irish nationalism and the unity of the United Kingdom.[99] The Bill did not attempt to give Ireland full fiscal autonomy, as it recognised that Ireland was in no position to support herself, but still gave Ireland sufficient fiscal power to 'work untold mischief'. The government, as Hewins told a British audience, were 'going to give Ireland a weapon by means of which they can split up the United Kingdom and introduce a wedge into the British Empire, and the most humorous thing is that you have got to pay for it'.[100]

Unionists argued that 'vague sentiment' and 'slosh' about 'good feeling' could not disguise these contradictions in the Bill.[101] They contended that tariff reform and Ireland's 'economic salvation under the Union' would constitute a cleaner alternative.[102] Ireland, the tariff reformers felt, had been impoverished by Britain's nineteenth-century free trade policies. The real source of her grievance was fiscal, not political; Ireland's interests had not been considered sufficiently in past British fiscal policy.[103] Appropriate import taxes, therefore, would form the final step in Ireland's incorporation into the British economic and political system. An Imperial tariff on foodstuffs might prove an enormous economic boon to Ireland by ensuring for her agriculturalists a larger share of the British market.[104] This proposal avoided awkward questions of whether Ireland could pay for herself. Federalism had little relevance to such a vision of economic unity; Hewins was 'absolutely and unalterably opposed' to such schemes, while Amery was at best lukewarm.[105]

Ultimately, tariff reformers showed some foresight in predicting that any effort to make Ireland an autarkical economic entity would be unsuccessful.[106] But tariff reformers' own policy also suffered from serious defects. In 1909, Hewins had dismissed the idea that there might be difficulties in reconciling industrial England to a tariff which would consider the interests of predominantly agricultural Ireland. He argued that Ireland could 'rest perfectly sure that we are not going to drop that particular side of the tariff reform propaganda', because revenue was relatively easy to collect from agricultural tariffs, and because food taxes would be required as part of a preferential tariff arrangement with the colonies. However, his other contention, that import taxes on foodstuffs would be too beneficial in electoral terms for Unionists to dispense with, proved to be wide of the mark.[107] Home rule was certainly not popular in England and was not an issue Liberals raised with much confidence.[108] Import duties on food, however, while fundamental to the preservation of the Anglo-Irish Union in the views of tariff reformers, were not popular in England either. It followed that if Unionists could only disengage themselves from the embarrassing commitment to food taxes, they would stand a good chance of discomfiting the Liberal government. Early in 1913, the temptation became irresistible, and the Unionist leader Andrew Bonar Law promised to put the question to a referendum in the event of a Unionist election victory.[109] The tariff reformers were more than a little irritated with their party's leadership for depriving them of their favoured constructive argument in support of the Union:[110] Garvin was particularly horrified to see the hand of his ex-proprietor Northcliffe in the shelving of the policy.[111] Liberals meanwhile, not surprisingly, were delighted by this turn of events.[112]

The fundamental problem for Unionists had been identified by Amery; there was simply a failure in Edwardian Britain to perceive the United Kingdom as a single political entity.[113] In spite of the pluralism of some British political traditions, narrow nationalism was actually more common in England than Imperialists liked to believe. England and Ireland may have had economically complimentary interests, but the perceived *political* interests of the majority in each country diverged. The anti-pluralism of British political institutions exacerbated tensions between the two countries by consistently failing to represent more than one of these political interests at any one time – either the Unionism of the predominant partner held sway, as for long periods between 1886 and 1906, or Ireland's majority's desire for autonomy held the balance of power. It was certainly possible to envisage a benign free and equal economic and political partnership between England and Ireland in 1912, with or without tariffs: but such visions were ceasing to seem politically compatible with the defence of the Union.

Imperialists had hoped to find 'firmer' grounds for resisting home rule than what Oliver described as Ulster's 'blind unreasoning religious jealousy and hatred'.[114] However, with tariff reform in abeyance, the Orange card was again a shrewd one for Unionists to play. If nationalist Ireland could claim the right to self-government embodied in the Home Rule Bill, Protestant Ulster was logically in a strong position to claim exemption from the same measure. Moreover, if the Unionists could focus public attention on fears that the Irish Catholic majority might persecute the Protestant minority in a home rule Ireland, they would enlist Britain's traditional Protestant prejudices on their side.[115]

Milner had taken little part in politics after being censured by the Liberal-dominated House of Commons in 1906 after his return from South Africa. He believed that an imperial opportunity had been lost in South Africa; if concerted efforts had been taken to ensure a numerical predominance of the British population, the country could have been made 'a source of strength to the Empire as a whole and a factor on the side of consolidation and not of disintegration'.[116] He believed the concession of self-government by the Campbell-Bannerman government to the conquered Boer provinces of Transvaal and the Orange Free State had wrecked this prospect. Milner's regret that South Africa had therefore become 'the weakest link in the Imperial chain' was a prominent theme of his sparse public activity in the years 1906–13.[117]

Consequently, the Ulster agitation caught Milner's imagination for several reasons. As a result of the policies of a Liberal ministry, largely the same ministry as that of 1906, the Ulster Unionists like the British of South Africa, had been betrayed and 'relieved by what has happened from any obligations to the mother-country'.[118] He thus told the Ulster Unionist leader Sir Edward Carson: 'I am completely in accord with you about Ulster, and what I want to know is whether there is not something which men like myself, who disbelieve in mere talk at this juncture, can do to help you'.[119] Milner returned from effective political retirement to fulfil this promise of assistance. Together with Amery, who was extremely suspicious of Liberal intentions towards Ulster,[120] he organised the British Covenant. This document invited signatories to pledge assistance for Unionist Ulster in the event of the Liberal government's use of the armed forces to enforce the Home Rule Bill. An echo of Ulster's own Covenant of September 1912, it was launched on the world on 3 March 1914 in the pages of Robinson's *Times.*[121] Milner also edited an associated publication, the *Covenanter.*[122] Members of the 'moot' were soon closely considering their attitude to the Covenant, and some actually signed.[123] But although Amery did ponder the question of how a provisional Unionist government of Ulster might be activated should the Home Rule Bill come into law,[124] the British Covenant was primarily designed simply to avert home rule rather than to strengthen the case for partition. The constitutional issue was paramount. Amery felt that Ulster was merely a 'symptom' of the wider danger of home rule to the Empire.[125] Significantly, Amery, like most of the moot, was not as pessimistic as Milner about South Africa.[126] Yet there was even ambiguity in Milner's attitude to Ulster Unionism.[127]

In this difficult context of intense political controversy, Grigg was faced with the task of writing two articles on Ireland for the *Round Table*, in December 1913 and March 1914.[128] Grigg was reasonably successful in avoiding the suggestion of partisanship, though he could not avoid expressing his deeply held conviction that the Liberal government had been guilty of treating a constitutional question in a party spirit.[129] However, he also felt that the Unionist opposition had unnecessarily complicated the vital constitutional issue by keeping the unpopular policy of tariff reform in its political programme.[130] The articles regretted that neither political party had wholeheartedly cultivated O'Brien's Independent Nationalist movement, which it was suggested had a far more realistic appreciation of the Irish political landscape than the Redmondite Nationalists.[131] Grigg's first article of December 1913 suggested that a system of four provincial councils in Ireland would be a better settlement than federalism. However, the limitations of the scheme and its association with the name of Joseph Chamberlain, did not commend it to Liberals such as the editor of the *Westminster Gazette* J.A. Spender.[132] Grigg's second article was written with the advice of G.L. Craik, whose interpretation of the crisis was similar to Oliver's. By this time the political crisis had deepened, and it seemed, in spite of Britons' 'sovereign' gifts of political sagacity, that an 'interval of conflict' was possible. This second essay was more favourably inclined to federalism and came closer to satisfying Spender.[133] Grigg rejected the enactment of home rule for southern Ireland with Ulster or part of Ulster excluded; this would have been a makeshift compromise which, he felt, failed to address the fundamental constitutional issue.[134]

Like Grigg, Hewins did not 'care a rap about the Ulster case, qua Ulster'.[135] In Dublin in April 1913 Hewins declared that Unionist 'Ulster was not fighting merely for herself [but] fighting for the Empire', and that he was happy to associate with her.[136] However, he had already refused to contribute to *Against home rule*, a collection of Unionist essays published in 1912, because he was offended by 'the religious line taken', i.e., the collection's emphasis of Unionist Ulster's fears of the influence of the Catholic Church in a home rule Ireland, or, as the apprehension was frequently expressed, of 'Rome Rule'.[137] And Hewins quickly regretted that he had not used his Dublin speech to express his sympathy with Roman Catholicism in a more emphatic fashion.[138] The extent to which Unionist leaders' support of Ulster began to take on the connotations of a Protestant crusade surprised and disgusted him.[139]

A letter that Hewins sent to the *Times* in September 1913 detailed what he saw as the essential bases for a negotiated settlement of the home rule question; these were the maintenance of undivided sovereignty, of fiscal and economic unity and of the principle of religious toleration, all over the United Kingdom. A speech made at Newcastle by Redmond six weeks later was criticised by the *Times* for trivialising the strength of Ulster's Unionism.[140] However, Hewins believed there was enough in the speech to suggest that settlement was truly possible along the bases that Hewins himself had proposed. In the autumn of 1913, Hewins also suspected that the Liberal government was moving towards a more imaginative fiscal policy. Thus, he interpreted political events in a characteristically idiosyncratic fashion; the 'Ulster fooling', and the consequent tension in Ireland, had been deliberately organised by elements in the Unionist party opposed to tariff reform.[141] He believed that Unionist support of the Ulster agitation was unwise from the point of view of both politics and statesmanship, and threatened to produce religious and social conflict all over the Empire. The British Covenanters, no less than the home rulers, were 'separatist', 'exclusionist wreckers', advocates of the 'policy of disintegration'.[142] A wiser defence of the Union would have consisted of an appeal to Roman Catholics in Ireland, and of 'the broader policy of Empire economics' (i.e., tariff reform).[143] Hewins had friends among the southern Unionists,[144] and was conscious of the dangers of focusing Unionist resistance to home rule too heavily on Ulster, creating the possibility of a home rule settlement for nationalist Ireland with Ulster excluded which would have left southern Unionists isolated. He also believed that such a policy would not have been popular within the ranks of the Unionist party.[145] And Hewins was also apprehensive that this would have meant the practical separation of three Catholic provinces from the Empire, with the retention of one predominantly Protestant area, adversely changing the denominational balance in the population of the United Kingdom.

Hewins thus believed that the amount of serious consideration given to this scheme by the Unionist leadership was linked to a hidden Protestant agenda. A group of influential politicians were out to create a coalition government of 'Whig anti-Catholic reactionaries',[146] aiming to effect all the policies Hewins opposed; Ulster exclusion, free trade and reactionary social legislation.[147] His interpretation of the famous Curragh incident of March 1914 was similarly idiosyncratic; it *was* a conspiracy, but *not*, as Amery and Oliver felt, a ham-fisted ministerial plot to coerce Ulster,[148] but an attempt by both front benches to make the exclusion of Ulster seem a more plausible settlement.[149] He suspected 'we could turn the Gov[ernmen]t out if our front bench meant business'.[150] Instead, Hewins was forced to rely 'on the Catholic forces here in Ireland and at Rome to defeat all separatist designs'.[151]

During 1914, British Imperialists were still endeavouring to maintain a distinction between their wider and deeper considerations in Ireland and that of Ulster.[152] The extent to which the political crisis was focusing solely on Unionist Ulster constituted, as Oliver appreciated, 'a very real danger to the principle of union': it was diverting attentions away from the wider need to resist the implementation of the Home Rule Bill, with its 'vicious principle of nationality', in any part of the United Kingdom.[153] This affected Imperialists' compromise proposals; self-government for Ireland with Ulster excluded was a 'wretched form of compromise'. Garvin supported exclusion only 'pending federation',[154] and in the nine months before July 1914, his *Observer* persistently reiterated this formula. Garvin continued to believe that the temporary exclusion of Ulster would have the merit of forcing the Nationalists to reconsider their political strategy and ideals, and would be likely to produce an Ireland united under a more moderate measure of autonomy than the Liberal home rule scheme.[155]

In the spring of 1914, the moot were also endeavouring to 'stave off the impending nightmare of civil war' with some scheme of 'exclusion pending federation'.[156] In April and May they circulated memoranda to several leading politicians. These proposed a settlement whereby Ulster might ultimately be 'won over' to union with Ireland. Ireland, with six counties of Ulster excluded, would receive home rule, and steps would be taken towards the creation of further federal assemblies for England, Scotland and Wales, thereby easing the problem of parliamentary congestion. The six counties could then send representatives to the new southern Irish Parliament, thus acknowledging the unity of Ireland, whenever they chose. The 'inducement' for 'Ulster' to do this was that she would not otherwise receive the benefit of local government: 'Ireland could not be permanently dismembered except by her own wish'. Many political leaders were apparently impressed by this scheme, but not the Nationalist leader John Redmond.[157] The moot's efforts to secure a settlement persisted after the outbreak of war in August 1914, when the Liberal government's plan to place home rule without Ulster exclusion on the statute book gave rise to problems with the wartime political truce.[158]

Imperialists' opposition to the permanent partition of Ireland was inspired by several considerations. Unity, rather than unnecessary political division, was the essence of Imperialism. If the glory of the British Empire truly was its ability to soothe national antagonisms and bring peoples together in a wider and peaceful association, the division of Ireland, no less than the division of the United Kingdom, would be a confession of failure. The 'perpetuation of two hostile camps' in Ireland was opposed to the anti-sectarian rhetoric of Imperialism.[159] The *Times* claimed that the partition of Ireland was a government scheme: 'we have never regarded the exclusion of Ulster as a wise or prudent alternative. We see little hope of peace for Ireland in a device which . . . merely deepens the rift which already cleaves the community in half'.[160] Imperialists saw that it was not a 'formula for conciliation', as virtually all the parties concerned were opposed to it.[161] The demographic reality of Ireland, with its intermixed populations, meant that any partition would merely create new minorities on both sides of the border.[162] Finally, the eventual inclusion of Ulster might offer some mechanism of alleviating the most objectionable features of the Home Rule Bill. Imperialists' consistent plan for the emergence of a united Ireland was for Ulster gradually to be 'won by sound administration with Nationalist loyalty to the Empire'.[163] If nationalist Ireland could win Ulster over in this way, felt Amery, 'by all means let them do so'. The temporary exclusion of Ulster would thus bring 'Redmond & Co. on their knees to Ulster before long'.[164]

In Ireland, as in South Africa, Imperialists perceived that in the event of the concession of self-government, the primary needs of the Empire would not have been served by keeping a loyal minority high and dry in a protected zone. It would have been better had the loyal minority tried to keep the majority as sound as possible through their influence.[165] The *Times* promised it would assist in 'passing the [Home Rule] Bill without delay' if a general election in 1914 had endorsed it, for resistance, in those circumstances, 'whatever may be said to the contrary would inevitably stand on an entirely different footing'.[166] In such circumstances, perhaps even Milner would not have disagreed.[167] The more fundamental point at stake was constitutional: the Parliament Act and home rule were 'inseparably associated', and the former 'destruction of the constitution must inevitably lead to unconstitutional resistance'.[168] Ulster was one tool in Imperialist efforts to win back constitutional advantages over the Liberal party that they had long enjoyed. There was a demand for ascendancy in 1914, but it was not an Ulster demand for ascendancy in Ireland as Liberals suggested, but the demand of Imperialists and Unionists for ascendancy in Britain, and all over the Empire. In so far as Imperialists saw themselves as the voice of Britain, Ulster was still 'the British garrison' in Ireland.[169]

Imperialists only came as close as they did to endorsing the idea of Ulster exclusion when it seemed to be the only 'alternative to civil war'. In the crisis of 1912–14, the effect of the Parliament Act in reducing the veto of the House of Lords to a suspensory power produced a period of tension in which Imperialists were increasingly aware that civil strife seemed inevitable.[170] But for the mainstream of backbench Unionism, Ulster exclusion, leaving 'an utterly unacceptable Home Rule Bill in force for the rest of Ireland', represented a totally undesirable compromise. Amery was satisfied by the collapse of negotiations between the parties' leaders at Buckingham Palace in July 1914. This was:

> a splendid opportunity . . . for clearing ourselves completely from the entanglement of this Ulster exclusion idea . . . nothing could have been more unsatisfactory from the national point of view and more disastrous from the Party point of view than such an agreement.[171]

In retrospect, Amery defended his resistance to separatist Redmondite Nationalism on the grounds that 'the kind of nationalism which demands complete political separation' was always likely to produce the partition of Ireland.[172]

For the time being, the outbreak of war did what Imperialists could not, in bringing a truce on the Irish question. This saved Unionists from having to face immediate concessions to separatist nationalism – but at the price of seeing Asquith's Home Rule Bill placed on the statute book. Hewins, grumbling in the *Morning Post*, realised that this action had placed home rule in a position of precedence *vis-à-vis* tariff reform; home rule was a fact with which Unionists would have to deal, whereas the political future of tariff reform was uncertain.[173] It is hard to see how serious political disorder in Ireland could have been averted had not the war intervened. Imperialists, no less than Liberals, were prepared only under extreme circumstances to consider the practical necessity of compromise over the Irish question before that event. In both cases, this must be explained by the fact that efforts at conciliation were heavily circumscribed by ideological predispositions. And ideological considerations continued to affect Imperialists' involvement with the Irish question over the next ten years.

CHAPTER NINE

'The Blame is not on England', 1916–25

THE CIRCUMSTANCES OF the Great War evoked important changes in the political orientation and discourse of proponents of imperial consolidation. They also tended to place pre-existing differences between Imperialists in sharper relief. These influences significantly affected Imperialist ideas on Irish policy.

THE GREAT WAR, IRELAND AND THE IMPERIALISTS

Imperialists recognised that the status and survival of the British Empire were clearly threatened during the war; Milner in particular feared on several occasions that the Germans were close to winning.[1] This meant that Imperialists had to adopt a more sensitive posture towards allies and potential allies, including the United States of America. Given the large immigrant Irish population on the other side of the Atlantic, this necessitated some liberalising of Imperialists' attitudes to Irish nationalism.[2]

However, the effect on Imperialists of crude arguments such as 'we ought to break up the United Kingdom in order to please the Irish vote in the United States' was always somewhat limited, and a more subtle (if similar) influence can be traced.[3] Propaganda by private individuals was an important part of the war effort, and Imperialists felt it was their duty to assist. The *Round Table*, for instance, justified its continuance during the war years as an organ of 'war propaganda'.[4] Imperialists represented the Allied cause as that of a 'family of nations . . . indissolubly united by a common humanity' in order to distinguish it in the eyes of all concerned, home and abroad, from German 'Machiavellianism gone mad'; German policy was based on an unchristian 'code of morals', whereas Britain fought for 'freedom and peace [and] the rights of humanity'.[5] The idealistic and frequently Liberal tone of this propaganda was in part set by the fact that the war began with Liberals in government.[6] Not all Imperialists were enamoured of this situation. Amery told Milner he objected to:

> All this harping on Prussian militarism as something that must be rooted out, as in itself criminal and opposed to the interest of an imaginary virtuous and pacific entity called Europe . . . This war against a German domination in Europe was only necessary because we had failed to make ourselves sufficiently strong and united as an Empire to be able to disregard the European balance.[7]

Oliver felt that the explanations commonly used to justify Britain's entry into the war were not only wrong, but counter-productive. Oliver believed that British policy was obviously morally unassailable, and thus that the pressing concern during the war was to ensure that Britain had a sufficiently efficient military organisation to make certain of victory. He did not believe that the liberal conventions of parliamentary democracy were conducive to this organisation, and advocated their relaxation.[8] Milner also declared himself 'indifferent' about democracy.[9] Yet, the idealistic justification of Allied policy as a 'war against war' did infiltrate the language even of Imperialists who were suspicious of its tone; it was necessary to draw as stark a distinction as possible between the British and German Empires.[10]

During the war, many Imperialists served or supported a coalition led by a Liberal. Although their actual influence on the Lloyd George coalition can be exaggerated, Imperialists had previously been sympathetic to the idea of coalition government (which had been aired by Lloyd George in 1910), and in some cases had previously been admirers of Lloyd George himself.[11] Hewins became Under-Secretary at the Colonial Office, Oliver served on a committee on economic strategy, Milner joined the War Cabinet and in 1917 Kerr became Lloyd George's secretary, a position in which he was eventually succeeded by Grigg. In some cases these new associations placed Imperialists in a new political perspective, at least so far as outsiders perceived them. C.P. Scott discerned that Kerr was 'quite a good Liberal (though an opinionated and rather cranky one)'.[12] Garvin also supported the Lloyd George coalition, and in 1919 wrote a book entitled *The economic foundations of peace*. He explained to A.G. Gardiner that this publication showed he was 'destined to become very advanced in my views . . . my intention is to give the rest of my life to the cause of the League of Nations and the constructive peace'.[13] The book was praised in the liberal press.[14]

Imperialists' use of a different discourse during the Great War certainly does not indicate that they retreated wholly from pre-war principles. Indeed Imperialists had always maintained that the British Empire embodied that 'free association, free development and voluntary cooperation' between states which advocates of a league of nations hoped to create.[15] Amery indeed maintained that the British Empire was a more practical international association than any league of nations.[16] As Hewins later contended 'in the British Empire we have already a great League of Nations . . . advanced many stages toward the solution of the difficulties we have to encounter'.[17] Garvin agreed that:

> A League of Nations already exists . . . beneath the Union Flag. It has come together and fought together for the very objects which the larger League will seek to perpetuate. An extension of the Pax Britannica to all the nations of the earth will be a complete consummation of the highest ideals . . . acclaimed by every nation, our late foes included – whether their acclaim be sincere or insincere.[18]

Nonetheless, the persistence of the wartime propagation of the league of nations idea did necessitate shifts in the emphases of Imperialist ideology, because it meant that the dominance of the British Empire in the market of 'larger ideas' was placed further under threat.[19] It was necessary to dwell to a greater extent on the liberal aspect of the Empire. In any case, the reality of the relations between the states of the white self-governing Empire was changing. The Imperial Conference of 1917 was ambiguous in its results for the moot, but it became increasingly clear that cooperative relations with the dominions, rather than imperial federation, were the best that could be hoped for.[20]

'Empire' was therefore being subtly transformed into 'Commonwealth', a looser alliance of freely associated states. Imperialist attitudes over a range of political issues were affected by this realignment. They reappraised their attitudes to Egyptian and Indian nationalism.[21] And significantly, the tone of the Imperialist press on Irish affairs seemed to change rather abruptly. Whereas some Imperialists had avowed an intention in 1912–14 to maintain the Anglo-Irish Union by force,[22] during the war they praised moderate Nationalists like the Redmonds. The 'cause of Home Rule, as hitherto understood' appeared to be 'absolutely won in England'.[23]

But this was also not as large a *volte-face* as it appeared. If the Empire was a valuable voluntary union of states fighting a just war, anarchic particularist nationalism without and within had to be resisted. Secessionist Irish nationalism seemed to be disrupting the war effort, and thus seemed as evil as 'Prussianism' itself. Imperialists believed that Sinn Féin nationalists were guilty of 'abandoning the general cause of human liberty'.[24] Amery argued:

> It is quite true that we entered this War in defence of certain small nations against unjust aggression. But we have not fought, and are not fighting for, the principle of nationalism carried to all lengths. That is the principle of our enemies. Germany is fighting for the right of German nationalism to prevail over all other interests. Those who maintain that Ireland comes first and last and all the time, and that nothing else counts but the wishes of Nationalist Ireland, are adopting the same line as the Germans. Sinn Féin is simply *Deutschland über alles* writ small.[25]

Consequently, Imperialists were still intractably opposed to the separatist culture of Irish nationalism; but they had adjusted their position to take account of wartime circumstances. In 1916, many Imperialists and Unionists were prepared to accept a compromise Irish settlement involving the temporary exclusion of Ulster, perhaps pending federation, and home rule for the rest of Ireland. Robinson's *Times* accepted the idea of negotiating a settlement in the aftermath of the Easter Rising with some reluctance, but like the *Observer*, it was sorry to see the opportunity presented by Lloyd George's efforts in 1916 wasted.[26] In the *Round Table*, Kerr criticised both Irish Unionists and Nationalists for intolerance and intransigence. He realised however that 'the principle of union' – grasped wholeheartedly by the British people, and so valuable in a variety of political contexts – had to be reconciled in Ireland with nationalist sentiment. His solution was 'the principle of federation': 'Either Ireland must become a self-governing unit within a federated Empire, or it must form one or more units in a federated United Kingdom'.[27] His reasons for opposing a larger measure of self-government for Ireland appear slightly tautological in retrospect, but were consistent with the ideas he had expounded to Curtis in 1910. He told Lord Monteagle: 'If you don't start from the point of view that for certain purposes the Irish and the Great

British peoples are only one people you will never get away from the underlying assumption that the interests of Great Britain and Ireland are separate'. Kerr also explained that it was necessary to preserve 'the unity of the United Kingdom' because 'Ulster has got to be won' to the idea of Irish unity.[28] Curtis' *Commonwealth of nations*, which appeared around this time, endorsed Kerr's attitude. Although Curtis' book was in some ways surprisingly radical,[29] he argued there was no middle ground between United Kingdom unity or independence for Ireland. While some system of home rule all round could therefore safely be adopted, Kerr and Curtis remained opposed to giving Ireland what was vaguely called 'Dominion home rule'.[30]

There were significant exceptions to Imperialists' and Unionists' general acceptance of home rule in 1916. Many of these joined the Imperial Unionist Association, which appears to have had the support of over a hundred Unionist MPs.[31] Hewins, although reluctant to have anything to do with Irish affairs at this time,[32] joined his friend John Gretton in this organisation. Gretton was not impressed by the fact that the Ulster Unionists seemed willing to accept home rule for the rest of Ireland, regarding this as a selfish and parochial betrayal.[33] For his part, once Lloyd George's compromise proposal of July 1916 was successfully averted, Hewins accepted the political need for autonomy in Ireland. So far as Hewins was concerned, the question of self-government was not fundamental to any permanent settlement in Ireland: the crucial principles remained the maintenance of the economic and fiscal unity of the United Kingdom, and 'no partitioning of Ireland'.[34]

Stability in Ireland became a vital Imperial interest throughout the years 1916–18. An accommodation with Irish nationalism would certainly have enhanced this stability, and whenever Ulster Unionism seemed to be exerting an influence against such a settlement, the tone of Imperialists such as Garvin was not particularly flattering to Unionist Ulster. In March 1917, in editorials praised by his proprietor Waldorf Astor and by Kerr, Garvin declared that Unionist Ulster took a 'pre-war attitude' to the Irish question:[35] Ulster had to 'put itself right with the English-speaking world', declared the *Observer* later.[36] There was a hint of at least moral coercion in Garvin's attitude to Ulster Unionism post-1916 and this clearly disorientated some Ulster Unionists. Joseph Fisher noted that Unionist Ulster's 'lack of agility in turning a political somersault is made the subject of grave reproach in the most diverse and unexpected quarters', and claimed that the same British Unionist leaders who in 1914 had urged

Ulster to resist home rule 'to the last ditch' for the sake of the Empire were now telling her that such resistance was in fact 'narrow and selfish' and pressing her 'incontinently [to] surrender to save the party'.[37] In justification, Garvin said that the world had changed since 1912–14, and that 'declarations more solemn' than those made in support of Ulster, such as the Covenant, had been overturned by the tide of events. But in fact Garvin and other Imperialists had never liked the idea of partition.[38]

Early in March 1917, Lloyd George, newly in place as Prime Minister, was due to make a statement on government Irish policy. Kerr sent him some advice. This constituted an intense test of the more idealistic of Britain's (and the Round Table's) wartime professions. Kerr responded shrewdly, suggesting Lloyd George should:

> refuse to be drawn into a discussion of the past, even of events since the beginning of the war, and . . . concentrate on pointing out what a bright future is possible if all concerned co-operate with one another in bringing it about . . . England has been an obstacle in the past, but she is not to-day.

'The principle of Home Rule has been almost universally conceded', Kerr argued, again emphasising the importance of reconciling home rule 'with the welfare and safety of the Empire'.[39]

The calling of the Irish Convention of 1917 had much in its favour in Imperialist eyes. It enabled them to delay pronouncing any specific Irish policy with the suggestion that 'the destinies of Ireland rest with the people themselves'.[40] When the Convention failed to reach agreement, Kerr, with self-conscious even-handedness, blamed both Irish Unionists and Nationalists. Or as F.E. Smith put it more crudely: 'Let them keep on talking. If they don't agree it's the fault of Irishmen and not of the English, for there is not an Englishman on the Convention. It's an Irish problem and not an English problem'.[41]

Oliver was given a chance to influence the course of discussion at the Convention by the appointment of his friend Plunkett as its Chair. Oliver was still hoping for a united Ireland as part of a federal settlement. He told Plunkett that he sympathised with:

> the nationalist view that the exclusion of Ulster 'temporarily' (in the hope that she would shortly clamour to be admitted into the privileges of union with the rest of Ireland) was dangerous . . . I

> think history is on my side when I protest against Ulster exclusion [and] Fiscal Autonomy to the utmost of my strength on the same grounds. . . .[42]

Oliver maintained: 'As love of the Union is a nobler sentiment than Irish patriotism, so, even the Ulsterman would freely admit, is love of Ireland a nobler sentiment than attachment to any particular province of Ireland'.[43] Oliver was still protesting 'about the false analogy between Ireland and a Dominion' and working for a 'United Empire, a United Kingdom and a United Ireland'.[44] Amery echoed this diagnosis, and joined the ranks of the Unionist advocates of federalism during the war. Even before the Convention was formally called, he told Carson that he hoped that its Unionist members would 'use the desire of the Nationalists for the Unity of Ireland . . . as a lever to secure the maintenance of the essentials of the Union in Ireland and reduce the compass of the Home Rule scheme to comparatively innocuous proportions'.[45]

This pressure on Ulster Unionists was eased somewhat due to the nationalist resistance to conscription in April 1918. Curtis, Kerr, Oliver and Milner found this hard to forgive. In 1919, Erskine Childers believed Curtis held 'the official view of Ireland as a stab-in-the-back rebellious province which didn't help in the war'.[46] As early as 1917 Oliver had warned Plunkett that there would be a growing 'desire for vengeance' in England and Scotland against Ireland unless nationalist Ireland accepted conscription.[47] Garvin explained to Sidney Colvin:

> In Ireland there's absolutely no exit unless we can bring Ulster round and make moderate Nationalist opinion at the same time courageously and effectively loyal. Conscription was far more than a military policy and offered the only means [of producing] Irish unity or the beginnings of it under Home Rule. Now that chance is smashed to atoms.[48]

He blamed Nationalist weakness and the Irish Catholic hierarchy's resistance to conscription for this development, telling Astor Ireland was 'bedevilled by Bishops and Bolshevists'.[49] Oliver was equally perplexed by the frustration of his federal plans. Subsequently, in 1919, E.R. Thompson observed that Oliver had 'explored the Irish question, and, for all practical purposes, given it up'; so out of sympathy had he become with even moderates in nationalist Ireland.[50]

In April 1918, Hewins and Curtis assisted a committee under Walter Long in drafting a home rule measure. Some time later Hewins publicly declared that he had encountered no hostility to Ireland on that committee.[51] However, the patience of the committee's Chair with Nationalist resistance to conscription was certainly wearing thin at this time.[52] Amery like Long believed that resistance to conscription had neither moral nor material force behind it. Indeed, Amery felt that April 1918 was a great 'opportunity' for 'settling the endless Irish controversy' by decisively defeating the extreme elements in Irish nationalism, and by bringing in federal self-government for a united Ireland which:

> more moderate elements in Nationalist Ireland will be prepared to accept when our firmness over conscription brings them to their senses. A bill definitely dividing Ireland in two would be misunderstood abroad and is fundamentally unacceptable to Irish national sentiment. In the last resort the unity of Ireland is far more important in Nationalist eyes than any question of Irish powers.[53]

Federalism had become, as the *New Statesman* saw, Unionism's 'second line of defence'.[54] However, when the federalists' case was put to the Prime Minister, the lack of interest in England was cited as the paramount and decisive obstacle to the policy.[55] Conscription was also not enforced in Ireland.

THE GOVERNMENT OF IRELAND ACT, 1920

For two years after the war had ended, Imperialists agreed that law had to be enforced with determination in nationalist Ireland until the country saw sense. The *Round Table*, briefly under the editorship of Geoffrey Dawson[56] after he had left the *Times*, complained in 1920 that Ireland was in the grip of an organisation financed from abroad, 'concerned not so much with the well-being of the Irish people as with hatred of England'. Britain had to follow the lead of Abraham Lincoln, 'take up the challenge, and employ all the resources of the State to suppress murder and crime and so make it possible for reasonable men . . . to play their part'.[57] The idea of such an international conspiracy against the British Empire appears particularly to have affected Kerr.[58] Garvin's *Observer* regarded the increasing popularity in Ireland of Sinn Féin as a bout of 'madness [that] will pass'.[59]

Occasional annoyance at the Roman Catholic Church still manifested itself. In January 1921, the Cabinet Secretary Maurice Hankey depicted

Cabinet discussions on Ireland for Nevinson, claiming: 'Philip Kerr is a malign influence, always urging to blood. He was a Catholic, now a [Chris]tian Scientist: agreeable but baleful, like all the Round Table'.[60] Hewins, of course, did not accept this assumption that Catholicism was as much a disruptive force as was Bolshevism. In 1918, Hewins had argued that the Irish Catholic hierarchy could be used as intermediaries to obtain the required enlistment from Ireland, and a settlement in Ireland. Hewins felt Leo XIII's encyclical on labour relations could be used as the basis of a social policy to defeat 'the revolutionary movement' and split Sinn Féin. Like Kerr and Garvin, Hewins was waiting for Ireland to recover from the Sinn Féin fever.[61]

The old scheme of United Kingdom federation, to the chagrin of Garvin and other Imperialists, was ceasing to have much relevance to the problem of Anglo-Irish relations.[62] The articles by Irish correspondents which had begun to appear in the *Round Table* expressed sympathy for a dominion style settlement in Ireland.[63] But Kerr, who as Lloyd George's secretary was actively involved in the quest for a settlement in Ireland, continued to believe that in spite of the difficulties of reconciling the respective majority political faiths of nationalist Ireland, Ulster and Britain, the destinies of each were intertwined, and they had to learn to live closely together.[64] The secession of nationalist Ireland from the Empire thus had to be resisted, and even a measure such as 'dominion home rule' had to be avoided if at all possible. Therefore, when churchmen protested about government Irish policy in April 1921, Kerr's draft response depicted Britain's cause in Ireland as 'exactly the same' as that of the North in the American Civil War:

> It is to fight secession and to maintain the fundamental unity of our kingdom of many nations . . . I believe that our ideal of combining Unity with Home Rule is a finer and a nobler ideal than that excessive nationalism which will take nothing less than isolation, which is Sinn Féin's creed today, and which if it had full play would Balkanise the world.[65]

Kerr reminded Archbishop Clune of:

> the South African precedent where, after the fundamental question of whether South Africa was to be under the Dutch or British flag

> had been fought out . . . General Botha had abandoned the Dutch and accepted the British flag and within four years had become Prime Minister of United South Africa. I thought . . . we [could] reach the same ultimate result in the case of Ireland also.[66]

Kerr hoped that a moderate nationalist movement would emerge in Ireland to make possible a settlement on the basis of a limited measure of home rule. Horace Plunkett, who had begun to advocate dominion status for Ireland, was not, Kerr believed, a likely representative of such moderate nationalist forces. Kerr had decided that 'Plunkett was much better as an agricultural organiser than as a constructive politician'.[67] Ironically, while the ex-Unionist Plunkett had become too much of a nationalist for Kerr's taste, Kerr much preferred the counsel of the Redmondite Nationalist, Stephen Gwynn.[68] Plunkett equally failed fully to understand Kerr, feeling that Kerr, 'as trainer of Ll[oyd] G[eorge]', assumed that 'there are three irreconcilables – S[inn] F[éin], Ulster and the British people', and aimed to encourage 'a bloody fight between Ulster and the South . . . hoping they will then shake hands'.[69]

The alternative to the policy of 'dominion home rule' which Kerr helped to devise in the course of 1919–20 was the coalition's Government of Ireland Act of 1920. The broad terms of this Act were determined in the autumn of 1919 by another committee chaired by Walter Long. The Act proposed to set up two parliaments in Ireland, one for the six counties of north-east Ulster and a second for the remaining territory of Ireland, both without full fiscal autonomy. It also suggested a central Council of Ireland, made up of equal-sized delegations from these two parliaments, to discuss matters common to the whole of Ireland.[70] Kerr considered this Act a serious proposal for the better government of Ireland and hoped that in spite of its proposed temporary partition of the country, the Act would promote political unity in Ireland.[71]

The inspirations of the 1920 Act were many and varied. An influential article in the *Times* in July 1919 had propounded a similar settlement, and Kerr considered a memorandum probably written by the newspaper's editor, Henry Wickham Steed (1871–1956), when working on the Act.[72] Moderate Irish opinion, through men like Northcliffe, Gwynn, and particularly Long, undoubtedly had an influence.[73] But the Act is also uncannily reminiscent of a few passages that appeared in the *Observer* back in October 1910, written undoubtedly by Garvin.[74] Both the *Observer* and the *Round Table* praised the Act, though Garvin would have preferred all nine counties of Ulster to be represented by the Northern Parliament, feeling that this would have created a less sectarian region more likely ultimately to accept Irish unity.[75] Nonetheless, Garvin could tell Hammond in March 1921, with only slight exaggeration: 'My policy . . . has never varied for ten years since I first proclaimed it': 'every facility for cooperation by agreement between North and South'. 'I have followed Irish affairs all my life, probably as closely as anyone in this country', he claimed. The 'triumph of the Sinn Féin extremists' in the Anglo-Irish conflict would make 'irreparable the breach between Ulster and the rest': 'I have not the least hope of any solution through any policy whatever operating from the side of Great Britain alone'.[76] Kerr indeed recognised the affinity between the assumptions underlying the 1920 Act and Garvin's.[77]

More distantly, therefore, the 1920 Act can be associated with the pre-war idea of Monypenny and others that there were two nations in Ireland which needed British intervention or control to enhance their prospects of coming together peacefully. This conception had been initially articulated by Unionists as part of a movement to resist any separate self-government for Ireland whatsoever. However, in the period after the Great War, the latent tendency of this rhetoric in the direction of partition had been revealed. Unionists and Imperialists were beginning to realise that while they had correctly identified the most significant division in Ireland, this rift was going to produce a very different political settlement from the kind they had desired.

'PUTTING US RIGHT WITH THE WORLD', 1921–5

As one historian has noted, it might have been possible to implement the 1920 Act in nationalist Ireland if 'Sinn Féin had first been destroyed' militarily.[78] With the military position uncertain at the start of 1921, however, there was scope for private attempts to initiate negotiations. W.A.S. Hewins was central to one such forgotten episode. The government had apparently considered Hewins in September 1918 as a possible Chief Secretary for Ireland, a post he claimed was the only one 'in the Government which I had ever desired'.[79] He was ultimately overlooked, however. The coalition also thought of sending Hewins to Ireland or Rome in 1920 as its emissary on the Irish question, but political difficulties frustrated such plans. He had also been interested in arranging an unofficial conference on Ireland in 1919 involving Joseph Devlin and the ubiquitous Gwynn, but this also fell flat. A letter Hewins sent to the *Times* in 1920 detailing his proposals had gone unpublished.[80]

What Hewins felt was needed was a policy to split Sinn Féin and win over Irish opinion. He believed that the 1920 Act was 'not a bad bill and could be made to work'.[81] An opportunity appeared in January 1921, when Hewins used his presidential address to the Birmingham Catholic Union to articulate his proposals for an economic and political settlement. He still firmly opposed fiscal autonomy for Ireland: there was no analogy:

> between the economic relations of Great Britain and Ireland, and those which exist between any part of Great Britain and any other part of the world – You simply cannot separate the economic interests of Great Britain and Ireland, without destroying most of the important things that at present exist.[82]

Hewins did however acknowledge Ireland's national aspirations. He suggested the creation of an exchequer board, with Irish representation, with responsibility for Anglo-Irish budgetary policy. Ireland should also have representatives involved in the negotiation of commercial treaties between the United Kingdom and other countries.[83]

In retrospect this scheme seems extremely unambitious. Hewins had been reluctant to speak about Ireland at all, but the gratifying reception to his address encouraged him further to pursue the line he had taken.[84] His ideas were welcomed in conservative and Catholic circles; Cardinal Francis Bourne, Archbishop of Westminster, apparently regarded it as 'the only really constructive suggestion wh[ich] had been made on the Irish question'.[85] Hewins' friends the Saundersons, Edward Aremberg (a disaffected recent secretary of the then Lord Lieutenant of Ireland Lord French) and Somerset, the sons of the former Irish Unionist leader Colonel Edward Saunderson,[86] lobbied the press on his behalf and it took more notice of what Hewins had to say than it had in 1920. Hewins' scheme was also communicated to Lloyd George and Irish political leaders.[87] Bourne, who was increasingly occupied with Ireland at this time,[88] offered to sponsor a pre-conference of Englishmen, whose conclusions might then be presented to moderate Sinn Féiners. Invitees were mostly businessmen, tariff reformers, bankers, aristocrats and/or Catholics. The pre-conference was delayed however by technical difficulties, the apathy of those invited and disputes between some of its organisers, including the Earl of Derby and the tariff reformer Sir Vincent Caillard. When it eventually met on 30 June 1921, only nine people attended in two separate sessions. Nevertheless, the small attendance could be regarded as a blessing in disguise since Hewins' proposals were approved without much criticism.[89]

However, at this point Lloyd George intervened, and official negotiations were opened with de Valera. In July 1921, Hewins noted in his diary:

> nothing can be done while the present negotiations are going on . . . I find no great confidence as to the outcome of the conversations with De Valera and very much objection to them. But I suppose they will lead at any rate to a new phase of the Irish question.[90]

To some extent Hewins associated himself with the criticisms of the progress of the negotiations voiced by Gretton and others in the House of Commons and at the Unionists' Liverpool conference in November 1921; but he was again a little uneasy that there was 'too much Ulster' about Unionist attacks on the Irish policy of a Liberal Prime Minister. Hewins believed that the influence of the Papacy in Anglo-Irish relations was more likely to prove beneficial than that of Ulster.[91] Hewins was far from impressed with the Anglo-Irish Treaty of December 1921, and not surprised by the Dáil opposition to it. Some time later a 'prominent Irish leader' told Hewins that the Irish Treaty was the worst thing Britain had ever done to the country:[92] and Hewins certainly regarded the erection of tariff walls between the United Kingdom and the Irish Free State as a disaster.[93] Pragmatically, however, Hewins saw that an attack on the Treaty in the House of Lords could achieve little.[94]

Hewins squarely attributed the non-implementation of the type of Anglo-Irish settlement he had sought to coalition fiscal policy: 'whenever we seemed to be getting near a solution of the Irish question, which was after all, very largely economic, progress was stopped by the obscurantism of liberal doctrinaire politicians, and it is to that cause . . . that I attribute many of the Irish troubles'.[95] In 1921, Hewins had believed that Ireland was 'by no means a question of the Lib[eral] or Lab[our] view of the conduct of the Black and Tans' – this at the precise time when the attitudes of radicals (as well as those of churchmen and some moderate conservatives) to suppression in Ireland were becoming politically crucial. Much later, Leopold Amery (Parliamentary Secretary to the Admiralty in 1921) still regarded the opposition to coalition Irish policy as the product of 'skilful Irish propaganda' – a feeling of bitterness no doubt in part inspired by the fact that the Irish Chief Secretary in 1921, Hamar Greenwood, was Amery's brother-in-law.[96] Indeed, at the start of the negotiations between de Valera and Lloyd George, Amery found his disgust for the government's admission of the hated principle that Ireland was a separate nation, and his contempt for Irish nationalism itself, literally inexpressible.[97]

J.L. Garvin was more aware of the nature of the political opposition in Britain to repression in Ireland. His *Observer* was critical of what it described as the 'stupendous stupidity' of 'martyring' Terence MacSwiney, and of the activities of the Black and Tans in Balbriggan in September 1920: 'No Government could have done worse'.[98] But the *Observer*'s attention was still at this time concentrated on political violence on the nationalist side. The state of British opinion, the shrewd observations of the *Observer*'s Irish correspondent Stephen Gwynn and Brigadier-General Crozier's allegations (in February 1921) that military superiors had discouraged his efforts to keep a tighter rein on 'reprisals', however, led the paper's tone to change early in 1921. 'The basis of the British Commonwealth is a theory of free association, free development and voluntary cooperation', it declared. 'The theory cannot be destroyed in Ireland and long survive elsewhere . . . Our political credit is lowered throughout the world'.[99] The paper began pressing for the government to open negotiations with Sinn Féin.

Garvin was honeymooning in Florence in September and October of 1921 following his second marriage,[100] but there was little change in the *Observer*'s attitude to the Anglo-Irish negotiations in his absence. It resisted de Valera's claims to 'unqualified self-determination' as geographically and historically unreal, and would still have preferred a federal settlement or the 1920 Act.[101] The bait for nationalists to accept this was Ulster; nationalists could win Ulster over only if they accepted a limited form of self-government. Thus, in 1920 the *Observer* had declared sincerely, if somewhat patronisingly:

> It is the policy of Britain which is working for Irish unity – working for it by the slow, gradual and voluntary means which are the only means on earth of bringing about some ultimate reconciliation. It is the policy of extreme nationalist Irishmen themselves which is madly seeking to destroy the last hope of any Irish unity.

'The unity of Ireland and the Republican claim are patently, utterly and eternally incompatible'.[102] Therefore, in November 1921, the *Observer* suggested that Sinn Féin should accept that Ireland continue to send representatives to Westminster when foreign policy matters were discussed in order to strengthen the prospect of Irish unity.[103]

The *Observer*'s plan for Irish settlement was, in other words: 'Ulster will sit tight and Ireland will come right'. Indications that Unionist Ulster was not minded to act as bait disconcerted Garvin; he regarded this as 'unhelpful dourness'.[104] His proprietor Waldorf Astor was equally unsympathetic when Ulster Unionists protested at having to make sacrifices; he argued that all had to for the greater good of the Empire.[105] When Unionists such as Gretton were mounting their defence of Ulster Unionism at the Liverpool conference of November 1921, Garvin reminded his readers that 'Ulster has its duties as well as its rights. For Great Britain and the Empire a policy of Irish settlement is an inexorable condition of every hope of our commercial and political recovery from the shaking sequels of Armageddon': '2 per cent of the United Kingdom' had no right to 'a veto over the other 98 per cent with respect to the only kind of proposal . . . which can have the least chance' of bringing peace between Britain and Ireland.[106] Garvin denied that he had any desire to exasperate, abuse or coerce Ulster Unionists, rather contending that he had Ulster's true interests at heart: 'There can be no quietness, no settled well-being nor permanent safety for Ulster as at present constituted, except within some all-Irish system'. He felt that the 'unresponsive attitude of Ulster to the entirely new situation [of late 1921] has been a reinforcement to her detractors and a very deep disappointment to her friends'.[107] In Garvin's absence, the *Observer* could fairly assert: 'this journal has never advocated partition'; for as it had said in 1920: 'A permanently divided Ireland would be no source of strength or comfort to the other partners in the United Kingdom . . . Irish peace is the first of British interests'.[108]

'British interests', Garvin thus declared in December 1921, were in 'Ulster's power': 'Ulster interests, British interests, Imperial interests, stand or fall equally with success or failure in the great task of reconciling the Irish race to the British Commonwealth'. The threat to 'British interests' from a divided Ireland was, Garvin believed, revealed at this time during negotiations between Britain and the United States on naval armament: 'The Irish element has contributed powerfully to form the new American attitude to sea power by deepening every misunderstanding and fanning every suspicion of British policy . . . So much, in one direction alone, the Jingo mind has lost for us. Will it lose the rest?'[109] The Anglo-Irish Treaty agreed a few days later was not ideal from Garvin's view; he felt that too much had been conceded to the Free State. But in one sense at least, in Garvin's eyes, British interests were satisfied: 'The great thing which no chance can reverse is that Britain has cleared her own conscience and vindicated her own position in the eyes of all the world'. The Treaty, Garvin felt, gave a significant boost to Britain's moral and practical strength in the world. If peace and unity did not result in Ireland, 'the blame' was once again 'not on England'.[110] It was the fault of the Irish themselves. The resistance to the Treaty of de Valera and especially Erskine Childers quickly jeopardised Irish unity and Irish peace: 'The new won repute of the Irish race has been endangered by this threat of a return to all the old weaknesses . . . An English convert like Mr Erskine Childers is more irreconcilable than the Irish themselves'.[111] The *Observer* felt that the Free State government erred badly in associating with such extremists. Meanwhile, the parochialists in the North were little better than the barbarians down South. In future, Britain would not 'take sides' in Ireland.[112]

Lionel Curtis and Edward Grigg are to be even more closely associated with the Treaty policy. In March 1921, Curtis, with John Dove, who was by then editor of the *Round Table*, journeyed to Ireland to research an article for the journal. The two were sincerely (if perhaps naively) shocked by the thought that the repression that they observed was being applied in the name of the British Empire to a part of the United Kingdom. Their article declared, in Gladstonian tones, that such a conflict degraded Britain 'in the eyes of the civilised world':

> the temptation to fight Sinn Féin with its own methods has not been resisted . . . blame is [due] to those at a distance who failed . . . to condemn and prohibit these methods. If the British Commonwealth can only be preserved by such methods it would become a negation of the principle for which it has stood.[113]

The article echoed some of Curtis' recurrent concerns, bemoaning the facts that the nationalist Irish had no 'affection for the larger community in which they are merged' and had been taught to believe in 'the efficacy of force'. But the *Round Table*'s editorial committee took fright and resolved that words be inserted into this article 'to show that the present situation in Ireland was not exclusively the fault of Great Britain'. It also recommended that subsequent articles on Ireland contain only 'a minimum of comment'.[114]

Curtis and Dove's article suggested that the autonomy granted to the two parts of Ireland under the 1920 Act should be increased, and hoped for an ultimate settlement on the basis of Irish unity.[115] Increasing criticism of government repression in nationalist Ireland was already being voiced in other formerly Unionist journals such as the *Times* and the *Observer.*[116] But Curtis and Dove's article appeared at a key psychological moment and caught the mood of changes in the emphases of British policy, epitomised by King George V's speech in June 1921 at the opening of the Parliament for six counties of Ulster created under the 1920 Act. Grigg, who had just succeeded Kerr as Lloyd George's secretary, was instrumental in persuading the Cabinet to use this speech to try to initiate negotiations with the Sinn Féin leaders, and also in part wrote the speech.[117]

Curtis and Grigg, however, were not dogmatic opponents of repression in nationalist Ireland at this time, and were suspicious of 'the Bentinck crowd' (i.e., the Peace with Ireland Council).[118] In the language of 1921, part of the logic of initiating negotiations with de Valera was that the British government would thus put Britain 'right with the . . . world'; having justified British good faith, it would then be possible, if negotiations were to break down, to combat the IRA without the difficulties with British public opinion which had been experienced in late 1920 and early 1921.[119] Through most of the summer of 1921, while Lloyd George sent de Valera increasingly irritated letters (which Grigg helped to draft), Grigg and Curtis probably believed that this was likely to occur.[120] They also believed that the issue of such a conflict could be resolved successfully from the British government's point of view. Kerr had foreseen in 1920 that further efforts at conciliation would be necessary before British public opinion would accept that there was no alternative to repression in Ireland. Consequently, Kerr was entirely consistent when acting as director of United Newspapers in 1921, the group which controlled the *Daily Chronicle*, a paper which defended government policy during the Irish negotiations.[121]

In spite of this unpromising prologue, however, an Anglo-Irish peace conference did begin in October 1921. Curtis, acting as a secretary to the conference, argued that Ireland should remain part of the Empire/ Commonwealth. Like Garvin, he felt that in such a context it was legitimate to exert moral pressure on Ulster to make some concession to Irish unity. In a memorandum which he wrote in November 1921, Curtis argued:

> In Ireland we have to deal with a state of mind disordered through centuries of violence and wrong . . . There is no cure for the radical

> disease from which Ireland is suffering but the fullest measure of responsible Government which can be granted within the British Commonwealth. The situation is such that this cure cannot be applied unless Ulster as part of Ireland will agree to its application.[122]

'Ulster' was not entirely willing to fulfil the role Curtis had outlined. Nonetheless, with Curtis' assistance, the British government was able to obtain the agreement of the Sinn Féin representatives to the Treaty in December 1921.[123]

After the Treaty, as an advisor on Irish affairs at the Colonial Office, Curtis was still concerned about the demoralised state of Irish opinion, and still endeavouring to cultivate 'constitutional habits' in Ireland.[124] Threats to the Treaty settlement, however, came on all sides. Curtis believed that there *was* a moderate majority of opinion in Ireland which was represented faithfully among his Irish contacts, such as the Presbyterian Bolton Waller and John Joseph Horgan, later the Irish correspondent of the *Round Table.*[125] The pressing concern of this moderate majority was to reunify Ireland. Nevertheless, in the months before and following the signing of the Treaty, the *Round Table* argued that Irish nationalist leaders were disproportionately influenced by extremists. As a result, the Free State sought to obtain as much independence as possible from the United Kingdom at the expense of serious consideration of the fundamental aspects of the question of Irish unity.[126] Curtis never quite understood the unwillingness of the leaders of the new Irish Free State, Arthur Griffith, Michael Collins and William Cosgrave, to disown 'vindictives' like de Valera and Curtis' fellow ex-Haileyburyian Erskine Childers, and Curtis certainly believed that the indulgence shown by the first Free State governments towards the anti-Treatyites reduced the chances of the reunification of Ireland.[127]

The source of exasperation for Curtis and Dove was that they continued to believe that a final settlement in Irish politics, and an end to the threat to the stability of Britain and of the Empire/Commonwealth implicit in disorder in Ireland, could only come with Irish unity. They defined the policy of the Treaty as 'partition for unity's sake'.[128] But Imperialists again wished to impress on Irish nationalists the fact that Irish reunion could only come 'through Ulster and not in spite of her', through respect for 'the heritage which the people of Ulster share with the people of Great Britain'.[129] Hence Curtis and Garvin continued to fear that while British policies were promoting the prospect of union in Ireland, the policies of nationalist Ireland's leaders were offending 'the susceptibilities of the North' and thus having the opposite effect.[130] Curtis also worried that disproportionate influence was being exercised in British Conservative circles by Protestants who had fled the Free State,[131] and that Winston Churchill was becoming exasperated by the policies of the Free State leaders. Curtis believed that visible reluctance by British governments in fully carrying out their obligations under the Treaty would bring the Irish settlement into peril, and might adversely affect Britain's position in the world.[132] In Curtis' view, Ireland certainly needed statesmanship and moderate leadership, 'one hour of Botha', in order to resolve her problems.[133]

The Boundary Commission promised by clause twelve of the Treaty was a considerable obstacle to such efforts to improve relations within Ireland, and between Britain and nationalist Ireland. The boundary between Northern Ireland and the Free State was certainly perceived by Imperialists as far from ideal. Garvin would have preferred a settlement of this difficult question by agreement between the North and the Free State.[134] Curtis believed that moderate Irish opinion realised that an award of Ulster territory to the Free State through compulsory arbitration would embitter Ulster Unionists and would 'defer the day of Irish Union'.[135] Unionist Ulster was obviously reluctant to become involved in the Boundary Commission and refused to appoint a representative to the Commission – the British government eventually had to do this on behalf of the North in 1924. Dove believed it imprudent to resist nationalist Irish leaders' insistence on the calling of the Boundary Commission.[136] Fortunately, the report of the Commission, which was chaired by the ex-Kindergarten member Richard Feetham, recommended little territorial change. Indeed, under an agreement sealed in December 1925, the Free State government accepted financial compensation from the British government rather than the proposed transfers of territory.[137] Though the formal union of North and South in Ireland was no longer an immediate prospect, Garvin believed that this settlement of the boundary question had increased the ultimate possibility by facilitating practical cooperation between the two.[138]

Amery also regarded this as a 'sensible' resolution to the problem of the Boundary Commission.[139] Amery was initially extremely sceptical about the Treaty of 1921;[140] but as Secretary of State for Dominion Affairs from 1925–9, and thus effectively directly responsible for Britain's relations with Ireland, he had to take a diplomatic attitude.[141] As he later explained in his autobiography: 'Whatever my objections to the partition of the

United Kingdom, I knew there could be no other policy, once the ill-advised concession had been made, than to accept the situation whole-heartedly and with good-will, and to base our relations on the same frankness and friendliness of personal intercourse as marked our relations with other Dominions'.[142] The role of 'friendliness of personal intercourse' was something Curtis was keen to impress on Amery when Amery first took up the office. Curtis himself had established a close personal rapport with Irish leaders such as William Cosgrave and Kevin O'Higgins who seemed prepared to be loyal to the Empire / Commonwealth.[143] In Amery's case, his relations with O'Higgins and the Free State's first Governor-General Tim Healy were particularly good: Amery was greatly distressed by O'Higgins assassination in 1927.[144] Amery believed that the good atmosphere created by such cordial interaction assisted the settlement of the boundary dispute.[145] Amery was sympathetic to the prospect of unity in Ireland, but like most Imperialists, he felt that closer relations between Britain and Ireland were the precondition.[146] In spite of his regret at the Treaty, his occasional impatience with the intricacies of Irish politics and, at times, even his disgust with all things Irish, Amery's disposition certainly eased the birth pangs of the new Anglo-Irish relationship.[147] His period in office, like Curtis', also helped to establish, in difficult circumstances, that pattern of generally convivial relations between British ministers and leaders of moderate nationalist Irish opinion which stretches forward to the present day.

Periods of difficulty in Anglo-Irish relations were however by no means over when Amery left office in 1929. Another commenced with the return to power of Eamon de Valera. Cosgrave's defeat in the Free State elections of 1932 was regretted by the Imperialists.[148] Garvin believed that de Valera's short-sighted subsequent action in upsetting the delicate fabric of the Treaty in an effort to secure more independence from the United Kingdom compromised further the prospects of unity in Ireland.[149] Yet, Imperialists could only with difficulty evade the assumption that Irish unity was the most likely foundation of stable Anglo-Irish relations.[150] Thus, in 1940, both Curtis and the Prime Minister Neville Chamberlain believed that such a reorganisation might be effected if de Valera's Ireland wholeheartedly supported the Allies in the Second World War. Chamberlain declared around this time that 'the interests of Northern Ireland could not be allowed to stand against the vital interests of the British Empire'.[151]

Although nothing came of such aspirations, the tone of such statements, and of British policy in Ireland for years to come, is strangely reminiscent of that of an Irish patriot, Neville Chamberlain's father's official biographer, James Louis Garvin. Garvin's direct influence on British policy in Ireland was certainly slight: but he had consistently argued that Unionist Ulster be given autonomy from a self-governing nationalist Ireland. This suggestion, embodied in the 1920 Government of Ireland Act, was to serve as the basis for the administration of Northern Ireland until direct rule came into force in 1972.[152] However, Garvin had also expected and desired, in Britain's as well as in Ireland's interest, that Ulster would gravitate to an intimate relationship with the rest of Ireland. And when 'Ulster' had proved unwilling, Garvin, along with his fellow Imperialists, had been prepared to give her a nudge.

Not all Imperialists reconciled themselves so easily to the application of this policy from 1921 onwards. Milner, Oliver and the Selbornes all found themselves greatly 'out of sympathy' with government policy, towards Ireland and in general.[153] The role of their former associates in negotiating the Treaty of 1921 added to their feelings of frustration – for Oliver, such rifts were always difficult.[154] But for those of their colleagues who were more stoical about the concessions which had been made to separatist Irish sentiment, this policy had great advantages. It had created the kind of bipartisan unity in Britain about Irish politics which Imperialists and Unionists (not least Oliver) had sought for so long.[155] As for Ireland itself, one could but wait: 'neither North nor South want peace', wrote Curtis in 1924: 'They are slowly but surely learning the limitations of force by the bitter experience of having to run a gov[ernmen]t of their own . . . there can be no solution of the Irish problem till that lesson is learned'.[156]

Three-quarters of a century later, and over a century since Bryce identified Ireland's lack of political training as the source of her instability,[157] British commentators are still waiting for 'Ireland' to learn her lessons.

Anglo-Irish Relations in the Age of Empire and the Age of Commonwealth

It is the character of the British people, or at least of the higher and middle classes who pass muster for the British people, that to induce them to approve of any change it is necessary that they should look upon it as a middle course: they think every proposal extreme and violent unless they hear of some other proposal going still further upon which their antipathy to extreme views may discharge itself.

John Stuart Mill, 1873[1]

The Prussian theory of war was the most terroristic in Europe. That fact was an important element in strengthening and maintaining the resistance of the Allies . . . This terrorism not only failed to bring victory to the Germans but succeeded in bringing death and maltreatment to many of them who, had ruthlessness never been adopted as a policy, would have been living today . . . It is the future of England, not the future of Ireland, that Mr Lloyd George is imperilling. He is destroying all those conventions of decency and discipline on which English civilisation is based. He has flung the boomerang of terrorism. But the boomerang always comes home.

Robert Lynd, 1920[2]

Ransack the literature of all countries, find, if you can . . . a single book . . . in which the conduct of England towards Ireland is anywhere treated except with profound and bitter condemnation . . . a sad exception to the glory of our country . . . what we want to do is . . . make our relations with Ireland conform to the other traditions of our country . . . so we hail the demand of Ireland for what I call a blessed oblivion of the past.

William Ewart Gladstone, 1886[3]

Hodson: I'm a Owm Ruler, I am . . . because I want a little attention paid to my own country; and thetll never be as long as you chaps are ollerin at Westminster as if nobody mettered but your own bloomin selves. Send em

back to hell or C'naught, as good oul English Cromwell said. I'm jast sick of Ireland. Let it gow. Cut the cable. Make it a present to Germany to keep the oul Kyzer busy for a while; and give poor oul England a chance; thets wot Oi say.
Matthew: . . . have yanny Coercion Acts in England . . . ?
Hodson: We can beyive ahrselves withaht sich things.

George Bernard Shaw, 1907[4]

our business is with the future, not with the past . . . There is no use in reproaches. Everybody can make them, and everybody has deserved them. There is no use recalling the wrongs and just resentments of the past. Nothing will help in the Irish Question but absolute forgiveness and absolute concentration on the future.

Gilbert Murray, 1917[5]

The English people live in their past as much as any people. Happily for them it is a past in which they can, for the most part, feel a just pride.

James Cotter Morison, 1868[6]

IN 1865, ALMOST NO educated Britons supported the concession of separate self-government to any part of Ireland. Two such measures were however conceded in 1920–1 after a long and violent struggle. Due to the want of systematic consideration given to this transition by serious historians, it is tempting to assume that this was just an episode of conflict and friction in the history of Anglo-Irish relations. It is therefore important to emphasise that there was a very different dimension to this development. In the late nineteenth and early twentieth centuries, increasing numbers of observers on both sides of the Irish sea began to believe that self-government in nationalist Ireland would contribute to the mutual respect and amity of the peoples of both islands. The growth of this conviction helped to shape the present pattern of relations between the Republic of Ireland and the United Kingdom, and is thus a significant, if overlooked, historical reality.

Four contentions were crucial to the initial advocacy of 'home rule' or 'Irish self-government' in late Victorian Britain; that the Union weakened Britain internally and externally, that Ireland should be treated as a nation, that the advocacy of such unpopular political principles was neither unnecessary nor undesirable and that Irish home rule could make a beneficial contribution to a desirable arrangement of international relations. Although the first advocates of Irish self-government were able to exert little or no direct influence on the political process, after the rise of Parnell's movement and the acceptance of Irish home rule by prominent British political figures, arguments similar to the first two became politically respectable, if not attractive – the third contention ceased to be relevant. Yet, in themselves these first two propositions were considered by British commentators in the main to be inadequate; even if Britons could never be expected to grant Irish self-government willingly, a plausible rationalisation for such a large constitutional change was necessary before they could reconcile themselves to it. This was eventually provided by cooperative ideas of international relations. The assumption that a potent or actual set of moral or legal bonds between nations limited the exercise of the national sovereignty of the United Kingdom outside of the British Isles reinforced the arguments of those who proposed the establishment of some kind of microcosm of these co-operative relations between Britain and Ireland. Therefore, the advocacy of home rule in Britain was complemented by such notions of the relations between states. Not all British home rulers were influenced by the Positivist and new Liberal model of international community. But many absorbed Gladstone's rhetorical assumptions that an Irish home rule settlement, a cooperative Anglo-Irish union of hearts, was in accordance with the practice and ideals of a 'civilised world' community, and with the best of English traditions.[7]

This kind of discourse was common particularly to those who saw Ireland as a case especially requiring the solvent of self-government, and who thus supported Gladstonian home rule until about 1918, and 'dominion home rule' for Ireland thereafter. The Imperialists dealt with in the third part of this book did not fall into this category. Some, like Oliver, Curtis and Kerr, were sympathetic to United Kingdom federation before 1914. These were usually supporters of imperial federation who advocated some formal division of political sovereignty within the Empire, and who thus encountered difficulties when they attempted to resist a similar division of sovereignty within the United Kingdom. As one MP observed during the home rule debates: 'it is impossible to conceive of any system of Imperial federation in which it will not be necessary that the decisions of the Imperial authorities should be enforced by the various State and Dominion officials'. If Unionist criticisms of home rule legislation were therefore correct, 'we should now have to conclude that a scheme of Imperial federation was bound to lead to such friction that it would collapse and have forthwith to be abandoned'.[8] However, Imperialists had a self-consciously realistic attitude to the relationships of Great Britain and states outside the Empire; before 1914, at least, they emphasised that these relationships were competitive, not cooperative. In this respect, Round Table Imperialism is to be placed on the Unionist side of the political divide.[9] Unionists argued that, in the hostile global environment, only large states could survive; it was necessary for the sake of the Empire to maintain the existing undivided nature of political sovereignty in the British Isles.[10] As Austen Chamberlain understood therefore, the Unionist vision of the Empire could only with very great difficulty ever be reconciled with the ideal of 'Ireland a nation'.[11]

During 1886–7, Unionists like Chamberlain and Balfour suggested that a separate Irish *state* (i.e., the creation of a new political sovereignty instead of a division of an existing one) was a more logical idea than any sort of quasi-federal distribution of power, and was less likely to hamper the Empire.[12] According to Unionists' rigorously *realpolitik* assumptions about the nature of world politics, Gladstonian home rule could, *on purely logical grounds*, be criticised for offering Ireland too little independence as well as too much.[13] Systems of divided sovereignty such as Irish home rule (introduced, in Amery's phrase, amidst 'slosh' about 'good feeling')[14] were impractical simply because different countries were frequently in dispute and rivalry. Westminster's Imperial veto over the legislation of an Irish home rule parliament would produce continued friction between the two countries. However, if Britain and Ireland were separate and independent countries, there would be no constitutional necessity for the British and Irish governments to cooperate, and Anglo-Irish relations might produce some equilibrium which would be advantageous to the stronger British state. Of course, Unionists felt that the preservation of the Union would be even better than this, in part because, they maintained, Ireland possessed greater powers of self-government within the Union than she could outside.[15]

However, languages of cooperative international relations gained some ground in the early twentieth century. Two particular developments can be associated with this. First of all, there was the apparent success of the grant of separate self-government to the conquered Boer provinces of South Africa. The latter certainly considerably strengthened the receptivity of British public opinion to Irish home rule. A similar analogy, pointing to the success of self-government in Canada, was used around the time of the first home rule crisis;[16] but by 1886, this example was less immediate, whereas disorder in Ireland, the land war of the 1880s, was fresh in the public memory. The status of colonies such as Canada in the 1880s was also ambiguous. John Stuart Mill had considered that a shift to an analogous position for Ireland would involve a degradation.[17] Reference to imperial experience by supporters of home rule at this time was thus relatively defensive.[18] Conversely, by 1911 Irish disorder was a distant memory compared to the Boer War and its sequel. As the *Nation* noted: 'We have in South Africa an object lesson far more vivid and recent than any of the examples which Gladstone could quote in 1886 or 1893'.[19] In January 1910, *Punch* depicted the dilemma of what it assumed to be the typical 'perplexed' elector, torn between rival Unionist and Liberal policies. The elector 'mistrusts Home Rule (when conceded to people with a record like that of the present Irish Party), yet realises the astounding success of Liberal Policy in South Africa'. Liberals were keen to dispel the feeling of mistrust by reference to the 'astounding success'.[20] The developing status and dignity of the self-governing dominions was ultimately to provide a suitable context for the creation of the Irish Free State.

Secondly, the First World War promoted a public discourse which juxtaposed the supposedly cooperative, liberal nature of British imperial and international relations with 'Prussian militarism'. In this context, some form of autonomy for nationalist Ireland was hard to resist. The effect of the Great War on contemporaries in many ways ought not to be underrated, and it can be seen to have had significant effects on the structures of political language.[21]

Both the Boer War and the Great War were associated with the perceived transition from 'Empire' to 'Commonwealth'. This transition is hard to define and hard to fix chronologically, but it is clear that it was associated with the growing prevalence of separate self-government in the states of the Empire, and of the conception of the Empire as an alliance of equal states. This interacted closely with 'the Irish question', as contemporaries conceived it; the Anglo-Irish Treaty offered the first official attempted definition of Dominion status (a definition influenced by Curtis), and the first official documentary use of the phrase 'British Commonwealth'. The *Nation* declared: 'we regard the Pacification of Ireland as one step in the transmutation of the political character of the Empire'.[22] Consequently, it is not surprising to find that, despite their differences, the Positivists, the new Liberals and the Imperialists, who all contributed with varying degrees of significance to the process which produced the Anglo-Irish settlement of 1921, also helped to develop the idea of commonwealth by articulating the 'larger idea' of a union of self-governing states. Indeed, during and immediately after the First World War, former critics and

THE PERPLEXED PATRIOT.

A sketch of an unhappy Elector who is most anxious to follow the advice of Lord Rosebery, to consider well his vote and save his country, but is somewhat hampered by the following considerations.

He dislikes much of the Budget, yet hates Tariff Reform; is strongly in favour of a Second Chamber, yet is infuriated by the partisan action of the House of Lords in recent years; has great faith in Mr Asquith, Sir Edward Grey, John Burns and others of the Ministry, yet non-contributory Old Age Pensions and all pandering to the Extreme Labour Party make him dreadfully unwell; mistrusts Home Rule (when conceded to people with a record like that of the present Irish Party), yet realises the astounding success of Liberal Policy in South Africa.

Will some charitably disposed person kindly tell him how to save his country by his vote this month?

Fig. 2: 'The Perplexed Patriot', *Punch*, cxxxviii, (5 Jan. 1910), p. 16.

partisans of empire articulated schemes for 'international government' which differed little. Imperialism and new Liberalism, which had seemed so bitterly opposed in the Edwardian period, were shown during the Great War to have much in common.[23]

British imperialism had always contained an idealistic, 'liberal' undertone which emphasised that Britain's was as an 'empire of appeasement', and a progressive influence for peace and cooperation in the world.[24] Imperialists needed only subtly to alter the emphases of their language to prepare themselves for a different global environment. Kerr, Curtis and their colleagues have been seen increasingly as idealistic advocates of international federation, but in their dealings with Irish nationalism, the limits to their idealism were initially demonstrated. It was possible to maintain for some time a language of cooperation and amity in imperial and foreign affairs, and yet regard Ireland as a 'rebellious stab-in-the-back province'.[25] Indeed, it was precisely the strength of the ideological justification for the Empire which initially seemed to legitimate the use of force against Irish nationalism. But the disjuncture ultimately proved impossible to maintain. Imperialist ideology remained unitarian; but in 1920, Kerr's thought had more in common with Gladstonian Liberalism than many of the manifestations of Balfourian Unionism.[26] During 1921, the idealistic elements of the Imperialism of men like Kerr, Curtis, Dove and Garvin inspired them to advocate opening negotiations with Sinn Féin.

Even before 1914, any dichotomy between the 'competitive' Unionist and Imperialist model of international relations and Liberals' and home rulers' cooperative vision, can be overemphasised. Outspoken critics of empire in the 1860s such as Goldwin Smith and John Bright did not become supporters of Irish home rule, but convinced opponents. From the 1860s Irish nationalism could be regarded not as a movement of national liberation, but merely as a regressive particularism inspired by religion or social grievance, analogous to contemporary movements in the southern states of the United States and in southern Italy. Such Liberals had supported unitarian nationalism in Italy and the United States, and consequently found the disintegrative nationalism of the Irish hard to accept.[27] But this was an interpretation which Liberals found increasingly unpalatable. Liberals such as Morley and Mill, who were sympathetic to Comte's strong assumptions against the coercion of 'opinion', were among the first to accept the idea of Irish self-government. After Gladstone established home rule as among the most sacred of his party's missions, it became difficult to oppose the policy and be regarded as a Liberal. Thus, though Liberal efforts to enact home rule were dormant after Gladstone's retirement in 1894, political circumstances, and events in South Africa, not only breathed new life into them in 1910, but gave them a strength which they had not had before.

There were other factors associated with the increasing acceptance in Britain of the idea of Irish self-government, including developments in Ireland itself. The relative pacification of the country after the Land Act of 1903, and the early twentieth-century respectability of the Redmondite movement (symbolised most effectively by Redmond's support of Britain in the Great War) could be used by supporters of home rule. This kind of appeal was not without effects on some such as Garvin, who subsequently hitched his wagon to the memory of 'the gallant Redmonds' in Ireland.[28] But these were ambiguous developments. Before 1914, it was still possible for Unionists and Imperialists to advocate the preservation of the Union, pointing out that, contrary to the confrontational imagery widely employed by Irish Nationalists, extensive and generous reforms had been implemented in Ireland by British governments.[29] Such arguments held their own before English audiences up until 1914. It is clear that when the policy of the existing Union finally proved insufficient, developments external to Ireland, as well as internal changes, had made it untenable.

There was a broad symmetry between Liberal and Unionist attitudes to domestic problems (such as Ireland) on the one hand and to international relations on the other. The policies of coercion and cooperation, within and without, were logical and coherent positions; cooperation within and coercion without, and vice versa, ultimately proved impossible to sustain politically and logically. Modern sociologists have argued that to seek to settle disputes in a conciliatory fashion can set a powerful precedent, even in a world accustomed to competition and antagonism; cooperation, and avoidance of conflict, is an inexpensive and inherently attractive solution to problems.[30] It can be argued that this kind of process occurred within British political thought in the 1910s. Yet, cooperation can also seem a fragile and dangerous strategy for dealing with hostile groups. Problems of ethnic and national antagonisms, which pose the same dilemma of cooperation or coercion, are of course still very common, and they continue to cause much consternation in Britain, Europe and the world.[31]

Speculation as to whether the Liberal or the Unionist vision was most applicable to the particular context of Anglo-Irish relations is dangerous. The Unionist view won over most contemporaries in Britain before 1914, and has won over some historians.[32] The manner in which the home rule issue was revived by the Liberal government after 1906 is certainly open to serious criticism.[33] However, it is clear that Unionist rhetoric had some serious effects on nationalist politics in Ireland. Unionists often claimed to feel no ill-will towards the Irish people. There seems no reason to doubt the sincerity of Unionist conviction that 'a change in the spirit rather than in the constitution of England', a greater tendency for the English to regard the Irish as 'fellow citizens', would be better for nationalist Ireland than a concession to the separatism of her political leaders.[34] Indeed, some Unionists challenged the predominant influence of a narrow nationalistic interpretation of England's interest, economic and political, over the government of the Anglo-Irish Union.[35] However, perhaps characteristically,[36] Unionists erred in underestimating the political symbolism of their rejection of home rule, the extent to which their dismissive attitude to the demands of the country's majority's political leaders committed Unionists to an attitude of suspicion and hostility towards the nationalist Irish people.

The long years of Unionist hegemony in England seemed to legitimate the Irish nationalist image of England as an imperialist robber and invader of Ireland, and gave a powerful impetus to some extreme anti-English developments of Irish nationalism. The arguments of separatists came to seem more plausible: 'The English people, either collectively or individually', P.S. O'Hegarty could maintain:

> do not want to give Ireland freedom. Some of them are willing to concede the name of freedom whilst reserving its machinery, but they are few. Most of them do not understand the Irish question, which is an international one, as being a dispute between two Sovereign Nations, and not an Imperial or Domestic one, and none of them want to understand it.[37]

Owing to the fact that Ulster remained as (according to such rhetoric) an English (or British) imperialist presence in Ireland, this tradition of nationalism survived the Treaty of 1921. After the assassination of Field Marshal Sir Henry Wilson in June 1922, the *Daily News* declared that not even the most 'distorted intelligence' could have seen Wilson as an oppressor of Ireland. Unfortunately, intelligences far more depraved than the *Daily News* could conceive of, continued to attach themselves to Irish republican traditions.[38]

British liberals have never been able to understand this indiscriminate hostility of Irish republicans to the British people. C.P. Scott, for instance, was bewildered by his first meeting with de Valera, particularly since Scott himself was an eminent representative of a significant radical tradition in British politics which was highly committed to Irish self-government.[39] The Positivists, Morley and Gladstone were not as isolated as is sometimes suggested; a persistent (if naive) radical enthusiasm for nationalist Ireland and Irish independence survived in the Labour and Liberal movements of the 1920s and beyond. Indeed, the commitment of Liberalism as a whole to the cause was not unimpressive. One historian of the Irish policy of the Liberal government of the years 1905–1910 judges that: 'It is to the House of Lords and not to the Asquithian Liberals that we must look primarily, in order to explain why the Liberal Party failed to make more progress in Ireland during this period'.[40] This is also true for the years immediately before and after.

Dichotomies between the British people and the Irish people, which are depicted in stereotypes on both islands, are strongly refuted by the commitment of some British Liberals, some of their Irish nationalist allies and others to ideas of a genuine Anglo-Irish partnership, grounded in particular interpretations of the traditions and needs of both countries. It is true that any unconditional sympathy with Irish nationalism was very much a minority tradition within Britain, and was consistently obstructed by the inertia of British institutions. Nonetheless, the idea of a self-governing Ireland and resistance to the coercion of nationalist Ireland, obtained substantial, ready and ultimately decisive support from long-standing and self-consciously 'British' traditions. Unless one accepts the highly dubious essentialist assumptions of Irish nationalism,[41] it must be conceded that without such assistance, Irish nationalists would have found it much harder to establish the Irish Free State, not to mention the Republic. After all, Irish nationalism, like the particularism of southern Italy or of the southern states of America, *might* have been politically defeated after the application of overwhelming military force by the stronger neighbouring power.[42] British politicians considered this option, on occasion very closely, particularly in 1921. However, wholehearted military coercion was never applied in this period to nationalist Ireland, a fact which must be attributed in large measure to the state of British public opinion,[43] and particularly to the influence of liberal ideologies over it. Interpretations of British politics which minimise the role of ideology, even when emanating from Unionist sources, complement the distortions of extreme Irish nationalism.

It is sometimes suggested (especially by Irish nationalists) that the Treaty of 1921 changed little; the modern problems of Northern Ireland are merely the reappearance of the pre-1921 problems of the whole country on a smaller scale.[44] But the Anglo-Irish Treaty did bequeath considerable gains to many different parties in Ireland and Britain. The Treaty was a 'solution' in that it took the question off political platforms in Britain; a broad cross-party consensus on Northern Ireland in Britain still exists. Ulster Unionists were protected from Irish nationalist rule and southern nationalists were also able 'to have their cake and to eat it as well: to posture about the wickedness of divisions "imposed" by Britain while enjoying the psychological, economic, and political comforts which the border provided'.[45] What the Treaty of 1921 left in Ireland was the residue of earlier disputes, the zero-sum game which is the essence of modern problems in Northern Ireland.[46]

British observers had long wished for an agreement in Britain on Irish policy which would remove the problems of Ireland from British party politics. This consensus was not achieved until both Liberal and Unionist parties had experienced internal divisions and political weakness (not to mention political violence). Neither ideology had a sufficiently accurate conception of Ireland and Irish politics to be able to settle the problem unilaterally, principally because both ideologies had been fashioned in other very different contexts. The settlement of 1921 contained at least one major aspect which was regrettable to all British observers, whether they be Liberal, Unionist, Positivist or Imperialist. Blood was shed in Ireland because Irish Unionists and Irish Nationalists had an insufficient appreciation of each others' needs and permanence; but blood was also shed because British political creeds did not impart a sufficient appreciation of Irish circumstances. Even the long-sought British consensus on Ireland after 1921 had its drawbacks; the bipartisan acceptance after the Treaty of the need to regard 'the Irish question' as 'settled' tended to leave Northern Irish issues neglected in Britain. Elements on all sides of British politics grumbled about having to give Ireland time, money and attention. This neglect contributed to the recurrence of significant levels of political violence in the North in the 1970s.[47]

Before 1921, there *was* consensus in Britain on two negative points about the likely nature of a settlement in Ireland. First of all, although frequently articulating different ideals of empire, British observers consistently believed that the separation of nationalist Ireland from the Empire was unlikely to produce peaceful Anglo-Irish relations. The

English Positivists, with their somewhat arbitrary 'hypothetical' Irish nationalism, were the most radical supporters of Irish self-government in British public life in their day; but even they were a little tentative in proposing the separation of Ireland from the Empire. Noticeably, it was the most dogmatic and politically inactive Positivists, associated with Chapel Street, who were most determined in insisting on separation in full; the more mainstream Positivists voiced more moderate proposals.[48] In 1921, elements associated with the radical wings of Liberalism and the Labour movement displayed a similar reluctance to be drawn into outright advocacy of an Irish republic, partly because a non-separatist solution and Irish unity were seen by just about all British commentators as symbiotic. Clearly, Irish home rule itself before about 1880, and the separation of Ireland thereafter, were not serious political demands at all in Britain.

The 'whole fabric of our Empire is built up on the endeavour, constantly renewed, to ascertain . . . the maximum of willing cooperation' declared the *Manchester Guardian* in 1916.[49] As developments in the post-1914 period only tended further to vindicate the need of cooperative relations within some 'society of nations', assertive separatist visions of Irish nationality seemed increasingly retrograde and anti-social. In the early 1920s, Labour, Liberal and moderate Conservative commentators rejected Irish republicanism, the 'Balkanisation' of the United Kingdom, while 'Die-Hard' Conservatives, logically enough, called for the creation of a republic in southern Ireland.[50] But the isolationist imperialism of the Tory 'Die-Hards' was increasingly peripheral to British politics, defeated over Ireland and India.[51] A culture favourable to the peaceful settlement of international disputes, based on the idea of international mutual dependence, became dominant in British politics in 1921, if not before. As Paul Kennedy has written:

> a 'tradition' of 'appeasement' can be detected in British foreign policy from the mid-nineteenth century onwards, and . . . this was, in a sense, the 'natural' policy for a small island state gradually losing its place in world affairs, shouldering military and economic burdens which were increasingly too great for it, and developing internally from an oligarchic to a more democratic form of political constitution in which sentiments in favour of a pacific and rational settlement of disputes were widely prevalent.[52]

In this context, the resistance to Irish home rule from 1886 to 1921 can be seen as an aberration. 'Appeasement', thus defined as the 'pacific and rational settlement of disputes' based on notions of mutuality and interdependence, largely survived the Second World War, in spite of the unfortunate associations of the word: 'Even today, while a foreign policy rooted in those traditional elements of morality, economy and prudence may be – indeed, probably is – being carried out, the last thing its executioners would desire would be to have the word attached to it'.[53] Cooperation only became discredited as a method for dealing with movements which were widely seen as utterly depraved. The isolationist attitude adopted by Irish governments, particularly during the Second World War, not only challenged British national self-interest, but was out of sympathy with the most entrenched aspects of British political culture. Irish governments' policies seemed trivial and narrow-minded, even to the Irishman Garvin: 'our relations with the Free State are only a detail in a very big day's work'. The Irish had failed to deal successfully with 'their own problem of appeasement'.[54] In 1949, Britain responded by presenting Northern Ireland with her strongest legislative guarantee yet. As Dennis Kennedy suggests, 'not for the first time, Irish Nationalism proved itself Unionism's greatest ally'.[55]

Nevertheless, the second element of consensus in British ideas on constitutional settlement in Ireland before 1921 was reluctance towards the partition of Ireland. Partition was a solution to imperial and Irish problems which British governments employed with a good deal of hesitation.[56] To Liberals and home rulers, partition in Ireland could only be based on obsolete, unprogressive bigotry. To Imperialists, Irish partition seemed to make the secession of southern Ireland from the Empire more likely. To practically all British commentators, it seemed an intrinsically unlikely form of final settlement (an assumption vindicated by subsequent events), involving continued British intervention in Irish politics (and thus the thorny issue of British responsibility), and a virtually insoluble boundary question. As John Bowman has shown, partition violated the Irish people's 'map-image' of their country; yet it no less created an incongruent position for people in the United Kingdom, whose map-images of their country usually include only Britain (i.e., exclude Northern Ireland, among other areas) or the whole 'British' Isles (i.e., include a foreign country). Because partition itself seemed to British commentators to be an implausible policy, the precise parameters of the Irish boundary mattered little; the whole question merely produced a good deal of impatience in Britain. The boundary provisionally agreed in 1921 has thus never been altered, and its apparent unfairness to the nationalist community of Northern Ireland has intensified the hostility of Irish republicans to the Northern state.[57] Of course, there have been some traditions in British public life, not dealt with in this study, which have been more fundamentally supportive of partition; but it is questionable how significant these have been. For Unionists such as Balfour, the exclusion of Ulster from the operation of Irish self-government became a desirable proposition only when it had become impossible to defend the Union as a whole.[58]

On both these points of consensus, British observers failed to anticipate the eventual settlement which emerged in Ireland in the years 1921–49. This was due to their fundamental aversion to recognising the possibility of a rooted sectarian disunity in Irish life, a product of ignorance about the nature of Irish politics. British commentators professed recurrent faith in a 'moderate majority amongst the general public' in Ireland,[59] North and South, as yet concealed by some political trickery of nationalists or unionists, but sufficiently overwhelming in numbers to be readily apparent once the right policy incantation were uttered. Redmond, Griffith, de Valera, Carson and others were all dismissed as extremists, ready to be displaced by far more acceptable leaders (such as William O'Brien, Stephen Gwynn, or Horace Plunkett) if such leaders could only be appropriately encouraged. The preferred tactic for encouraging such moderates was some relatively limited concession of devolution or self-government, treating Ireland as one unit. Of course, by the time it was perceived that Redmond may himself be the relative moderate, it was too late;[60] and Ireland was quickly charged with perversity for not keeping faith with such leaders for quite long enough. Kerr's fears of August 1914 were typical: 'the trouble is that the nationalist Volunteers are in the hands of people who are not too loyal. The rank and file I think are loyal enough, but the leaders aren't'.[61] The assumption that 'the rank and file' will prove more moderate than 'the leaders' was the wishful thinking of outsiders, particularly of outsiders brought up on 'the political experience of mainland Britain', which was conducive to 'a belief in negotiation; that all problems have accessible solutions; and, most importantly, the concept of "the centre"'.[62]

Nationalism has increasingly been regarded less as a series of identifiable political movements than as views of the world in which a plethora of clichés which assume 'nations to be the basic and natural units of analysis' occupies conceptual space which might have been taken up by more careful consideration of political and social phenomena: 'Nationalism is now envisaged less as an essentially political body of ideas, and more as a mode of sensibility, projected and elaborated across a range of cultural fields'.[63] On this definition, most British commentators on Irish politics in the period on which this study concentrates based their analyses on nationalistic assumptions. Notions of British national identity were of fundamental importance in the transformation of British opinion towards Irish self-government. Initially, British observers were concerned by the fact that proposals of Irish autonomy, whether federal, colonial or dualistic in nature, did not suit the wishes or interests of the 'predominant partner' in the United Kingdom:[64] The majority of English people were ultimately content with a state of affairs where 'England' and 'Britain' could be conveniently elided and confused.[65] British home rulers meanwhile were convinced, like Shaw's Hodson,[66] that Irish home rule would purify the British polity of a foreign and distracting element.[67]

Most importantly, however, British commentators were continually challenged by the dichotomy between their assumptions of the unique tolerance and decency of British traditions on the one hand, and global perceptions of British policy in Ireland on the other. The government of Ireland through the Union, contended Gladstone, was contrary to the tendencies of British history, 'a history in most respects so noble'.[68] When changes in the global environment and in the institutions of the Empire, led Britons to emphasise these liberal elements of their national identity more earnestly and persistently, significant advances were made towards Irish self-government. British home rulers believed it best that Britain did not dirty her hands on the Union; the methods necessary to maintain full legislative unity between Britain and nationalist Ireland, they argued, would prove intolerable to an electorate habituated to revere British traditions. Unionists sympathised with these sentiments but felt that within limits it was justifiable forcibly to maintain England's liberal and benign hegemony. When these limits were reached, as Mill and Dicey had anticipated, it was revealed that British home rulers had correctly anticipated the process, but not the outcome.[69] In the years 1916–21, British critics of government policy in Ireland were moved to a hysterical pitch of indignation because they could not reconcile visible policies of coercion in nationalist Ireland – in spite of their moderation compared to policies elsewhere in the British Empire – with their patriotic faith in Britain's uniqueness. In the end, such critics carried British public opinion with them. The British national myth was not immune from the contradictions and irrationalities which also characterised contemporary continental nationalism; its proponents invoked crude stereotypes and categories as a substitute for thought in just the same way. These contradictions helped to push Ireland out of the British Empire / Commonwealth altogether.

In advocating a British constitutional convention, Oliver wrote: 'The American and South African precedents are always in my mind'.[70] Because British commentators were really concerned with 'larger' themes, they frequently used analogies, especially with American, Canadian and South African experience, in their analyses of Irish politics. But British observers rarely saw Irish events themselves as likely to enlighten other imperial problems by analogy. In retrospect, the most relevant such inference that could have been drawn from Ireland in this period was that the United Kingdom ultimately would not be able to resist radical separatist nationalism in the colonies;[71] and naturally, Liberals and Imperialists were alike unwilling to accept this conclusion. Therefore, Massingham was insulting Gandhi in the columns of the *Nation* long after he had come to terms with Sinn Féin.[72] In 1921, Garvin's *Observer* declared, 'separatism for Ireland inevitably means separatism for India'; yet after the Treaty, it insisted that there was 'no analogy between Ireland and India', and like Massingham, dismissed Gandhi as 'childish'.[73] Lionel Curtis and the *Round Table* lagged in the other direction; they accepted ultimate dominion status for India in 1917, when they were still convinced that the geographical proximity of Ireland to Britain made dominion status in Ireland highly undesirable.[74] Curtis seems to have much preferred the Indians to the Irish, feeling the former possessed greater aptitude in manifesting a spirit of national unity.[75]

The Anglo-Irish Treaty placed Anglo-Irish relations on an entirely different footing. It was associated with no great discontinuity in British political thought, in which the idea of commonwealth, of free cooperation between self-governing states, had a long tradition. But British supporters of the Treaty, Liberal and Unionist, adopted a discourse which emphasised the discontinuity in Anglo-Irish relations. They were keen to close an 'unhappy episode in our history'.[76] It is not, of course, surprising that British commentators should wish rather hastily to draw a veil over some of their governments' past acts in Ireland, to wish for a 'blessed oblivion' of the past – and the value of the Treaty policy was that it went a long way to putting Britain 'right with the world'. 'Great Britain has gone to lengths of generosity greater than any of her sternest critics would have demanded', said the *Times*. 'No party in this country ever could go beyond it. There is nothing more [to] give', asserted the *Observer*.[77]

Oliver MacDonagh has explored the theme of ideas of continuity and discontinuity in Anglo-Irish history in an arresting essay. He argues that British views of history are generally developmental and evolutionary: 'in such a framework, a sudden turnabout in attitude . . . might be a matter not for apology, but for satisfaction. The corollary of such moral expansionism was a corresponding diminution of any sense of responsibility for the past'. Irish nationalist views (and, indeed, Ulster unionist views), however, are characterised by 'historical cyclicalism'. They assume 'an absolute repetitive form to lie at the heart of Anglo-Irish dealings'. The past lives on 'in that it had generated still unexpiated and irredeemed injustices; the mere intervention of years, however many, could do nothing whatever to change this ethical reality'.[78]

Unionists in the 1880s usually admitted that 'all men of whatever party, of whatever nation, who have seriously studied the annals of Ireland are agreed' that Britain had misgoverned or oppressed the country in the past. Unionists, however, denied that this fact was relevant to the issue of the Union, or sought to mitigate its significance by comparing past British policies in Ireland with the standards of the relevant age.[79] During and immediately after the First World War, British commentators again tacitly admitted the fact of a recent past of British error, obstruction and oppression in Ireland. But they argued that this was of little account as Britain had experienced 'a sudden turnabout in attitude'. Garvin's *Observer* said in 1921: 'material and possessive conceptions of Empire finally disappeared in face of the political development of the Dominions themselves. The war brought further enlightenment. It was in English eyes itself a crusade against domineering materialism. . . . Neither the British people nor the Government desire to "dominate" Ireland'.[80] As Kerr suggested Lloyd George emphasise in March 1917: 'England has been an obstacle in the past, but she is not to-day'.[81] Three years later in 1920, Kerr explained why he thought Irish nationalists should adopt an attitude of 'appeasement' to Ulster Unionism:

> The refusal of G[rea]t Britain to recognise the persistence of Irish Nationalism has kept both Ireland and England in a fever of distress for half a century. Are Irishmen, with this lesson before their eyes, going to make the same mistake with the same result by refusing to recognise the determination of Ulster to have separate treatment from the rest of Ireland for [the] present [?].[82]

Kerr here expressed assumptions common to many British political observers of Ireland in these years. 'English perceptions of Ireland', one historian has observed, 'were increasingly informed by abstract ideas of progress and civilisation. These took shape around a growing assumption – not peculiar to Englishmen – that English society demonstrated the pattern of universal political and economic progress'.[83] There was one path of political evolution down which all nations had to go, and the British, who had advanced farthest, were in the best and most impartial position to judge the progress of all others. Even advanced British commentators on Irish affairs supposed that Ireland was deficient in 'political training', and that the Irish lacked the education in moderation undergone by the British people; only some of the Positivists, peripheral as they were to British politics, articulated a more relativistic view. British governments' past mistakes in Ireland, according to the commonest views, did not justify Irish nationalist suspicion of Britain, but rather formed a stock of political learning on which all countries could draw. Such 'progressive' assumptions tacitly inform much British comment on Irish politics even today.

According to MacDonagh, Irish nationalist thought is characterised by the elision of time: 'the Irish do not forget, and . . . the English do not remember'.[84] According to Irish nationalist and Ulster unionist mindsets, political communities do not develop in a linear manner, but experience a cyclical and repetitive pattern of events. On these assumptions, contrary to Kerr's 1920 memorandum, British Unionist resistance to Irish nationalism was not an expression of an obsolete political faith, a 'mistake' from which all political societies should learn and become immune, but an attitude which any people is likely to adopt towards its national rivals at any time. The best policy is thus to protect oneself from hostile nationalism and imperialism wherever they may appear. This non-progressive faith has not been without expressions in British political culture; Leopold Amery and Correlli Barnett, for instance, have argued that Britain should never have admitted the strength of Irish nationalism.[85] An Irish nationalist interpreting the history of Anglo-Irish relations in a similar spirit could quite feasibly argue that there is no reason why any separate Unionist Ulster identity should be recognised.

Therefore, the elision of time in this way tends to produce a confrontational interpretation of the present reality of Anglo-Irish relations. It has thus intermittently been in British interests to de-legitimise this interpretation and compartmentalise the past and the present. The concept of the 'fresh start', the 'turning point' in Anglo-Irish relations, has consequently had distinct advantages from British perspectives. 'Fresh starts' abound in Anglo-Irish history.[86] J.A. Froude argued that Cromwell established the best chance for starting again and left Ireland a 'blank sheet of paper';[87] John Morley argued that the 1881 Land Act had placed relations on a new footing.[88] Suggested caesura also appeared after the Treaty; the Anglo-Irish settlement of 1938 was supposed to have opened another new era of appeasement, created another 'clean slate' between Britain and Ireland.[89] More recently, the Anglo-Irish Agreement of 1985, the Downing Street Declaration of 1993 and the Good Friday Agreement of April 1998 have constituted further attempts to put Britain 'right with the world'. British governments again have asserted that they have no desire to 'dominate' Ireland, and have endeavoured to create the image of a 'new climate of friendship and cooperation'.[90] With each fresh start it is insinuated that because the basis of Anglo-Irish relations has been utterly changed, only 'history-mad Irish minds', the perverse and the retrograde, would try to perpetuate 'fruitless wrangles about the past'.[91]

The construction of 'fresh starts' undoubtedly could improve Britain's reputation and self-image. But the strategy has also had drawbacks. The effort to brush history impatiently aside is not just anti-intellectual – it is opposed to human instinct. Indeed, almost all British commentators on Irish politics throughout the period 1865–1925 professed a timeless and essentialist view of British national identity, presupposing the existence of a mystical corporate personality known as 'England' or 'Britain', consisting of homogeneous 'English' or 'British' citizens; in other words they committed exactly the same error (if error it was) that they found intolerable in Irish nationalists.[92] Forms of national identity are necessarily rooted at least partly in history, and Irish nationalism has therefore defined itself in opposition to Englishness. Consequently, there has been a residual level of suspicion of Britain among Irish nationalists which no new departure in British policy, no matter how bold, has eroded. The attempt to treat this suspicion as perverse has itself been irritating and provocative, since it has seemed hypocritical.

A quest for a 'fresh start' tacitly assumed that there was some practically perfectly legitimated basis for British policy in Ireland, from which Anglo-Irish relations could proceed on a free and equal footing, cleansed from the associations of an unfortunate past. In pursuit of this elusive, perhaps unattainable position, British governments have thus encountered a series of seemingly ridiculous Irish nationalist suspicions which could only be explained by a persistent awareness of some 'black' pages in Anglo-Irish history. The holy grail of placing British good faith in Ireland 'beyond doubt'[93] has therefore tempted British governments into a series of cumulative concessions to Irish nationalism.

A reversal of this strategy would, logically enough, have been the soundest basis on which Unionist Ulster's position within the United Kingdom could have been consolidated. British policy-makers arguably might have evaded the encumbrance of what was held by mutual consent (rightly or wrongly) to have been a past of British oppression in Ireland by frankly admitting the reality and significance of this past. Such an admission would have necessitated an adjustment of some of the clumsy generalisations and stereotypes of British (which largely meant English) nationalism. The problem was that such national myths were (and perhaps still are) especially cherished in Britain. On British nationalist assumptions, Britain had a uniquely peaceable political culture. In the nineteenth century, Ireland, as 'sensational press reporting of Irish rural backwardness, crime and "anarchy"' in Britain suggested, did not fit this model.[94] Thus, it was insinuated that 'the Irish problem' (which was in itself of course largely a British stereotype)[95] could be relieved by integrating Ireland further into the British political system. Yet the very fact that Ireland required further integration merely highlighted its supposed exceptionality, and measures designed to unite consolidated the general awareness of differences. Even Unionists rarely regarded the Irish as fellow citizens.[96] An 'unEnglish' settlement was accordingly made all the more likely; and the separation of nationalist Ireland from the United Kingdom and the subsequent renewed conflict, merely seemed to fulfil British nationalist assumptions that Ireland was a violent country, and that Britain was unique in its political culture of 'fair play' and moderation.

More recently, British governments' efforts to maintain the comforting conventional national self-image and evade the stigma of Britain's past involvement in Ireland have led them to give more and more substance to their claims that they bear no ill-will to the people of nationalist Ireland and have no 'selfish' aims in the country. The oft-repeated formula that the Union with Northern Ireland is merely dependent on the will of the majority in the province has been pushed to the limit. British public opinion seems to be barely aware of the extent to which British governments' efforts to avoid entanglement in the politics of Northern Ireland have not only committed British politicians to greater involvement,[97] but logically propelled them further and further towards accepting a united

Ireland. Ulster Unionists, however, are keenly aware of this. Since the Anglo-Irish Agreement of 1985, Ulster Unionists have thus become more and more insecure due to apparent pressure from British sources to have the whole issue resolved in what seemed in Britain to be this most logical way.[98]

The roots of this unwillingness of Britons to perceive Northern Ireland as truly part of the United Kingdom were similar to the causes of Britain's eventual acceptance of the secession of Southern Ireland from the United Kingdom. The historic longevity and extent of nationalistic prejudice in Britain about the Southern Irish (and indeed in Southern Ireland about the British) is hardly a new or surprising observation.[99] The longevity, extent and historic significance of nationalistic prejudice about Ulster Unionism in Britain is a little more surprising. As James Loughlin writes: 'definitions of the national interest arrived at in London depended on an evolving political context in which the relevance of Ulster Unionism was largely a matter of political chance . . . the bonds of identity holding Ulster within the British "national family" were – compared to those that held the communities of Britain together on the same land mass – fragile'.[100] Northern Irish political culture, Unionist no less than Nationalist, was (and perhaps still is), in British views, dominated by unattractive features.[101] Accordingly, in the 1970s, Britons tended to perceive 'both sides to the [Northern Ireland] conflict as morally equivalent, with the British security forces neutral between the two and trying to maintain order . . . '.[102] Even elements on the Right of British politics, ostensibly the keenest supporters of the retention of Northern Ireland within the United Kingdom, persistently articulated the national myth that the British are moved by a unique spirit of tolerance and compromise in its most rarefied form. This narrowly defined, exclusive vision of 'Britishness' seemed alien to Britain's image of Ulster, and thus significantly exacerbated the perception of difference between Northern Ireland and the rest of the United Kingdom, therefore increasing the fragility of the Union.[103]

Stereotypical notions in Britain about Unionist Ulster, a failure to grasp its diversity,[104] have consequently placed Ulster Unionists in an almost impossible position. Britons have been irritated by the fervour of Unionist Ulster's very insistence on being British, and suspicious of the sincerity of this determination, regarding Ulster Unionism as a form of regionalism.[105] Even the spirit of Unionist Ulster's attachment to the symbols of British patriotism has been said to place her outside 'the British world'.[106] 'Settlements' for Ulster proposed by outsiders have therefore largely involved political structures which mark out its distinctness (with the Irish Republic) from the whole British political system. British proposals in the 1920s and 1930s frequently suggested some form of system to get Irish nationalists and Ulster Unionists 'round a table' together. This was the notion behind the Council of Ireland scheme proposed by Garvin in 1910, endorsed by Kerr in the Government of Ireland Act of 1920 and by Curtis for many years afterwards. More recently, the British and Irish governments' 'Framework documents' of 1995, which heavily influenced the Good Friday Agreement of 1998, proposed a structure of all-Ireland institutions of limited power which bears more than a passing resemblance to this Council as mentioned in the 1920 Act.[107] Such structures are disliked in Unionist Ulster, which desires rather to be integrated further into the British political community; they offer more (though by no means absolute) satisfaction for the unitarian Irish nationalist. The contradictions in pre-1921 Unionist attitudes to Irish nationalists were replicated in many Britons' views of Unionist Ulster in that era and later; Ulster could neither be severed entirely from the United Kingdom, nor accepted as full members on a par with the English.[108]

There was nothing inevitable about this developing application of exclusive British sentiments towards Unionist Ulster after the 1921 Treaty. Although the hyperbolic self-praise of British commentators should be dismissed, "Britishness" had in certain historic circumstances shown a capacity to produce a cohesive if fluid equilibrium between constituent national identities.[109] Arguably, if more had been done to direct these inclusive tendencies towards Northern Ireland after the Treaty, the intricate dilemmas of modern British policy in the province could have been evaded. It would be very wrong to assume, however, as some Irish nationalists do, that this trend is irreversible and that British governments and the British people will casually (or actively) allow the fraying bonds of the Union to break so that Northern Ireland will fall into nationalist hands.[110]

Collini writes:

> The absence of challenges to fundamental moral and political legitimacy [in nineteenth-century Britain] removed what would otherwise have been a major stimulus to defining the nature and limits of this 'national community' . . . For these and other reasons, explicit nationalism did not become a permanent feature of public debate with the result that to some ears there may be a discordant oddity in speaking of 'English nationalism' at all. Certainly, the

> conventional view was for long that 'in England patriotism takes the place of nationalism'.[111]

Given this tendency to assume that there is no such thing as English nationalism, it is not surprising that most historians have failed to suggest that the contradictions of English nationalism were a crucial dimension to the 'Irish problem'. Yet, this study has suggested that it is the inconsistencies, irrationalities and crude stereotypes of nationalism *all over* the United Kingdom which underlie the violent history of Northern Irish politics. British nationalism may, in Billig's phrase, have been banal, but in Ireland its consequences have not always been benign.[112]

It would be a mistake to underestimate the flexibility of conventional ideas of British national identity, or to ignore the extent to which they have helped the British people to deal successfully with a wide variety of crises.[113] Some historians have marvelled at the way in which British writers managed to move from articulating the Unionist Imperialism of the early twentieth century, to an ideology adapted to the liberal world order of the mid- and late twentieth century, without perceptible discontinuity.[114] The idealistic aspects of British national identity certainly provided a context crucial to the success of nationalist Ireland's demand for self-government. But in spite of (or perhaps because of) this proud, almost haughty heritage of liberal imperialism, Britons continued to regard Ireland as a violent country which lacked the British political wisdom which allows a majority to exercise power over a minority with sensitivity. Ireland, North and South, was perceived as lacking in political civilisation, requiring some steadying British guidance. Nationalists were usually blamed for this by British commentators; but the British attachment to Irish Unionism was not much greater. This notion that outside intervention was necessary to keep the two intolerant Irish factions from each others' throats is fundamentally the same one Walter Alison Phillips used in 1923 to defend the old policy of the Union of Britain and Ireland.[115]

Much has been written about the great theatrical political crisis initiated by Gladstone's conversion to home rule in late 1885, apparently on the assumption that this irrevocably changed the face of British politics. But this study has emphasised just how much was unaltered by Gladstone's change of heart. The movement in British public opinion towards Irish self-government was ultimately also successful because many individuals besides Gladstone, frequently on the fringes of politics and frequently motivated by ideological considerations, chose to accept and persevered in supporting such a measure. Some of these began to advocate Irish self-government enthusiastically and before Gladstone – others, with equal importance, accepted it reluctantly and belatedly. But nearly all of these commentators argued within a tradition of ideas about politics, British nationality and progress common to their Unionist opponents, and their advocacy did surprisingly little to change British political culture. In March 1919, the *Times* declared that 'we are all Home Rulers to-day'.[116] This was by no means the first nor the last claim that a new era in Anglo-Irish relations was about to begin. Yet, eight decades later, it is worth considering the extent to which, just as unreflective nationalist cliché and prejudice still infects the politics of Ireland, anachronistic unionist presumption still distorts British perceptions of the neighbouring island.[117]

Endnotes

INTRODUCTION

1 M. Freeden, *Ideologies and political theory: a conceptual approach* (Oxford, 1996), especially p. 1: T. Eagleton (ed.), *Ideology* (Harlow, 1994).
2 Definition based on Freeden, *Ideologies and political theory*, p. 3.
3 A.B. Cooke and J. Vincent, *The governing passion: cabinet government and party politics, 1885–1886* (Cambridge, 1974), pp. 21–2.
4 'Intellectual' is in fact an anachronistic term for this period. However, Collini's definition, that intellectuals were a group 'marked out by their involvement in the business of articulating reflections on human activities and exercising some kind of cultural authority acknowledged by the attentions of the wider society', is useful. S. Collini, *Public moralists: political thought and intellectual life in Victorian Britain, 1850–1930* (Oxford, 1991), p. 28.
5 M. Cowling, *Mill and liberalism* (Cambridge, 2nd ed., 1990, first published 1963), pp. xliv, xlii, 160–1, and *passim*.
6 Cooke and Vincent, *Governing passion*: Vincent, *The formation of the Liberal party, 1857–1868* (London, 1966): *Cowling, The impact of Labour, 1920–1924: the beginning of modern British politics* (Cambridge, 1971); *The impact of Hitler: British politics and British policy, 1933–1940* (Cambridge, 1975); 1867: *Disraeli, Gladstone, and revolution: the passing of the second Reform Bill* (Cambridge, 1967). The work of writers such as D. Hamer (see *Liberal politics in the age of Gladstone and Rosebery: a study in leadership and policy* (Oxford, 1972)), and C. Harvie (*The lights of liberalism: university liberals and the challenge of democracy* (Oxford, 1976), pp. 218–32; 'Ideology and home rule: James Bryce, A.V. Dicey and Ireland, 1880–7', *Eng.Hist.Rev.*, xci (1976), 298–314; 'Ireland and the intellectuals, 1848–1922', *New Edinburgh Review*, nos xxxviii–xxxix (1977), 35–42; 'Gladstonianism, the provinces and popular culture, 1880–1906', in R. Bellamy (ed.), *Victorian liberalism: nineteenth-century political thought and practice* (London, 1990), pp. 152–74) is informed by assumptions which are more sophisticated but similar.
7 J. Parry, *Democracy and religion: Gladstone and the Liberal party, 1867–1875* (Cambridge, 1986), pp. 438–52; *The rise and fall of Liberal government in Victorian Britain* (New Haven, 1993), pp. 295–306: C. Harvie, *Lights of liberalism*, pp. 218–32; 'Ireland and the intellectuals'; 'Ideology and home rule': M. Bentley, *The climax of Liberal politics: British liberalism in theory and practice, 1868–1918* (London, 1987), especially pp. 134–7: W.C. Lubenow, 'Liberals

and the national question', *Parliamentary History*, xiii (1994), 119–42; 'Irish home rule and the social basis of the great separation in the Liberal party in 1886', *Hist.Journ.*, xxviii (1985), 125–42; *Parliamentary politics and the home rule crisis: the British House of Commons in 1886* (Oxford, 1988): T. Dunne, '*La traihson des clercs*: British intellectuals and the first home rule crisis', *Ir.Hist.Stud.*, xxiii (1982–3), 134–73; 'Ireland, England and the empire, 1868–1886: the ideologies of the British political leadership' (Cambridge University, Ph.D. thesis, 1975): T.A. Jenkins, *Gladstone, whiggery and the Liberal party, 1874–1886* (Oxford, 1988).

8 *Ibid.*, pp. 284–5.

9 Parry, *Democracy and religion*, pp. 438–9.

10 Cooke and Vincent, *Governing passion*, p. 163.

11 R. Nisbett and L. Ross, *Human inference: strategies and shortcomings of social judgement* (Englewood Cliffs, 1980).

12 R. Shannon, *Gladstone: heroic minister, 1865–98* (London, 1999), especially pp. 365–405: Jenkins, *Gladstone, whiggery and the Liberal party*, pp. 292–3: Parry, *Rise and fall of Liberal government*, pp. 295–311.

13 E. Biagini, *Liberty, retrenchment and reform: popular liberalism in the age of Gladstone, 1860–1880* (Cambridge, 1992), *passim.*, especially, pp. 3–4: Parry, *Rise and fall of Liberal government*, pp. 17–8; *Democracy and religion*, pp. 446, 450: Vincent, *Formation of the Liberal party*, *passim.*, especially pp. 68–9, 257–8.

14 M. O'Callaghan, *British high politics and a nationalist Ireland: criminality, land and the law under Forster and Balfour* (Cork, 1994), p. 107. Also see O'Callaghan, 'Irish history, 1780–1980', *Hist.Journ.*, xxix (1986), 492.

15 Cowling, *Mill and liberalism*, p. xliii: Cooke and Vincent, *Governing passion*, pp. 17–9: G.A. Jones, *The politics of reform, 1884* (Cambridge, 1972), pp. 10–3.

16 Cooke and Vincent, *Governing passion*, pp. 79–82: Shannon, *The age of Salisbury, 1881–1902: Unionism and empire* (London, 1996), pp. 201–2.

17 Cooke and A.P. Malcomson (eds), *The Ashbourne papers* (Belfast, 1974), p. ix: O'Callaghan, *British high politics*, pp. 119, 148–152: V. Crossman, *Politics, law and order in nineteenth-century Ireland* (Dublin, 1996), pp. 153–4.

18 Cooke and Vincent, *Governing passion*, p. 167.

19 S. Pedersen and P. Mandler, 'The British intelligentsia after the Victorians', in Pedersen and Mandler (eds), *After the Victorians: private conscience and public duty in modern Britain* (London, 1994), pp. 1–28: E.M. Sigsworth, *In search of Victorian values: aspects of nineteenth-century thought and society* (Manchester, 1988).

20 L. Goldman, 'The Social Science Association, 1857–1886: a context for mid-Victorian liberalism', *Eng.Hist.Rev.*, ci (1986), 95–134: Collini, *Public moralists*, pp. 199–250.

21 *Ibid.*, p. 4, *passim.*

22 B. Stuchtey, *W.E.H. Lecky (1838–1903): historisches Denken und politisches Urteilen eines anglo-irischen Gelehrten* (Göttingen, 1997), pp. 259–89: D. McCartney, *W.E.H. Lecky: historian and politician, 1838–1903* (Dublin, 1994), pp. 114–50. On Lecky see below pp. 39–40, 42.

23 R. Cosgrove, 'The relevance of Irish history: the Gladstone-Dicey debate about home rule, 1886–7', *Éire-Ireland*, xiii (1978), no. 4, 6–21.

24 M. Bentley, *The liberal mind, 1914–1929* (Cambridge, 1977), pp. 205, 160–2, 172.
25 M. Laffan, 'Insular attitudes: the revisionists and their critics', in M. Ní Dhonnchadha and T. Dorgan (eds), *Revising the rising* (Derry, 1991), p. 106.
26 B. Harrison, 'Mrs. Thatcher and the intellectuals', *Twentieth-century British History*, v (1994), 245.
27 Bentley, *Climax of Liberal politics*, pp. 69, 96–7.
28 Bentley, *Liberal mind*, p. 4; 'Party, doctrine and thought', in M. Bentley and J. Stevenson (eds), *High and low politics in modern Britain: ten studies* (Oxford, 1983), pp. 123–53, especially p. 144.
29 Bentley, *Liberal mind*, p. 4.
30 Parry, *Rise and fall of Liberal government*, p. 311: E. Green, *The crisis of Conservatism: the politics, economics and ideology of the British Conservative party, 1880–1914* (London, 1995), pp. 1, 59–60: M.I. Francis and I. Zweiniger-Bargielowska (eds), *The Conservatives and British society, 1880–1990* (Cardiff, 1996): B. Evans and A. Taylor, *From Salisbury to Major: continuity and change in Conservative politics* (Manchester, 1996).
31 G.S. Jones, *Languages of class: studies in English working-class history, 1832–1982* (Cambridge, 1983), p. 22.
32 S. Koss, *The rise and fall of the political press in Britain* (London, 1981–4, 2 vols), ii.10, 4, 9.
33 S. Inwood, 'The role of the press in English politics during the first world war, with special reference to the period 1914–1916' (Oxford University, D.Phil. thesis, 1971), p. 390: A.J. Lee, *The origins of the popular press, 1855–1914* (London, 1976), *passim.*, especially pp. 125–9: Koss, *Political press, passim.*: R. Ellins, 'Aspects of the new Liberalism, 1895–1914' (University of Sheffield, D.Phil. thesis, 1980), pp. 110–87: *Scott diary, passim.*: A.M. Gollin, *The 'Observer' and J.L. Garvin, 1908–14: a study in great editorship* (London, 1960).
34 N. Blenett, quoted in Koss, *Political press*, ii.136.
35 Lee, *Origins of the popular press*, p. 185.
36 Koss, *Political press*, ii.125, 119, 7, 17, 234: D.G. Boyce, 'The fourth estate: the reappraisal of a concept', in Boyce, J. Curran and P. Wingate (eds), *Newspaper history from the seventeenth century to the present day* (London, 1978), pp. 320–38.
37 R. Blake (ed.), *Ireland after the Union* (Oxford, 1989), p. viii: Dunne, 'Response to Gladstonian home rule and land reform', *Ir.Hist.Stud.*, xxv (1986–7), 432.
38 Hamer, *Liberal politics in the age of Gladstone and Rosebery, passim.*; 'The Irish question and Liberal politics, 1886–1894', *Hist.Journ.*, xii (1969), 511–32: Bentley, *Climax of Liberal politics*, p. 98.
39 M. Cunningham, *British government policy in Northern Ireland, 1969–89: its nature and execution* (Manchester, 1991), pp. 243–9, *passim.*: D.G. Boyce, *The Irish question and British politics, 1868–1996* (Basingstoke, 2nd ed., 1996, first published 1988), pp. 130, 151.
40 *Governing passion*, p. 18.
41 Definitions of 'home rule' or 'self-government' which draw upon a specific legal or constitutional framework are of limited utility to historians of British opinion towards Irish self-government, since such precise definitions were so often

eschewed by the proponents of these policies themselves. This broad (if ambiguous) definition, resting on political criteria, is a more useful tool of analysis for present purposes. See A. O'Day, *Irish home rule, 1867–1921* (Manchester, 1998): A.J. Ward, *The Irish constitutional tradition: responsible government and modern Ireland, 1782–1992*, (Blackrock, 1994), pp. 84–7. Also see pp. 18, 36 below on some of the problems of defining 'self-government' in this context.

42 See above, pp. 2–7.

43 P. Bew, H. Patterson, and P. Teague, *Northern Ireland, between war and peace: the political future of Northern Ireland* (London, 1997), especially p. 63: Boyce, *Irish question and British politics*, pp. 130, 152.

44 R. Kearney, *Postnationalist Ireland: politics, culture, philosophy* (London, 1997).

45 *Scott diary*, pp. 348–9: P. Jalland and J.O. Stubbs, 'The Irish question after the outbreak of war in 1914: some unfinished party business', *Eng.Hist.Rev.*, xcvi (1981), 797.

46 Bew, Patterson, and Teague, *Northern Ireland, between war and peace*, p. 207.

47 O'Callaghan, *British high politics*, pp. 3–4, 11–12, 153: Boyce, *Englishmen and Irish troubles: British public opinion and the making of Irish policy, 1918–22* (London, 1972).

48 Definitions of Imperialism are discussed below, pp. 112–14.

CHAPTER ONE

1 R.F. Foster, *Modern Ireland, 1600–1972* (London, 1985), p. 427: A. O'Day, *Irish home rule*, p. 106. On Bradlaugh see F. D'arcy, 'Charles Bradlaugh and the Irish question: a study in the nature and limits of British radicalism, 1853–91', in A. Cosgrove and D. McCartney (eds), *Studies in Irish history presented to R. Dudley Edwards* (Dublin, 1979), pp. 228–56.

2 William Gladstone papers, (British Library, London), MS.44,519, f.318–19; 44,518, f.92, Harrison to Gladstone, 31 Dec., 7 Mar. 1894.

3 R. Harrison, 'E.S. Beesly and Karl Marx', *International Review of Social History*, iv (1959), 37: *PR*, xxiii (1915), pp. 176–7.

4 Comte, *System of Positive polity: a treatise in sociology, instituting the religion of humanity* (London, 1875–7, 4 vols), trans. R. Congreve et al from *Système de politique positive, ou traité de sociologie instituant la religion de l'humanité* (Paris, 1851–1854, 4 vols), iii.174, ii.262–5, iv.333–4; *A general view of Positivism* (London, 1865), trans. J. Bridges from *Discours sur l'ensemble du positivisme* (Paris, 1848), pp. 121–30; *A discourse on the Positive spirit* (London, 1903), trans. E.S. Beesly from *Discours sur l'esprit positif* (Paris, 1844), p. 145.

5 Comte, *Positive polity*; *The catechism of Positive religion* (London, 3rd ed., 1891, first published 1858), trans. Congreve from *Catéchisme positiviste* (Paris, 1852); *Discourse*; *General View*: H. Martineau (ed.), *The Positive philosophy of Auguste Comte* (London, 1896, 3 vols, first published 1853 in 2 vols), based on A. Comte, *Cours de philosophie positive* (Paris, 1830–42, 6 vols). For recent publications on Comte see Pickering, *Auguste Comte*: H.S. Jones (ed.), *Auguste Comte: early political writings* (Cambridge, 1998): G. Lenzer (ed.), *Auguste*

Comte and Positivism: the essential writings (New Brunswick, 1998): K. Thompson (ed.), *Auguste Comte* (London, 1976).

6 W.M. Simon, 'Auguste Comte's English disciples', *Vict.Stud.*, vii (1963–4), 161–72: J. MacGee, *A crusade for humanity: the history of organised Positivism in England* (London, 1931): R. Harrison, *Before the socialists: studies in labour and politics, 1861–1881* (Aldershot, 1994, first published 1965), especially pp. 251–342.

7 Pickering, *Auguste Comte*, p. 615.

8 T.R. Wright, *The religion of humanity: the impact of Comtean Positivism on Victorian Britain* (Cambridge, 1986): C. Kent, *Brains and numbers: elitism, Comtism and democracy in mid-Victorian England* (Toronto, 1978).

9 M.S. Vogeler, *Frederic Harrison: the vocations of a Positivist* (Oxford, 1984): P. Adelman, 'The social and political ideas of Frederic Harrison, in relation to English thought and politics, 1855–1886' (London University, D.Phil. thesis, 1977): F. Harrison, *Autobiographic memoirs* (London, 1911, 2 vols): A. Harrison, *Frederic Harrison, thoughts and memories* (London, 1926).

10 C. Kent, *Brains and numbers*, especially p. xiii: Harvie, *Lights of liberalism*, pp. 41–2, 147–9: S. Eisen, 'Huxley and the Positivists', *Vict.Stud.*, viii (1964–5), 338.

11 Wright, *Religion of humanity*, especially pp. 6–7.

12 Kent, *Brains and numbers*, pp. 66–8, 90: R. Harrison, *Before the socialists*, pp. 254, 262–5, 328–33: Comte, *Appeal to conservatives* (London, 1889), trans. Congreve and T. Donikin from *Appel aux conservateurs* (Paris, 1855), pp. 130–1, 137–8.

13 *Positivist comments on public affairs: occasional papers issued by the London Positivist Society, 1878–1892* (London, 1896): LPS papers (British Library of Political and Economic Science, London School of Economics and Political Science), 1/1.

14 H. Pelling, *A history of British trade unionism* (Harmondsworth, 4th ed, 1987, first published 1963), pp. 51–64: S. and B. Webb, *The history of trade unionism* (London, new ed, 1902, first published 1894), pp. 248–57: H.W. McCready, 'British labour and the Royal Commission on Trade Unions, 1867–9', *University of Toronto Quarterly*, xxiv (1953–4), pp. 390–409.

15 R. Harrison, *Before the socialists*, pp. 277–313, 271–2; 'Beesly and Marx'; 'Professor Beesly and the working-class movement', in A. Briggs and J. Saville (eds), *Essays in labour history* (London, 1960–77, 3 vols), i.205–41: R. Harrison (ed.), *The English defence of the commune, 1871* (London, 1971): Vogeler, *Frederic Harrison*, pp. 63–70: Beesly, 'Trades' unions', *Westminster Review*, lxxvi (Oct. 1861), pp. 510–542: F. Harrison, *Order and progress* (London, 1875), pp. 151–2, 171–5, 195.

16 H. Crompton, 'Foreign policy and the working classes', *Bee-Hive*, (11 July 1874), p. 4: Comte, *General view*, p. 211: *PR*, i (1893), pp. 34–9; xiii (1905), pp. 121–5; xv (1907), pp. 104–8.

17 Martineau (ed.), *Philosophy of Comte*, ii.238.

18 Comte, *Positive polity*, ii.251, 378–82, iii.306–7.

19 Beesly, 'The unnamed dead', *PR*, xxiii (1915), p. 218. On Comte's anti-imperialism, see B. Semmel, *The liberal idea and the demons of empire: theories of imperialism from Adam Smith to Lenin* (Baltimore, 1993), pp. 43–7.

20 Beesly, 'The Indian frontier war', *PR*, v (1897), p. 182: Congreve (ed.), *International policy* (London, 1866): Semmel, *The Governor Eyre controversy* (London, 1962), pp. 130–41.
21 *PR*, vii (1899), pp. 137–40; xii (1904), pp. 9–14, 27, 49–57.
22 F. Harrison, 'International arbitration', *PR*, xix (1911), p. 77: H. Crompton, 'International policy', *Bee-Hive*, (3 Feb. 1872), pp. 2–3.
23 Bridges, 'England and China', in Congreve (ed.), *International policy*, pp. 327–448, especially p. 431.
24 Swinny, 'Time and tide in India', *PR*, xi (1903), p. 80: H. Cotton, 'Is British imperialism a moral factor in the progress of humanity?', *PR*, xii (1904), pp. 241–50. Sir Henry Jones Stedman Cotton (1845–1915) acted as president of the Indian National Congress in 1904–5, and was a prominent critic of the policies of the then Secretary of State for India, John Morley, in the House of Commons from 1906–10. Cotton, *India and home memories* (London, 1911), pp. 287–308: *PR*, xxiii (1915), pp. 273–5: S. Koss, *John Morley at the India Office, 1905–1910* (New Haven, 1969), pp. 131–3, 76, 126, 105, 158.
25 'India' and 'Gibraltar: or the foreign policy of England' (both first published in 1857), in R. Congreve, *Essays, political, social, and religious* (London, 1874–1900, 3 vols), i.67–106, 1–65.
26 FHP, 1/11, f.53–8, n.d.; Harrison to Beesly: Kent, *Brains and numbers*, p. 87. On Goldwin Smith's 'separatism', see C. Bodelsen, *Studies in mid-Victorian imperialism* (London, 1924), pp. 52–9: C.C. Eldridge, *England's mission: the imperial idea in the age of Gladstone and Disraeli* (London, 1973), pp. 34–5, 45.
27 *Times*, (4 May 1867), pp. 5–6, (15 June 1867), p. 9: RCP, MS.Eng.lett.c.180, f.185, Bright to Congreve, 11 Apr. 1867: R. Harrison, *Before the socialists*, p. 279.
28 'Ireland', *Commonwealth*, (3 Mar. 1866), p. 4. Compare the articles by P. Fox, *Commonwealth*, (10 Feb. 1866), p. 5, (17 Feb. 1866), pp. 4–5, (24 Feb. 1866), p. 5, (3 Mar. 1866), p. 5, (17 Mar. 1866), p. 5.
29 G. Baden-Powell 'Introductory', and the Duke of Argyll, 'Some inconsistencies of Gladstonian home rule', in Baden-Powell (ed.), *The truth about home rule: papers on the Irish question* (London, 2nd ed, 1888), pp. 1–36, especially pp. 6–9, 30.
30 G. Smith, *Irish history and Irish character* (Oxford, 1861), pp. 192–3: J.C. Morison, *Irish grievances shortly stated* (London, 1868), pp. 82–5: F.H. Hill, 'Ireland', in F.H. Hill, et al, *Questions for a reformed parliament* (London, 1867), pp. 1–36.
31 FHP, 1/18, f.32–4, Harrison to Beesly, n.d.: *Commonwealth*, (24 Nov. 1866), p. 1, (1 Dec. 1866), p. 1: *Bee-Hive*, (10 Nov. 1866), p. 4.
32 J.H. Bridges, *Irish disaffection: four letters addressed to the editor of the 'Bradford Review'* (Bradford, 1868), [reissued as *The home rule question eighteen years ago* (London, 1886)], p. 3.
33 *Ibid.*, p. 7.
34 *Ibid.*, p. 24.
35 *Ibid.*, p. 7.
36 For the importance of this analogy to British supporters of home rule, see below, pp. 61–2, 69–70, 132.

37 Congreve, 'Ireland' (first published in 1868), in *Essays*, i.179–207, especially p. 179: FHP, 1/14, f.85–6, Harrison to Beesly, 11 Dec. 1867.
38 Congreve, *Essays*, i.189, 190, 186.
39 D'arcy, 'Bradlaugh and the Irish question', p. 240: ESBP, 23, Beesly, 'Great states': F. Harrison, 'Public affairs', *FR*, xxi (1874), p. 146; 'Empire and humanity' *FR*, xxxiii (1880), p. 292; 'The radical programme', *CR*, il (1886), p. 278.
40 Comte, *Positive polity*, vol iv: Congreve, 'The west', in Congreve (ed.), *International policy*, pp. 1–49.
41 Comte, *Positive polity*, ii.251.
42 JKIP, D2808/14/3, Comte to Ingram and G. Allman, 16 Oct. 1852: Comte, *Catechism of positive religion*, pp. 233–4: Comte, *Positive polity*, ii.121, 302–5, iv.267.
43 Congreve, *Essays*, i.206, 188.
44 Harrison, 'England and France', in Congreve (ed.), *International policy*, p. 140: Swinny, 'England and Germany', *PR*, xvii (1909), p. 83.
45 Congreve, 'Ireland' (paper first read 1 Dec. 1880), in *Essays*, ii.128–37, especially ii.132.
46 Bridges, *Irish disaffection*, p. 24: Beesly, *Home rule* (London, 1886), p. 16.
47 *Weekly Dispatch*, (18, 25 Nov. 1877), p. 9: F. Harrison, 'How to drive home rule home', *FR*, lviii (1892), pp. 285, 287.
48 S. and B. Webb, *History of trade unionism*, pp. 348–9n.
49 Beesly, 'English, workmen and Ireland', *Labour Standard*, (8 Oct. 1881), p. 5: H. Crompton, *The Irish state trial* (London, 1881): 'The Irish tenant farmer and the law', *Labour Standard*, (4 June 1881), p. 5: JKIP, D2808/17/7, H. Crompton to Ingram, 7 Mar. 1881.
50 Beesly, 'Incendiary government', *Labour Standard*, (22 Oct. 1881), p. 5.
51 'Anti-coercion meeting in Liverpool', *Liverpool Daily Post*, (28 Feb. 1881), p. 7f-h: ESBP, 23, 'Great states'.
52 Congreve, 'The Irish crisis', *Labour Standard*, (5 Nov. 1881), p. 5, reprinted in Congreve, *Essays*, ii.39–42, especially p. 41: *RO*, vi (1881), pp. 296–304; ix (1882), p. 289.
53 RCP, MS.Eng.lett.c.185, f.62, Congreve to Parnell, 23 Nov. 1880.
54 P. Bull, *Land, politics and nationalism: a study of the Irish land question* (Dublin, 1996), pp. 106, 113: O'Callaghan, *British high politics*, pp. 96, 95–103, 52–4, 46–7: Crossman, *Politics and law and order*, pp. 130–2, 137–8, 143–4, 153–81.
55 Argyll, 'Some inconsistencies of Gladstonian home rule', pp. 33–5.
56 Comte, *General view*, pp. 397–8: Beesly, 'Coercion in Ireland', *PR*, x (1902), pp. 227–8.
57 Beesly, 'The Galway judgement', *FR*, xviii (1872), pp. 39–50; 'Positivists and workmen', *FR*, xxiv (1875), pp. 68–72: Swinny, *The history of Ireland: three lectures given in Newton Hall* (London, 1890), pp. 38, 17–8: Bridges, 'From the Union to Catholic emancipation, 1801–1829', in J. Bryce (ed.), *Two centuries of Irish history* (London, 1888), pp. 204–314, especially pp. 241–3, 269, 293–6.
58 Beesly, 'England and the sea', in Congreve (ed.), *International policy*, p. 208.
59 Beesly, 'Our foreign and our Irish policy', *FR*, xxxv (1881), pp. 242–3.

60 Congreve, *Essays*, i.191–8: *FR*, xxxv (1881), p. 242.
61 Comte, *General View*, pp. 145, 169, 175–7: F. Harrison, *Order and progress*, pp. 1–122: Harvie, 'Ireland and the intellectuals', 37.
62 Bridges, *Irish disaffection*, p. 23: F. Harrison, *Autobiographic memoirs*, ii.227–9: *CR*, il (1886), pp. 278–9.
63 *Labour Standard*, (20 May 1882), p. 1: *MG*, (2 Jan. 1886), p. 6d: *RO*, vii (1882), pp. 285–7.
64 Simon, 'Comte's English disciples', 161–72: Wright, *Religion of humanity*, pp. 81–2, 88–101: Peatling, 'British ideological movements and Irish politics, 1865–1925' (Oxford University, D.Phil. thesis, 1997), pp. 32–4, 68–73.
65 Hutton, *Comte, the man and the founder: personal recollections* (London, 1891), p. 16. On the general development of Chapel Street Positivism after 1878, see Congreve, *Essays*, ii–iii, *passim*.
66 FHP, 1/4, f.95–8, Harrison to Beesly, n.d. [1857?], quoted in Kent, *Brains and numbers*, p. 87: FHP, 1/57, f.58–61, Harrison to Morley, 9 Oct. 1873: Vogeler, *Harrison*, pp. 153–9.
67 PP, MS 45,231, f.83–4, Congreve to H. Crompton, 3 Dec. 1890; MS 45,233, f.51–2, Congreve to Ingram, 16 Mar. 1887: Congreve, *Essays*, ii.405–8.
68 *Ibid.*, ii.133.
69 PP, MS 45,228, f.54–8, A. Crompton to Congreve, 1 Dec. 1890.
70 *Essays*, ii.56, 388.
71 RCP, MS.Eng.lett.c.182, f.38, Congreve to H. Cotton, 9 June 1886.
72 *Essays*, ii.56: RCP, MS.Eng.lett.c.182, f.169, Congreve to A. Crompton, 23 Apr. 1887: A. Gailey, 'Failure and the making of a new Ireland', in D.G. Boyce (ed.), *The revolution in Ireland, 1879–1923* (Basingstoke, 1988), pp. 47–70: PP, 45,233, f.141–4, Congreve to Ingram, Oct.–Nov. 1895.
73 This argument is distinct from that occasionally used by some Unionists, that Irish home rule was no better, or was even worse, than the separation of Ireland from Britain (see A.V. Dicey, *England's case against home rule* (London, 3rd ed, 1887, first published 1886), pp. 19, 142–6; 'Home rule from an English point of view', *CR*, xlii (1882), pp. 67, 84–5: Harvie, 'Ideology and home rule', 307–9, misses this distinction).
74 LPS papers, 1/3, Committee minutes, 5 June 1886 to 11 July 1887: *PMG*, (18, 19, 21 May 1886), pp. 2, 2, 5.
75 *MG*, (4 Jan. 1886), p. 6c. Positivists did occasionally speak of Irish political discontent in such a tone of contempt, see below p. 30: Morison, 'Ireland for the English', *FR*, ix (1867), pp. 89–94. On Morison see Wright, *Religion of humanity*, pp. 120–2: 'Morison, James Augustus Cotter (1832–1888)', in *DNB*, vol xxxix.
76 JKIP, D2808/7/8, Beesly to Ingram, 9 Oct. 1899: Beesly, *Home rule*, pp. 3, 10–3.
77 *Ibid.*, p. 2.
78 Bridges to F.H. Torlesse, 16 Apr. 1886, quoted in M.A. Bridges (ed.), *Recollections of John Henry Bridges* (London, 1908), p. 144.
79 Bridges to Beesly, 10 Feb. 1886, quoted in S. Liveing (ed.), *A nineteenth-century teacher: John Henry Bridges* (London, 1926), p. 221.
80 Harrison, *Mr Gladstone – or anarchy!* (London, 1886), p. 9.

81 *Ibid.*, p. 4: *Order and progress*, pp. 171–5, 195: *FR*, xix (1873), pp. 18, 10, 22–4: *NC*, iii (1878), p. 816: *RO*, viii (1882), pp. 88–9.
82 Beesly, *Home rule* (London, 1886), pp. 14–6.
83 FHP, 1/116: *PMG*, (28 June 1886), p. 8: R. Harrison, (ed.), *English defence of the Commune*, p. 41.
84 Bridges to Beesly, 10 Feb. 1886.
85 Bridges, 'From the Union to Catholic emancipation, 1801–1829': James, Viscount Bryce papers (Bodleian Library), MS Bryce 11, f.143–4, Bryce to Gladstone, 10 July 1886. See above, p. 5.
86 Congreve, *Essays*, ii.870, iii.6–10, 26: RCP, MS.Eng.lett.c.182, f.52, Congreve to Cotton, 1 Nov. 1887.
87 F. Harrison, *Autobiographic memoirs*, ii.219–22.
88 *Labour Standard*, (8 Oct. 1881), p. 5: Beesly, 'Tests of national union', *PR*, iii (1895), p. 11.
89 Beesly, 'National cohesion', *PR*, iii (1895), p. 30: Harrison, 'The big fight', *PR*, xi (1903), p. 246.
90 Swinny, 'Sociological view of the history of Ireland', *SR*, i (1908), pp. 280–90, especially p. 289: *Indian Review*, vi (1905), pp. 7–8.
91 F. Harrison, 'Ireland', *PR*, xx (1912), p. 152.
92 Bridges, *Irish disaffection*, p. 8.
93 Swinny, *History of Ireland*, pp. 30, 19.
94 Swinny, 'Minor currents in Irish life', *PR*, xv (1907), p. 61.
95 JKIP, D2808/54/53, Swinny to Ingram, n.d.
96 'Irish notes', *PR*, xx (1912), p. 234.
97 Bridges, *Irish disaffection*, p. 18: Swinny, *History of Ireland*, pp. 28–31.
98 *PR*, xvi (1908), pp. 44; xv (1907), pp. 57–8.
99 JKIP, D2808/54/52, Swinny to Ingram, 22 Feb. 1907.
100 *PR*, i (1893), pp. 88–92; xxi (1913), pp. 226–7, 239–40; xxii (1914), p. 3; xxvii (1919), pp. 226–7; xxviii (1920), p. 167: *FR*, lviii (1892), p. 286.
101 Harrison, *Mr Gladstone – or anarchy!*, pp. 14, 13.
102 Harrison's preface to F.W. Pim, *Home rule through federal devolution* (London, 1919), pp. 7–10, especially p. 9.
103 National Library of Ireland (Dublin), MS 9,769; A. Crompton, 'In Memoriam: Henry Dix Hutton': R.B. MacDowell, 'Henry Dix Hutton – Positivist and Cataloguer', *Friends of the Library of Trinity College Dublin: Annual Bulletin* (1952), pp. 6–7: C.L. Falkiner, *Memoir of John Kells Ingram* (Dublin, 1907): 'Ingram, John Kells (1823–1907)', and 'Allman, George Johnston (1824–1904)', in *DNB*, 1901–10: Hutton, *Comte, man and founder*; *Comte's life and work: exceptional, but finally normal; an address* (London, 1892): Ingram, Outlines of the history of religion (London, 1900), especially pp. 20–2; *Human nature and morals according to Auguste Comte* (London, 1901); *Practical morals: a treatise on universal education* (London, 1904).
104 Ingram, *Sonnets and other poems* (London, 1900), pp. 104–6, 6.
105 On Ingram's life and political thought see Peatling, 'Who fears to speak of politics? John Kells Ingram and hypothetical nationalism', *Ir.Hist.Stud.*, xxxi (1998–9), 202–21. I am grateful to *Irish Historical Studies* for the opportunity

here to summarise arguments and material which had previously appeared in that journal.

106 Ingram, 'National presage', in *Sonnets and other poems*, p. 76.

107 Crompton, 'In Memoriam: Henry Dix Hutton', p. 18.

108 JKIP, D2808/54/27, Swinny to Ingram, 4 May 1905: *PR*, xiii (1905), p. 141; xv (1907), pp. 132–3: Ingram, *Final transition*, p. 59n.

109 JKIP, D2808/47/1–77, especially /4, 6, 20, 19, 55, Quin to Ingram, 1896–1904: Quin, *The politics of the proletariat: a contribution to the science of citizenship based chiefly on the sociology of Auguste Comte* (London, 1920), pp. 61–70.

110 PP, MS 45,228, f.265–8, Ingram to Congreve, 4 Aug. 1898.

111 Comte, *General view*, pp. 383–4: Bridges, 'Right and wrong', *PR*, xi (1903), p. 227.

112 Beesly, 'Fashoda', *PR*, vi (1898), p. 181.

113 FHP, 1/16, f.62–5, Harrison to Beesly, 6 July 1870: M. Quin, *Memoirs of a Positivist* (London, 1924), p. 171.

114 J. Carey Hall, 'The Irish Presbyterians', *PR*, xxiv (1916), pp. 252, 253. Hall, like Cotton, had spent much of his life in Imperial service in the east, see *PR*, xxix (1921), pp. 258–60.

115 Harrison, 'Moral and religious socialism – II, social morality', *PR*, xxvi (1918), p. 126: B. Anderson, *Imagined communities: reflections on the rise and spread of nationalism* (London, rev. ed, 1991, first published 1983), p. 6.

116 *Times*, (27 Oct. 1916), p. 7d: Harrison, *Autobiographic memoirs*, i.309, ii.238; Harrison, 'A critical year', *PR*, xxi (1913), p. 32.

117 Pim, *Home rule through federal devolution*, p. 8. Harrison nearly visited Ireland in 1888–9, but was apparently discouraged by the recent arrest of his friend and fellow home ruler Wilfrid Blunt; FHP, 1/67, f.13–18, Harrison to Morley, 1888. Bridges and Beesly did visit Ireland, and Swinny returned every year; *PR*, i (1893), pp. 186–7; xxiii (1915), p. 247; xxxi (1923), p. 223.

118 FHP, 1/30, f.21–2, Davitt to Harrison, 1 Mar. 1890: Harrison, 'The report of the special commission', *New Review*, ii (1890), pp. 199–211.

119 FHP, 1/46, f.8–9, Lecky to Harrison, 18 Jan. 1886. On Lecky also see pp. 5, 37–40.

120 On this see F.S.L. Lyons, *The fall of Parnell, 1890–91* (London, 1960): F. Callanan, *The Parnell split, 1890–91* (London, 1992).

121 Harrison, 'The Irish leadership', *FR*, lv (1891), p. 125: FHP, 1/70, f.15–6, 19–22, Harrison to Morley, Sept. 1891, 29 Nov. 1891.

122 Harrison, *Autobiographic memoirs*, ii.238–9.

123 *Times*, (18 Nov. 1913), p. 5b: *WG*, (19 Feb. 1914), pp. 3c, 8a, (18 Feb. 1914), p. 8d: *PR*, xxi (1913), pp. 31–2.

124 *MP*, (1 May 1917), p. 4c–e, (12 May 1917), p. 4d, (15 May 1917), p. 4d, (18 May 1917), p. 4b-c, f: William O'Brien papers, National Library of Ireland, 8,557/6, Harrison to O'Brien, 13 July 1917, 21 May 1917, O'Brien to Harrison, 17 July 1917: FSMP, MS.Eng.lett.c.263, f.221–2, Harrison to Marvin, 28 Oct. 1916: *FR*, cix (1918), pp. 650–1.

125 Harrison to Rosebery, 16 Dec. 1919, quoted in Vogeler, *Harrison*, p. 378.

126 R. Harrison, 'E.S. Beesly and Karl Marx', pp. 214–15.

127 Beesly, *Mind your own business: some plain words to the Gladstonians about Mr Parnell* (London, 1890): RCP, MS.Eng.lett.c.182, f.57, Congreve to Cotton, 9 Dec. 1890: FSMP, MS.Eng.lett.d.251, f.70–1, Swinny to Marvin, 22 Mar. 1891: F.H. Torlesse, *Some account of John Henry Bridges and his family* (London, 1912), pp. 209–10.
128 The is discussed at greater length in Peatling, 'British ideological movements', pp. 84–92, especially p. 90.
129 Lubenow, 'Liberals and the national question', p. 130.
130 Harrison, *Autobiographic memoirs*, ii.239, 9: *PR*, ix (1901), pp. 27–9.
131 Bridges, *Essays and addresses* (London, 1907), p. 110: Congreve, *Essays*, ii.59: Beesly, *Socialists against the grain: or, the price of holding Ireland* (London, 1887), pp. 15–16.
132 *PR*, xxx (1922), p. 28; xxviii (1920), p. 167; xxvii (1919), pp. 228, 238–9; xxv (1917), p. 239.
133 F.H. Hayward and E.M. White, *The last years of a great educationist: the work and thought of F.J. Gould from 1923 to 1938* (Bungay, n.d.), pp. 74–6.
134 Harrison, *Autobiographic memoirs*, ii.238.

CHAPTER TWO

1 'The dawn of a better era', *PR*, xxx (1922), p. 22.
2 T.W. Heyck, *The dimensions of British radicalism: the case of Ireland, 1874–95* (Urbana, Illinois, 1974), pp. 25–6, 95, 109–10.
3 R. Harrison, *Before the socialists*, p. 313.
4 See above, pp. 4–5.
5 Parry, *Democracy and religion*, pp. 238, 239–49, 445–50: E. Biagini, *Liberty, retrenchment and reform*, especially pp. 380–1: R. Harrison, *Before the socialists*, pp. 319–42, 50, 68–77, 311–13: G. Goodlad, 'Gladstone and his rivals: popular liberal perceptions of the party leadership in the political crisis of 1885–6', in E. Biagini and A. Reid (eds), *Currents of radicalism: popular radicalism, organised labour and party politics in Britain, 1850–1914* (Cambridge, 1991), pp. 163–83: A.P. Saab, *Reluctant icon: Gladstone, Bulgaria and the working class, 1856–1878* (Cambridge, Mass., 1991).
6 Parry, *Democracy and religion*, pp. 438–9: H.C.G. Matthew, *Gladstone* (Oxford, 1986–95, 2 vols), ii.211–58. See above, pp. 2–7.
7 Comte, *Discourse*, p. 26n: J.S. Mill, 'A system of logic, ratiocinative and inductive' (first published 1843), *Collected works of John Stuart Mill*, eds J.M. Robson et al (Toronto, 1963–88), vols vii–viii.
8 Wright, *Religion of humanity*, pp. 40–50: I.W. Mueller, *John Stuart Mill and French thought* (Urbana, Illinois, 1956), pp. 92–133: B. Knights, *The idea of a clerisy in the nineteenth century* (Cambridge, 1978), pp. 140–77.
9 Mill, 'Autobiography' (first published 1873), in *Collected works*, i.1–290, especially p. 221; 'Auguste Comte and Positivism' (first published 1865), in *Collected works*, x.261–368, and the response by J.H. Bridges, *The unity of Comte's life and doctrine* (London, 1866).

10 E.D. Steele, 'J.S. Mill and the Irish question: the principles of political economy, 1848–1865', 'J.S. Mill and the Irish question: reform and the integrity of the empire, 1865–1870', *Hist.Journ.*, xiii (1970), 216–36, 419–50: L. Zastoupil, 'Moral government: J.S. Mill on Ireland', *Hist.Journ.*, xxvi (1983), 707–17: B.L. Kinzer, 'J.S. Mill and Irish Land: a reassessment', *Hist.Journ.*, xxvii (1984), 111–27: B.L. Kinzer and A.P. and J.M. Robson, *A moralist in and out of parliament: John Stuart Mill at Westminster, 1865–1868* (Toronto, 1992), pp. 149–83.
11 Mill, 'England and Ireland' (first published 1868), in *Collected works*, vi.507–32, especially p. 520; Mill, 'Autobiography', pp. 279–82.
12 Mill, 'England and Ireland', pp. 521–4, 526, 530–2.
13 *Ibid.*, p. 532.
14 FHP, 1/80, f.19–24, Morley to Harrison, 6 Apr. 1873. Morley omitted Mill's acceptance of the ultimate separation of Ireland when reproducing details of this letter in the *Fortnightly Review* after Mill's death; see *FR*, xxi (1874), p. 6.
15 Wright, *Religion of humanity*, pp. 137–42: Kent, *Brains and numbers*, pp. 104–35, especially pp. xiv, 108–9: D. Hamer, *John Morley: liberal intellectual in politics* (Oxford, 1968), especially, pp. 18–31.
16 FHP, 1/60, f.48–9, Harrison to Morley, 12 Nov. 1874; 1/80, f.64–5, Morley to Harrison, 17 July 1873.
17 F. Harrison, 'Public affairs', *FR*, xxi (1874), p. 291, p. 293n: FHP, 1/58, 1/60, Harrison to Morley, 1873–4, especially 1/60, f.48–9, 12 Nov. 1874; FHP, 1/80, Morley to Harrison, 1873: F.W. Hirst (ed.), *Early life and letters of John Morley* (London, 1927, 2 vols), i.21, 72, 178–301: E.M. Everett, *The party of humanity: the 'Fortnightly Review' and its contributors, 1865–1874* (New York, 1939), pp. 74–105.
18 Morley, 'Mr Mill's autobiography', *FR*, xxi (1874), p. 11.
19 Hamer, *Intellectual in politics*, especially pp. 210–12, 281.
20 P. Fraser, *Joseph Chamberlain: radicalism and empire, 1868–1914* (London, 1966), pp. 81–2.
21 Parry, *Democracy and religion*, pp. 239–49.
22 *FR*, x (1868), pp. 234–6.
23 *PMG*, (23 Aug. 1881), p. 1: Morley, 'Conciliation with Ireland', *FR*, xxxvi (1881), pp. 2–4; Morley, 'Irish revolution and English Liberalism', *NC*, xii (1882), pp. 653–5.
24 Morley, 'Home and foreign affairs', *FR*, xxxi (1879), pp. 642–3.
25 P. Jay, *Joseph Chamberlain: a political study* (Oxford, 1981), pp. 104, 125: Matthew, *Gladstone*, ii.207: Ward, *Irish constitutional tradition*, pp. 87–9.
26 T. Moody and R. Hawkins (eds), *Florence Arnold-Forster's Irish journal* (Oxford, 1988), pp. 160, 201, 445–9, 460, 473: *PMG*, (13, 14, 17 Oct. 1881, 3 & 4 Apr. 1882), p. 1.
27 O'Callaghan, *British high politics*, especially pp. 96, 89.
28 *MG*, (3 May 1886), p. 5b–d.
29 Morley, *The life of William Ewart Gladstone* (London, 1908, 2 vols, first published 1903 in 3 vols), ii.402, n.2; 'Some arguments considered', in J. Bryce, (ed.), *Handbook of home rule* (London, 1887), p. 250.
30 Morley, 'Irish policy in the eighteenth century', *FR*, xvii (1872), pp. 196–203, especially, p. 203.

31 Lecky, *History of the rise and influence of the spirit of rationalism in Europe* (London, 1910, 2 vols in 1, first published 1865), i.vi; *A history of European morals: from Augustus to Charlemagne* (London, 1911, first published 1869).
32 Lecky, 'Ireland in the light of history', *North American Review*, clii (1891), p. 11.
33 *PR*, xix (1911), pp. 115–16: Lecky, *Rationalism*, ii.174: H. Montgomery Hyde (ed.), *A Victorian historian: private letters of W.E.H. Lecky, 1859–1878* (London, 1947), pp. 40–1, 53. For Lecky's view of Comtean Positivism, see Lecky, *Rationalism*, ii.374–5n.
34 Lecky, *History of European morals*, pp. 142–3.
35 Lecky, *Rationalism*, ii.101.
36 *Ibid.*, ii.375.
37 Lecky, *Democracy and liberty* (London, 1899, 2 vols, first published 1896), ii.92–6.
38 Lecky, *Rationalism*, ii.28–30.
39 Comte, *Discourse*, p. 18, 44.
40 Huxley, 'On the physical basis of life', *FR*, xi (1869), p. 141: Eisen, 'Huxley and the Positivists', 357, 339–42.
41 'Catholicism', *PR*, xix (1911), p. 175; 'The institutions of the Catholic Church', *PR*, xix (1911), pp. 321–8.
42 Congreve, *Essays*, ii.235.
43 'The Protestant Reformation', *PR*, xxxv (1917), p. 278: *PR*, xix (1911), pp. 1–12, pp. 341–52.
44 Lecky, *History of European morals*, pp. 148–9.
45 Lecky, *Historical and political essays* (London, 1908), pp. 43–67; *Democracy and liberty*, i.503; *A history of Ireland in the eighteenth century* (London, new ed, 1892, 5 vols), v.491.
46 Lecky, *The leaders of public opinion in Ireland* (London, 1871, first published 1861), p. xix; *Clerical influences: an essay in Irish sectarianism and English government*, eds. W. Lloyd and F. Cruise O'Brien (Dublin, 1911), pp. 51–2.
47 Lecky, *History of Ireland*, i.396–7, 371–95, 170–1; Lecky, 'Mr Froude's *English in Ireland*', *MacMillan's Magazine*, xxvii (1873), pp. 246–64, xxx (1874), pp. 166–84: Froude, *The English in Ireland in the eighteenth century* (London, 1881, 3 vols, first published 1872–4), i.453–96.
48 Lecky to Knightley Chetwoode, 21 Mar. 1866, quoted in J.P. von Arx, *Progress and pessimism: religion, politics and history in late Victorian nineteenth-century Britain* (New Haven, 1985), p. 84: Lecky, *Leaders of public opinion* (1871 ed.), pp. xix–xx.
49 Lecky, *History of Ireland*, i.402. Also see E.R. Norman, *Anti-Catholicism in Victorian England* (London, 1968).
50 On the Irish Positivists see above, pp. 28–9.
51 Peatling, 'Who fears to speak of politics?', pp. 214–16.
52 Stuchtey, *Lecky*, pp. 260–7: D. McCartney, 'Lecky's *Leaders of public opinion in Ireland*', *Ir.Hist.Stud.*, xiv (1964–5), 119–41: Lecky, 'Why I am not a home ruler', in G. Baden-Powell (ed.), *Truth about home rule*, pp. 163–87, especially p. 178 n.

53 Lecky, *History of Ireland*, iii.324; *The leaders of public opinion in Ireland* (London, new ed, 1903, 2 vols), ii.105–6; 'Why home rule is undesirable', *North American Review*, clii (1891), pp. 356–8; 'A Nationalist parliament', *NC*, xix (1886), pp. 639, 644; 'Some aspects of home rule', *CR*, lxiii (1893), pp. 635–7.
54 Quoted in von Arx, *Progress and pessimism*, p. 115.
55 See above, p. 22.
56 Swinny, *History of Ireland*, p. 17: *Bee-Hive*, (8 July 1871), p. 1: Bridges, 'From Union to Catholic emancipation', pp. 241–3, 269, 293–6.
57 Swinny, *History of Ireland*, p. 38.
58 *PR*, xix (1911), pp. 114–16: Swinny, *History of Ireland*, p. 37n.
59 See above, pp. 17–18.
60 *FR*, xvii (1872), p. 196: Smith, *Irish history and Irish character*.
61 E. Wallace, *Goldwin Smith: Victorian liberal* (Toronto, 1957), especially pp. 253–80, 27–130.
62 A. Haultain (ed.), *A selection from the correspondence of Goldwin Smith* (London, 1913), pp. 345–6.
63 Goldwin Smith to Fanny Hertz, 1 Jan. 1885, quoted *Ibid.*, p. 164. Also see *Ibid.*, pp. 151–3, 179–82, 345–6.
64 Smith, 'The administration of Ireland', *CR*, xlviii (1885), p. 8; Smith, 'The greatness of England', *CR*, xxxiv (1878), pp. 1–18.
65 Haultain (ed.), *Correspondence of Goldwin Smith*, pp. 397–8, 375–7: Smith, *Irish history and the Irish question* (Toronto, 1905), pp. 222–6
66 J.M. Robertson, *The saxon and the celt* (London, 1897), especially, pp. 266–93.
67 Smith, 'What science is saying about Ireland', Pall Mall Gazette (25 Mar. 1882) p. 2; *Dismemberment no remedy* (London, 1886), p. 22.
68 Smith, *CR*, xlviii (1885), pp. 5–7; 'What science is saying about Ireland', *PMG*, (25 Mar. 1882), p. 2: L.P. Curtis Jr., *Anglo-Saxons and Celts: a study of anti-Irish prejudice in Victorian England* (Bridgeport, Connecticut, 1968).
69 Smith, *Irish history and Irish character*; *Irish history and the Irish question*.
70 [E.L. Godkin], 'Two English writers on the Irish question', *NYN*, xxxvi (21 June 1883), pp. 524–5.
71 Bryce, 'How we became home rulers', in Bryce (ed.), *Handbook*, pp. 24–54; 'Alternative policies in Ireland', *NC*, xix (1886), pp. 312–28. On Bryce see H.A.L. Fisher, James Bryce (London, 1927, 2 vols): H. Tulloch, *James Bryce's American commonwealth: the Anglo-American background* (Woodbridge, 1988): Harvie, 'Ideology and home rule', pp. 311–12.
72 Bryce, *Committee on Irish affairs, paper no. 1: England and Ireland; an introductory statement* (London, 1884), pp. 34–5. Compare Morley, 'Irish revolution and English Liberalism', *NC*, xii (1882), pp. 657, 661.
73 Smith, *Irish history and Irish character*, p. 194: *CR*, xlviii (1885), pp. 5–7, xxxiv (1878), p. 15
74 Lord Salisbury's speech, 15 May 1886, known to posterity as the 'Hottentot' speech, quoted in Shannon, *Age of Salisbury*, p. 201.
75 K.T. Hoppen, 'Nationalist mobilisation and governmental attitudes: geography, politics and nineteenth-century Ireland', in L.W.B. Brockliss and D. Eastwood (eds), *A union of multiple identities: the British Isles, c.1750–c.1850* (Manchester, 1997), pp. 173–4: O'Callaghan, *British high politics*, pp. 153, 3–4, 11–12, 16.

76 Beesly, *Socialists against the grain*, p. 11.
77 Dunne, 'Ireland, England and the Empire', pp. 93–4.
78 FHP, 1/68, f.1–4, Harrison to Morley, 9 Jan 1889: Harrison, 'An appeal to Liberal Unionists', *CR*, liv (1888), pp. 769–82: Argyll, 'A reply to our appellant', and Harrison, 'A rejoinder to the Duke of Argyll', *CR*, lv (1889), pp. 1–23, 301–16.
79 Quoted in McCartney, *Lecky*, p. 137: R.B. O'Brien, 'The Unionist case for home rule', in Bryce (ed.), *Handbook*, pp. 154–93.
80 Bryce (ed.), *Two centuries of Irish history*, p. xxxiv
81 Bryce, 'The past and future of the Irish question', in Bryce (ed.), *Handbook*, pp. 242–3; *England and Ireland*, p. 49: Morley, 'The government of Ireland: a reply, I', 'The government of Ireland: a reply, II', *NC*, xxi (1887), pp. 19–39, 301–20, especially pp. 25, 319.
82 Gladstone to Forster, 12 Apr. 1882, quoted in Morley, *Life of Gladstone*, ii.223.
83 Dicey, *England's case*, pp. 103–10.
84 Bryce, 'Past and the future of the Irish question', pp. 217–20.
85 See above, p. 41.
86 Dicey, *England's case*, pp. 121, 138–41, 288.
87 *CR*, liv (1888), pp. 769–82.
88 *PMG*, (14 Mar. 1882), p. 1: Gladstone, 'Notes and queries on the Irish question', *NC*, xxi (1887), pp. 182–5.
89 Morley, 'The new phase of the Irish crisis', *PMG*, (17 Oct. 1881), p. 1: Bryce 'How we became home rulers', p. 45: *FR*, xxxvi (1881), pp. 24–5, 407, 418, 805–6, 125.
90 *NC*, xxi (1887), pp. 168, 176, 186: Gladstone, *The Irish question* (London, 1886), p. 40: *Hansard's Parliamentary Debates*, 3rd ser., cccvi, c.1236–40 (Gladstone, 7 June 1886).
91 *FR*, xxi (1874), p. 291, p. 293n: FHP, 1/59, f.53–6, Harrison to Morley, 29 Jan. 1874.
92 Beesly, 'Coercion in Ireland', *PR*, x (1902), pp. 226–7; *Socialists against the grain*.
93 Dicey, *England's case against home rule*, p. 287–8: on Mill see above, p. 35. On Dicey see R. Cosgrove, *The rule of law: Albert Venn Dicey, Victorian jurist* (London, 1980): H. Tulloch. 'A.V. Dicey and Ireland, 1870–1922', *The Irish Jurist*, new series, xv (1980), pp. 825–40; Harvie, 'Ideology and home rule', especially p. 301.
94 Morley, 'Some arguments considered', p. 247; *NC*, xxi (1887), p. 25.
95 Bryce, 'How we became home rulers', pp. 47, 46, 38–9, 42, 44, 45. Bryce's account in this essay of his acceptance of home rule, and that of like-minded Liberals, though retrospective, is moderately stated and worthy of consideration.
96 See above pp. 20–1, 26; Beesly, *Home rule*, pp. 7–8.
97 Harvie, 'Ideology and home rule', p. 312.
98 *Hansard*, 3rd. ser., cccvi, c.1239, 1224 (7 June 1886); ccciv, c.1081–2 (8 Apr. 1886): Matthew, *Gladstone*, ii.216, 249–50, 257: Dunne, 'Ireland, England and the Empire', pp. 30–3, 171, 209, 239–41: *NC*, xxi (1887), pp. 303–4, 306, 310–11.

99 Ward, *Irish constitutional tradition*, pp. 81–4.
100 A.V. Dicey, *Lectures on the relation between law and public opinion in England during the nineteenth century* (London, 2nd ed, 1914, first published 1905), pp. 455–7, especially p. 456; *A fool's paradise: being a constitutionalist's criticism on the Home Rule Bill of 1912* (London, 1912), p. xxxi: *NC*, xix (1886), p. 644: Dunne, 'Ireland, England and the Empire', pp. 280–1, 292–3.
101 Stuchtey, *Lecky*, pp. 220, 256–8: Lecky, 'Why I am not a home ruler', pp. 165–9, 172–3: Dicey, *England's case*, p. 6.
102 S. Evans, 'The Conservatives and the redefinition of Unionism, 1912–21', *Twentieth-century British History*, ix (1998), 2–8: D.G. Boyce, 'Federalism and the Irish question', in A. Bosco (ed.), *The federal idea* (London, 1991–2, 2 vols), i.126: A. O'Day, *Parnell and the first home rule episode, 1884–1887* (Dublin, 1986), p. 229.
103 Dicey, 'What is the state of English opinion about Ireland?', *NYN*, xxxiv (2 Feb. 1882), pp. 95–7; 'A sign of the times in England', 'Notes on the relation between home rule and English politics', *NYN*, xxxvii (12, 26 July 1883), pp. 30–1, 72–4: 'Y' [Bryce], 'Paralysis of parliamentary government', *NYN*, xxxv (13 July 1882), pp. 28–9; 'The troubles of England', *NYN*, xl (26 Feb. 1885), pp. 175–6; 'The Irish elections and the struggle in Ulster', 'England: Mr Gladstone and the Irish question', *NYN*, xlii (7, 14 Jan. 1886), pp. 8–9, 29–30; Bryce, 'England's case against home rule', *NYN*, xliv (20 Jan. 1887), p. 59: MS Bryce 2, f.64–8. Dicey to Bryce, 3 Jan. 1885: Dicey, *Fool's paradise*, pp. ix, 114–15; *England's case*, pp. 126, 137–8: Lecky, 'Why home rule is undesirable', *North American Review*, clii (1891), p. 370.
104 Quoted in Shannon, *Age of Salisbury*, p. 202.
105 Lubenow, 'Liberals and the national question', 119–42: E. Biagini, 'Introduction: citizenship, liberty and community' in Biagini (ed.), *Citizenship and community: liberals, radicals and collective identities in the British isles* (Cambridge, 1996), p. 13: Harvie, 'Ireland and the intellectuals', 36.
106 See above, p. 40–1.
107 *PR*, v (1897), p. 182.
108 *PR*, ii (1894), pp. 31–2, 36, 62–3.
109 FHP, 1/68, f.1–4, Harrison to Morley, 9 Jan. 1889: *PR*, v (1897), pp. 73–5, 157–63, 170–1.
110 FSMP, MS.Eng.lett.d.256, f.36–7, Beesly to Marvin, 2 Jan. 1905. Philip Henry Thomas (1854–1920) is perhaps best remembered as the father of the poet Edward Thomas (1878–1917): see J. Moore, *The life and letters of Edward Thomas* (London, 1939), pp. 3–23: Wright, *Religion of humanity*, pp. 243–5.
111 Wright, *Religion of humanity*, pp. 250–5: Quin, *Memoirs*.
112 Frederick James Gould (1855–1938) was a prominent educationalist, secularist and activist in Leicester local politics in the Edwardian years, but his attempt to found a Positivist Church in Leicester in 1908 rapidly failed. D.S. Nash, 'F.J. Gould and the Leicester Secular Society: a Positivist commonwealth in Edwardian politics', *Midland History*, xvi (1991), 126–40: Nash, *Secularism, art and freedom* (Leicester, 1992), especially pp. 134–5, 152–5: Gould, *The life-story of a humanist* (London, 1923): Hayward and White, *Last years of Gould*.

113 Wright, *Religion of humanity*, pp. 255–60: S. Style, *In memoriam, Albert Crompton* (Liverpool, 1908).

114 Koss (ed.), *The pro-Boers: the anatomy of an anti-war movement* (Chicago, 1973), pp. 63–6, 81, 131, 173, 210–13, xxx–xxxiv: *PR*, viii (1900), pp. 107–10, 93–4. On new Liberals' reaction to the Boer War, see below, pp. 61–3.

115 Swinny's speech to the Subject Races Congress at the Hague on 8–9 July 1907 in *PR*, xv (1907), pp. 210–11: Swinny, 'The dangers of empire', *PR*, xiii (1905), pp. 33–42: ESBP, 35–6; Annual reports of the EPC, 1905–12.

116 *The sociological society* (London, 1904): Bridges, 'Some guiding principles in the philosophy of history', in *Essays and addresses*, pp. 114–40: JKIP, D2808/54/16, 22, Swinny to Ingram, 22 June 1904, Bridges to Ingram, 24 June 1904.

117 Hobhouse and new Liberalism are discussed below, pp. 53–107, especially pp. 56–8, 102: Hobhouse, 'The law of the three stages', *SR*, i (1908), pp. 262–79: *PR*, xii (1904), pp. 283–4; xiv (1906), pp. 284–5; xvi (1908), pp. 209–12; xviii (1910), pp. 183–6: Collini, *Liberalism and sociology: L.T. Hobhouse and political argument in England, 1880–1914* (Cambridge, 1979), *passim.*, especially pp. 198–208: J.E. Owen, L.T., *Hobhouse: sociologist* (London, 1974): Collini, 'Hobhouse, Bosanquet and the State: philosophical Idealism and political argument in England, 1880–1918', *Past & Present*, no. 72 (1976), 86–111: J. Hobson and M. Ginsberg, *L.T. Hobhouse: his life and work* (London, 1931), especially pp. 103–5.

118 Hobhouse, *Sociology and philosophy* (London, 1966), p. 296: *PR*, xiv (1906), p. 180: Collini, *Liberalism and sociology*, p. 152 n.16, p. 216 n.28.

119 Swinny, 'The annual address', *PR*, xviii (1910), p. 32; 'England and Germany', *PR*, xvii (1909), p. 83.

120 Harrison, 'England and France', in Congreve (ed.), *International policy*, pp. 51–152: Congreve, et al, *Papers on the war between France and Germany* (London, 1871): FHP, 1/59, f.37–50, Harrison to Morley, 10 Feb. 1874: Comte, *Positive polity*, ii.112–16, iv.347.

121 Harrison, *The German peril* (London, 1915): Vogeler, *Harrison*, pp. 269–70, 275, 366–71: Harrison, 'The ministerial programme', *PR*, xvii (1909), pp. 57–62: FHP, 1/90, f.4–5, Morley to Harrison, 14 Mar. 1909: *DN*, (28 Dec. 1912), pp. 4b–c, 5a. Harrison's hostility to Germany and Asquithian Liberalism was echoed at this time by the most famous of his sons, Austin, editor of the *Observer* and of the *English Review*. Though not a Positivist, Austin Harrison (1873–1928), like his father, predicted war with Germany long before the beginning of the Great War. During the conflict, he advocated conscription (including in Ireland) and a relaxation of the conventions of parliamentary democracy. Later he became a critic of Lloyd George and actually stood as an independent Liberal against the Prime Minister in the December 1918 Election. See Gollin, *'Observer' and Garvin*, pp. 7, 10, 20: A.J.A. Morris, *The scaremongers: the advocacy of war and rearmament, 1896–1914* (London 1984), p. 82: *English Review*, xxii (1916), pp. 76–95, 178–86, 587–91: Vogeler, *Harrison*, p. 376.

122 *PR*, xxii (1914), pp. 193–200, 215, 231–41, 233–4, 237–8: Swinny, 'Trial and endurance', *PR*, xxiv (1916), p. 30.

123 Bridges, 'England and China', and Congreve, 'The west', in Congreve (ed.), *International policy*, pp. 431, 1–49.
124 Swinny, 'War and peace', *PR*, xxiii (1915), pp. 25–35, especially p. 30; 'Humanity and the nations', *PR*, xxv (1917), p. 32.
125 *PR*, xxiii (1915), p. 30: F.J. Gould, 'The war and the spiritual outlook', *PR*, xxiv (1916), p. 53.
126 *PR*, xxvi (1918), pp. 223–5; xxx (1922), pp. 22, 27–30.
127 *PR*, xxix (1921), pp. 193–4.
128 *PR*, xxx (1922), pp. 12, 13–15, 28.
129 Gilbert Murray papers (Bodleian Library), MS Gilbert Murray 160, *passim*. On Murray, see below p. 59.
130 F.S. Marvin (ed.), *Western races and the world* (London, 1922), pp. 9–10.
131 F.S. Marvin, *The century of hope: a sketch of western progress from 1815 to the Great War* (Oxford, 1919), pp. 271–5, especially p. 275; Marvin (ed.), *England and the world* (London, 1925), especially, pp. 269–70; Marvin (ed.), *The unity of western civilisation* (London, 2nd ed, 1922, first published 1915); Marvin (ed.), *Progress and history* (London, 1916); Marvin (ed.), *Western races and the world*. On Marvin see Wright, *Religion of humanity*, pp. 242–3.
132 FSMP, MS.Eng.lett.c.264, f.48–9, Gould to Marvin, 1 Apr. 1917: LPS papers, 1/7, EPC minutes, 12 Apr., 30 May 1923.
133 LPS papers, 1/16.

CHAPTER THREE

1 Scott to Lloyd George, 18 Jan. 1914, quoted in *Scott diary*, p. 75.
2 M. Freeden, *The new Liberalism: an ideology of social reform* (Oxford, 1978); 'The new Liberalism and its aftermath', in R. Bellamy (ed.), *Victorian liberalism*, pp. 175–92: P. Weiler, *The new Liberalism: Liberal social theory in Great Britain, 1889–1914* (New York, 1982): H.V. Emy, *Liberals, radicals and social politics, 1892–1914* (Cambridge, 1973): P.F. Clarke, *Lancashire and the new Liberalism* (Cambridge, 1971); *Liberals and social democrats* (Cambridge, 1978); 'The progressive movement in England', *Trans.Royal.Hist.Soc.*, 5th ser., xxiv (1974), pp. 159–81: D. Blaazer, *The popular front and the progressive tradition: Socialists, Liberals and the quest for unity, 1884–1939* (Cambridge, 1992): B. Gilbert, *The evolution of national insurance in Great Britain: the origins of the welfare state* (London, 1966): I. Packer, 'The Liberal cave and the 1914 Budget', *Eng.Hist.Rev.*, cxi (1996), 620–35: R. Douglas, 'Labour in decline, 1910–1914', in K.D. Brown (ed.), *Essays in anti-Labour history: responses to the rise of Labour in Britain* (London, 1974), pp. 105–25: M. Hart, 'The decline of the Liberal party in parliament and in the constituencies, 1914–1931' (Oxford University, D.Phil. thesis, 1982).
3 H. Pelling, *Popular politics and society in late Victorian Britain* (London, 1968), pp. 1–18, 101–20: R.I. McKibbin, *The evolution of the Labour party, 1910–1924* (Oxford, 1991, first published 1974): G.L. Bernstein, 'Liberalism and the progressive alliance in the constituencies, 1900–1914 – three case studies',

Hist.Journ., xxvi (1983), 617–40: D. Powell, 'The new Liberalism and the rise of Labour', *Hist.Journ.*, xxix (1986), 369–93: D.Tanner, 'The strange death of Liberal England', *Hist.Journ.*, xxxvii (1994), 971–9.

4 J. Grigg, 'Liberals on Trial', and C. Cook, 'Labour and the downfall of the Liberal party', in A. Sked and C. Cook (eds), *Crisis and controversy* (London, 1976), pp. 23–65: Tanner, *Political change and the Labour party, 1900–1918* (Cambridge, 1990): P. Thompson, *Socialists, Liberals and Labour: The struggle for London, 1885–1914* (London, 1964): M.D. Pugh, '"Yorkshire and the new Liberalism"?', *Journ.Mod.Hist.*, i (Sept. 1978), no. 3, on demand supplement, D1139–D1155: K.O. Morgan, 'The new liberalism and the challenge of labour: the Welsh experience, 1885–1929', in Brown (ed.), *Essays in anti-Labour history*, pp. 159–82: H.C.G. Matthew, R.I. McKibbin and J.A. Kay, 'The franchise factor in the rise of the Labour party', *Eng.Hist.Rev.*, xci (1976), 723–52: P.F. Clarke, 'Liberals, Labour and the franchise', *Eng.Hist.Rev.*, xcii (1977), 582–90.

5 Bentley, 'Party, doctrine and thought': Ellins, 'New Liberalism'. This literature is reviewed in Bentley, *Climax of Liberal politics*, pp. 111–27, 137–45: G. Searle, *The Liberal party: triumph and disintegration, 1886–1929* (Basingstoke, 1992), especially pp. 77–120.

6 Freeden (ed.), *Minutes of the rainbow circle, 1894–1924* (London, 1989), p. 9. Also see S. Howe, *Ireland and Empire: colonial legacies in Irish history and culture* (Oxford, 2000), pp. 73–4.

7 Jalland, *The Liberals and Ireland: the Ulster question in British politics to 1914* (Aldershot, 1993, first published 1980), pp. 30, 36–7, 13–17. The quotation from the *Nation* is from 'The government's threefold task', x (30 Dec. 1911), no. 13, p. 539.

8 Jalland, *Liberals and Ireland*, p. 56.

9 *Ibid.*, p. 264.

10 *Ibid.*, p. 267.

11 Jalland and Stubbs, 'Irish question after the outbreak of war', 778. Hamer, in *Liberal politics in the age of Gladstone and Rosebery*, pp. 309–29, and in 'The Irish question and Liberal politics', 511–32, and P. Stansky, *Ambitions and strategies: the struggle for the leadership of the Liberal party in the 1890s* (Oxford, 1964), also suggest that the commitment to home rule hampered Liberal social reform after 1886.

12 See A. Jackson, 'British Ireland: what if home rule had been enacted in 1912', in N. Ferguson (ed.), *Virtual history: alternatives and counterfactuals* (London, 1997), pp. 175–227, especially pp. 193–4.

13 Freeden, *New Liberalism*, pp. 195–250.

14 See above, pp. 7–8.

15 See above, pp. 33–46.

16 See also, Peatling, 'New Liberalism, J.L. Hammond and the Irish question, 1897–1949', *Historical Research*, lxxiii (2000), 48–65. I am grateful to *Historical Research* for permitting here a small overlap with arguments and material first published in that journal.

17 *Bee-Hive* (21 Jan. 1871), pp. 1–2: L. Atherley-Jones, 'The new Liberalism', *NC*, xxvi (1889), pp. 186–93: 'From old to new Liberalism', *Nation*, vii (20 Aug.

1907), no. 21, pp. 724–5: C.F.G. Masterman, *The new Liberalism* (London, 1920): N. Mansfield, *Failure of the left, 1919–1939: a plea for a new liberalism* (London, 1947).

18 Hobson, *The crisis of Liberalism: new issues of democracy* (Hassocks, 1974, first published 1909), p. xii: Hobhouse, *Social evolution and political theory* (Washington, 1911), pp. 167–74: Weiler, *New Liberalism*, p. 113.

19 J.S. Mill, 'On Liberty', in *Collected works*, xviii.213–310, especially pp. 228–75; *Collected works*, viii.831–52: J. Gibbins, 'J.S. Mill, liberalism and progress', in Bellamy (ed.), *Victorian liberalism*, pp. 91–109.

20 A. Vincent and R. Plant, *Philosophy, politics and citizenship: the life and thought of the British Idealists* (Oxford, 1984), pp. 90–3: Freeden, *New Liberalism*, pp. 76–116; 'Biological and evolutionary roots of the new Liberalism in England', *Political Theory*, iv (1976), 471–90; 'J.A. Hobson as new Liberal theorist: some aspects of his social thought until 1914', *Journ.Hist. Ideas*, xxxiv (1973), 421–43: Collini, 'Hobhouse, Bosanquet and the State'.

21 *DN*, (1 June 1914), p. 4e: Hobson, *Crisis*, p. 166.

22 *Ibid.*, p. 81.

23 Hobhouse, *Mind in evolution* (London, 1901): Freeden, *New Liberalism*, pp. 96–7: Hobson and Ginsberg, *Hobhouse*, pp. 112–22, 126–7.

24 Hobson, *Crisis*, pp. 81–2.

25 'Introductory', *Progressive Review*, i (1896), no. 1, p. 4, quoted in Freeden (ed.), *Rainbow Circle*, p. 9.

26 *MG*, (22 Feb. 1912), p. 4b–c: Freeden, *New Liberalism*, pp. 89–91, 103–9, 253, p. 222n: Weiler, *New Liberalism*, pp. 21–2, 153: Freeden, *Liberalism divided: a study in British political thought, 1914–1939* (Oxford, 1986), pp. 224–5, 292: Masterman, *New Liberalism*, pp. 30, 154.

27 Hobson, *Crisis*, pp. 248–55, especially p. 248: Hobhouse, *Morals in evolution: a study in comparative ethics* (London, 1951, first published 1915), pp. 266–9; *The metaphysical theory of the state* (London, 1918), pp. 112–13: B. Semmel, *Imperialism and social reform: English social-imperialist thought, 1895–1914* (London, 1960).

28 F.W. Hirst, G. Murray and J.L. Hammond, *Liberalism and the empire: three essays* (London, 1900), pp. 196–9. On the Hammonds see S.A. Weaver, *The Hammonds: a marriage in history* (Stanford, Calif., 1997).

29 'A larger Liberalism', *Nation*, xiv (20 Dec. 1913), no. 12, p. 527: 'The Irish plea of self-determination', *Nation*, xxiv (1 Feb. 1919), no. 18, p. 507: G.P. Gooch, 'Imperialism', in C.F.G. Masterman (ed.), *The heart of the empire: discussions of the problem of city life in England with an essay on imperialism* (London, 1901), pp. 308–97, especially pp. 332–4.

30 Hobhouse, *The world in conflict* (London, 1915), pp. 96–104, especially p. 104. On Hobhouse's relationship to Bridges, see above, p. 47.

31 Hobson, *Towards international government* (London, 1915): Hobhouse, *Social development: its nature and conditions* (London, 1966, first published 1924), p. 293; *World in conflict*, p. 91: D. Long, *Towards a liberal internationalism: the international theory of J.A. Hobson* (Cambridge, 1996), pp. 65–6, 183–5.

32 Masterman, *New Liberalism*, p. 32: Hirst et al, *Liberalism and empire*, pp. 167–8: Hobhouse, *Liberalism* (New York, 1964, first published 1911), pp. 57–8: J.L.

Hammond, 'Gladstone and the League of Nations mind', in *Essays in honour of Gilbert Murray* (London, 1936), pp. 95–118.

33 *DN*, (26 May 1917), p. 2c–d.

34 Masterman, *New Liberalism*, p. 32: Hobhouse, 'Democracy and nationality', *Speaker*, v (11 Jan. 1902), no. 119, pp. 415–16; Hobhouse, *World in conflict*, p. 82; *Social development*, pp. 116–19: Hobson, *Imperialism: a study* (London, 3rd ed, 1988, first published 1902), p. 185. On Masterman see E. David, 'The new liberalism of C.F.G. Masterman, 1873–1927', in Brown (ed.), *Essays in anti-labour history*, pp. 17–41

35 Hobhouse, *Questions of war and peace* (London, 1916), p. 30; *Morals in evolution*, pp. 267–8.

36 *Ibid.*, pp. xli–xliii.

37 Hobson, *Crisis*, p. 260.

38 H.N. Brailsford, *A league of nations* (London, 1917), pp. 89–131.

39 *DN*, (8 May 1912), p. 4b–c: Hobson, *Imperialism*, pp. 124–5, 141–51: Hobhouse, *Democracy and reaction* (London, 1904), pp. 144–57.

40 Hobhouse, 'The limitations of democracy', *Speaker*, v (28 Dec. 1901), no. 117, p. 360.

41 Hobhouse, *Democracy and reaction*, pp. 54–5.

42 Hobson, *Imperialism*, p. 141: Masterman, 'Realities at home', and Gooch, 'Imperialism', in Masterman, (ed.), *Heart of the empire*, pp. 3–4, 308, 396–7.

43 Hobhouse, 'The foreign policy of collectivism', *Economic Review*, ix (Apr. 1899), no. 2, p. 198.

44 Hobson and Ginsberg, *Hobhouse*, p. 269.

45 'The meaning of home rule', *Nation*, ix (27 July 1912), no. 17, p. 609: Hobson, *Crisis*, pp. 242–3.

46 Hobhouse, 'Irish nationality and Liberal principle', in J.H. Morgan, *The new Irish constitution: an exposition and some arguments* (London, 1912), p. 367; L.T. Hobhouse, *The elements of social justice* (London, 1922), pp. 45–6.

47 On Goldwin Smith see above, pp. 40–1: G.M. Trevelyan, *The life of John Bright* (London, 1913), pp. 446–61: G.P. Gooch, *The life of Lord Courtney* (London, 1920), pp. 235–61.

48 'A German Ireland', *Nation*, viii (24 Dec. 1910), no. 13, p. 527: *DN*, (10 Apr. 1912), p. 4b–c.

49 See above, pp. 20–1.

50 *CR*, cxii (1917), p. 631: Hobson and Ginsberg, *Hobhouse*, p. 326.

51 *MG*, (6 Mar. 1908), p. 6c.

52 Murray to B. Russell, 27 July 1953, quoted in J. Smith and A. J. Toynbee (eds), *Gilbert Murray: an unfinished autobiography* (London, 1960), p. 210: D. Wilson, *Gilbert Murray, OM, 1866–1957* (Oxford, 1987).

53 *Oxford University Home Rule League: list of members, 1891* (Bodleian Library): *Oxford Magazine*, v (2, 9 Feb. 1887), pp. 42, 65; vii (6, 20, 27 Feb., 6, 13 Mar. 1889), pp. 188–9, 220–1, 238–9, 255, 271–2.

54 See above, p. 54: H.W. Massingham, *The Gweedore hunt: a story of English justice in Ireland* (London, 1890): H.J. Massingham (ed.), *H.W.M.: a selection from the writings of H.W. Massingham* (London, 1925), pp. 93–4.

55 *Nation*, xxiii (29 June 1918), no. 13, p. 333.
56 On Scott see D. Ayerst, *'Guardian': biography of a newspaper* (London, 1971): J.L. Hammond, *C.P. Scott of the 'Manchester Guardian'* (London, 1934): Clarke, *Lancashire and new Liberalism*, pp. 153–96.
57 Ayerst, *'Guardian'*, pp. 204, 231–2: Lee, *Origins of the popular press*, pp. 139–40. Curiously, Jalland hardly mentions the *Guardian* in *Liberals and Ireland*.
58 Ayerst, *'Guardian'*, pp. 217–19, 240: M. Ward and C. Montague, *William Thomas Arnold* (Manchester, 1907), pp. 35–6, 44, 77–80. Arnold (1852–1904) was the nephew of Matthew Arnold and the grandson of Thomas Arnold of Rugby.
59 *MG*, (9 Apr. 1886), p.5a–b: Hammond, *Scott*, pp. 60–1, 65–8: CPSP, reel 11, 129/36–41, J.E. Taylor to Scott, 1886.
60 *C.P. Scott, 1846–1932: the making of the 'Manchester Guardian'* (London, 1946), p. 54: CPSP, reel 3, 118/64, T.P. O'Connor to Scott, 28 June 1886.
61 *MG*, (8 June 1886), p.5b–c.
62 *MG*, (8 May 1886), p.7b–d. See above, pp. 19, 44–5.
63 *MG*, (6 May 1886), p.5a–b.
64 *MG*, (15 & 19 Mar. 1886), p.5c–d: A.L. Warren, 'Gladstone, land and social reconstruction in Ireland, 1881–7', *Parliamentary History*, ii (1983), 153–73.
65 Gladstone, *The Irish question* (London, 1886), p. 45: *MG*, (1 Dec. 1886), p.5b–c. On the unpopularity of Gladstone's land reform plans, see G. Goodlad, 'The Liberal party and Gladstone's Land Purchase Bill of 1886', *Hist.Journ.*, xxxii (1989), 627–41.
66 O. Elton, *C. E. Montague: a memoir* (London, 1929), pp. 1, 3, 5–6, 135.
67 M. K. Barker, *Gladstone and radicalism: the reconstruction of liberal policy in Britain, 1885–94* (Hassocks, 1975), pp. 54–75: *Hansard*, 3rd ser., ccciv, c.1053–4 (Gladstone, 8 Apr. 1886).
68 H.J. Massingham (ed.), *H.W.M.*, p. 95: A.F. Havighurst, *Radical journalist: H.W. Massingham (1860–1924)* (Cambridge, Mass., 1974), pp. 29–32: Barker, *Gladstone and radicalism*, pp. 241–56: T.W. Heyck, 'Home rule, radicalism and the Liberal party', in A. O'Day et al, *Reactions to Irish nationalism* (London, 1987), pp. 259–84: Searle, *Triumph and disintegration*, pp. 29–48.
69 CPSP, reel 4, 120/47, Scott to Rosebery, 30 Sept. 1894.
70 See the printed copy of the resolution in HLRO, Historical Collections 192, Lloyd George papers, A/8/1/3: Clarke, *Lancashire and new Liberalism*, p. 160.
71 Havighurst, *Radical journalist*, p. 107.
72 L.T. Hobhouse, *Democracy and reaction*, p. 12: *Economic Review*, ix (1899), pp. 197–220: *Speaker*, v (11 Jan. 1902), no. 119, pp. 415–16: Hobson, 'Socialistic imperialism', *International Journal of Ethics*, xii (1900), pp. 44–58: Blaazer, *Popular front*, pp. 60–72: B. Porter, *Critics of empire: British radical attitudes to colonialism in Africa* (London, 1968), pp. 109–17: A. McBriar, *Fabian Socialism and English politics, 1884–1918* (Cambridge, 1962), pp. 120–30, 119n: 'Fabianism and the empire', *Speaker*, iii (6 Oct. 1900), no. 53, pp. 5–6: Webb, 'Lord Rosebery's escape from Houndsditch', *NC*, l (1901), p. 371: B. Shaw, *Fabianism and the empire: a manifesto* (London, 1900).
73 On Liberal Imperialism, see H.C.G. Matthew, *The Liberal imperialists: the ideas and politics of a post-Gladstonian Élite* (London, 1973): T. Boyle, 'The Liberal

imperialists, 1892–1906', *Bulletin of Instit.Hist.Research*, lii (1979), 48–82: P. Jacobsen, 'Rosebery and Liberal imperialism, 1899–1903', *Journ.Brit.Stud.*, xiii (1973–4), 83–103.

74 CPSP, reel 14, 132/124, Hobhouse to Scott, 5 Jan. 1902.

75 *Speaker*, v (8 Mar., 22 Feb. 1902), nos 127, 125, pp. 633, 577–8: H.W. McCready, 'Home rule and the Liberal party, 1899–1906', *Ir.Hist.Stud.*, xiii (1962–3), 316–48: A. Gautzke, 'Rosebery in Ireland, 1899–1903', in A. O'Day et al, *Reactions to Irish nationalism*, pp. 285–96.

76 *DN*, (22 May 1907), p. 6.

77 *DN*, (20 June 1901), p. 5d–e, (10, 13, 17, 24, 27 June 1901), pp. 5.

78 See T. Wilson's introduction, *Scott diary*, p. 30.

79 R. Koebner and H. Schmidt, *Imperialism: the story and significance of a political word, 1840–1960* (Cambridge, 1964), pp. 164–71: P. Marshall, 'The imperial factor in the Liberal decline, 1880–1885', in J. Flint and G. Williams (eds), *Perspectives of empire* (London, 1970), pp. 130–47: E. Green, *Crisis of Conservatism*, pp. 62–9. On the relationship between Unionism, Imperialism and English nationalism, see below, pp. 112–21.

80 *Speaker*, iii (2 Mar. 1901), no. 74, pp. 596–7. On Milner see below, pp. 114, 138–9.

81 *Speaker*, iii (23 Mar. 1901), no. 77, p. 663.

82 H.J. Massingham (ed.), *H.W.M.*, pp. 33–9: *Speaker*, ii (29 Sept. 1900), no. 52, pp. 687–9.

83 'The government's three-fold task', *Nation*, x (30 Dec. 1911), no. 13, p. 538: 'A happy revolution', *Nation*, vii (28 May 1910), no. 9, p. 303.

84 *DN*, (26 Nov. 1910), p. 6, (21 Nov. 1910), p. 6, (27 Apr. 1907), p. 6: Masterman, *New Liberalism*, pp. 209, 59–63, 174–6: *Nation*, i (3 Aug. 1907), no. 23, pp. 822–3; viii (24 Dec. 1910), no. 13, p. 527: G.P. Gooch, 'The nineteenth century', in Marvin (ed.), *England and the world*, pp. 132–52, especially pp. 135–6: Gooch, 'Imperialism', in Masterman (ed.), *Heart of the empire*, pp. 310–11.

85 See below, pp. 69–70.

86 'To pacify and regenerate Ireland', *Speaker*, viii (9 May 1903), no. 188, p. 133.

87 *Speaker*, ii (23 June 1900), no. 38, pp. 320–1: D. Dutton, *'His Majesty's loyal opposition': the Unionist party in opposition, 1905–1915* (Liverpool, 1992), pp. 257–60: E. Green, *Crisis of Conservatism*, pp. 71, 73, 77, 245, 249: Semmel, *Imperialism and social reform*, pp. 235–9: *Hansard*, 4th ser., clxxxviii, c.480 (Asquith , 7 May 1908); clxxii, c.1211 (Asquith, 18 Apr. 1907): *DN*, (16, 19, 23 Apr. 1907), p. 6: J.L. Hammond et al, *Towards a social policy: or, suggestions for constructive reform* (London, 1905).

88 Hirst *et al.*, *Liberalism and empire*: Koss (ed.), *The pro-Boers*, especially pp. xxx–xxxii, 81, 99: J.W. Auld, 'The Liberal pro-Boers', *Journ.Brit.Stud.*, xiv (1974–5), 78–101: Collini, *Liberalism and sociology*, pp. 83–7, 94–7. On Positivists' reaction to the Boer War see above, pp. 46–7.

89 MS Gilbert Murray 8, f.208, J. Hobson to Murray, 17 Aug. 1902: CPSP, reel 6, 120/60, Scott to Hobson, 16 July 1899.

90 Scott to Courtney, quoted in Collini, *Liberalism and sociology*, p. 81.

91 A.J.A. Morris, *Radicalism against war, 1906–14* (London, 1972): H.S. Weinroth, 'The British radicals and the balance of power, 1902–1914', *Hist.Journ.*, xiii (1970), 653–82: D. McClean, 'British radicals and the fate of Persia, 1907–1913', *Eng.Hist.Rev.*, xciii (1978), 338–53: A.J.P. Taylor, *The trouble makers: dissent over foreign policy, 1792–1939* (London, 1957), pp. 95–131.

92 Unionists certainly suggested this; see below, pp. 123, 126.

93 Hobhouse, *Liberalism*, p. 92: *DN*, (9 Sept. 1913), p. 4b–c.

94 'Persons and politics', *Speaker*, viii (9 May 1903), no. 188, pp. 139: 'A Frenchman on Ireland', *Speaker*, viii (6 June 1903), no. 192, p. 224: 'Devolution and federation', *Nation*, viii (5 Nov. 1910), no. 6, p. 222.

95 *Speaker*, viii (9 May, 4, 11 Apr. 1903), nos 188, 183–4, pp. 129, 133, 5, 38: Brailsford, *Some Irish problems* (London, 1903): *DN*, (10, 20 June 1901), p. 5: Nevinson, 'The chance in Ireland', *CR*, lxxxiii (1903), pp. 337–43.

96 MS Gilbert Murray 140, f.51–3, Hammond to Murray, 24 Nov. 1905.

97 Havighurst, *Radical journalist*, pp. 140, 143.

98 John Alfred Spender (1862–1942), editor of the *Westminster Gazette* from 1896 to 1921, was a close friend of the Liberal Imperialists Asquith and Grey, and his editorial policy before 1914 was moderate. Meanwhile, the *Daily Chronicle* became the 'accredited organ' of Lloyd George's coalition Liberals after a change of ownership in 1918: *MG*, (9 Feb. 1920), p. 6a–b: Koss, *Political press*, ii.210–11, 333–7, 10, 46–7, 55: Ellins, 'New Liberalism', pp. 162–6. On Gardiner, see Koss, *Fleet Street radical: A.G. Gardiner and the 'Daily News'* (London, 1973), especially pp. 45–8.

99 *MG*, (22 Feb. 1912), p. 4b–c, (1 July 1908), p. 6, (24 July 1914), p. 7a–b: *Nation*, xiii (24 May 1913), no. 8, p. 312: *DN*, (1 July 1912), p. 6d: Koss, *Fleet Street radical*, pp. 173–4.

100 R.B. McDowell, *Alice Stopford Green: a passionate historian* (Dublin, 1967), especially pp. 83–4: R. Dunlop, 'Truth and fiction in Irish history', *QR*, ccx (1909), pp. 254–75: *Eng.Hist.Rev.*, xxiv (1909), pp. 129–35, xxviii (1913), pp. 811–12.

101 Ayerst, *'Guardian'*, pp. 249–51, 419–29.

102 On Plunkett see below, pp. 90, 122–3, 150–1, 154: On Gwynn, pp. 122, 154: On Casement, pp. 83–5.

103 Nevinson, *Changes and chances* (London, 1923), pp. 206–15, 310–14: Hammond papers (Bodleian Library), MS Hammond 165, f.189–229; account of a visit to Ireland in Feb. 1921 by the Hammonds, Margaret Buckmaster and Desmond McCarthy: L. O'Broin, *Protestant nationalists in revolutionary Ireland: the Stopford connection* (Dublin, 1985).

104 Havighurst, *Massingham*, pp. 155–72: *Nation*, xxviii (8 Jan. 1921), no. 15, p. 525: CPSP, reel 18, 332/179–92; papers relating to a legal adjudication by Scott in favour of the Abbey Theatre, 1911: R.F. Foster, *W.B. Yeats: a life. 1: the apprentice mage, 1865–1914* (Oxford, 1997), pp. 290–3: R. Schuhard, '"An attendant lord": H.W. Nevinson's friendship with W.B. Yeats', in W. Gould (ed.), *Yeats Annual*, no. 7 (Basingstoke, 1990), 90–130.

105 For the Scott-Dillon correspondence, see Dillon papers (Trinity College Dublin Library), MS 6843/1–97. Also CPSP, reel 7, 124/109–10, Elizabeth

Dillon to Scott, 11 Nov. 1902, Scott to Elizabeth Dillon, 18 Nov. 1902; reel 8, 126/18, 54, J. Dillon to Scott, 27 Feb. 1905, J. Muldoon to Scott, 3 May 1905.

106 E.g., *DN*, (28 Nov. 1913), p. 8f, (27 Sept. 1913), p. 8e, (3 June 1914), p. 4d.

107 Lynd, *Galway of the races: selected essays*, ed. S. MacMahon (Dublin, 1990); *Ireland a nation* (London, 1919); *'Y.Y.': an anthology of essays* (London, 1933).

108 HWNP, MS.Eng.hist.c.621/3, f.73; diary, 9 Aug. 1920.

109 Havighurst, *Massingham*, p. ix.

110 *Nation*, i (15 June, 25 & 4 May 1907), nos 16, 13 & 10, pp. 585, 478, 367: *DN*, (8 May 1907), p. 6: *MG*, (8 May 1907), p. 6b.

111 *MG*, (23 May 1907), p. 6b–c: A.C. Hepburn, 'Liberal policies and Nationalist politics in Ireland, 1905–10' (University of Kent, Ph.D. thesis, 1968), pp. 312–13: *DN*, (22 May 1907), p. 6b–c: F. Eyck, *G.P. Gooch: a study in history and politics* (London, 1982), pp. 115–16.

112 *Nation*, i (22 June, 11 May, 6 Apr. 1907), nos 17, 11, 6, pp. 620–1, 404, 213–14: *DN*, (4 June 1907), p. 6.

CHAPTER FOUR

1 *PMG*, (12 Oct. 1912), p. 6.

2 Jalland, *Liberals and Ireland*, pp. 23–8.

3 Redmond papers (National Library of Ireland), MS 15,171; conversation with Campbell-Bannerman, 14 Nov. 1905: Chartwell trust papers (Churchill Archives Centre, Churchill College, Cambridge), Char.4/20, f.19–20; W.S. Churchill's responses to electoral test questions at the north-west Manchester by-election, 1908.

4 CPSP, reel 15, 132/153, Hobhouse to Scott, 20 Feb. 1910.

5 A.G., Gardiner, *The life of George Cadbury* (London, 1923), pp. 73–4: AGGP, 1/8, Cadbury to Gardiner, n.d. [1904–5].

6 F.S.L. Lyons, *The Irish parliamentary party, 1890–1910* (London, 1950), pp. 125–9: Hepburn, 'Liberal policies and Nationalist politics', pp. 729–808, *passim.*: P. Bew, *Conflict and conciliation in Ireland, 1890–1910*; *Parnellites and radical agrarians* (Oxford, 1987), pp. 192–3, 199. On O'Brien see below, pp. 78, 128–9.

7 Bew, *Ideology and the Irish question: Ulster Unionism and Irish Nationalism, 1912–1916* (Oxford, 1994), pp. 125–7: P. Bull, *Land, politics and nationalism*, pp. 169–70: *Hansard*, 5th ser., iv, c.579–82 (Redmond, 29 Apr. 1909), c.2026–134 (T. Kettle, S.L. Gwynn, Devlin, Dillon, etc., 13 May 1909), v, c.861–6, 872 (O'Connor and Healy, 24 May 1909), vi, c.302–13 (Redmond, 9 June 1909): CPSP, reel 19, 332/74–6, O'Connor to Scott, 1913–14.

8 CPSP, reel 1; diary, 4 Dec. 1916, 27 July 1914 quoted in *Scott diary*, pp. 246, 91: Dillon papers, MS 6843/16–17; Scott-Dillon correspondence, 20–2 Sept. 1912: *MG*, (19 Apr. 1910), p.8b–c: F.S.L. Lyons, *John Dillon: a biography* (London, 1968).

9 CPSP, reel 15, 132/160, Hobhouse to Scott, Mar. 1910: B. Murray, *The people's Budget, 1909–10: Lloyd George and Liberal politics* (Oxford, 1980).

10 CPSP, reel 10, 128/147, /140, /142, Scott to Churchill, 24 Feb. 1910, Scott to Grey, 8 and 13 Feb. 1910.

11 CPSP, reel 15, 132/156, Hobhouse to Scott, 24 Feb. 1910; reel 10, 128/148, Churchill to Scott, 2 Mar. 1910: Hobson, 'A new way with the Lords', *Independent Review*, vi (1905), pp. 59–62: *MG*, (15 June 1907), p. 8a–b: Hobson, *Crisis*, pp. 17–49: P. Kelvin, 'The development and use of the concept of the electoral mandate in British politics, 1867–1911' (University of London, D.Phil. thesis, 1977), especially pp. 240–5, 283–5.

12 *Nation*, ix (29 Apr. 1911), no. 5, pp. 152–3: A.K. Russell, *Liberal landslide: the General Election of 1906* (Newton Abbot, 1973), pp. 65, 74–5, 83, 92–3: N. Blewett, *The peers, the parties and the people: the general elections of 1910* (London, 1972), pp. 124–5.

13 Dillon papers, MS 6843/10–11; Scott-Dillon correspondence, 25–6 Jan. 1912: CPSP, reel 18, 332/33, Scott to Kemp, 15 Aug. 1911.

14 [Massingham], '"War on everybody"', *DN*, (24 Feb. 1913), p. 6e.

15 *Nation*, vii (23 Apr. 1910), no. 4, p. 110: *MG*, (26 Feb. 1910), p. 8b–c, (19 Apr. 1910), p. 8b–c, (17 Feb. 1910), p. 4b–c, (18 Nov. 1910), p. 8.

16 *DN*, (3 Feb. 1910), p. 4: R. Fanning, 'The Irish policy of Asquith's government and the cabinet crisis of 1910', in Cosgrove and McCartney (eds), *Studies in Irish history*, pp. 279–303: C. Weston, 'The Liberal leadership and the Lords' veto', *Hist.Journ.*, xi (1968), 508–37: Blewett, *Peers, parties and people*: Hepburn, 'Liberal policies and Nationalist politics', pp. 725–45.

17 Jalland, 'Irish home rule finance: a neglected dimension of the Irish question, 1910–1914', in O'Day, et al., *Reactions to Irish nationalism*, pp. 297–318.

18 See below, pp. 126–8: Kendle, *Ireland and the federal solution: the debate over the United Kingdom constitution, 1870–1921* (Kingston, 1989), pp. 104–76; *Federal Britain: a history* (London, 1997), pp. 67–73: Jalland, 'United Kingdom devolution, 1910–14; Political panacea or tactical diversion?', *Eng.Hist.Rev.*, xciv (1979), 757–85.

19 CPSP, reel 1; diary, 21 June 1911: *Ward, Irish constitutional tradition*, pp. 72–5.

20 'New aspects of home rule', *Nation*, x (6 Jan. 1912), no. 14, p. 574. For the problems of home rule finance see below, pp. 134, 136–7.

21 *Nation*, viii (24 Dec. 1910), no. 13, p. 527: Also see above, pp. 61–3. For Imperialists' reactions to this argument see below, pp. 130–2.

22 *DN*, (24 Apr. 1912), p. 4c: *Nation*, viii (3 Dec. 1910), no. 10, pp. 392–3.

23 *MG*, (15 Jan. 1912), p. 6c.

24 B. Williams (ed.), *Home rule problems* (London, 1911): Morgan (ed.), *New Irish Constitution*.

25 E. Childers, *The framework of home rule* (London, 1912); 'The basis of home rule, II', *DN*, (2 Feb. 1912), p. 4d–e: Erskine Childers papers (Trinity College Dublin Library), MS 7901; assorted reviews of Childers' *Framework of home rule*: J.H. Morgan, 'The constitution: a commentary', in Morgan (ed.), *New Irish Constitution*; 'The constitutional problem', in Williams (ed.), *Home rule problems*, pp. 111–26: *MG*, (14 Feb. 1912), p. 8b–c, (19 Feb. 1912), p. 9e.

26 G.A. Wells (ed.), *J.M. Robertson (1856–1933), liberal rationalist and scholar* (London, 1987), pp. 37–8: M. Page, *Britain's unknown genius: an introduction to the life-work of John MacKinnon Robertson* (London, 1984): J. Cathcart Wason,

Home rule all round versus fiscal independence, separation and tariff reform (Westminster, 1912): Kendle, *Federal Britain*, pp. 64–8, 70: Freeden (ed.), *Rainbow Circle*, pp. 125–6.

27 On Childers and Williams, see Basil Williams papers (Rhodes House Library, Oxford), MSS.Afr.s.130–5: Williams, 'How Erskine Childers worked', *Irish Times*, (6 Dec. 1941), pp. 8–9; *Erskine Childers* (London, 1925): J. Ring, *Erskine Childers* (London, 1996). On Milner's Kindergarten see below, p. 114.

28 *DN*, (2 Feb. 1912), p. 4d–e.

29 Williams, 'The exclusion or retention of Irish members in the imperial parliament', in Williams (ed.), *Home rule problems*, p. 177.

30 'Union through liberty', *Nation*, viii (17 Dec. 1910), no. 12, p. 490: *MG*, (13 Sept. 1912), p. 6b–c: J.L. Garvin papers (Harry Ransome Humanities Research Center, University of Austin at Texas), Scott to Garvin, 7 May 1914.

31 Kendle, *Federal Britain*, pp. 60–1: O'Day, *Irish home rule*, pp. 242–50. Also see below, pp. 134, 136.

32 *Nation*, xiv (29 Nov. 1913), no. 9, p. 392: Childers papers, MS 7825a; collection of pre–1914 articles by Childers: *DN*, (4 Apr. 1914), p. 6f.

33 *DN*, (1 Feb. 1912), p. 4c: 'What the Liberal party asks', *Nation*, viii (29 Oct. 1910), no. 5, p. 184: *Nation*, xi (8 June 1912), no. 10, pp. 354–9.

34 *MG*, (12 Apr. 1912), p. 8b–c, (1 May 1912), p. 8b–c: Robertson, *Saxon and celt*, pp. 1–3, 281.

35 CPSP, reel 1; diary, 3 Apr. 1917; reel 10, *passim*.

36 *DN*, (7 Jan. 1913), p. 8c.

37 Dillon papers, MS 6843/11, Dillon to Scott, 26 Jan. 1912: D. Morgan, *Suffragists and Liberals: the politics of women's suffrage in England* (Oxford, 1975), pp. 106–14.

38 Hammond, *Scott*, pp. 112–16: *MG*, (13 Mar. 1912), p. 6d–e.

39 F.M. Leventhal, *The last dissenter: H.N. Brailsford and his world* (Oxford, 1985), pp. 64–5.

40 HWNP, MS.Eng.misc.e.621/6, f.22, 618/2, f.35; diary, 25 May 1921, 14 Mar. 1914: Alice Green papers, (National Library of Ireland), MS 15,084/8, Nevinson to Green, 5 Mar. 1914. On Nevinson, see his autobiographic *Changes and chances*, especially pp. 181–2, 201–15, 310–14; *More changes and more chances* (London, 1925); *Last changes, last chances* (London, 1928): Schuhard, 'Attendant lord'.

41 HWNP, MS.Eng.misc.e.619/4, f.79–87; 620/1, f.11; diary, Aug.-Sept. 1916.

42 See E. Sharp, *Unfinished adventure: selected reminiscences from an Englishwoman's life* (London, 1933), especially pp. 204–30: M. Nevinson, *Life's fitful fever: a volume of memories* (London, 1926): A.V. John, 'Men, manners and militancy: literary men and women's suffrage', in John and C. Eustance (eds), *The men's share: masculinities, male support and women's suffrage, 1880–1920* (London, 1997), pp. 102–3. Professor Angela John is currently working on a collective biography of Evelyn Sharp and Margaret and Henry Nevinson.

43 Brailsford, 'Suffrage and the Irish vote', *DN*, (22 Jan. 1913), p. 6e: CPSP, reel 1; diary, 15–16 Jan. 1913, quoted in *Scott diary*, pp. 64–5.

44 HWNP, MS.Eng.misc.e.618/2, f.23; diary, 4 Mar. 1914.
45 B.M. Walker, 'The 1885 and 1886 General Elections: a milestone in Irish history', in P. Collins (ed.), *Nationalism and unionism: conflict in Ireland* (Belfast, 1994), pp. 1–15: Walker, *Ulster politics: the formative years, 1868–1885* (Belfast, 1989).
46 'The Irish need of home rule', *Nation*, xi (11 May 1912), no. 6, p. 202.
47 *MG*, (19 Feb. 1914), p. 8c–d: A. Mitchell, *Labour in Irish politics, 1890–1930: the Irish labour movement in an age of revolution* (Dublin, 1972), pp. 21–42.
48 'Home rule in the modern eye', *Nation*, xi (4 May 1912), no. 5, p. 148: *DN*, (9 Feb. 1912), p. 4b–c: *MG*, (12 Aug. 1912), p. 6b–c: 'The Irish situation', *Progressive Review*, i (1896), no. 1, pp. 18–19.
49 *DN*, (14 Nov. 1913), p. 8d, (22 Nov. 1913), p. 6d–e: *Nation*, xiv (8 Nov. 1913), no. 6, pp. 248–51.
50 'The curse of history', *Nation*, xi (3 Aug. 1912), no. 18, p. 656: 'The party, the Bill and the closure', *Nation*, xii (12 Oct. 1912), no. 2, p. 90.
51 *MG*, (13 Oct. 1913), p. 8c–d, (10 Oct. 1919), p. 6a-c.
52 *DN*, (17 Oct. 1913), p. 6b–c.
53 'Ways and means of settlement', *Nation*, xv (27 June 1914), no. 13, p. 476.
54 *MG*, (8 Sept. 1913), p. 6b–c: *DN*, (18 Jan. 1913), p. 4c, (10 Aug. 1912), p. 4b–c: *Nation*, ix (12 Aug. 1911), no. 20, pp. 697–8.
55 Nevinson, 'The stroke in Ireland', *Nation*, xxiii (25 May 1918), no. 8, p. 197.
56 *MG*, (11 Mar. 1914), p. 8b–c, (17 July 1913), p. 6d.
57 *DN*, (7 Dec. 1912), p. 8c.
58 *DN*, (4 Apr. 1914), p. 6d–e.
59 *DN*, (25 Feb. 1914), p. 6b–c, (19 June 1912), p. 6b–c: *MG*, (19 June 1912), p. 8c.
60 A. Jackson, *The Ulster party: Irish Unionists in the House of Commons, 1884–1911* (Oxford, 1989), pp. 6–7, 17: P. Buckland, *Irish Unionism* (Dublin, 1972–3, 2 vols): Buckland (ed.), *Irish Unionism, 1885–1923: a documentary history* (Belfast, 1973): Jackson, 'Irish Unionism', and Buckland, 'Carson, Craig and the partition of Ireland', in Collins (ed.), *Nationalism and Unionism*, pp. 35–46, 75–90.
61 *DN*, (1 Dec. 1913), p. 6b–c. On the extent to which Unionists were most interested in upsetting the Liberal government in 1912–14, and were ambivalent about Ulster exclusion, see below, pp. 134–44.
62 Hobson, *Traffic in treason: a study in political parties* (London, 1914).
63 HWNP, MS.Eng.misc.e.618/2, f.29–30; diary, 10 Mar. 1914: B. Webb, *My apprenticeship* (London, 1926), pp. 95–6.
64 *Nation*, xxvii (12 June 1920), no. 11, p. 336.
65 Nevinson, 'Carson, Smith & Co.', *Nation*, xii (5 Oct. 1912), no. 1, p. 10; 'Man of the week: Sir Edward Carson', *New Weekly*, i (18 Apr. 1914), no. 5, pp. 136–7.
66 *MG*, (17 June 1913), p. 8b–c: *DN*, (15 May 1912), p. 6b–c.
67 'The mind of Ulster', *Nation*, xi (27 Apr. 1912), no. 4, p. 120.
68 *MG*, (9 Apr. 1912), p. 4b–c: *DN*, (18 Jan. 1912), p. 4c–d.
69 *MG*, (26 Jan. 1912), p. 6b–c.
70 *MG*, (17 Jan. 1912), p. 6d.

71 For further interpretation of British attitudes to Unionist Ulster in these years see below, pp. 185–8.
72 See for instance T. Sinclair, 'The position of Ulster', in S. Rosenbaum (ed.), *Against home rule: the case for the union* (London, 1912), p. 173.
73 *MG*, (26 Sept. 1912), p. 6b–c.
74 [Childers], *Nation*, xi (7 Sept. 1912), no. 23, pp. 837–8: Lynd, *Ireland a nation*, pp. 89–91.
75 Hobhouse, 'Irish nationality and Liberal principle', pp. 369–70.
76 *MG*, (10 June 1913), p. 8c–d: *Nation*, xiii (12 July 1913), no. 15, pp. 552–3.
77 Hobhouse, *Morals in evolution*, pp. 362–3.
78 'Compromise and no compromise', 'What the government can do', *Nation*, xv (4 Apr., 13 June 1914), nos 1, 11, pp. 5, 404.
79 'Ulster for home rule', *DN*, (1 Feb. 1913), p. 1c: *DN*, (1 Oct. 1913), p. 6c, (19 May 1914), p. 6b–c, f: Casement, 'The Irishry of Ulster', *Nation*, xiv (11 Oct. 1913), no. 2, pp. 100–1. The Gladstonian Liberals of 1885–94 had also been misled by the existence of Protestant home rulers; see J. Loughlin, 'The Irish Protestant Home Rule Association and nationalist politics', *Ir.Hist.Stud.*, xxiv (1984–5), 341–60.
80 For the context of the Liberal dilemma, see E.A. Muenger, *The British military dilemma in Ireland, 1886–1914* (Kansas, 1991).
81 *DN*, (24 Mar. 1914), p. 6f.
82 Hobson, *Traffic in treason: DN*, (11 Oct. 1913), p. 6d, (10 Mar. 1914), p. 6f: *MG*, (20 May 1914), p. 7a–b.
83 *Times*, (11 Sept. 1913), pp. 7–8: *DN*, (13, 27, 16 Sept. 1913), pp. 6f, 8f, 4f: G.L. Bernstein, *Liberalism and Liberal politics in Edwardian England* (Boston, 1986), pp. 158–163. Earl Loreburn (1846–1923) had been Lord Chancellor in the Liberal government from 1905–12 before resigning through ill-health. His letter was thus taken as a semi-official statement from the government and its conciliatory spirit served as a cue for renewed efforts at settlement.
84 A.J. Lee, 'The radical press', in A.J.A. Morris (ed.), *Edwardian radicalism, 1900–1914: some aspects of British radicalism* (London, 1974), pp. 56–7: Clarke, *Liberals and social democrats*, p. 47.
85 *DN*, (16 Sept. 1912), p. 6.
86 Redmond papers, MS 15,254, Massingham to Redmond, 4, 19 Feb. [1912?]
87 *Nation*, x (27 Jan. 1912), no. 17, pp. 683–4.
88 *Nation*, xi (27 Apr. 1912), no. 4, p. 120.
89 *Nation*, xii (12 Oct. 1912), no. 2, p. 90.
90 *MG*, (15 Oct. 1912), p. 8c–d, (7 Oct. 1912), p. 8b–c.
91 Jalland, *Liberals in Ireland*, p. 57.
92 *DN*, (29 Sept. 1913), p. 6d.
93 *DN*, (24 Mar. 1914), p. 6b–c.
94 In mid-March 1914, a large number of officers at the army garrison at the Curragh just outside Dublin offered to resign rather than face the imminent prospect of involvement in military manoeuvres against the increasingly organised and powerful Unionist resistance to home rule in Ulster. Many accusations and counter-accusations between the political parties resulted.

95 Massingham, 'Order in Ulster', *DN*, (23 Mar. 1914), p. 6d. At this time, the *Daily News* was once more 'overwhelmed with letters on "The menace of militarism"'; *DN*, (27 Mar. 1914), p. 6f.
96 *Nation*, xv (23 May 1914), no. 8, p. 285.
97 Scott to Hobhouse, 19 June 1914, quoted in *Scott diary*, pp. 87–8.
98 'The great concession', *Nation*, xiv (14 Mar. 1914), no. 24, p. 988.
99 Jalland, *Liberals in Ireland*, p. 92: Ayerst, *'Guardian'*, pp. 373–8.
100 *DN*, (16 Sept. 1912), p. 6: *Nation*, xi (13 Apr. 1912), no. 2, p. 38; xv (4 Apr. 1914), no. 1, pp. 4–9: *NS*, i (7 June, 20 Sept., 4 Oct. 1913), nos 9, 24, 26, pp. 260–1, 741–2, 804–5.
101 CPSP, reel 1; diary, 23 June 1914: *DN*, (1 Dec. 1913), p. 6d.
102 On O'Brien see pp. 67–8, 128–9.
103 Michael MacDonagh papers (National Library of Ireland), MS 11439/1 and 14, Loreburn to O'Brien, 1913: CPSP, reel 19, 333/40, Loreburn to Scott, 4 Oct. 1913: *MG*, (12 Sept. 1913), p. 6b–c, (14 Nov. 1913), p. 8b–c: *DN*, (15 Sept. 1913), p. 4d.
104 *DN*, (23 Mar. 1914), p. 6d, (4 Apr. 1914), p. 6d–e.
105 AGGP, 1/26, T.P. O'Connor to Gardiner, 11 Mar. 1914: CPSP, reel 19, 333/42, /44, O'Connor to Scott, 17, 20 Oct. 1913.
106 Dillon papers, MS 6843/20–3; Dillon-Scott correspondence, 1914; CPSP, reel 1; diary, 26 Apr. 1914.
107 CPSP, reel 1; diary, 13 Apr. 1914: HWNP, MS.Eng,misc.e.618/2, f.30–1; diary, 11 Mar. 1914: *Nation*, xv (4 Apr. 1914), no. 1, pp. 4–9: *DN*, (13 July 1914), p. 4d.
108 Scott to Hobhouse, 19 June 1914, quoted in *Scott diary*, p. 88; Scott to Dillon, 9 Aug. 1914, quoted *ibid.*, p. 100.
109 CPSP, reel 19, 333/88, Hobhouse to Scott, 2 May 1914, partly quoted in *Scott diary*, p. 84.
110 See above, p. 74.
111 CPSP, reel 19, 333/127–8, O'Connor to Scott, 19, 22 Aug. 1914: *MG*, (11 Aug. 1914), p. 4b: *DN*, (9 Sept. 1914), p. 4c: *Nation*, xv (19 Sept. 1914), no. 25, p. 852: J. McEwan, 'The Liberal party and the Irish question during the First World War', *Journ.Brit.Stud.*, xii (1972–3), 110–11.
112 Jalland, *Liberals and Ireland*, p. 71.
113 *Ibid.*, pp. 68–9
114 Koss, *Asquith* (London, 1976), pp. 134–8: G. Cassar, *Asquith as war leader* (London, 1994), pp. 9, 236: J. Grigg, 'Liberals on Trial', pp. 23–37.
115 Foster, *Modern Ireland*, p. 463.
116 Massingham, 'No excuse for civil war', *DN*, (10 Mar. 1914), p. 6d: *MG*, (10, 11 Mar. 1914), pp. 8b–c: *Nation*, xiv (14 Mar. 1914), no. 24, pp. 988–9, 992.
117 See Nicholas Mansergh's review of *Liberals and Ireland* in *Ir.Hist.Stud.*, xxiii (1982–3), pp. 82–4.

CHAPTER FIVE

1 On Liberalism after 1914 see Freeden, *Liberalism divided*: M. Bentley, *Liberal mind*: Hart, 'Decline of the Liberal party', *passim.*: Searle, *Triumph and disintegration*, pp. 121–64. On the political context, see J. Turner, *British*

politics and the Great War: coalition and conflict, 1915–1918 (New Haven, 1992): K. Morgan, *Consensus and disunity: the Lloyd George coalition government* (Oxford, 1979): C. Wrigley, *Lloyd George and the challenge of Labour: the post-war coalition, 1918–1922* (New York, 1990).

2 Scott was so distressed by the outbreak of war that initially he seems to have delegated the writing of leaders on the conflict to Montague. See Inwood, 'Press in English politics', pp. 80–2.

3 MS Hammond 30, f.65, Murray to Hammond, 18 June 1915: Reginald McKenna papers (Churchill Archives Centre), McK 5/9, f.21, Massingham to McKenna, 1 Jan. 1916: Arthur Ponsonby papers (Bodleian Library), MS.Eng.hist.c.660, f.102–3, Hammond to Ponsonby, 7 Aug. 1914: John Burns papers (British Library), MS 40,503, f.63–4, Hobhouse to Burns, 6 Aug. 1914.

4 Hobhouse, *Metaphysical theory*, p. 24; *World in conflict*, p. 52–3.

5 *Ibid.*, pp. 91, 73–4: Murray, *Faith, war and policy: lectures and essays* (Boston, 1918): D.S. Birn, *The League of Nations Union, 1918–1945* (Oxford, 1981): M. Swartz, *The Union of Democratic Control in British politics during the First World War* (Oxford, 1971): S. Wallace, *War and the image of Germany: British academics, 1914–1918* (Edinburgh, 1988): J.C. Heim, 'Liberalism and the establishment of collective security in British foreign policy', *Trans.Royal Hist.Soc.*, 6th ser., v (1995), 91–110.

6 See below, pp. 145–6. On Positivists' reactions to changes in views of the relationships between states during the Great War, see above, pp. 47–8.

7 Hobhouse, *World in conflict*, p. 65.

8 *Nation*, xix (29 Apr. 1916), no. 5, pp. 120, 117, 120–1, 125, 149–50: *MG*, (26 Apr. 1916), p. 4a–b.

9 *DN*, (15 May 1916), p. 4d–e. On the Unionist response to the Rising see below, pp. 147–9.

10 Sheehy-Skeffington papers (National Library of Ireland), MS 21,651; notes on the Molesworth Hall meeting, 17 Mar. 1914: M. Ward, *Hanna Sheehy-Skeffington: a life* (Cork 1997), pp. 19–162, especially p. 33.

11 *Ibid.*, pp. 153–83: *MG*, (10 May 1916), p. 5c.

12 HWNP, MS.Eng.misc.e.619/4, f.11; diary, 9 May 1916.

13 *MG*, (12 May 1916), p. 4a–b.

14 HWNP, MS.Eng.misc.e.619/4, f.19; diary, 23 May 1916: *Nation*, xix (20, 27 May 1916), nos 8–9, pp. 207, 247–8.

15 B. Inglis, *Roger Casement* (London, 1973): Casement papers (National Library of Ireland), MS 13,073/34, 13,080(i), correspondence between Nevinson and Casement.

16 HWNP, MS.Eng.misc.e.617/3, f.11; diary, 29 Sept. 1912. Also see above, p. 64.

17 HWNP, MS.Eng.misc.e.619/4, *passim.*: Nevinson, *Last changes, last chances*, pp. 87–116.

18 Lloyd George papers, E/3/7: AGGP, 1/32, G.B. Shaw to Gardiner, 7, 13 July 1916: Casement papers, MS 13,075/10: *MG*, (30 June 1916), p. 6a–b: *DN*, (3 July 1916), p. 4f: Murray, *Faith, war and policy*, pp. 129–43.

19 *Nation*, xix (6, 13, 20 May 1916), nos 6–8, pp. 159–60, 188, 222: HWNP, MS.Eng.misc.c.497/1, f.109–10; MS.Eng.misc.e.619/4, f.13–14, 41, 50–1; diary, 13 May, 27 June, 6 July 1916.

20 *Guardian*, (29 Mar. 1994), p. 24.
21 HWNP, MS.Eng.misc.e.617/3, f.7, 621/4, f.92; diary, 21 Sept. 1912, 6–7 July 1921.
22 Nevinson, 'Sir Roger Casement and Sinn Féin: some personal notes', *Atlantic Monthly*, cxviii (Aug. 1916), pp. 236–44: Baron MacDonnell of Swinford papers (Bodleian Library), MS.Eng.hist.c.395, f.33–4, A.S. Green to MacDonnell, 14 July 1916.
23 HWNP, MS.Eng.misc.e.619/4, f.43; diary, 26 June 1916.
24 *DN*, (27 Mar. 1917), p. 2e.
25 *MG*, (5 May 1917), p. 4a–b: 'The new movement in Ireland', *Nation*, xxi (12 May 1917), no. 6, p. 132.
26 *MG*, (25 July 1916), p. 4a–b, (5 May 1917), p. 4a–b: *DN*, (1 Aug. 1916), p. 4b–c.
27 CPSP, reel 15, 132/223, Scott to Hobhouse, 16 Oct. 1916: *Nation*, xix (23 & 30 Sept. 1916), nos 26–7, pp. 781, 811–12; xx (14 Oct. 1916), no. 2, pp. 69–70. For the thoughts of some of these 'conscriptionists' see below, pp. 146, 148, 151–2.
28 'Hopes and fears in Ireland', *Nation*, xix (17 June 1916), no. 12, p. 338; *DN*, (13 June 1916), p. 4b–c.
29 Massingham, ' The violated treaty', *Nation*, xix (5 Aug. 1916), no. 19, pp. 525–6: D.W. Savage, 'The attempted home rule settlement of 1916', *Éire-Ireland*, ii (1967), no. 3, 132–45.
30 *Nation*, xx (31 Mar. 1917), no. 26, p. 837.
31 *DN*, (28 Feb. 1918), p. 2f.
32 A.S. Green, *Ourselves alone in Ulster* (London, 1918): *DN*, (26 Feb. 1918), p. 2d, (22 Mar. 1917), p. 2c–d: *Nation*, xxi (21 July 1917), no. 16, p. 392.
33 *DN*, (26 Feb. 1918), p. 2d, (14 Apr. 1917), p. 2e-f.
34 *Nation*, xxi (12 May 1917), no. 6, p. 132.
35 *DN*, (11 June 1917), p. 2d–e.
36 *MG*, (20 June 1916), p. 4a–b, (17 May 1917), p. 4a–b: *DN*, (11 July 1916), p. 4b–c.
37 Bodleian Library, MS.Eng.lett.d.310, f.232, Massingham to Curran, 17 June 1917.
38 Lloyd George papers, F/45/2/6, Scott to Lloyd George, 4 Mar. 1917.
39 CPSP, reel 15, 132/236, Scott to Hobhouse, 9 Apr. 1917: *MG*, (22 May 1916), p. 4a–b, (13 June 1916), p. 4a–b.
40 'Ireland, 1916 and beyond', *Atlantic Monthly*, cxviii (1916), p. 845: *Nation*, xix (17 June 1916), no. 12, p. 338.
41 CPSP, reels 1–2; diary 2, 6, 10, 15 May 1917.
42 CPSP, reel 2; diary 22 Feb. 1919.
43 *DN*, (17 May 1917), p. 2d–e.
44 MS.Eng.lett.d.310, f.229, Massingham to Curran, May 1917.
45 *Nation*, xxii (19 Jan., 9 Feb. 1918), nos 16, 19, pp. 507, 587–8: *MG*, (22 Jan. 1918), p. 4b: *DN*, (18 Jan. 1918), p. 2d.
46 On the Convention and its chairman Plunkett, see below, pp. 150–1: R.B. McDowell, *The Irish Convention, 1917–1918* (London, 1970): S. Lawlor, *Britain and Ireland, 1914–23* (Dublin, 1983), pp. 16–21.
47 MS.Eng.lett.d.310, f.226–36, Massingham to Curran, 1917–18. Curran's collection of cuttings on the rise of Sinn Féin survives in the uncatalogued section of the Curran collection in University College Dublin Library.

48 [Massingham], 'A London diary', *Nation*, xxi (21 July 1917), no. 16, p. 397: *Nation*, xx (17 Feb., 10 Mar. 1917), nos 20, 23, pp. 675–6, 752.
49 Scott to Hobhouse, 29 Mar. 1918, quoted in *Scott diary*, p. 341.
50 Scott to Lloyd George, 7 Apr. 1918, quoted in *Scott diary*, p. 341: *DN*, (3 Apr. 1918), p. 2d.
51 *MG*, (17 Apr. 1918), p. 4a–b: *Nation*, xxiii (25 May 1918), no. 8, p. 197.
52 *MG*, (11 Apr. 1918), p. 4a–b.
53 *Nation*, xxiii (25, 18 May, 13 Apr. 1918), nos 8, 7, 2, pp. 197, 168–9, 28, 25, 32–3: A.J. Ward, 'Lloyd George and the 1918 conscription crisis', *Hist.Journ.*, xvii (1974), 107–29.
54 *DN*, (13 Apr. 1918), p. 2e-f, (11 Apr. 1918), p. 2d–e.
55 Dillon papers, MS 6843/57, /59, Dillon to Scott, 22 Apr. 1918, Scott to Dillon, 23 Apr. 1918: Lyons, *John Dillon*, pp. 435–7.
56 Hammond, 'The catastrophe of Paris', *Nation*, xxv (7 June 1919), no. 10, p. 288: Hobson, *Problems of a new world* (London, 1921), pp. 113–14: *MG*, (15 May 1919), p. 6a–b: Hammond, *The terror in action* (London, 1921), p. 10. On new Liberalism, the Versailles Treaty and the December 1918 Election, see Hart, 'Decline of the Liberal party', pp. 73–9: Havighurst, *Radical journalist*, pp. 265–75: *Hammond, Scott*, pp. 246–66: L.B. Masterman, *C.F.G. Masterman: a biography* (London, 1939), pp. 307–13: Bentley, *Liberal mind*, pp. 46–83, especially, pp. 63–7: Morgan, *Consensus and disunity*, pp. 26–45, 192–204.
57 AGGP, 1/8, G. Cadbury to Gardiner, 30 Dec. 1918.
58 AGGP, 1/48; letters to Gardiner on his resignation: Koss, *Political press*, ii.361–2, 366, 375; *Fleet Street radical*, pp. 169, 192–4, 252–3, 262, 268–9, 290. The editorship was initially offered to Hammond on Gardiner's resignation, but Stuart Hodgson (1877–1950) was eventually appointed.
59 Blaazer, *Popular front*, pp. 101, 105–6, 108–15: Lord Oxford and Asquith papers (Bodleian Library), MS Asquith 17, f.266, Gardiner to Asquith, 20 Dec. 1916: *DN*, (19 Nov. 1918), p. 4b, (13 Dec. 1918), p. 4b, (14 Dec. 1918), p. 4e–f: *Nation*, xxiv (23 Nov. 1918), no. 8, p. 209.
60 *MG*, (11 May 1918), p. 4a–b, (24 May 1918), p. 4a–b.
61 *MG*, (8 Feb. 1919), p. 8b–c: 'The only way in Ireland', *Nation*, xxiii (18 May 1918), no. 7, p. 160: *Nation*, xxvii (3 Apr. 1920), no. 1, pp. 4–5.
62 Masterman, *New Liberalism*, p. 173: G. Bell, 'The British working-class movement and the Irish national question, 1916–1921' (University of Leeds, Ph.D. thesis, 1992), *passim.*, especially pp. 143–53.
63 CPSP, reel 15, 132/266, Scott to Hobhouse, 28 Apr. 1918: *Nation*, xxiii (18 May 1918), no. 7, p. 160.
64 AGGP, 1/26, letters from O'Connor to Gardiner, 1917–21: CPSP, reel 21, 335/42, /111, O'Connor to Scott, 27 July 1918, A. Wilson to Scott, 26 July 1919; reel 2; diary, 1 Dec. 1919. O'Connor (1872–1931) had been Solicitor-General and then Attorney-General for Ireland during the Great War, and was at this time Lord Justice of Appeal.
65 'The dominion of Ireland', *Nation*, xxv (5 July 1919), no. 14, p. 411: *DN*, (10 Oct. 1919), p. 4b.

66 *Scott diary*, p. 382, entry for 16–17 Mar 1920: H.A.L. Fisher, *An unfinished autobiography* (London, 1940), pp. 126–7, 130.
67 *MG*, (29 Mar. 1920), p. 8b–c, (8 Mar. 1920), p. 6b–c: *Nation*, xxvii (3 Apr. 1920), no. 1, pp. 4–5.
68 *MG*, (31 Mar. 1920), p. 8b–c: 'From Russia to Ireland', *Nation*, xxvi (14 Feb. 1920), no. 20, p. 660. On this Act see below, pp. 154–5.
69 *MG*, (24 Nov. 1920), p. 8b–c, (31 Mar. 1920), p. 8b–c.
70 *Nation*, xxv (9 Aug., 12 Apr. 1919), nos 19, 2, pp. 553, 39: Nevinson, 'Ireland – the one solution', *NYN*, cx (29 May 1920), pp. 715–16.
71 'Back to the pale', *Nation*, xxvi (6 Mar. 1920), no. 23, p. 764: Masterman, *New Liberalism*, pp. 179–81.
72 HWNP, MS.Eng.misc.e.621/6, f.19–20; diary, 23 May 1921.
73 *Nation*, xxvii (17 June 1920), no. 11, p. 331.
74 *MG*, (23 Aug. 1920), p. 6d.
75 HWNP, MS.Eng.misc.e.621/3, f.78–80; diary, 22–5 Aug. 1920: *Daily Herald*, (10 Sept. 1920), p. 1: *NS*, xv (11 Sept. 1920), no. 387, p. 612. For other reactions to the MacSwiney incident, see below, p. 158.
76 On Balbriggan, and government policy at this time, see C. Townshend, *The British campaign in Ireland, 1919–1921: the development of political and military policies* (London, 1975), especially pp. 113–17.
77 George F.–H. Berkeley papers (National Library of Ireland), MS 10,924; 'My experiences with the Peace with Ireland Council', ch.11.
78 *MG*, (22 Sept. 1920), p. 6c. The *New Statesman* copied this description; see xv (25 Sept. 1920), no. 389, pp. 664–5.
79 *MG*, (22 Sept. 1920), p. 6c: 'From the book of von Bissing', *Nation*, xxviii (8 Jan. 1921), no. 15, pp. 496–7.
80 *MG*, (20 Dec. 1919), p. 8c, (1 Mar. 1920), p. 8a–b.
81 Hammond, *Terror in action*, pp. 24–5, 32, 16.
82 Masterman, *New Liberalism*, pp. 170–1. For Masterman's criticism of coalition Irish policy in the *Daily News* at this time, see (8 Sept. 1920), p. 4d, (7 Oct. 1920), p. 4d, (3 Nov. 1920), p. 4d–e, (11 Apr. 1921), p. 4e, (4 May 1921), p. 4d.
83 On the Council see Berkeley papers, MS 10,920–1, 10,924–8, especially 10,924, chs 4, 6–8, 10: National Library of Ireland, MS 11,426; biographical account by Edith Stopford: D.G. Boyce, *Englishmen and Irish troubles*, pp. 64–70: MS Hammond 18, *passim.*: Sir Horace Plunkett papers (Plunkett Foundation Library, Long Hanborough, Oxfordshire); diary, 20 Oct. 1921. For examples of Hammond's work from 1920–1, see Hammond, 'A tragedy of errors', *Nation* supplement, xxviii (8 Jan. 1921), no. 15, pp. 525–32: Hammond, 'The red terror in Ireland', *DN*, (29 Sept. 1920), p. 4d–e.
84 Berkeley papers, MS 10,924, ch.10, appendix: HWNP, MS.Eng.misc.e.621/4, f.68, 74; diary, 12 Apr., 1 May 1921.
85 *MG*, (27 Oct. 1920), p. 6b–c.
86 *MG*, (30 Oct. 1920), p. 8c–d.
87 P. Gibbs' preface to H. Martin, *Ireland in insurrection: an Englishman's record of fact* (London, 1921), pp. 9–18, especially p. 9.

88 *MG*, (21 June 1920), 6c: Nevinson, 'The obvious in America', *CR*, cxviii (Sept. 1920), p. 346: E. Sharp, *Unfinished adventure*, p. 214.
89 Nevinson (ed.), *England's voice of freedom: an anthology of liberty* (London, 1929), especially pp. 5, 270–3.
90 *DN*, (8 May 1916), p. 4d–e.
91 Hammond, *Terror in action*, p. 15: Clarke, *Liberals and social democrats*, p. 124.
92 'The guilt of the government', *Nation*, xxviii (9 Oct. 1920), no. 2, p. 34.
93 MS Gilbert Murray 142, f.22–3, Barbara Hammond to Murray, 9 Mar. 1921.
94 *MG*, (31 Mar. 1921), p. 6b–c, (1 Jan. 1921), p. 6b–c.
95 *Nation*, xxviii (8, 29 Jan. 1920), nos 15, 18, pp. 525, 603–4. See below, pp. 151–2.
96 See A. Mitchell, *Revolutionary government in Ireland: Dáil Éireann, 1919–21* (Dublin, 1995): Boyce, *Englishmen and Irish troubles*, p. 101.
97 *MG*, (21 Oct. 1920), p. 6b–c, (15 Oct. 1920), p. 8b–c.
98 See below, pp. 157–8: *Nation*, xxviii (22 Jan. 1920), no. 17, p. 577.
99 Mitchell, *Revolutionary government in Ireland*, pp. 33–4, 99–119: Boyce, *Englishmen and Irish troubles*, pp. 84–8, 92–3.
100 Childers papers, MS 7815/1189, Scott to M.A. Childers, n.d.; MS 7811; diary, 1919–20, *passim.*: Childers, 'Military rule in Ireland', *DN*, (29 Mar., 7, 12, 14, 19, 27 Apr., 11, 20 May 1920), pp. 6d, 6d, 6e, 6d, 6d, 6d, 4d, 4d, republished as *Military rule in Ireland* (Dublin, 1920).
101 *Nation*, xxvii (7 Aug. 1920), no. 19, p. 578; xxix (4 June 1921), no. 10, p. 356: Nevinson in *DH*, (26 Nov. 1920), p. 1a.
102 MS Hammond 30, f.78, Murray to Hammond, 2 Jan. 1921.
103 *MG*, (31 Jan. 1921), p. 6d.
104 G.S. Messinger, *British propaganda and the state in the First World War* (Manchester, 1992), pp. 7, 255: M.L. Sanders and P.M. Taylor, *British propaganda during the First World War, 1914–18* (London, 1982), pp. 146–8, 263–4: Freeden, *Liberalism divided*, pp. 18–44: M. Grant, *Propaganda and the role of the State in inter-war Britain* (Oxford, 1994), pp. 11–12.
105 Hammond, 'Government by propaganda', *DN*, (2 Dec. 1920), p. 4e.
106 HWNP, MS.Eng.misc.e.621/3, f.80; diary, 25 Aug. 1920.
107 Hobhouse, *Social development*, p. 296.
108 Murray, *Essays and addresses* (London, 1921), p. 181.
109 'The Liberal party', *Speaker*, v (8 Mar. 1902), no. 127, p. 633.
110 MS Hammond 165, f.196–8: K. Bradby, 'What an Englishwoman saw: an appeal to her sisters', *DN*, (17 Mar. 1921), p. 4d: HWNP, MS.Eng.misc.e. 621/4, f.1–2, 621/5, f.19; diary, 6–7 Oct., 1 Dec. 1920: Martin, *Ireland in insurrection*, pp. 93–4, 117–21, 134, 137, 187–92.
111 *DN*, (3 Nov. 1920), pp. 1a-c, 3a.
112 *DN*, (5 Nov. 1920), p. 1b: *Nation*, xxviii (6 Nov. 1920), no. 6, pp. 177, 180: *NS*, xvi (13 Nov. 1920), no. 396, pp. 161–2: Boyce, *Englishmen and Irish troubles*, pp. 58–9.
113 Gardiner, 'Stop the terror', *DN*, (6 Nov. 1920), p. 4d–e.
114 CPSP, reels 1–2; diary, 2 May 1917, 22 Feb. 1919.
115 Koss, *Political press*, ii.309.

116 *MG*, (11 Oct. 1920), p. 6b–c.
117 Lloyd George to Scott, 23 July 1921, quoted in *Scott diary*, p. 394.
118 CPSP reel 16, 135/163, Scott to Lloyd George, 4 May 1921.
119 Scott to Hobhouse, 27 Oct. 1921, quoted in *Scott diary*, p. 402: [Massingham], 'A London diary', *Nation*, xxx (17 Dec. 1921), no. 12, p. 464. See also *Scott diary*, pp. 381, 389–90.

CHAPTER SIX

1 On the context of Anglo-Irish relations at this time, see J. Curran, *The birth of the Irish Free State, 1921–13* (Alabama, 1981), pp. 64–80.
2 *DN*, (15 Aug. 1921), pp. 4b, 3b-f.
3 Hammond papers, MS.Eng.c.5787, f.99, Scott to Hammond, 9 Sept. 1921.
4 Berkeley papers, MS 10,920/2, J.L. Hammond to Berkeley, 22 Sept. 1921: Hammond, 'Ireland under the truce', *Nation*, xxx (15 Oct. 1921), no. 3, p. 107.
5 MS Gilbert Murray 549, f.5–8, Barbara Hammond to Mary Murray, 5 Sept. 1921: *Nation*, xxix (27 Aug. 1921), no. 20, p. 758.
6 Lloyd George to Scott, 23 July 1921.
7 Herbert Fisher papers (Bodleian Library), MS Fisher 55, f.10–13, 14–17, Fisher to Gilbert Murray, 27 June, 21 July 1921: Lawlor, *Britain and Ireland*, pp. 70, 82–3: Townshend, *British campaign in Ireland*, p. 201.
8 *Nation*, xxiv (25 Jan., 1 Feb. 1919), nos 17–18, pp. 473–4, 514: Childers papers, MS 7812; diary, 22–3 Feb. 1921. For a collection of republican articles by Childers, see Childers papers, MS 7825b.
9 'Order and anarchy in Ireland', *Nation*, xxvii (24 Apr. 1920), no. 4, p. 102: Clarke, *Liberals and social democrats*, pp. 170, 188–9.
10 *MG*, (15 Dec. 1921), p. 6b–c, (18 July 1921), p. 6b–c.
11 *DN*, (9 Sept. 1921), p. 4b.
12 'Illusive independence', *Nation*, xxix (27 Aug. 1921), no. 22, p. 760.
13 Martin in *DN*, (18 Aug. 1921), p. 1a–b, (18 Oct. 1921), p. 3b, and in regular *Daily News* articles in July and August 1921.
14 *MG*, (26 Nov. 1921), p. 9b–c, and regularly in the *Guardian* in October and November 1921 (on Hammond's authorship of these articles, see Berkeley papers, MS 10,920/5, B.C. Waller to Berkeley, 8 Dec. 1921).
15 'The Empire and Ulster', *Nation*, xxx (12 Nov. 1921), no. 7, p. 241: *MG*, (19 Aug. 1921), p. 6b–c.
16 See *Scott diary*, pp. 394, 392–3; diary entries, 28, 15 July 1921.
17 Brailsford, 'Ireland and sea power', *DH*, (30 Aug. 1921), p. 4d–e: HWNP, MS.Eng.misc.e.621/3, f.20–1, 621/1, f.71; diary, 10 May 1920, 4 Aug. 1919.
18 HWNP, MS.Eng.misc.e.622/1, f.19; diary, 29 Aug. 1921: *DH*, (3 Nov. 1921), p. 4b (italics in the original): *NS*, xv (17 Apr., 15 May, 2 Oct. 1920), nos 366, 370, 390, pp. 32–3, 153, 689: *Nation*, xxvii (24 Apr. 1920), no. 4, pp. 102–3.
19 Bell, 'Working-class movement', p. 116: *DH*, (12 Dec. 1921), p. 4b.
20 *DN*, (22 Jan. 1919), p. 4e, (23 Aug. 1919), p. 1a–b: Martin, *Ireland in insurrection*, pp. 214–16.

21 *MG*, (7 Dec. 1921), p. 6b–c, (8 Dec. 1921), p. 6b–c: MS Hammond 4, f.55–6, J.L. Hammond to B. Hammond, n.d.
22 *Nation*, xxix (27 Aug. 1921), no. 22, p. 760.
23 Hobhouse, *Social development*, p. 258n, p. 258.
24 'Ireland a nation', *Nation*, xxx (10 Dec. 1921), no. 11, p. 425.
25 *MG*, (7 Dec. 1921), p. 6b–c, 10c.
26 *MG*, (8 Dec. 1921), p. 10a–b: Nevinson, *Last changes, last chances*, pp. 179–200, especially, p. 200.
27 *MG*, (7 Dec. 1921), p. 6b–c.
28 [Massingham], 'A London diary', *Nation*, xxx (17 Dec. 1921), no. 12, p. 464.
29 *MG*, (8 Dec. 1921), p. 6b–c: *Scott diary*, pp. 412, 403; diary entries, 5 Dec., 28 Oct. 1921: *MG*, (5 Dec. 1921), p. 6b–c
30 Childers papers, MS 7851/1305–6, Dorothy Williams to Childers, 6, 12 Dec. 1921; MS 7847/73, Berkeley to Childers, 7 Dec. 1921.
31 MS Hammond 4, f.61, J.L. Hammond to B. Hammond, 1921: *DN*, (21 Dec. 1921), p. 4b: HWNP, MS.Eng.misc.e.622/2, f.9; diary, 8 Dec. 1921.
32 'The making of the new Ireland', *Nation*, xxxi (19 Aug. 1922), no. 21, p. 677.
33 *MG*, (21 June 1922), p. 6b–c, (7 Dec. 1921), p. 7f-g, (8 Dec. 1921), p. 6b–c: *Nation*, xxx (10 Dec. 1921), no. 11, pp. 421–2.
34 Fisher, *Unfinished autobiography*, p. 132: *Nation*, xxxi (8 Apr. 1922), no. 2, p. 46.
35 MS Gilbert Murray 549, f.82–3, J.L. Hammond to Mary Murray, 4 Feb. 1933; MS Gilbert Murray 141, f.216–17, Hammond to Gilbert Murray, 27 Nov. 1948.
36 MS Hammond 18, f.199–200, B. Williams to J.L. Hammond, 7 Dec. 1922: Williams, *Erskine Childers*, pp. 31–4.
37 *DN*, (17 June 1922), p. 4b.
38 *Nation*, xxxi (3 June 1922), no. 10, p. 327: *MG*, (27 June 1922), p. 8b–c.
39 *MG*, (24 May 1922), p. 6c–d: [Massingham], 'A London diary', *Nation*, xxxi (3 June 1922), no. 10, p. 335.
40 *Nation*, xxxi (27 May 1922), no. 9, pp. 298, 295.
41 *MG*, (25 May 1922), p. 8b–c.
42 'Gilbert and Sullivan in Ireland', *Nation*, xxxi (6 May 1922), no. 6, p. 182.
43 Sharp, *Unfinished adventure*, p. 230.
44 Scott to Margot Asquith, 31 Aug. 1922, quoted in *Scott diary*, p. 412: 'A republic of Alsatia', *Nation*, xxxi (27 May 1922), no. 9, p. 298.
45 Hobhouse, *The labour movement* (London, 1894), pp. 93–4.
46 Hammond papers, MS.Eng.c.5786, f.231–3, J.L. Hammond to B. Hammond, 5 Aug. 1924.
47 *DH*, (18 Aug. 1921), p. 1a–b: HWNP, MS.Eng.misc.e.622/1, f.9; diary, 16 Aug. 1921.
48 HWNP, MS.Eng.misc.e.622/4, f.1–14; diary, 1 July 1922: *Nation*, xxxi (8 July 1922), no. 15, pp. 497–9.
49 *DN*, (14 June 1922), p. 5b.
50 'The success of Sinn Féin', *Nation*, xxx (7 Jan. 1922), no. 15, p. 553: *MG*, (9 Feb. 1922), p. 6c–d, (3 May 1912), p. 8b–c, (8 Dec. 1921), p. 6b–c.
51 Berkeley papers, MS 10,920/5, B.C. Waller to Berkeley, 16 Oct. 1922: *MG*, (22 Aug. 1924), p. 8.

52 A. Morgan, *Labour and partition: the Belfast working class, 1905–23* (London, 1991).
53 *DN*, (12 Aug. 1924), p. 4b: *MG*, (22 Feb. 1922), p. 6c.
54 'The only way in Ireland', *Nation*, xxiii (18 May 1918), no. 7, p. 160: Morley 'Some arguments considered', p. 254.
55 *Nation*, xxvi (14 Feb. 1920), no. 20, p. 660: *DN*, (17 Nov. 1920), p. 4c.
56 Collini, *Liberalism and sociology*, pp. 215–16: Soffer, 'Why do disciplines fail? The strange case of British sociology', *Eng.Hist.Rev*, xcvii (1982), 792–3. On Positivist teleology see above, pp. 30–2, 46–7.
57 MS Hammond 4, f. 217, J.L. Hammond to B. Hammond, 20 Aug. 1924: C. Townshend, 'British policy in Ireland, 1906–21', in Boyce (ed.), *Revolution in Ireland*, p. 189.
58 Massingham to Lady Gregory, 7 June 1923, cited in Havighurst, *Radical journalist*, p. 285.
59 Sharp papers, MS.Eng.lett.d.280, f.29, D. Coffey to E. Sharp, 10 Nov. 1941: Gwynn, 'Ebb and flow: a book commentary', *FR*, clxiii (1945), pp. 201–2: Bodleian Library, MS.Eng.lett.d.310, f.256, H.J. Massingham to Curran, 15 Sept. 1924: Dillon papers, MS 6843/95, Dillon to Scott, 25 Oct. 1926: MS Hammond 18, f.134, Æ to Hammond, n.d.
60 *MG*, (1, 2, 8, 16 Aug. 1924), p. 8: *DN*, (1 Aug. 1924), p. 4, (11 Aug. 1922), pp. 3a, 4b.
61 *MG*, (22 Aug. 1924), p. 8, (8 Aug. 1924), p. 8.
62 Dillon papers, MS 6843/91, Scott to Dillon, 10 Feb. 1925.
63 On the commission, see below, pp. 163–4.
64 P. Canning, *British policy towards Ireland, 1921–1941* (Oxford, 1985), pp. 226, 231–2, 315–16: *FR*, cliii (1940), pp. 114–15.
65 *MG*, (22 Aug. 1924), p. 8.
66 *Irish Independent*, (4 Jan. 1932), p. 9b.
67 *MG*, (12 May 1932), p. 8b–c, (21 May 1932), p. 10c, (20 May 1932), p. 8b–c: D. McMahon, *Republicans and imperialists: Anglo-Irish relations in the 1930s* (New Haven, 1984).
68 *News Chronicle*, (12 May 1932), p. 8b, (11 Apr. 1932), p. 5c–d, (11 May 1932), p. 8b: Koss, *Political press*, ii.447.
69 *News Chronicle*, (25 May 1932), p. 8b
70 Hobhouse to Scott, 7 Nov. 1924, in *Scott diary*, p. 468: Herbert, Viscount Gladstone papers (British Library), MS 46,476, f.95–6, Scott to Gladstone, 3 Feb. 1922: Hobson, *Democracy after the war* (London, 1917), pp. 172–3: Freeden, *Liberalism divided*, pp. 199–202.
71 D. Harkness, 'England's Irish question', in G. Peele and C. Cook (eds), *The politics of reappraisal, 1918–1939* (London, 1975), pp. 39–63, especially p. 62.
72 Dillon papers, MS 6843/96, /93, Scott to Dillon, 26 Oct., 22 Feb. 1926.
73 MS Gilbert Murray 141, f.99, Hammond to Murray, 12 Sept. 1935.
74 Hammond, *Gladstone and the Irish nation* (London, 1938), pp. 738, x.
75 *Ibid.*, p. 64. This analysis is developed in Peatling, 'New Liberalism, J.L. Hammond and the Irish question'.
76 *News Chronicle*, (25 Apr. 1938), p. 10, (24 Apr. 1938), p. 10.
77 *MG*, (17 June 1938), p. 10b–c, (6 May 1938), p. 10c.
78 N. Mansergh, *The unresolved question: the Anglo-Irish settlement and its undoing, 1912–72* (London, 1991), pp. 336–51: MS Hammond 30, f. 195, Murray to Hammond, 26 Nov. 1948:, Hammond to Murray, 27 Nov. 1948.

CHAPTER SEVEN

1 See below, pp. 133–9 (especially pp. 138–9 on Milner): J. Wrench, *Geoffrey Dawson and our times* (London, 1955), pp. 94–101: L.S. Amery, *My political life* (London, 1950–3, 3 vols), i.397–407, 436–66: Gollin, *'Observer' and Garvin*, pp. 403–5.

2 See below, pp. 126–9, 133, 139–42: J.M. Kendle, 'The Round Table movement and home rule all round', *Hist.Journ.*, xi (1968), 332–53; *Ireland and the federal solution*, pp. 104–76: A.C. May, 'The Round Table, 1910–1966' (Oxford University, D.Phil, thesis, 1995), pp. 143–50: Jalland, 'United Kingdom devolution', *passim.*: D.G. Boyce and J.O. Stubbs, 'F.S. Oliver, Lord Selborne and Federalism', *Journ.Imp. and Comm.Hist.*, v (1976–7), 53–81: Gollin, *'Observer' and Garvin*, pp. 209–27.

3 See below, pp. 153–4.

4 See below, pp. 160–3, 155–7: D. Lavin, *From empire to international commonwealth: a biography of Lionel Curtis* (Oxford, 1995), pp. 180–226: Hewins, *The apologia of an Imperialist: forty years of empire policy* (London, 1929, 2 vols), ii.206–39.

5 See below, p. 163.

6 See below, pp. 163–4.

7 Porter, *Critics of empire*: Koebner and Schmidt, *Imperialism*.

8 See above, pp. 60–2: Hobson, *Crisis*, pp. 248–60: *DN*, (16 Apr. 1907), p. 6: *Nation*, xix (1 July, 19 Aug. 1916), nos 14, 21, pp. 393–4, 638–40.

9 See above, p. 100.

10 F.S. Oliver, 'From empire to union', *NR*, liii (March 1909), special supplement, p. 16: Hewins, *Empire restored* (London, 1927), p. 118.

11 L. Curtis (ed.), *The commonwealth of nations, Part 1* (London, 1916), p. 698.

12 'Empire day', *PMG*, (24 May 1913), p. 6.

13 Oliver, 'From empire to union', p. 15: Hewins, *Empire restored*, pp. 15, 123–6.

14 Amery, *Union and strength: a series of papers on imperial questions* (London, 1912), p. 17.

15 See above, pp. 57–8: Amery, *Union and strength*, p. 20.

16 Hewins, *Trade in the balance* (London, 1924), pp. 47, 134, 47.

17 Kerr to F. Lascelles, 24 Dec. 1920, quoted in J. Turner and M. Dockrill, 'Philip Kerr at 10 Downing Street, 1916–1921', in J. Turner (ed.), *The larger idea: Lord Lothian and the problem of national sovereignty* (London, 1988), p. 61.

18 Amery (ed.), *The 'Times' history of the war in South Africa* (London, 1900–9, 7 vols), i.21–2.

19 Geoffrey Dawson papers (Bodleian Library), MS Dawson 61, f.51–62, Milner to Robinson, 14 Sept. 1907: Lord Northcliffe papers (British Library), MS 62,236A, f.6–20, Garvin to Northcliffe, 1 Dec. 1906: *Round Table studies* (London, 1910–15, two series, 7 vols), first series, i.vii–xv: W. Nimocks, *Milner's young men: the Kindergarten in Edwardian imperial affairs* (London, 1970, first published 1968), pp. 123–4: Hewins, *Apologia*, i.53–6.

20 *Round Table studies*, first series, i.250–2, 352: Curtis (ed.), *The problem of the commonwealth* (London, 1916), pp. 56–7, 103–5, 132–4, 148–57: RTP,

MS.Eng.hist.c.808, f.147–50, Curtis to Glazebrook, 3 Nov. 1914: J.L. Garvin, 'Imperial and foreign affairs', *FR*, xcii (1909), pp. 189–206.

21 Oliver, 'From empire to union', p. 17.

22 E. Green, *Crisis of Conservatism*, pp. 12–14, 27–77, 194–206.

23 Hewins, *Empire restored*, pp. 15, 83, 109–10.

24 See above, pp. 61–3.

25 C. Headlem (ed.), *The Milner papers (South Africa)* (London, 1931–3, 2 vols), ii.381–2: Lavin, *Empire to international commonwealth*, pp. 40–62: Nimocks, *Milner's young men*, pp. 17–53. On Milner see J. Marlow, *Milner, apostle of empire* (London, 1976): J. Wrench, *Alfred Lord Milner: the man of no illusions, 1854–1925* (London, 1958): T.H. O'Brien, *Milner: Viscount Milner of St James's and Cape Town, 1854–1925* (London, 1979).

26 Lavin, *Empire to international commonwealth*, pp. 63–104: Nimocks, *Milner's young men*, pp. 75–122: D.G. Boyce (ed.), *The crisis of British power: the imperial and naval papers of the second Earl of Selborne, 1895–1910* (London, 1990), pp. 198–429: D. Torrance, *The strange death of the Liberal empire: Lord Selborne in South Africa* (Liverpool, 1996), pp. 146–59, 166–78.

27 Curtis to Selborne, 18 Oct. 1907, quoted in Boyce (ed.), *Crisis of British power*, pp. 330–1.

28 For more detail see Peatling, 'The last defence of the Union? The Round Table and Ireland, 1910–1925', in A. Bosco and A. May (eds), *The Round Table, the Empire/Commonwealth, and British foreign policy* (London, 1997), pp. 283–303, especially pp. 283–4. I am grateful to the editors of this collection for their permission to summarise some arguments and material taken from this essay here.

29 Bosco and May, 'Introduction', in Bosco and May (eds), *Round Table and British foreign policy*, especially pp. iii–xv: Lavin, *Empire to international commonwealth*, pp. 100–1, 105–32: Nimocks, *Milner's young men*, pp. 123–37. On Zimmern and Coupland, see 'Zimmern, Sir Alfred Eckhard (1879–1957)', and 'Coupland, Sir Reginald (1884–1952)', in *DNB*, 1951–60: Zimmern, *Nationality and government* (London, 1918); *The League of Nations and the rule of law, 1918–1935* (London, 1936): T. Fraser, 'Sir Reginald Coupland, the Round Table and the problem of divided societies', in Bosco and May (eds), *Round Table and British foreign policy*, pp. 407–19: Sir Reginald Coupland papers (Rhodes House Library).

30 May, 'The London "moot", dominion nationalism and imperial federation', in Bosco and May (eds), *Round Table and British foreign policy*, especially pp. 226–30; 'Round Table', especially pp. 3–4, 42–8, 56–7, 88–95, 110–19: Lavin, *Empire to international commonwealth*, p. 111: Kendle, *Federal Britain*, pp. 83–90; *The Round Table movement and imperial union* (Toronto, 1977), pp. 288–9: R.H. Brand papers, (Bodleian Library), MS Brand 182, Kerr to Brand, 1 Nov. 1909.

31 May, 'Round Table', pp. 95–109: Curtis (ed.), *The commonwealth of nations, Part 1; Problem of the commonwealth.*

32 Amery, *Political life*, i.269–71, 348–50: Hewins, *Apologia*, ii.65, 109: Nimocks, *Milner's young men*, pp. 206, 210–13.

33 W.D. Rubenstein, 'The secret of Leopold Amery', *History Today*, il (Feb 1999), 17–23: Amery, *Political life*, i.21–43, 52, 61: A. Sykes, *Tariff reform in British politics, 1903–13* (Oxford, 1979), pp. 20–1, 23–4, 36: Green, *Crisis of conservatism*, pp. 59–77. On Amery also see W.R. Louis, *In the name of God, go! Leopold Amery and the British empire in the age of Churchill* (London, 1992). Deborah Lavin is currently working on a biography of Leopold Amery.

34 Oxford University Home Rule League papers (Bodleian Library); list of college secretaries, 1888.

35 R. Dahrendorf, *LSE: a history of the London School of Economics and Political Science* (Oxford, 1995), especially pp. 10–13, 63–71.

36 Hewins, *Empire restored*, p. 118; *Trade in the balance*, pp. 9–11, 71–89; *Apologia*, i.4, 37–8, 52–7: WASHP, 21, f.6–50, especially f.11–13; notes on a lecture entitled 'Ireland's interest in tariff reform', delivered by Hewins at Plunkett House, 2 Feb. 1909: Green, *Crisis of Conservatism*, especially pp. 177–80: Sykes, *Tariff reform in British politics*, pp. 127–35.

37 Hewins, *Apologia*, i.66–81.

38 On Hewins' political activities, see J.O. Stubbs, 'The Conservative party and the politics of war, 1914–16' (Oxford University, D.Phil. thesis, 1973), especially pp. 126–7.

39 WASHP, 179; diary, 1 Nov. 1912.

40 WASHP, 179; diary, 3–4 Sept. 1914.

41 E. Oldmeadow, *Francis Cardinal Bourne* (London, 1940, 2 vols).

42 WASHP, 179; diary, 1 May 1919, 3 Mar. 1913.

43 WASHP, 179; diary, 31 July 1916, 15 Nov. 1913.

44 WASHP, 179; diary, 1 Nov. 1912: Hewins, *Empire restored*, pp. 123–6.

45 WASHP, 179; diary, 28 Oct. 1913.

46 WASHP, 179; diary, 16–20 May 1912: *Hansard*, 5th ser., xliv, c.311–15 (Hewins, 31 Dec. 1912).

47 'Howard, Henry FitzAlan–, fifteenth Duke of Norfolk, 1847–1917', in *DNB*, 1911–20: 'Howard, Edmund Bernard FitzAlan–, first Viscount FitzAlan of Derwent, 1855–1947', in *DNB*, 1941–50.

48 *DN*, (11 Apr. 1921), p. 4e: D. Quinn, *Patronage and piety: the politics of English Roman Catholicism, 1850–1900* (Basingstoke, 1993), pp. 181–3.

49 Hewins, *Apologia*, ii.34–5.

50 [J.L. Garvin], 'The future of Irish politics', *FR*, lxiii (1895), pp. 685–702: D. Ayerst, *Garvin of 'The Observer'* (Beckenham, 1985), pp. 10–28: K. Garvin, *J.L. Garvin: a memoir* (London, 1948), pp. 13, 32–3. On Garvin also see J.O. Stubbs, 'Appearance and reality: a case study of the *Observer* and J.L. Garvin', in Boyce, Curran and Wingate (eds), *Newspaper History*, pp. 320–38.

51 [J.] Louis Garvin, 'Parnell and his power', *FR*, lxx (1898), p. 878.

52 AMP, MS Milner dep. 41, f.75, Garvin to Milner, 30 Mar. 1914: Garvin papers, Garvin to Scott, 25 Nov. 1913.

53 *Observer*, (21 Sept. 1913), p. 8: *PMG*, (6 July 1912), p. 6, (9 Apr. 1912), p. 6. I am grateful to Professor John Ledingham for allowing me to see a collection of Garvin's articles from the early phase of his career.

54 LM, GD40/17/456/14, Kerr to his father, 25 Mar. 1907: Amery (ed.), *'Times' history of the war in South Africa*, i.2, 12: Milner, *The Nation and the Empire: speeches and addresses* (London, 1913), p. xxxvii.

55 *Observer*, (14 May 1911), p. 10: Garvin papers, Garvin to J. St Loe Strachey, 13 Feb. 1909.
56 Garvin to Astor, 27 Dec. 1912, quoted in Gollin, *'Observer' and Garvin*, pp. 376–7: LM, GD40/17/491/2, R.M. Barrington-Ward to Curtis, 1 Oct. 1919.
57 Ayerst, *Garvin*, pp. 51–4, 235–9: Garvin, *The life of Joseph Chamberlain* (London, 1932–4), vols i–iii.
58 Gollin, *'Observer' and Garvin*, p. 15. On Austin Harrison see above, p. 207.
59 Gollin, *'Observer' and Garvin*, pp. 279–307: Koss, *Political press*, ii.147, 167.
60 There is a highly amusing caricature of Garvin in H.G. Wells' novel *The new Machiavelli* (London, 1994, first published 1911), pp. 243–4.
61 *Observer*, (20 Nov. 1910), p. 10: Gollin, *'Observer' and Garvin*, pp. 251–3.
62 See below, pp. 127–9.
63 *DN*, (15 Apr. 1912), p. 4b–c.
64 A.G. Gardiner, *Prophets, priests and kings* (London, 1908), pp. 300–7: *DN*, (29 Nov. 1910), p. 6: *Nation*, viii (19 Nov. 1910), no. 8, pp. 317, 325–6: Garvin papers, Garvin to Walter Long, 24 Nov. 1910.
65 John Satterfield Sandars papers (Bodleian Library), MS.Eng.hist.c.760, f.29–30, Garvin to Sandars, 29 Jan. 1910.
66 See Peatling, 'Who fears to speak of politics?', pp. 217–19.
67 H. Cunningham, 'The Conservative party and patriotism', in R. Colls and P. Dodd (eds), *Englishness: politics and culture, 1880–1920* (London, 1986), pp. 283–307. See above, pp. 61–2.
68 *Observer*, (22 Jan. 1911), p. 8.
69 *Observer*, (14 Mar. 1920), p. 12: Garvin, *Life of Joseph Chamberlain*, ii.413, 607–9.
70 Milner, *Nation and empire*, p. 153: John, Viscount Simon papers (Bodleian Library), MS Simon 52, f.91–3, Amery to Simon, 8 Jan. 1916.
71 May, 'Round Table', pp. 49–50, 70, 77–8: LM, GD40/17/11/16–23; memorandum of 'Kindergarten' discussions in South Africa, 1909: Maud, Countess Selborne papers (Bodleian Library), MS.Eng.lett.d.430, f.147–50, Curtis to Lady Selborne, 11 Nov. [1912?].
72 RTP, MS.Eng.hist.c.870, f.25–41, Curtis to Oliver, 18 Aug. 1910. See also Peatling, 'Last defence of the Union?', p. 284.
73 A. Bosco, 'National sovereignty and peace: Lord Lothian's federalist thought', in Turner (ed.), *Larger idea*, p. 122; A. Bosco, *Lord Lothian: un pionere del federalismo, 1882–1940* (Milan, 1989): G. Guderzo (ed.), *Lord Lothian: una vita per la pace* (Florence, 1986): J. Pinder and A. Bosco (eds), *Pacifism is not enough: collected lectures and speeches of Lord Lothian* (Philip Kerr) (London, 1990), pp. 5–36: Kendle, *Federal Britain*, especially p. 103: J.M. Brown, *Lord Lothian (Philip Kerr) 1882–1940* (London, 1955).
74 *Times*, (27 July 1925), p. 13f: Lionel Curtis papers (Bodleian Library), MS Curtis 1, f.228–32, Milner to Curtis, 1 Dec. 1908.
75 WASHP, 77, f.46–64, especially f.54; notes on Hewins' presidential address to the Birmingham Catholic Union, 31 Jan. 1921.
76 Sir Alfred Zimmern papers (Bodleian Library), MS Zimmern 17, f.158–69, Curtis to Zimmern, 30 Dec. 1922: MS Milner dep. 13, f.109–10, Oliver to Milner, 13 Jan. 1921.

77 *PMG*, (24 Apr 1913), p. 6: Garvin papers, Garvin to Balfour, 25 Oct. 1910.
78 T. Dunne, 'Ireland, England and the Empire', pp. 273–4: Matthew, *Gladstone*, ii.235: J. Loughlin, 'Chamberlain, Ulster and English nationalism', *History*, lxxvii (1992), 202–19.
79 Lavin, *Empire to international commonwealth*, p. 172.
80 *RT*, iv (Dec. 1913), p. 65: Hewins, *Empire restored*, pp. 83–5: Curtis, *Problem of the commonwealth*, p. 3.
81 Milner, *Nation and Empire*, pp. xxxviii, xxxix.
82 'Mr Gladstone's monument', *Outlook*, xvi (11 Nov. 1905), no. 406, p. 657: Milner, *Questions of the hour* (London, 1923), pp. 98–101, 119–20, 172–3.
83 'The meaning of home rule', *Nation*, xi (27 July 1912), no. 17, p. 610.
84 'The pessimism of imperialism', *Speaker*, viii (8 Aug. 1903), no. 203, pp. 473–4.
85 May, 'Round Table', pp. 143–7: Kendle, *Round Table movement*, pp. 154–5.
86 Howe, *Ireland and Empire*, p. 230.
87 Many Round Table articles have been conveniently attributed. See May, 'Round Table', especially pp. 469–86.
88 Koss, *Political press*, ii.167–9, 349–51: Wrench, *Geoffrey Dawson*, pp. 173–91: *History of the 'Times': the 150th anniversary and beyond, 1912–48*, vol IV (London, 1952), part I, pp. 370–479.
89 Inwood, 'Press in English politics', pp. 1–5: CPSP, reel 1; diary, 4 May 1914: MS Dawson 20; diary, 2 Mar. 1914: Koss, *Political press*, ii.207–8.

CHAPTER EIGHT

1 *Hansard*, 5th ser., lxii, c.1066 (12 May 1914).
2 Plunkett papers; diary entry, 18 Nov. 1912: Garvin to Milner, 30 Mar. 1914.
3 [Brand and G.L. Craik], 'Home rule', *RT*, ii (1912), pp. 422–46, especially p. 422.
4 May, 'Round Table', pp. 469–72, 454: MS Brand 2/ii, Brand to Oliver, 7 Jan. 1913; MS Brand 182, Brand to Kerr, 7 Jan. 1913.
5 [Grigg], 'The Irish question', *RT*, iv (1913), pp. 1–67.
6 MS Fisher 59, f.8–12, Kerr to Fisher, 21 May 1905.
7 [Grigg and Craik], 'The Irish crisis', *RT*, iv (1914), pp. 209–10.
8 On Gwynn see above, p. 64: Peatling, 'Last defence of the Union?', pp. 285, 290, 293. Gwynn eventually edited the collection *The anvil of war: letters between F.S. Oliver and his brother, 1914–1918* (London, 1936).
9 M. Digby, *Horace Plunkett: an Anglo-American Irishman* (Oxford, 1949): T.West, *Horace Plunkett: co-operation and politics, an Irish biography* (Gerrards Cross, 1986): Plunkett, *Ireland in the new century* (London, 1904).
10 Peatling, 'Last defence of the Union?', pp. 285–6.
11 *Times*, (10 Feb. 1914), p. 9b–c.
12 Milner, *Nation and empire*, pp. xl–xli: WASHP, 21, f.6: 'Pacificus' [Oliver], 'A constitutional conference – VII', *Times*, (2 Nov. 1910), p. 10a–c.
13 'The temptation of Sir Anthony', *Outlook*, xv (25 Feb. 1905), no. 369, p. 247.
14 Foster, *Modern Ireland*, p. 427: Gailey, 'Failure and the making of a new Ireland'; 'Unionist rhetoric and local government reform', *Ir.Hist.Stud.*, xxiv

(1984–5), 52–68; *Ireland and the death of kindness: the experience of constructive Unionism* (Cork, 1987).

15 MS Milner dep. 6, f.221–8, Milner to Goschen, 17 Oct. 1886.

16 MS Dawson 62, f.95–100; Robinson's notes, 28 Aug. 1911.

17 Garvin papers, Garvin to Balfour, 17 Oct. 1910: *Observer*, (23 Oct. 1910), p. 10, (30 Oct. 1910), p. 8.

18 'Home rule on all fours', *Outlook*, xvi (2 Dec. 1905), no. 409, p. 769: *Outlook*, xv (25 Feb. 1905), no. 369, p. 247: Lyons, 'The Irish Unionist party and the devolution crisis of 1904–5', *Ir.Hist.Stud.*, vi (1948–9), 1–22.

19 'Pollex' [Garvin], 'Ireland and sea power', *FR*, lxxxvii (1907), pp. 573–89.

20 Sandars papers, MS.Eng.hist.c.761, f.297–9, Garvin to Sandars, 31 Oct 1910: J.R. Fanning, 'The Unionist party and Ireland, 1906–10', *Ir.Hist.Stud.*, xv (1966–7), 147–71.

21 J. Barnes and D. Nicholson (eds), *The Leo Amery diaries* (London, 1980, 2 vols), i.92: *Hansard*, 5th ser., lviii, c.240–1 (11 Feb. 1914). See above, pp. 45, 112–14, 118–21.

22 Selborne and Oliver, *A method of constitutional co-operation: suggestions for the better government of the United Kingdom* (London, 1918), p. 23 n.2.

23 E. Marjoribanks and I. Colvin, *The life of Lord Carson* (London, 1932–6, 3 vols), ii.382, iii.347–9.

24 Curtis to Kerr, 19 Sept. 1910, quoted in Kendle, 'Round Table and home rule', 339: MS Brand 2(i); [Curtis], *An analysis of the system of government throughout the British Empire* (London, 1912), part 1(c), p. 48.

25 *RT*, ii (1912), p. 445.

26 Speech by Curtis in Johannesberg, 30 Oct. 1906, reproduced in Curtis, *With Milner in South Africa* (Oxford, 1951), pp. 352–3: RTP, MS.Eng.hist.c.807, f.18–19, Curtis to Grigg, 1 Oct. 1913.

27 *Times*, (3 May 1918), p. 8d, (9 Sept 1912), p. 7b–c: *PMG*, (12 July 1912), p. 6, (1 Oct. 1912), pp. 6–7: *Observer*, (11 Jan. 1914), p. 8.

28 Sinclair, 'The position of Ulster', in Rosenbaum (ed.), *Against home rule*, p. 173: G. Walker, 'Thomas Sinclair: Presbyterian Liberal Unionist', in R. English and G. Walker (eds), *Unionism in modern Ireland : new perspectives on politics and culture* (Basingstoke, 1996), pp. 19–40.

29 'Monypenny, William Flavelle (1866–1912)', in *DNB*, 1911–21.

30 MS Dawson 20; diary, 6 Jan. 1914.

31 *Times*, (16 Jan. 1914), p. 51c–d: Monypenny, *The two Irish nations* (London, 1913), p. 12.

32 *Ibid.*, pp. 68, 15.

33 *PMG*, (6 July 1912), p. 6: *Observer*, (22 Sept. 1912), p. 8: *Times*, (9 May 1912), p. 14a–b.

34 W.A. Phillips, *The revolution in Ireland,1906–23* (London, 1923), p. vii. Phillips occasionally advised Robinson on *Times* policy towards Ireland. See *History of the 'Times'*, vol. IV, part II, p. 551.

35 *Times*, (31 Jan. 1914), p. 9b–c: Amery, *The case against home rule* (London, 1912), *passim.*, especially pp. 8–9, 39.

36 HLRO, Historical Collections 191, Bonar Law papers, 25/1/33, Amery to Bonar Law, 17 Jan. 1912: J. Loughlin, *Ulster Unionism and British national identity since 1885* (London, 1995), pp. 60–1.

37 W. Rodner, 'Leaguers, Covenanters, moderates: British support for Ulster, 1913–14', *Éire-Ireland*, xvii (1982), no. 3, 68–85: J. Smith, 'Conservatives, ideology and representations of the Union with Ireland, 1885–1914', in Francis and Zweinger-Bargielowska (eds), *Conservatives and British society*, pp. 18–38: R. Murphy, 'Faction in the Conservative party and the home rule crisis', *History*, lxxi (1986), 222–34: G.D. Phillips, 'Lord Willoughby de Broke and the politics of radical toryism, 1909–1914', *Journ.Brit.Stud.*, xx (1980–1), 205–24.

38 J.D. Fair, *British interparty conferences: a study of the procedure of conciliation in British politics, 1867–1921* (New York, 1980), pp. 77–102.

39 *Times*, (2 Nov. 1910), p. 10a–c, (22 Oct. 1910), p. 10a–b.

40 Oliver, 'From empire to Union': Balfour papers (British Library), MS49861, f.1–25; memorandum by Oliver [1910]: *Times*, (20, 22, 24, 26, 28, 31 Oct., 2 Nov. 1910).

41 Garvin papers, Oliver to Garvin, 17 Oct. 1910.

42 Garvin to Balfour, 17 Oct. 1910.

43 *PMG*, (13 Mar. 1912), p. 6.

44 Garvin, 'Imperial and foreign affairs: a review of events', *FR*, xciv (1910), pp. 765–82, especially p. 768: *Observer,* (30 Jan. 1910), p. 8: Garvin papers, Garvin to Balfour, 17, 25 Oct. 1910, Garvin to Austen Chamberlain, 20, 22 Oct. 1910: Sandars papers, MS.Eng.hist.c.762, f.14–17, Garvin to Sandars, 6 Nov. 1910: West Sussex Record Office, Leo Maxse papers, vol. 462, no. R750, Garvin to Maxse, 6 Nov. 1910.

45 *MG*, (20 July 1912), p. 8c–d: *Nation*, viii (5 Nov. 1910), no. 5, pp. 221–2.

46 Northcliffe papers, MS 62,165A, f.17, Oliver to Buckle, 2 Nov. 1910.

47 *FR*, xciv (1910), p. 769.

48 *Hansard*, 5th ser., lx, c.1734 (Amery, 6 Apr. 1914): MS Milner dep.13, f.11–17, Oliver to Milner, 11 Oct. 1911.

49 MS Milner dep.13, f.47–52, Milner to Oliver, 12 Nov. 1913.

50 Lloyd George papers, F/2/1/22, Amery to Lloyd George, 29 Apr. 1918.

51 Kendle, *Federal Britain*, pp. 73, 77–8.

52 *Observer*, (2 Feb. 1913), p. 10.

53 On O'Brien see above, pp. 67–8, 80: J.V. O'Brien, *William O'Brien and the course of Irish politics, 1881–1918* (London, 1976): W. O'Brien, *The Irish revolution and how it came about* (London, 1923).

54 Amery, 'The home rule crisis and a national settlement', *QR*, ccxx (1914), pp. 266–90, especially p. 280.

55 O'Brien, *Irish revolution*, pp. 170–2: *RT,* iv (1914), pp. 204–5.

56 *PMG*, (11 Apr. 1912), p. 6: *Observer*, (23 Oct. 1910), p. 10: *RT*, iv (1913), p. 32.

57 *Observer*, (23 Oct. 1910), p. 10: *PMG*, (27 May 1912), p. 6.

58 *Observer*, (23 Oct. 1910), p. 5.

59 *Outlook*, xv (25 Feb. 1905), no. 369, p. 243: Garvin to Long, 24 Nov. 1910

60 Plunkett papers, Gar.1, Garvin to Plunkett, 1 Aug. 1910.

61 Sandars papers, MS.Eng.hist.c.760, f.29–30, Garvin to Sandars, 29 Jan 1910.

62 Northcliffe papers, MS 62,237, f.82–4, Garvin to Northcliffe, 21 Nov. 1910: A. Ward, 'Frewen's Anglo-American campaign for federalism, 1910–1921', *Ir.Hist.Stud.*, xv (1966–7), 256–75.

63 Garvin papers, Balfour to Garvin, 22 Oct. 1910, Garvin to Austen Chamberlain, 22 Oct. 1910.
64 *Observer*, (30 Oct. 1910), p. 8: Garvin to Balfour, 25 Oct. 1910.
65 MS Milner dep.13, f.3–5, Oliver to Milner, 7 Nov. 1910.
66 G.P. Taylor, 'Cecil Rhodes and the second Home Rule Bill', *Hist.Journ.*, xiv (1971), 771–81.
67 Kerr to Curtis, 30 Sept. 1910, quoted in 'The Lionel Curtis-Philip Kerr (Lord Lothian) correspondence, 1909–1940', *Lothian foundation annals*, i (1991), pp. 273–86, especially pp. 281, 280.
68 *Ibid.*, pp. 275, 279–80.
69 *Ibid.*, pp. 281, 275, 278.
70 *Ibid.*, pp. 280; Kendle, *Federal Britain*, pp. 85–8.
71 May, 'Round Table', pp. 43–4, 103.
72 'Curtis-Kerr correspondence', pp. 284, 282.
73 Oliver papers (National Library of Scotland, Edinburgh), Acc. 7726/148, [Æ] to F.S. Oliver, 24 Mar. 1917.
74 Dove to Brand, 14 Mar. 1925, cited in Brand (ed.), *The letters of John Dove* (London, 1938), p. 204.
75 Curtis (ed.), *Commonwealth of nations*, p. 519: Amery, 'Home rule and the colonial analogy', 'The economics of separation', in Rosenbaum (ed.) *Against home rule*, pp. 128–52, 282–94, especially pp. 135–6: *Times*, (8 May 1912), p. 7e–f.
76 *Professor Hewins, MP, on the Home Rule Bill* (Irish Unionist Alliance Pamphlet, no. 209) (Dublin, 1913), pp. 2–5. See below, p. 136.
77 *RT*, ii (1912), p. 429.
78 'Curtis-Kerr correspondence', p. 280: *RT*, ii (1912), pp. 445, 428–32, 429.
79 *Hewins on the Home Rule Bill*, p. 3.
80 *Times*, (13 Sept. 1912), p. 5b–c, (16 Oct. 1912), p. 7e: *Observer*, (2 Nov. 1913), p. 10: *RT*, iv (1913), pp. 29–30, 39, 61–2, 65: Oliver papers, MS 24,848, f.62–7, Milner to Oliver, 12 Oct. 1911.
81 'Home rule and the colonial analogy', especially p. 150.
82 Monypenny, *Two Irish nations*, p. 80.
83 See fig 1, p. 135.
84 *Hansard* 5th ser., xxxvii, c.1787 (30 Apr. 1912); lviii, c.237–46 (11 Feb. 1914): Bonar Law papers, 26/2/4, Garvin to Bonar Law, 2 Apr. 1912.
85 Milner to Oliver, 12 Oct. 1911. See below, pp. 138–9.
86 Sandars papers, MS.Eng.hist.c.762, f.21, Garvin to Sandars, 9 Nov. 1910: Dutton, *'His Majesty's loyal opposition'*, p. 103.
87 Northcliffe papers, MS 62,237, f.70, Garvin to Northclifffe, 3 Nov. 1910: *Observer*, (21 May 1911), p. 10.
88 *Observer*, (11 Jan. 1914), p. 8: *PMG*, (2 Apr. 1914), p. 3. See above, p. 129.
89 *PMG*, (29 Oct. 1913), p. 6, (16 Oct. 1913), p. 6.
90 *Observer*, (27 Oct. 1912), p. 12: Amery, 'The home rule crisis and a national settlement', 'The home rule crisis', *QR*, ccxx (1914), pp. 266–90, 570–90, 'The home rule crisis', *QR*, ccxxi (1914), pp. 275–94: Bonar Law papers, 32/2/68, 32/3/25, Amery to Bonar Law, 30 Apr. 1914, 13 May 1914.
91 *Observer*, (16 June 1912), p. 8.

92 *Observer*, (10 May 1914), p. 10, (8 June 1913), p. 10, (24 Nov. 1912), p. 10, (14 July 1912), p. 10, (22 Sept. 1912), p. 8.
93 *MG*, (30 Sept. 1912), p. 6b–c.
94 *Atlantic Monthly*, cxviii (1916), p. 239.
95 *Hewins on the Home Rule Bill*, p. 7.
96 Jalland, 'Home rule finance': *PMG*, (8 Feb. 1912), p. 6: Hewins, *Apologia*, ii.230, i.292–3.
97 *Times*, (31 Oct. 1910), p. 9a–c: *PMG*, (31 Jan., 8 May 1912), p. 6.
98 B. Webb, *Our partnership*, ed. by B. Drake and M.I. Cole (London, 1948), pp. 328–9: Amery, 'The economics of separation', p. 288.
99 *Hansard*, 5th ser., xxxvii, c.1779 (Amery, 30 Apr. 1912); lx, c.1472–9 (W. Astor, 2 Apr. 1914): *Times*, (30 Apr. 1912), p. 7a-d, (18 Apr. 1912) p. 14f: Amery, 'The economics of separation', pp. 282–94: Hewins, *Tariff reform and home rule* (London, 1912), p. 8.
100 *Ibid.*, p. 15: *Hewins on the Home Rule Bill*, p. 4.
101 *Hansard*, 5th ser., xlii, c.1528, (Amery, 17 Oct. 1912), c.2260 (Hewins, 23 Oct. 1912).
102 'Home rule on all fours', *Outlook*, xvi (2 Dec. 1905), no. 409, p. 769.
103 WASHP, 21, f.23: Amery to Bonar Law, 18 Jan. 1913, quoted in Sykes, *Tariff reform and British politics*, p. 290.
104 *Hansard*, 5th ser., xliv, c. 941–6, 1093–1100 (Hewins, 25–6 Nov. 1912); xxxvii, c.1773–4 (Amery, 22 Apr. 1912): Hewins' preface to A.E. Murray, *A history of the commercial relations between England and Ireland from the period of the Restoration* (London, 1903), p. vii: Amery, *Case against home rule*, pp. 40–5, 52–8; 'Home rule and the colonial analogy' p. 152; 'The economics of separation', pp. 282, 285.
105 *QR*, ccxx (1914), pp. 283–90: *Hewins on the Home Rule Bill*, p. 2.
106 B. Girvin, *Between two worlds: politics and economy in independent Ireland* (Dublin, 1989).
107 WASHP, 21, f.47, 46.
108 See above, pp. 67–8.
109 Sykes, *Tariff reform in British politics*, pp. 258–84, especially pp. 271–5.
110 Hewins, *Apologia*, i.294–9: Amery to A. Chamberlain, 27 Dec. 1912, quoted in Barnes and Nicholson (eds), *Amery diaries*, i.88.
111 Waldorf, Viscount Astor papers (Reading University Library), MS 1066/1/1200, Garvin to Waldorf Astor, 19 Dec. 1912: Gollin, *'Observer' and Garvin*, pp. 272–85.
112 *MG*, (17 Jan. 1913), p. 8b–c: *DN*, (17 Jan. 1913), p. 6b–c.
113 See above, p. 124.
114 Oliver papers, MS 24,848, f.55–6, Oliver to Robinson, 27 Aug. 1911: *RT*, ii (1912), pp. 332–5, 704–6.
115 J. Smith, 'Bluff, Bluster and Brinkmanship: Andrew Bonar Law and the third Home Rule Bill', *Hist.Journ.*, xxxvi (1993), 161–78: A.T.Q. Stewart, *The Ulster crisis* (London, 1967).
116 MS Dawson 61, f.51–62, Milner to Robinson, 14 Sept. 1907.
117 Milner, *Nation and Empire*, especially pp. xxxvii, 279.

118 Milner to Robinson, 14 Sept. 1907.
119 MS Milner dep.40, f.204–5, Milner to Carson, 9 Dec. 1913.
120 Lord Craigavon papers (Public Record Office of Northern Ireland), T/3775/11/1, Amery to Mrs Mary Craig, 17 May 1914.
121 *Times*, (3 Mar. 1914), p. 7: MS Milner dep.85; diary, 2 Mar 1914: Amery, *Political life*, i.440–2: Marlow, *Apostle of empire*, pp. 218–35: A.M. Gollin, *Proconsul in politics: a study of Lord Milner in opposition and in power* (Letchworth 1960), pp. 171–220: N.C. Hamilton, 'Lord Milner and the Ulster crisis, 1912–14' (University of Kent, M.A. thesis, 1972).
122 The *Covenanter*, no. 1, (20 May 1914).
123 Peatling, 'Last defence of the Union?', pp. 288–9.
124 MS Milner dep.157, f.120–9; memorandum by Amery, May 1914.
125 *QR*, ccxx (1914), p. 279.
126 MS Milner dep.36, f.28–34, Amery to Milner, 5 July 1909: MS Curtis 2, f.1, Curtis to his mother, 1 Jan. 1910.
127 Milner to Oliver, 12 Oct. 1911: Peatling, 'Last defence of the Union?', pp. 289–90.
128 [Grigg], 'The Irish question', [Grigg and Craik], 'The Irish crisis', *RT*, iv (1913–14), pp. 1–67, 201–30.
129 *RT*, iv (1913–14), pp. 7–11, 44, 206–8, 228–9: Peatling, 'Last defence of the Union?', pp. 288–9.
130 *RT*, iv (1914), p. 216. Plunkett, visiting Cliveden (home of the Astor family) in February 1914, found Garvin and some of the moot 'all hopeless about the Unionist (some also the Liberal) party activities'; Plunkett papers; diary, 14–15 Feb. 1914.
131 *RT*, iv (1913–14), pp. 13–17, 32, 62, 209–11.
132 *RT*, iv (1913), pp. 58–62: RTP, MS.Eng.hist.c.790, f.12–13, Spender to Grigg, 11 Dec. 1913. Amery considered a similar plan; *QR*, ccxx (1914), pp. 266–90: Milner papers, MS.Eng.hist.c.689, f.248–55; memorandum by Amery, 22 June 1914.
133 *RT*, iv (1914), pp. 225, 224, 230: RTP, MS.Eng.hist.c.790, f.46–7, Spender to Grigg, 2 Apr. 1914: Oliver papers, MS 24,851, f.103–6, 133–4, Craik to Oliver, 23 Mar., 16 Apr. 1914.
134 *RT*, iv (1913), pp. 1, 43, 45–6, 49.
135 RTP, MS.Eng.hist.c.823, f.143, Grigg to Curtis, 24 Mar. 1914.
136 *Hewins on the Home Rule Bill*, p. 7.
137 WASHP, 179; diary, 10 Apr. 1912. In the event, Amery's essay 'The economics of separation' (Rosenbaum (ed.) *Against home rule*, pp. 282–94) probably differed little from any Hewins would have contributed.
138 WASHP, 179; diary, 7 May 1913.
139 WASHP, 179; diary, 27 May 1913.
140 *Times*, (15 Nov. 1913), pp. 16c, 15c, (30 Sept. 1913), p. 8b.
141 WASHP, 179; diary, 6, 15 Nov. 1913.
142 WASHP, 179; diary, 4, 30 Apr. 1914.
143 Hewins, *Apologia*, i.285: WASHP, 179; diary, 3 Jan. 1912.
144 WASHP, 179; diary, 27 Nov., 2 Dec. 1912.

145 WASHP, 179; diary, 28 Oct. 1913, 1 Oct. 1912.
146 WASHP, 179; diary, 26 Mar. 1914.
147 WASHP, 179; diary, 26 Sept. 1913, 9 Mar. 1914.
148 Amery, *A plot against Ulster: a lecture* (London, 1914): Oliver papers, Acc. 7726/147, v & vi, *passim.*: *Hansard*, 5th ser., lx, c.244–50 (Amery, 24 Mar. 1914); lxi, c.464–8 (Amery, 16 Apr. 1914). On the Curragh incident, see above, p. 219.
149 WASHP, 179; diary, 30 Apr., 28 Mar. 1914.
150 WASHP, 179; diary, 23 July 1912.
151 WASHP, 179; diary, 9 Mar. 1914: Hewins, *Apologia*, i.285–312.
152 *Times*, (1 May 1914), p. 9b–c.
153 Oliver, *Alternatives to civil war* (London, 1913), pp. 37, 36.
154 *PMG*, (25 Feb. 1914), p. 3, (1 Oct. 1913), p. 6: *Times*, (30 Apr. 1914), p. 9b–c.
155 *Observer*, (5 Apr. 1914), p. 12: Oliver papers, MS 24,851, f.30–1, Garvin to Oliver, 12 Feb. 1914: Garvin to Scott, 25 Nov. 1913.
156 Curtis to Feetham, 24 June 1914, quoted in Kendle, 'Round Table and home rule', 353.
157 AMP, MS.Eng.hist.c.689, f.228–33; Round Table memorandum, 24 Apr. 1914: MS Asquith 39, f.167–71, Redmond to Asquith, 5 May 1914: Kendle 'Round Table and home rule', pp. 349–52: Nancy, Lady Astor papers, (Reading University Library), 1416/1/4/47, Kerr to Nancy Astor, 7, 16 May 1914: Lloyd George papers, C/4/15/1–2, Grigg to Lloyd George, 25 Apr., 9 June 1914.
158 LM, GD40/17/464/36–7, Kerr to his mother, 17–20 Aug. 1914: Jalland and Stubbs, 'Irish question after the outbreak of war'.
159 MS Dawson 63, f.200, Robinson to Lovat Fraser, 3 Dec. 1913: Oliver, *What federalism is not* (London, 1914), pp. 114–15: Garvin papers, Oliver to Garvin, 11 Feb. 1914.
160 *Times*, (17 Nov. 1913), p. 9.
161 *Observer*, (7 Dec., 8 June 1913), pp. 12, 10: *RT*, iv (1913–14), pp. 27–8, 203: CPSP, reel 1; diary, 13 Apr. 1914.
162 Amery, *Case against home rule*, p. 121: *RT*, iv (1913–14), pp. 51, 221.
163 *Observer*, (2 July 1916), p. 8, (28 Sept. 1913), p. 10.
164 MS Dawson 63, f.171–6; Robinson's notes on conversations with Morley and Curzon, 1913: MS Milner dep.157, f.173–87, especially f.183–4; 'Some notes on the home rule issue', n.s., probably by Amery.
165 Amery to Milner, 5 July 1909: *Observer*, (28 Sept. 1913), p. 10: *Times*, (19 Sept. 1912), p. 7b–c.
166 *Times*, (9 Feb. 1914), p. 7b–c, (20 Mar. 1914), p. 9b–c.
167 Bonar Law papers, 31/4/27, Milner to Bonar Law, 17 Mar. 1914.
168 *PMG*, (13 Aug. 1912), p. 6: *Times*, (31 Jan. 1914), p. 9b–c.
169 See above, p. 73.
170 MS Dawson 63, f.177–9, Robinson to Lovat Fraser, 7 Oct. 1913: *Observer*, (12 Oct. 1913), p. 10: RTP, MS.Eng.hist.c.808, f.43–6, Curtis to Grigg, 1 Aug. 1914.
171 Amery to N. Chamberlain, 25 July 1914, quoted in Barnes and Nicholson (eds), *Amery diaries*, i.101: Bonar Law papers, 33/1/46, Amery to Bonar Law, 25 July 1914.

172 Amery, *Political life*, i.403.
173 *MP*, (9 Sept. 1914), p. 4e.

CHAPTER NINE

1 Marlow, *Apostle of empire*, pp. 269–70, 279, 284, 296–7: RTP, MS.Eng.hist.c.808, f.94, Grigg to Curtis, 28 Aug. 1914.
2 R. Fanning, 'Britain, Ireland and the end of the Union', in Blake (ed.), *Ireland after the Union*, pp. 105–20.
3 *PMG*, (9 Feb. 1912,) p. 6: S. Hartley, *The Irish question as a problem in British foreign policy, 1914–1918* (Basingstoke, 1987), especially pp. 4, 21, 98: Chamberlain papers (Birmingham University Library), JC 27/62, A. Chamberlain to Garvin, 21 Oct. 1910.
4 Waldorf Astor papers, MS 1066/1/780; Curtis, 'Memorandum on the present action of the Round Table', 24 Apr. 1918, p. 3: Sanders and Taylor, *British propaganda during the First World War*, pp. 2–3: Messinger, *British propaganda and the state*, p. 7.
5 *Times*, (28 Dec. 1918), p. 7b: Oliver, *Ordeal by battle* (London, 1915), p. x: *Observer*, (4 Mar. 1917), p. 6: [Kerr], 'The war for public right', *RT*, vi (1916), pp. 193–231, especially p. 202.
6 Messinger, *British propaganda and the State*, pp. 44–5.
7 MS Milner dep. 350, f.142–4, Amery to Milner, 25 May 1915.
8 Oliver, *Ordeal by battle*: Oliver papers, Acc. 7726/153; miscellaneous notes by Oliver; Chamberlain papers, AC 14/6/1–62, Oliver to A. Chamberlain, 1915: MS Milner dep.349, f.434, Oliver to Milner, 26 Dec. 1914.
9 MS Curtis 2, f.188–98, Milner to Curtis, 27 Nov. 1915
10 Lloyd George papers, F/89/1/10, Kerr to Lloyd George, 5 Dec. 1917: [Kerr], 'The harvest of the war', 'The war for public right', *RT*, vi (1915–16), pp. 1–32, 193–231.
11 Searle, *Country before party: coalition and the idea of 'national government' in modern Britain, 1885–1987* (London, 1995), pp. 73, 97, 103; *The quest for national efficiency* (Oxford, 1971), pp. 171–204: R. Scally, *The origins of the Lloyd George coalition: the politics of social imperialism, 1900–1918* (Princeton, 1975): J. Turner, 'The formation of Lloyd George's 'garden suburb': "Fabian–like Milnerite penetration"?', *Hist.Journ.*, xx (1977), 165–84.
12 *Scott diary*, p. 343; diary entry, 19–21 Apr. 1918: Turner, *Lloyd George's secretariat* (Cambridge, 1980), pp. 142, 115–16: Oliver papers, Acc. 7726/217; diary, Nov.–Dec. 1917: Hewins, *Apologia*, ii.165–6.
13 AGGP, 1/14, Garvin to Gardiner, 17 Mar. 1919: Garvin, *The economic foundations of peace: or, world partnership as the truer basis of the League of Nations* (London, 1919): Garvin papers, Massingham to Garvin, 18 Apr. 1919 (two letters).
14 *Nation*, xxv (12 Apr. 1919), no. 2, pp. 58–62.
15 *Observer*, (20 Mar. 1921), p. 12: see above, pp. 112–14, 119–20.
16 Amery to Cecil, 23 Dec. 1916, quoted in Barnes and Nicholson (eds), *Amery diaries*, i.133.

17 Hewins, *Trade in the balance*, p. 145: AMP, MS.Eng.hist.c.696, f.397–401, Milner to Lloyd George, 6 Sept. 1918.
18 *Observer*, (22 Dec. 1918), p. 6.
19 See above, pp. 82–3.
20 Kendle, *Round Table movement*, pp. 219–23: May, 'Round Table', pp. 108–9.
21 Lavin, 'Lionel Curtis and Indian Dyarchy', in Bosco (ed.), *Federal idea*, i.193–209: Kendle, *Round Table movement*, pp. 224–47: *Observer*, (18, 25 May 1919), pp. 10.
22 See above, pp. 138–9.
23 *Observer*, (20 May 1917), p. 6, (30 Apr. 1916), pp. 8–9: *Times*, (28 Apr., 4 July 1916), pp. 7a–b, 9a–b: *RT*, vii (1917), pp. 763–4.
24 *Observer*, (14 Apr. 1918), p. 6: *Times*, (3 May 1918), p. 8d, (19 Oct. 1916), p. 11a–b.
25 *Hansard*, 5th ser., civ, c.1940 (12 Apr. 1918): Peatling, 'Last defence of the Union?', pp. 290–1.
26 *Observer*, (14 May, 23 July 1916), pp. 8: *Times*, (25 July, 17 May 1916), pp. 9a, 9a–b: Stubbs, 'The Unionists and Ireland, 1914–1918', *Hist.Journ.*, xxxiii (1990), 881–3.
27 [Kerr], 'Ireland and the empire', *RT*, vi (1916), pp. 614–52, especially pp. 650, 648. Kerr was more consistent than most Imperialists in his criticism of the Easter rebels, since he had been one of the Round Table members most hostile to British Unionists' support of Unionist Ulster's threats to resist home rule with violence in 1914; see Nancy Astor papers, 1416/1/4/47, Kerr to Nancy Astor, 12 Mar. 1914.
28 RTP, MS.Eng.hist.c.790, f.151–2, 182–6, Kerr to Monteagle, 4 Aug., 3 Nov., 1916.
29 D. Lavin, 'History, morals and politics: Lionel Curtis and the Round Table', in J. Bossy and P. Judd (eds), *Essays presented to Michael Roberts* (Belfast, 1976), p. 127.
30 Curtis, *Commonwealth of nations*, pp. 518–19. See above, pp. 130–2.
31 WHLP, 947/402/8; list of members of the Imperial Unionist 'Committee', 1916: Stubbs, 'Conservative party and war', pp. 319–37, 398; 'Unionists and Ireland', 883–4.
32 WASHP, 179; diary, 29 July 1916.
33 WASHP, 60, f.4–7, Gretton to Hewins, 6 June 1916; section 179; diary, 18–29 July 1916. Gretton (1867–1947), later Baron Gretton of Stapleford, a Conservative and Unionist MP between 1895 and 1943, became a prominent critic of both the British government's negotiations with Sinn Féin in 1921, and of the eventual Treaty; see P. Canning, *British policy towards Ireland*, p. 21: Hewins, *Apologia*, ii.240, 242, 244, 248–51.
34 Conversations with Joseph Devlin, quoted *ibid.*, ii.127.
35 *Observer*, (11 Mar. 1917), p. 6: Garvin papers, Kerr to Garvin, 9[?] Mar. 1917: Waldorf Astor papers, MS 1066/1/1210, Astor to Garvin, 12 Mar. 1917.
36 *Observer*, (20 Jan. 1918), p. 6.
37 Fisher, 'The "unreasonableness" of Ulster', *NC*, lxxxiii (1918), p. 1088: *Belfast Evening Telegraph*, (14 Jan. 1918), p. 5b–c.

38 *Observer*, (13 Jan. 1918), p. 6: Boyce, 'British Conservative opinion, the Ulster question and the partition of Ireland, 1912–21', *Ir.Hist.Stud.*, xvii (1970–1), 90–112.
39 Lloyd George papers, F/89/1/3, Kerr to Lloyd George, 3 Mar. 1917.
40 Northcliffe papers, MS 62,245, f.43–7, Robinson to Northcliffe, 28 June 1917.
41 Quoted in Hartley, *Irish question in British foreign policy*, p. 161: [Kerr], 'The Irish crisis', *RT*, viii (1918), pp. 496–525.
42 Oliver papers MS 24,855, f.122–3, Oliver to Plunkett, 8 Nov. 1917: Peatling, 'Last defence of the Union?', p. 291.
43 *Times*, (6 May 1918), p. 6b.
44 Oliver, *Ireland and the Imperial conference: is there a way to settlement?* (London, 1917), p. 16: Baron Carson of Duncairn papers (Public Record Office of Northern Ireland), D1507/A/22/20, Oliver to Pembroke Wicks, 30 Mar. 1917: Oliver and Selborne, *Method of constitutional co-operation*: D.G. Boyce (ed.), *The crisis of British Unionism: the domestic papers of the second Earl of Selborne, 1885–1922* (Oxford, 1988), pp. 204–22: Boyce and Stubbs, 'Oliver and Selborne', 67–72.
45 Carson papers, D1507A/21/23, Amery to Carson, 13 Feb. 1917: Amery, 'The Irish demand for fiscal autonomy', *NC*, lxxxiii (1918), pp. 1157–67: Kendle, *Ireland and the federal solution*, pp. 177–209.
46 Childers papers, MS 7811; diary, July 1919.
47 Plunkett papers, Oli.27, Oliver to Plunkett, 28 Oct. 1917.
48 Garvin papers, Garvin to Colvin, 20 June 1918.
49 Waldorf Astor papers, MS 1066/1/1204, Garvin to Astor, 24 June 1918.
50 E.T. Raymund [pseud.], *All and sundry* (London, 1919), p. 130: *Times*, (8 May 1918), p. 7b: Peatling, 'Last defence of the Union?', pp. 291–2.
51 WASHP, 77, f.56; section 123, *passim.*, papers relating to the Long committee, 1918: Kendle, *Walter Long, Ireland and the Union, 1905–1920* (Montreal, 1992), p. 152.
52 Long to Hewins, 10 Apr. 1918, quoted *ibid.*, p. 147.
53 Lloyd George papers, F/2/1/23/22, Amery to Lloyd George, 1 May, 29 Apr. 1918.
54 'The English people and Ireland', *NS*, xi (18 May 1918), no. 267, p. 128: Boyce, 'British opinion, Ireland and the War, 1916–18', *Hist.Journ.*, xvii (1974), 589: Kendle, 'Federalism and the Irish problem in 1918', *History*, lvi (1971), 211–22, 229.
55 Kendle, *Ireland and the federal solution*, p. 207.
56 Robinson had changed his name in 1917, as part of the requirements of a will.
57 [Brand, et al], 'United Kingdom', *RT*, x (1920), pp. 639, 638: May, 'Round Table', p. 450.
58 Lloyd George papers, F/34/2/7, Kerr to Lloyd George, 14 Sept. 1921.
59 *Observer*, (29 Dec. 1918), p. 6.
60 HWNP, MS.Eng.misc.e.621/4, f.33; diary 23 Jan. 1921: Peatling, 'Last defence of the Union?', p. 292.
61 WASHP, 74, f.192–3, Hewins to Lloyd George, 27 July 1919; section 123, f.63–5, Hewins to Lloyd George, 24 Apr. 1918: WHLP, 947/258, Hewins to Long, 3 May 1918.

62 Waldorf Astor papers, MS 1066/1/1210, Garvin to Astor, 23 June 1919: *Observer*, (10 Aug. 1924), p. 10: [Curtis], 'The better government of the United Kingdom', *RT*, viii (1918), pp. 750–77.
63 *RT*, ix (1919), pp. 582–3; x (1920) pp. 124–7, 867: May, 'Round Table', pp. 203–4. The identity of these correspondents is unclear.
64 'Ireland and the empire', *RT*, vi (1916), pp. 616–17, 623, 648, 650–1.
65 Lloyd George papers, F/19/3/12; memorandum by Kerr, 11 Apr. 1921: Curran, *Birth of the Free State*, pp. 51–2: *RT*, viii (1918), pp. 522–3.
66 LM, GD40/17/627/2; interview between Clune and Kerr, 31 Dec. 1920 (see also Lloyd George papers, F/90/1/29).
67 CPSP, reel 2; diary, 1 Dec. 1919: Plunkett papers; diary, 21 July 1920: LM, GD40/17/80/166–72, Plunkett to Kerr, 1920–1.
68 Peatling, 'Last defence of the Union?', p. 293.
69 Plunkett papers; diary, 25 Aug., 21 July 1920.
70 O'Day, *Irish home rule*, pp. 294–9: Kendle, *Walter Long*, pp. 179–92: R. Murphy, 'Walter Long and the making of the Government of Ireland Act, 1919–20' *Ir.Hist.Stud.*, xxv (1986–7), 82–96.
71 On Kerr's involvement in this legislation, see Peatling, 'Last defence of the Union?', pp. 292–3.
72 LM, GD40/17/608; memorandum by Steed, n.s.: *Times*, (24 July 1919), p. 13b–e.
73 Kendle, *Walter Long*, p. 184: [Curtis], 'Cutting Ireland in two', *Atlantic Monthly*, cxxxiv (1924), pp. 823–37, especially p. 827.
74 See above, pp. 129, 133.
75 *Observer*, (7, 14 Mar. 1920), p. 12: *RT*, x (1920), pp. 378–80.
76 MS Hammond 18, f.59–61, Garvin to Hammond, 2 Mar. 1921.
77 LM, GD40/17/595; memorandum by Kerr, 18 Dec. 1919.
78 Murphy, 'Long and the Government of Ireland Act', p. 96.
79 Hewins, *Apologia*, ii.207: WASHP, 179; diary, 26 Sept. 1918.
80 WASHP, 76, f.274, Hewins to the *Times*, 14 Dec. 1920; section 179; diary, 30 Apr. 1919: Hewins, *Apologia*, ii.208–19.
81 Diary, 18 Dec. 1920, quoted *ibid.*, ii.223: WHLP, 947/259, Hewins to Long, 29 Jan. 1920.
82 WASHP, 77, f.58; section 38, f.194, 197; memorandum entitled 'Conditions for the economic settlement of the Irish question'.
83 WASHP, 77, f.46–65, especially f.61: Hewins, *Apologia*, ii.224–7.
84 WASHP, 181; diary, 3 Feb. 1921.
85 WASHP, 181; diary, 25 Mar. 1921.
86 On the Saundersons see A. Jackson, *Colonel Edward Saunderson: land and loyalty in Victorian Ireland* (Oxford, 1995), especially pp. 226–42.
87 WASHP, 181; diary, 25 Mar. 1921; section 77, f.68, C. Grigsby to Hewins, 9 Feb. 1921: *Times*, (24 Feb. 1921), p. 15g.
88 Oldmeadow, *Bourne*, ii.176–85: *Times*, (14 Feb. 1921), p. 10b, (12 Nov. 1920), p. 13e.
89 WASHP, 38 & 77, *passim.*; memoranda and letters; section 181; diary, Mar. –July 1921: Hewins, *Apologia*, ii.223–30. For Derby's involvement in Anglo-Irish politics at this time, see R.S. Churchill, *Lord Derby, 'King of Lancashire':*

the official life of Edward, seventeenth Earl of Derby, 1865–1948 (London, 1959), pp. 402–21.

90 WASHP, 181; diary, 15 July 1921.

91 *Ibid.*, 182; diary, 21, 20, 23 Oct., 14 Nov. 1921: Hewins, *Apologia* ii.240, 229–30, 239–44.

92 *Ibid.*, ii.294, 244–7.

93 Hewins, *Trade in the balance*, p. 125.

94 *Apologia*, ii.249: WASHP, 182; diary, 20 Dec. 1921.

95 *Apologia*, ii.229: WHLP, 947/258, Hewins to Long, 3 May 1918.

96 Amery, *Political life*, i.428, ii.229: WASHP, 181; diary, 14 Mar. 1921.

97 Baron Altrincham (Edward Grigg) papers (microfilm copies, Bodleian Library), MSS Films 999, Amery to Grigg, 28 Aug. 1921.

98 *Observer*, (12 Sept. 1920), p. 10, (5 Sept. 1920), p. 10, (26 Sept. 1920), pp. 12–13. See above, p. 91.

99 *Observer*, (20 Mar. 1921), p. 12: F.P. Crozier, *Ireland for ever* (London, 1932), pp. 89–134: Garvin papers, Gwynn to Garvin, 1920–1, *passim.*: P. Bew, 'Moderate Irish nationalism and the Irish revolution, 1916–1923', *Historical Journal*, xlii (1999), no. 3, 730–2.

100 Harcourt papers (Bodleian Library), MS Harcourt dep. 688, f.309, Garvin to Viscount Harcourt, 2 Nov. 1921: Garvin papers, Garvin to Amery, 24 Aug. 1921. During Garvin's absences, *Observer* editorial policy would have been conducted by Robert McGowan Barrington-Ward (1891–1948), Garvin's assistant editor 1919–27, and later editor of the *Times*.

101 *Observer*, (29 May 1921), p. 10, (28 Aug. 1921), p. 10.

102 *Observer*, (27 Nov. 1921), p. 12, (16 May 1920), p. 12.

103 *Observer*, (13 Nov. 1921), p. 13.

104 *Observer*, (13 Nov., 26 June 1921), p. 12.

105 Waldorf Astor papers, 727; notes for a speech by Astor.

106 *Observer*, (13 Nov. 1921), pp. 12, 13.

107 *Observer*, (27, 13, 20 Nov. 1921), pp. 12, 13, 12.

108 *Observer*, (14 Nov. 1920), p. 12, (30 Oct. 1921), p. 12.

109 *Observer*, (4 Dec. 1921), p. 12: Garvin papers, Garvin to Amery, n.d. [1921].

110 *Observer*, (20 May 1917), p. 6, (18 Dec. 1921), pp. 12–3, (11 Dec. 1921), p. 12.

111 *Observer*, (18, 25 Dec. 1921), pp. 12, 6.

112 *Observer*, (26 Mar. 1922), p. 12, (14 May 1922), p. 12, (20 Mar. 1932), p. 16, (10 Aug. 1924), p. 10.

113 [Dove and Curtis], 'Ireland', *RT*, xi (1921), pp. 465–534, especially pp. 505, 532.

114 Round Table additional papers (Bodleian Library); editorial committee meeting notes, 2 Aug., 3 May 1921: *RT*, xi (1921), pp. 475, 465: Curtis (ed.), *Commonwealth of nations*, pp. 517–21.

115 *RT*, xi (1921), p. 530.

116 *History of the 'Times'*, vol IV, part II, pp. 553, 561–74.

117 T. Jones, *Whitehall diary*, ed. K. Middlemas (London, 1969, 3 vols), iii.77–9: Altrincham papers, MSS Films 1010, *passim.*: Lloyd George papers, F/29/4/48–9, F/86/1/5–9; miscellaneous letters and drafts, June 1921: May, 'Round Table', pp. 206–7.

118 Altrincham papers, MSS Films 999, Curtis to Grigg, 25 June 1921, Grigg to Curtis, 27 June 1921. See above, p. 92, on the Council.
119 Lloyd George papers, F/86/1/5, Grigg to Lloyd George, 14 June 1921: *Observer*, (26 June 1921), p. 12: *Times*, (17 Aug. 1921), p. 9b–c.
120 Jones, *Whitehall diary*, iii.90, 96–8: Curran, *Birth of the Free State*, pp. 64–80.
121 *Daily Chronicle*, (24 Oct., 7 Dec. 1921), pp. 4, 6: Peatling, 'Last defence of the Union?', pp. 293–4.
122 Lloyd George papers, F/181/4/1; memorandum by Curtis entitled 'Proposals to Ulster', 8 Nov. 1921: [Dove], 'Ireland', *RT*, xii (1921), pp. 37–74, especially pp. 62, 72–4.
123 Lavin, *Empire to international commonwealth*, pp. 180–203: Jones, *Whitehall diary*, iii.119–83, *passim*.
124 Lloyd George papers, F/184/2/3; Curtis, 'Further memorandum on Provisional Government', 9 Dec. 1921: [Dove and Curtis], 'Ireland at the cross-roads', *RT*, xii (1922), pp. 517, 509. On Curtis' work at the Colonial Office in 1922–4, see Jones, *Whitehall diary*, iii.194–232: Canning, *British policy towards Ireland*, pp. 29–91, *passim.*: J. McColgan, 'Implementing the 1921 Treaty; Lionel Curtis and constitutional procedure', *Ir.Hist.Stud.*, xx (1976–7), 310–33.
125 Altrincham papers, MSS Films 999, *passim*. On Horgan see May, 'Round Table', pp. 298–305, 381–4: Horgan, *Parnell to Pearse* (Dublin, 1948).
126 [Dove and Curtis], 'Ireland at the cross-roads', [Barrington-Ward], 'Ireland', *RT*, xii (1922), pp. 507–37, 782–807, especially, 507–9, 520, 782, 796.
127 *Atlantic Monthly*, cxxxiv (1924), p. 837: Lloyd George papers, F/184/1; memoranda by Curtis for the Cabinet Provisional Government of Ireland Committee, 21 May, 6 June 1922.
128 *RT*, xii (1922), p. 524: [Curtis], 'The Irish boundary question', *RT*, xv (1925), pp. 38, 26.
129 *Observer*, (23 Jan. 1938), p. 14: Altrincham papers, MSS Films 999, Curtis to Grigg, 25 June 1921.
130 *Atlantic Monthly*, cxxxiv (1924), p. 835: MS Curtis 89, f.76–83, Curtis to Churchill, 19 Aug. 1924: *Observer*, (10 Aug. 1924), p. 10.
131 *RT*, xv (1925), pp. 35–7. The assumption made by Curtis, and by later historians, that the experience of such southern Unionists was unrepresentative is questioned in P. Hart, *The IRA and its enemies: violence and community in Cork, 1916–23* (Oxford, 1998), especially, pp. 312–14.
132 MS Curtis 89, f.76–83, 84–7, Curtis to Churchill, 19, 31 Aug. 1924; MS Curtis 90, f.30–54, Curtis to Churchill, 17 Dec. 1928.
133 Curtis and Kerr, *The prevention of war* (New Haven, 1923), p. 106.
134 *Observer*, (5 Feb. 1922), p. 10, (21 Sept. 1924), p. 12.
135 *Atlantic Monthly*, cxxxiv (1924), pp. 837, 836: Jones, *Whitehall diary*, iii.226: [Dove], 'A holiday in Ireland', *RT*, xiv (1924), pp. 320–2.
136 [Dove], 'The Irish Boundary Commission: editor's note', *RT*, xiv (1924), pp. 767–83, especially p. 778.
137 Sir Richard Feetham papers (Rhodes House Library, Oxford), box 7, *passim.*: *Times*, (18 Dec. 1925), p. 19a: *Report of the Irish Boundary Commission, 1925* (Dublin, 1969): Peatling, 'Last defence of the Union?', p. 295.

138 Garvin, '1925', *Observer*, (27 Dec. 1925), p. 12: [F.B. Bourdillon and Horgan], 'Ireland: the boundary settlement', *RT*, xvi (1926), pp. 344–67, especially pp. 344–55.
139 Amery, *Political life*, ii.373.
140 Barnes and Nicholson (eds), *Amery diaries*, i.286–7.
141 *Hansard*, 5th ser., cclxix, c.1205 (Amery, 20 Nov. 1931): Amery, *Political life*, iii.406, 244–5, ii.274.
142 *Ibid*., ii.371.
143 Lavin, *Empire to international commonwealth*, pp. 181, 196, 224–5: Barnes and Nicholson (eds), *Amery diaries*, i.390; diary entry, 6 Nov. 1924.
144 *Ibid*., i.515, 483; diary entries for 10 July 1927, 23 Nov. 1926: Amery, *Political life*, ii.371–2, 247.
145 Barnes and Nicholson (eds), *Amery diaries*, i.429; diary entries for 2–3 Dec. 1925.
146 *Ibid*., i.483; diary entry for 23 Nov. 1926: Garvin papers, Amery to Garvin, 16 Nov. 1921: Altrincham papers, MSS Films 999, Amery to Grigg, 22 Nov. 1921.
147 Barnes and Nicholson (eds), *Amery diaries*, i.515–16, 570; diary entries for 10, 13 July 1927, 8 Nov. 1928: Canning, *British policy towards Ireland*, pp. 101, 103, 112, 165, 180–1.
148 Peatling, 'Last defence of the Union?', pp. 294–5: R. Coupland, *The Empire in these days: an interpretation* (London, 1935), p. 59.
149 *Observer*, (22 May, 21 Feb., 20 Mar. 1932), pp. 16b, 14b, 16b.
150 Coupland, *The Empire in these days*, p. 77.
151 Canning, *British policy towards Ireland*, pp. 280, 258–74: MS Curtis 90, f.104–6, Curtis to E. Bevin, 12 June 1940.
152 B.A. Follis, *A state under siege: the establishment of Northern Ireland, 1920–25* (Oxford, 1995).
153 MS Milner dep.13, f.111, Milner to Oliver, 13 Jan. 1921: Oliver papers, MS 24,856, f.162–5, Oliver to Lord Lee of Fareham, 23 Sept. 1922: Selborne to the Marquess of Salisbury, 29 July 1921, quoted in Boyce (ed.), *Crisis of British Unionism*, pp. 231–2
154 Oliver, 'From empire to union', p. 31: Peatling, 'Last defence of the Union?', p. 295.
155 *Atlantic Monthly*, cxxxiv (1924), p. 833.
156 Countess Selborne papers, MS.Eng.lett.d.430, f.52–4, Curtis to Lady Selborne, 28 June 1924.
157 See above, pp. 41–3.

CONCLUSION

1 'Autobiography', p. 280.
2 'How the terror comes home', *NS*, xvi (20 Nov. 1920), no. 397, pp. 192–3.
3 *Hansard*, 3rd. ser., cccvi, c.1239–40 (7 June 1886).
4 *John Bull's other island*, (London, 1957, first published 1907), p. 129.
5 *Faith, war and policy*, pp. 145, 152.

6 *Irish grievances*, p. 73.
7 Dunne, 'Ireland, England and the Empire', pp. 30–60, 171, 209, 239–41.
8 *Hansard*, 5th ser., xlvi, c.654 (H.B. Lees Smith, 2 Jan. 1913).
9 See above, pp. 45, 120–1, 130–3.
10 Green, *Crisis of Conservatism*, pp. 62–9, 195: I. Colvin, 'The dead-hand of federalism', *National Review*, lxiii (1914), pp. 52–70.
11 Oliver papers, MS 24,851, f.56–9, A. Chamberlain to Oliver, 23 Feb. 1914: *Hansard*, 5th ser., lviii, c.240–1 (11 Feb. 1914).
12 Jay, *Joseph Chamberlain*, pp. 123–5: C.B. Shannon, *Arthur J. Balfour and Ireland, 1874–1922* (Washington, 1988), p. 284: Dicey, *England's case*, pp. 6, 120, 143–97, 263–5, 287–9.
13 *Hansard*, 5th ser., xlvi, c.1227 (Amery, 8 Jan. 1913): Amery, 'Home rule and the colonial analogy', p. 144.
14 See above, p. 136.
15 See above, p. 18.
16 See above, pp. 19, 45, 60.
17 Mill, 'England and Ireland', pp. 524–5.
18 Morley, 'Some arguments considered', pp. 259–60: Baden–Powell, 'Colonial self-government', in Baden-Powell (ed.), *Truth about home rule*, pp. 188–97, especially pp. 189–90.
19 'The conditions of home rule', *Nation*, x (4 Nov. 1911), no. 5, p. 189.
20 See fig.2, p. 171.
21 See above, pp. 91–5, 145–8.
22 'From Russia to Ireland', *Nation*, xxvi (14 Feb. 1920), no. 20, pp. 660–1: D. Harkness, *The restless Dominion: the Irish Free State and the British Commonwealth of Nations, 1921–31* (London, 1969), especially p. 12: N. Mansergh, *The Commonwealth experience*, (London, 2nd ed, 1982, 2 vols, first published 1969), especially i.233, 29: Lavin, *From empire to international commonwealth*, pp. 189–90, 194: M. Beloff, *Britain's liberal empire, 1897–1921* (London, 1969): Mansergh, *Unresolved question*, pp. 201–2.
23 Hobhouse, *Questions of war and peace*; *World in conflict*: Hobson, *Towards international government*: Murray, *Faith, war and policy*: C.R. Buxton (ed.), *Towards a lasting settlement* (London, 1915): Zimmern, *Nationality and government*: Curtis (ed.), *Commonwealth of nations*; *Problem of the commonwealth*: Garvin, *Economic foundations of peace*: Lavin, 'History, morals and politics', pp. 126–7; 'Lionel Curtis and the idea of commonwealth', in F. Madden and D. Fieldhouse (eds), *Oxford and the idea of commonwealth* (London, 1982), pp. 97–121: Bridges, 'England and China', in Congreve (ed.), *International policy*, p. 431: F.J. Gould, *Whither, British? A brief survey of social and political situation* (London, 1913), pp. 12–14. Also see above, pp. 47–9.
24 *PMG*, (24 May 1913), p. 6. Also see above, pp. 112–14, 119–20, 147.
25 See above, p. 151.
26 Turner and Dockrill, 'Philip Kerr at 10 Downing Street, 1916–1921', p. 60.
27 See above, pp. 40–1, 45, 59.
28 *Observer*, (16 Nov. 1924), p. 12b: Bew, *Ideology and the Irish question*, pp. 38, 83, 128, 118–52.

29 *Ibid.*, pp. 79–84: Bew, *Conflict and conciliation*, pp. 112–21, 134–40, 203–5: Bull, *Land, politics and nationalism*, pp. 153–8, 170–7, 190–1.
30 R. Axelrod, *The evolution of co-operation*, (New York, 1984).
31 A. Breton, G. Galeotti, P. Salmon and R. Winstable (eds), *Nationalism and rationality* (Cambridge, 1995).
32 Cooke (ed.), *The Ashbourne papers*, p. ix.
33 C. Townshend, 'British policy in Ireland, 1906–1921', in Boyce (ed.), *Revolution in Ireland*, pp. 173–92: Hepburn, 'Liberal policies and Nationalist politics', pp. 813–23: Jalland, *Liberals and Ireland*.
34 Dicey, 'Home rule from an English point of view', *CR*, xlii (1882), p. 86: Curtis, *Commonwealth of nations*, p. 518.
35 See above, pp. 136–8.
36 See above, p. 4.
37 P.S. O'Hegarty, *Sinn Féin: an illumination* (Dublin, 1919), p. 41: Bull, *Land, politics and nationalism*, pp. 105–6, 113.
38 *DN*, (23 June 1922), p. 4b: R. English, *Radicals and the Republic: socialist republicanism in the Irish Free State, 1925–37* (Oxford, 1994): M.L.R. Smith, *Fighting for Ireland? The military strategy of the Irish republican movement* (London, 1995).
39 *Scott diary*, pp. 392–4; see above, p. 100: Bryce, 'How we became home rulers', p. 38; 'Y' [Bryce], 'Symptoms of Irish feeling towards England', *NYN*, xxxvi (1 Mar. 1883), pp. 186–7.
40 Hepburn, 'Liberal policies and Nationalist politics', p. 816.
41 Hoppen, 'Nationalist mobilisation and governmental attitudes', in Brockliss and Eastwood (eds), *Union of multiple identities*, pp. 162–78: D. Fitzpatrick, 'The geography of Irish nationalism, 1910–21', *Past & Present*, no. 78 (1978), 113–44.
42 See above, p. 172.
43 C. Townshend, *British campaign in Ireland, passim.*, especially p. 186: Curran, *Birth of the Free State*, pp. 53–6. See above, pp. 91–7, 157–8, 160–1.
44 P. O'Farrell, *England and Ireland since 1800* (London, 1975), p. 106.
45 K.T. Hoppen, *Ireland since 1800: conflict and conformity* (London, 2nd ed, 1999, first published 1989), pp. 188, 187, 231, 234.
46 J. McGarry and B. O'Leary, *The politics of antagonism: understanding Northern Ireland* (London, 1993), p. 2.
47 P. Buckland, *A history of Northern Ireland* (Dublin, 1981), pp. 23, 72: D. Harkness, 'England's Irish question', pp. 61–2: E. Phoenix, *Northern nationalism: nationalist politics, partition and the Catholic minority in Northern Ireland, 1890–1940* (Belfast, 1994), pp. 391–9.
48 See above, pp. 23–6.
49 *MG*, (20 June 1916), p. 4a–b.
50 *RT*, xii (1922), p. 524: MS Curtis 89, f.89–90, Churchill to Curtis, 8 Sept. 1924.
51 S. Ball, *Baldwin and the Conservative party: the crisis of 1929–31* (New Haven, 1988), pp. 108–29.
52 P. Kennedy, *Strategy and diplomacy, 1870–1945: eight studies* (London, 1983), p. 38.
53 *Ibid.*, p. 39, 22–3.

54 See above, p. 103: *Observer*, (20 Mar. 1932), p. 16b, (8 Nov. 1925), p. 12.
55 D. Kennedy, *The widening gulf: Northern attitudes to the independent Irish state, 1921–49* (Belfast, 1988), p. 240: Mansergh, *Unresolved question*, pp. 334–41.
56 T. Fraser, 'Partitioning Ireland, India and Palestine', in Collins (ed.), *Nationalism and unionism*, pp. 177–86.
57 J. Bowman, *De Valera and the Ulster question, 1917–73* (Oxford, 1982), pp. 9–20.
58 Shannon, *Balfour and Ireland;* Canning, *British policy towards Ireland*, pp. 72–3: Loughlin, *Ulster unionism and British national identity*, pp. 193, 210, 213. According to some (though not all) opinion polls, a united Ireland is still popularly perceived in Britain as the likeliest specific long-term settlement. The strength of this belief has been reflected in British policy in Northern Ireland over the last fifteen years; See McGarry and O'Leary, *Politics of antagonism*, pp. 279–81.
59 Townshend, 'British policy in Ireland, 1906–21', p. 173.
60 Bew, *Ideology and the Irish question*, pp. 118–52, especially pp. 151, 128.
61 LM, GD40/17/464/37, Kerr to his mother, 20 Aug. 1914.
62 Loughlin, *Ulster unionism and British national identity*, p. 188.
63 G. Cubitt, 'Introduction', in Cubitt (ed.), *Imagining nations* (Manchester, 1998), especially pp. 3, 1: M. Billig, *Banal nationalism* (London, 1995): J. Breuilly, *Nationalism and the state* (Manchester, 2nd ed, 1993, first published 1982), p. 2: E. Gellner, *Nations and nationalism* (Oxford, 1983), p. 138: B. Anderson, *Imagined communities*: S. Wolff (ed.), *Nationalism in Europe, 1815 to the present: a reader* (London, 1996): A.D.S. Smith, *Nationalism in the twentieth century* (Oxford, 1979); *The ethnic origins of nations* (Oxford, 1986): L. Colley, *Britons: the forging of a nation, 1707–1837* (London, 1996, first published 1992).
64 Kendle, *Ireland and the federal solution*, p. 235; *Federal Britain*, especially pp. 70, 61, 75, 77–8, 169–76: Matthew, *Gladstone*, ii.215, 235: *CR*, lxiii (1893), pp. 636–7: Dicey, *Fool's paradise*, p. ix.
65 A fact which, of course, complicates the task of historians in conceptually demarcating 'English' and 'British' national identity in this period: G. Morton, *Unionist-nationalism: governing urban Scotland, 1830–1860* (Phantassie, East Lothian, 1999), pp. 2–3.
66 See above, pp. 166–7.
67 See above, pp. 21, 26, 43, 58–60, 62: Bryce, 'How we became home rulers', pp. 31, 47.
68 Gladstone, 'Notes and queries on the Irish question', *NC*, xxi (1887), p. 168: Matthew, *Gladstone*, ii.257.
69 See above, pp. 35, 44.
70 Chamberlain papers, AC 14/6/72; comment by Oliver in a memorandum by Oliver and Craik, p. 27.
71 As Beatrice Webb apparently realised. Webb, *Beatrice Webb's diaries, 1912–24*, ed. M.I. Cole (London, 1952), p. 220.
72 *Nation*, xxxi (15 Apr. 1922), no. 3, p. 82.
73 *Observer*, (12 Feb. 1922), p. 13, (5 Feb. 1922), p. 10, (2 Jan. 1921), p. 12.
74 Ellinwood, 'The Round Table movement and India, 1909–1920', *Journ.Imp. & Comm.Hist.*, ix (1971), 183–209.

75 Curtis and Kerr, *Prevention of war*, p. 122.
76 'The atrocity campaign of the *Morning Post*', *Nation*, xxix (13 Aug. 1921), no. 20, p. 703: *Nation*, xxx (10 Dec. 1921), no. 11, pp. 421–2: *MG*, (7 Dec. 1921), p. 6b–c.
77 *Observer*, (11 Dec. 1921), p. 12: *Times*, (7 Dec. 1921), p. 11b–c. Also see Balfour's comment, quoted in Jones, *Whitehall diary*, iii.64–5.
78 O. MacDonagh, *States of mind: a study of Anglo-Irish conflict, 1780–1980* (London, 1983), pp. 1–14, especially pp. 10–11, 14, 9, 1.
79 R. Cosgrove, 'The relevance of Irish history'. See for instance the writings of the influential Unionists Dicey and Lecky, especially Dicey, *England's case*, pp. 72–81 (the quotation is from p. 72); *CR*, xlii (1882), p. 86; [Dicey], 'England and Ireland', *NYN*, xxxv (28 Sept. 1882), pp. 267–8: Lecky, *History of Ireland*, i.188–90, ii.97, 420–1, v.198, 419, 483–94; *Leaders of public opinion* (1903 ed), ii.105–6. There were some Unionists, such as George Brodrick and the Duke of Argyll, who largely denied that British policy had ever been unkind or oppressive in Ireland; see Brodrick, *Home rule and justice to Ireland: a letter to the editor of the 'Times'* (Oxford, 1886), pp. 10–13; 'Plain facts about Ireland', *National Review*, xi (1888), pp. 87–102: Argyll, 'A reply to our appellant', *CR*, lv (1889), pp. 1–13. But Brodrick and Argyll were less influential because they were more obviously partisans, see Harvie, 'Ideology and home rule', p. 300: McCartney, *Lecky*, pp. 144–50.
80 *Observer*, (2 Oct. 1921), p. 12.
81 See above, p. 150.
82 LM, GD40/17/601/2; memorandum sent by Kerr to Lloyd George, n.d., [1920].
83 Townshend, *Political violence in Ireland: government and resistance since 1848* (Oxford, 1983), p. 2.
84 MacDonagh, *States of mind*, p. 11.
85 C. Barnett, *The collapse of British power* (London, 1972), pp. 184–5: Amery, *Political life*, ii.112–13.
86 R. Foster, 'Anglo-Irish relations and Northern Ireland: historical perspectives', in D. Keogh and M. Haltzel (eds), *Northern Ireland and the politics of reconciliation* (Cambridge, 1993), p. 16.
87 Froude, *English in Ireland in the eighteenth century*, i.134–53, especially i.144.
88 *PMG*, (9 Sept. 1881), p. 1.
89 *Times*, (26 Apr. 1938), p. 17b–c: *MG*, (26 Apr. 1938), p. 10b.
90 Anglo-Irish summit meeting, 15 Nov. 1985, joint communiqué: Boyce, *Irish question and British politics*, p. 130.
91 Chartwell trust papers, Char.22/14, f.77, Curtis to A. Cope, 14 Sept. 1922: 'The case for clemency', *Nation*, xix (6 May 1916), no. 6, p. 149.
92 See above, pp. 179–81: R. Porter (ed.), *Myths of the English* (Cambridge, 1992): R. Samuel (ed.), *Patriotism: the making and unmaking of British national identity* (London, 1989, 3 vols), vol.i: P.J. Ward, *Red flag and Union Jack: Englishness, patriotism and the British left, 1881–1924* (Woodbridge, 1998): B. Stuchtey, 'Literature, liberty and life of the nation: British historiography from Macaulay to Trevelyan', in S. Berger, M. Donovan and K. Passmore (eds), *Writing national histories: western Europe since 1800* (London, 1999), pp.

30–46: Dicey, *England's case*, pp. 142–5: M. MacColl, 'Professor Dicey on home rule', *CR*, lii (1887), pp. 102–3.

93 *MG*, (1 Aug. 1924), p. 8.

94 Townshend, 'British policy in Ireland, 1906–21', p. 175.

95 See above, p. 42.

96 See above, p. 174: Shannon, *Balfour and Ireland*, pp. 284–5; 'The legacy of Arthur Balfour to twentieth-century Ireland', in Collins (ed.), *Nationalism and Unionism*, pp. 17–33.

97 Boyce, *Irish question and British politics*, p. 115.

98 B. O'Duffy, 'The price of containment: deaths and debate on Northern Ireland in the House of Commons', and W. Harvey Cox, 'From Hillsborough to Downing Street – and after', in P. Catterall and S. McDougall (eds), *The Northern Ireland question in British politics* (London, 1996), pp. 122, 182–211: Bew, Patterson and Teague, *Northern Ireland, between war and peace*, pp. 39–68, 4, 214: Boyce, *Irish question and British politics*, pp. 138, 140: S. Bruce, *The edge of the Union: the Ulster loyalist political vision* (Oxford, 1994), *passim.*, especially pp. 64–70: A. Aughey, *Under siege: Ulster Unionism and the Anglo-Irish Agreement* (London, 1989).

99 L.P. Curtis Jr., *Anglo–Saxons and Celts*: R.F. Foster, 'Paddy and Mr Punch', in *Paddy and Mr Punch; connections in Irish and English history* (London, 1993), pp. 171–93

100 Loughlin, *Ulster Unionism and British identity*, p. 85.

101 *Ibid.*, p. 129. See above, pp. 73–6, 85–6, 90–1, 99, 102–5, 138, 140–4, 149–51, 157–62, 164.

102 Loughlin, *Ulster Unionism and British identity*, p. 200 and *passim.*: I. MacBride, 'Ulster and the British problem', in R. English and G. Walker (eds), *Unionism in modern Ireland*, pp. 1–18, especially pp. 14–15.

103 Loughlin, *Ulster Unionism and British identity*, pp. 105, 99–100, 210, 229.

104 P. Shirlow and M. McGovern (eds), *Who are 'the people'? Unionism, Protestantism, and Loyalism in Northern Ireland* (London, 1997).

105 Loughlin, *Ulster Unionism and British identity*, p. 133.

106 *RT*, iv (1914), p. 219.

107 Bew, Patterson and Teague, *Northern Ireland, between war and peace*, p. 221: Boyce, *Irish question and British politics*, pp. 150–1. As a result of the agreement of December 1925, the Council of Ireland itself never actually sat: see D. Kennedy, 'Politics of north-south relations in post-partition Ireland', in P. Rode and B. Barton (eds), *The Northern Ireland question: nationalism, unionism and partition* (Aldershot, 1999), pp. 76–7.

108 MacBride, 'Ulster and the British problem', p. 6.

109 B. Bradshaw and P. Roberts (eds), *British consciousness and identity: the making of Britain, 1533–1707* (Cambridge, 1998): M. Pittock, *Inventing and resisting Britain: cultural identities in Britain and Ireland, 1685–1789* (Basingstoke, 1997): Brockliss and Eastwood (eds), *Union of multiple identities*: K. Robbins, *Great Britain: identities, institutions and the idea of Britishness* (London, 1997): Loughlin, *Ulster Unionism and British identity*, pp. 37, 199, 229.

110 Bew, Patterson and Teague, *Northern Ireland, between war and peace*, pp. 204–5, 215: F. Cochrane, *Unionist politics and the politics of unionism since the Anglo-Irish Agreement* (Cork, 1997), p. 389.
111 Collini, *Public moralists*, p. 346.
112 Billig, *Banal nationalism*, pp. 6–7: P. Wright, *On living in an old country: the national past in contemporary Britain* (London, 1985).
113 Bradshaw and Roberts, 'Introduction', in Bradshaw and Roberts (eds), *British consciousness and identity*, p. 3: Brockliss and Eastwood, 'Introduction', and Brockliss, Eastwood and M. John, 'From dynastic union to unitary state: the European experience', in Brockliss and Eastwood (eds), *Union of multiple identities*, pp. 1–2, 194–6.
114 See above, p. 119.
115 See above, pp. 125–6.
116 *Times*, (26 Mar. 1919), p. 13c, quoted in Boyce, *Englishmen and Irish troubles*, p. 25.
117 Kearney, *Postnationalist Ireland*, p. 9.

Bibliography

MANUSCRIPT SOURCES

Republic of Ireland

Dublin

National Library of Ireland:

George F.H. Berkeley papers
Roger Casement papers
Alice Green papers
Michael MacDonagh papers
William O'Brien papers
John Redmond papers
Francis and Hanna Sheehy-Skeffington papers
Miscellaneous manuscripts: MS 9,769 (A. Crompton, 'In Memoriam: Henry Dix Hutton'); MS 11,0466 (Autobiographical account by Edith Stopford); MS 18,269–73 (John Joseph Horgan material)

Trinity College Dublin Library:
Erskine Childers papers
John Dillon papers

University College Dublin Library:
Constantine P. Curran collection

United Kingdom

Belfast

Public Record Office of Northern Ireland:

Baron Carson of Duncairn papers
Lord Craigavon papers
John Kells Ingram papers
Theresa, Lady Londonderry papers

Birmingham
University Library:
Chamberlain papers

Cambridge

Churchill Archives Centre, Churchill College:

Chartwell trust papers
Reginald McKenna papers

Edinburgh

National Archives of Scotland:

Lothian Muniments; the papers of the eleventh Marquess of Lothian (Philip Kerr)

National Library of Scotland:

Frederick Scott Oliver papers

London

British Library:

Arthur Balfour papers
John Burns papers
Henry Campbell-Bannerman papers
Viscount Cecil of Chelwood papers
Sir Charles Dilke papers
Baron Gladstone of Hawarden papers
Herbert, Viscount Gladstone papers
William Gladstone papers
Walter Hume Long, Viscount Long of Wraxall papers
MacMillan archive

Lord Northcliffe papers
Positivist papers

British Library of Political and Economic Science, London School of Economics and Political Science:

Alfred George Gardiner papers
Frederic Harrison papers
London Positivist Society papers

House of Lords Record Office:

Andrew Bonar Law papers
David Lloyd George papers
Herbert, Viscount Samuel papers
Robert Spence Watson–Viscount Morley of Blackburn (John Morley) correspondence

University College London Library:

Edward Spencer Beesly Papers

Long Hanborough, Oxfordshire

Plunkett Foundation Library:

Sir Horace Plunkett papers

Oxford

Bodleian Library:

Baron Altrincham (Edward Grigg) papers (microfilm copies)
Baron Brand papers
James, Viscount Bryce papers
Richard Congreve papers
Lionel Curtis papers
Geoffrey Dawson papers
Herbert Fisher papers
John Lawrence and Barbara Hammond papers
Sir William and Viscount Harcourt papers
Baron MacDonnell of Swinford papers
Francis Sydney Marvin papers
Alfred, Lord Milner papers
Gilbert Murray papers
Henry Woodd Nevinson papers
Lord Oxford and Asquith papers
'Oxford University Home Rule League: List of Members, 1891'
Oxford University Home Rule League papers
Oxford University Unionist League papers
Mark Pattison papers
Arthur Ponsonby papers
Round Table additional papers (1994 deposit, uncatalogued)
The Round Table papers of Lionel Curtis
John Satterfield Sandars papers
Charles Prestwich Scott papers (microfilm copies)
Maud, Countess Selborne papers
Second Earl of Selborne papers
Third Earl of Selborne papers
Evelyn Sharp papers
John, Viscount Simon papers
Goldwin Smith papers (microfilm copies)
Sir Alfred Zimmern papers
Miscellaneous manuscripts: MS.Eng. lett.c.41 (John Ruskin material): MS. Eng.lett. d.310 (letters to Constantine P. Curran): MS.Eng.misc.d.177 (Sir Sydney Lee material)

Jesus College Library:

John Richard Green papers

Rhodes House Library:

Sir Reginald Coupland papers
Sir Richard Feetham papers
Basil Williams papers

Reading

University Library:

Nancy, Lady Astor papers
Waldorf, Viscount Astor papers

Sheffield

University Library:

William Albert Samuel Hewins papers

Trowbridge

Wiltshire Record Office:

Walter Hume Long, Viscount Long of Wraxall papers

United States of America

Harry Ransome Humanities Research Center, the University of Texas at Austin:

James Louis Garvin papers

NEWSPAPERS AND PERIODICALS (CONTEMPORARY)

Albany Review
Atlantic Monthly
Bee-Hive
Belfast Evening Telegraph
Boston Sunday Globe
Commonwealth (formerly the *Working Man's Advocate*: 1866–7)
Contemporary Review
Covenanter
Daily Chronicle
Daily Herald
Daily News
Daily Telegraph
Eastern Post
Economic Review
English Historical Review
English Review
Fortnightly Review
Hibbert Journal
Highway
Independent Review
Indian Review
International Journal of Ethics
Irish Independent
Irish Times
Journal of the Statistical and Social Inquiry Society of Ireland
Justice
Law Quarterly Review
Liverpool Daily Post
MacMillan's Magazine
Manchester Guardian
Morning Post
Nation
National Review
New Review
New Statesman
New Weekly
New York Nation
New York Times
Nineteenth Century (and After)
North American Review
Observer
Outlook
Oxford Magazine
Pall Mall Gazette
Positivist Review
Proceedings of the British Academy
Progressive Review
Punch, or the London Charivari
Quarterly review
Revue Occidentale: Philosophique, Sociale et Politique
Round Table
Sociological Review
Speaker
Spectator
Sunday Westminster Gazette
Times
T.P.'s Weekly
University Review
Weekly Dispatch
Westminster Gazette
Westminster Review

HANSARD'S PARLIAMENTARY DEBATES

3rd–5th series.

UNPUBLISHED DISSERATIONS

Adelman, P., 'The social and political ideas of Frederic Harrison in relation to English thought and politics, 1855–1886' (University of London, D.Phil., 1967).

Bell, G., 'The British working class movement and the Irish national question, 1916–1921' (University of Leeds, Ph.D., 1992).

Dorey, A.J., 'Radical liberal criticism of the British foreign policy, 1906–1914' (Oxford University, D.Phil., 1964).

Dunne, T., 'Ireland, England and the Empire, 1868–1886: the ideologies of the British political leadership' (Cambridge University, Ph.D., 1975).

Ellins, R.E., 'Aspects of the new Liberalism, 1895–1914' (University of Sheffield, D.Phil., 1980).

Ellinwood, D.C. Jr., 'Lord Milner's "Kindergarten": the British Round Table group and the movement for imperial reform, 1910–1918' (Washington University, Ph.D., 1962).

Fitzpatrick, C., 'Labour, ideology and the states in Ireland, 1917–1932' (Cambridge University, Ph.D., 1993).

Forster, N.T.A., 'The religio Milneriana and the Lloyd George coalition, 1916–21' (Keele University, Ph.D., 1989).

Hamilton, N.C., 'Lord Milner and the Ulster crisis, 1912–14' (University of Kent, M.A., 1972).

Harrison, R., 'The activity and influence of the English Positivists upon labour movements, 1859–1885' (Oxford University, D.Phil., 1955).

Hart, M., 'The decline of the Liberal party in parliament and in the constituencies, 1914–1931' (Oxford University, D.Phil., 1982).

Hepburn, A.C., 'Liberal policies and Nationalist politics, 1905–1910' (University of Kent, Ph.D., 1968).

Inwood, S., 'The role of the press in English politics during the First World War, with special reference to the period 1914–1916' (Oxford University, D.Phil., 1971).

Kelvin, P., 'The development and use of the concept of the electoral mandate in British politics, 1867 to 1911' (University of London, D.Phil., 1977).

Kent, C., 'Aspects of academic radicalism in mid-Victorian England: a study in the politics of thought and action with particular reference to Frederic Harrison and John Morley' (University of Sussex, Ph.D., 1968).

Marley, M.E.P., 'Asquith, home rule and the Gladstonian tradition' (Queen's University of Belfast, D.Phil., 1972).

May., A.C., 'The Round Table, 1910–66' (Oxford University, D.Phil., 1995).

Morris, A.J.L., 'A study of John St Loe Strachey's editorship of the *Spectator*, 1901–1914' (Cambridge University, Ph.D., 1986).
Murphy, J.M., 'Positivism in England: the reception of Comte's doctrines, 1840–1870' (Columbia University, Ph.D., 1968).
O'Callaghan, M., 'Crime, nationality and the law: the politics of land in late Victorian Ireland' (Cambridge University, Ph.D., 1989).
Peatling, G.K., 'British ideological movements and Irish politics, 1865–1925' (Oxford University, D.Phil., 1997).
Russell, A.K., 'The General Election of 1906' (Oxford University, D.Phil., 1962).
Stubbs, J.O., 'The Conservative party and the politics of war, 1914–1918' (Oxford University, D.Phil., 1973).
Towey, T.F., 'The origin and development of dominion status as a constitutional settlement in Ireland, 1920–1923' (Oxford University, D.Phil., 1978).
Ward, P.J., '"Englishness", patriotism and the British left, 1881–1914' (University of London, Ph.D., 1994).

BOOKS AND PAMPHLETS

Abrams, P., *The origins of British sociology, 1834–1914* (Chicago, 1968).
Amery, L.S., *The fundamental fallacies of free trade* (London, 1907).
—, *The case against home rule* (London, 1912).
—, *Union and strength: a series of papers on imperial questions* (London, 1912).
—, *My political life* (London, 1950–3, 3 vols).
Amery, L.S. (ed.), *The 'Times' history of the war in South Africa* (London, 1900–9, 7 vols).
Anderson, B., *Imagined communities: reflections on the rise and spread of nationalism* (London, rev. ed, 1991, first published 1983).
Anderson, M., *Noel Buxton: a life* (London, 1952).
Annals of the Lothian Foundation, i (1991).
Ash, B., *The lost dictator: a biography of Field Marshall Sir Henry Wilson* (London, 1968).
Ashton, R., *G.H. Lewes: a life* (Oxford, 1991).
Auchmuty, J., *Lecky: a biographical and critical essay* (Dublin, 1945).
Aughey, A., *Under siege: Ulster Unionism and the Anglo-Irish Agreement* (London, 1989).
Axelrod, R., *The evolution of co-operation* (New York, 1984).
Ayerst, D., *'Guardian': biography of a newspaper* (London, 1971).
—, *Garvin of the 'Observer'* (Beckenham, 1985).
Baden-Powell, G., (ed.), *The truth about home rule: papers on the Irish question* (London, 2nd ed, 1888).
Ball, S., *Baldwin and the Conservative party: the crisis of 1929–1931* (New Haven, 1988).
Barker, M., *Gladstone and radicalism: the reconstruction of Liberal politics in Britain, 1885–94* (Hassocks, 1975).
Barnes, J., and Nicholson, D., (eds), *The Leo Amery diaries* (London, 1980, 2 vols).
Barnett, C., *The collapse of British power* (London, 1972).

Bartlett, T., and Jeffrey, K., (eds), *A military history of Ireland* (Cambridge, 1996).
Barton, F.B., *An outline of the Positive religion of humanity* (London, 1867).
Beesly, E.S., *The social future of the working class: a lecture* (London, 1869).
—, *A word for France, addressed to the workmen of London* (London, 1870).
—, *Letters to the working classes* (London, 1870).
—, *Home Rule* (London, 1886).
—, *Socialists against the grain: or, the price of holding Ireland* (London, 1887).
—, *Mind your own business: some plain words to the Gladstonians about Mr. Parnell* (London, 1890).
—, *A strong second chamber* (London, 1907).
Bellamy, R., (ed.), *Victorian liberalism: nineteenth-century political thought and practice* (London, 1990).
Beloff, M., *Britain's liberal empire, 1897–1921* (London, 1969).
Bentley, M., *The Liberal mind, 1914–1929* (Cambridge, 1977).
—, *The climax of Liberal politics: British Liberalism in theory and practice, 1868–1918* (London, 1987).
Bentley, M., and Stevenson, J., (eds), *High and low politics in modern Britain: ten studies* (Oxford, 1983).
Berlin, I., *Four essays on liberty* (Oxford, 1969).
Bernstein, G.L., *Liberalism and Liberal politics in Edwardian England* (Boston, 1986).
Bew, P., *Conflict and conciliation in Ireland, 1890–1910: Parnellites and radical agrarians* (Oxford, 1987).
—, *Ideology and the Irish question: Ulster Unionism and Irish Nationalism, 1912–1916* (Oxford, 1994).
—, *John Redmond* (Dundalk, 1996).
Bew, P., Patterson, H., and Teague, P., *Northern Ireland, between war and peace: the political future of Northern Ireland* (London, 1997).
Biagini, E., *Liberty, retrenchment and reform: popular liberalism in the age of Gladstone, 1860–1880* (Cambridge, 1992).
Biagini, E., (ed.), *Citizenship and community: Liberals, radicals and collective identities in the British Isles, 1865–1931* (Cambridge, 1996).
Biagini, E., and Reid, A., (eds), *Currents of radicalism: popular radicalism, organised labour and party politics, 1850–1914* (Cambridge, 1991).
Billig, M., *Banal nationalism* (London, 1995).
Birn, D.S., *The League of Nations Union, 1918–1945* (Oxford, 1981).
Blaazer, D., *The popular front and the progressive tradition: Socialists, Liberals and the quest for unity, 1884–1939* (Cambridge, 1992).
Blake, R., *The unknown Prime Minister: the life and times of Andrew Bonar Law, 1858–1923* (London, 1955).
—, *The Conservative party from Peel to Thatcher* (London, 1985).
Blake, R., (ed.) *Ireland after the Union* (Oxford, 1989).
Blewett, N., *The peers, the parties and the people: the general elections of 1910* (London, 1972).
Bodelsen, C., *Studies in mid-Victorian imperialism* (London, 1924).
Bolger, P., *The Irish co-operative movement: its history and development* (Dublin, 1977).

Bosco, A., *Lord Lothian: un pionere del federalismo, 1882–1940* (Milan, 1989).
Bosco, A., (ed.) *The federal idea* (London, 1991–2, 2 vols), vol.I.
Bosco, A., and May, A., (eds), *The Round Table, the Empire/Commonwealth, and British foreign policy* (London, 1997).
Bourassa, H., *'Independence or imperial partnership': a study of 'The problem of the commonwealth' by Mr Lionel Curtis* (Montreal, 1916).
Bowman, J., *De Valera and the Ulster question, 1917–73* (Oxford, 1982).
Boyce, D.G., *Englishmen and Irish troubles: British public opinion and the making of Irish policy, 1918–22* (London, 1972).
—, *Nationalism in Ireland* (London, 2nd ed, 1991).
The Irish question and British politics, 1868–1996 (Basingstoke, 2nd ed, 1996, first published 1988).
Boyce, D.G., (ed.), *The crisis of British Unionism: the domestic political papers of the second Earl of Selborne, 1885–1922* (London, 1988).
—, (ed.), *The revolution in Ireland, 1879–1923* (Basingstoke, 1988).
—, (ed.), *The crisis of British power: the imperial and naval papers of the second Earl of Selborne, 1895–1910* (London, 1990).
Boyce, D.G., Curran, J., and Wingate, P., (eds), *Newspaper history from the seventeenth century to the present day* (London, 1978).
Boyce, D.G., Eccleshall, R., and Geoghan, V., (eds), *Political thought in Ireland since the seventeenth century* (London, 1993).
Boyland, H., *A dictionary of Irish biography* (Dublin, 1978).
Lord Bradbourne, *Facts and fiction in Irish history: a reply to Mr Gladstone* (London, 1886).
Bradshaw, B., and Morrill, J., (eds), *The British problem, c. 1534–1707: state formation in the Atlantic Archipelago* (Basingstoke, 1996).
Bradshaw, B., and Roberts, P., (eds), *British consciousness and identity: the making of Britain,* 1533–1707 (Cambridge, 1998).
Brailsford, H.N., *Some Irish problems* (London, 1903).
—, *The war of steel and gold: a study of the armed peace* (London, 1914).
—, *A league of nations* (London, 1917).
—, *The life-work of J.A. Hobson* (London, 1948).
Brailsford, H.N., (ed.), *Essays, poems and tales of Henry W. Nevinson* (London, 1941).
Brand, R.H., *The Union of South Africa* (Oxford, 1909).
Brand, R.H., (ed.), *The letters of John Dove* (London, 1938).
Breton, A., Galeotti, G., Salmon P., and Winstable R., (eds), *Nationalism and rationality* (Cambridge, 1995).
Breuilly, J., *Nationalism and the state* (Manchester, 2nd ed, 1993, first published 1982).
Bridges, J.H., *The unity of Comte's life and doctrine* (London, 1866).
—, *Irish disaffection: four letters addressed to the editor of the 'Bradford Review'* (Bradford, 1868), [reissued as *The home rule question eighteen years ago* (London, 1886)].
—, *Essays and addresses* (London, 1907).
Bridges, M.A., (ed.), *Recollections of John Henry Bridges* (London, 1908).

Briggs, A., and Saville, J., (eds), *Essays in labour history* (London, 1960–77, 3 vols), vol.I.
Brockliss, L.W.B., and Eastwood, D., (eds), *A union of multiple identities: the British Isles, c.1750–c.1850* (Manchester, 1997).
Brodrick, G., *Home rule and justice to Ireland: a letter to the editor of the 'Times'* (Oxford, 1886).
—, *Unionism: the basis of a national party* (Oxford, 1888).
—, *Memories and impressions, 1831–1900* (London, 1900).
Bromage, M.C., *Churchill and Ireland* (Notre Dame, 1964).
Brown, A.W., *The Metaphysical Society: Victorian minds in crisis, 1869–1880* (New York, 1947).
Brown, K., (ed.), *Essays in anti-Labour history: responses to the rise of Labour in Britain* (London, 1974).
Bruce, S., *The edge of the Union: the Ulster loyalist political vision* (Oxford, 1994).
Bryce, J., *Committee on Irish affairs, paper no.1: England and Ireland: an introductory statement* (London, 1884).
—, *The American commonwealth* (London, 1893, 2 vols).
Bryce, J., (ed.), *Handbook of home rule* (London, 1887).
—, (ed.), *Two centuries of Irish history* (London, 1888).
Buchan, J., *Memory hold the door* (London, 1940).
Buckland, P., *Irish Unionism* (London, 1972–3, 2 vols).
Buckland, P., (ed.), *Irish Unionism, 1885–1923: a documentary history* (Belfast, 1973).
Budd, S., *Varieties of unbelief: atheists and agnostics in English society, 1850–1960* (London, 1977).
Bull, P., *Land, politics and nationalism: a study of the Irish land question* (Dublin, 1996).
Burgess, M., (ed.), *Federalism and federation in western Europe* (Beckenham, 1986).
Burrow, J.W., *Evolution and society: a study in Victorian theory* (Cambridge, 1970).
—, *A liberal descent: Victorian historians and the English past* (Cambridge, 1981).
Butler, J.R.M., *Lord Lothian (Philip Kerr), 1882–1940* (London, 1960).
Buxton, C.R., (ed.), *Towards a lasting settlement* (London, 1915).
C.P. Scott, 1846–1932: the making of the 'Manchester Guardian' (London, 1946).
Caird, E., *The social philosophy and religion of Comte* (New York, 1968, first published 1885).
Callanan, F., *The Parnell split, 1890–91* (London, 1992).
Campbell, C., *Emergency law in Ireland, 1918–1925* (Oxford, 1994).
A Canadian criticism on 'The problem of the Commonwealth' and the author's reply thereto (London, 1916).
Canning, P., *British policy towards Ireland, 1921–1941* (Oxford, 1985).
Carlyle, T., *Reminiscences of my Irish journey in 1849* (London, 1882).
Carsten, F.L., *War against war: British and German radical movements in the First World War* (London, 1982).
Cassar, G., *Asquith as war leader* (London, 1994).
Catterall, P., and McDougall, S., (eds), *The Northern Ireland question in British politics* (London, 1996).
Ceadel, M., *Pacifism in Britain, 1914–1945: the defining of a faith* (Oxford, 1980).

Viscount Cecil of Chelwood, *A great experiment: an autobiography* (London, 1941).
Chamberlain, A., *Politics from the inside* (London, 1936).
Chesterton, G.K., *Irish impressions* (London, 1919).
Childers, E., *The framework of home rule* (London, 1912).
—, *Military rule in Ireland* (Dublin, 1920).
Churchill, R.S., *Lord Derby, 'King of Lancashire': the official life of Edward, seventeenth Earl of Derby, 1865–1948* (London, 1959).
Churchill, W.S., *Liberalism and the social problem* (London, 1909).
—, *The world crisis, 1911–1918* (London, 1923).
Clarke, A., (ed.), *'A good innings': the private papers of Viscount Lee of Fareham* (London, 1974).
Clarke, P.F., *Lancashire and the new Liberalism* (Cambridge, 1971).
—, *Liberals and social democrats* (Cambridge, 1978).
Cline, C.A., *Recruits to Labour: the British Labour party, 1914–1931* (New York, 1963).
Cochrane, F., *Unionist politics and the politics of Unionism since the Anglo-Irish Agreement* (Cork, 1997).
Cocks, R.C.J., *Sir Henry Maine: a study in Victorian jurisprudence* (Cambridge, 1988).
Coetzee, F., *For party or country: nationalism and the dilemmas of popular conservatism in Edwardian England* (Oxford, 1990).
Coit, S., (ed.), *Ethical democracy: essays in social dynamics* (London, 1900).
Colley, L., *Britons: forging the nation, 1707–1837* (London, 1996, first published 1992).
Collini, S., *Liberalism and sociology: L.T. Hobhouse and political argument in England, 1880–1914* (Cambridge, 1979).
—, *Public moralists: political thought and intellectual life in Britain, 1850–1930* (Oxford, 1991).
Collini, S., Winch, D., and Burrow, J., *That noble science of politics: a study in nineteenth-century intellectual history* (Cambridge, 1983).
Collins, P., (ed.), *Nationalism and unionism: conflict in Ireland* (Belfast, 1994).
Collison Black, R.D., *Economic thought and the Irish question, 1817–70* (Cambridge, 1960).
Colls, R., and Dodd, P., (eds), *Englishness: politics and culture, 1880–1920* (London, 1986).
Comte, A., *A general view of Positivism* (London, 1865), trans. J.H. Bridges from *Discours sur l'ensemble du positivisme* (Paris, 1848).
—, *System of Positive polity: a treatise in sociology, instituting the religion of humanity* (London, 1875–7, 4 vols), trans. R. Congreve et al from *Système de politique positive, ou traité de sociologie instituant la religion de l'humanité* (Paris, 1851–1854, 4 vols.).
—, *Appeal to conservatives* (London, 1889), trans. Congreve and T. Donikin from *Appel aux conservateurs* (Paris, 1855).
—, *The catechism of Positive religion* (London, 3rd ed, 1891, first published 1858), trans. Congreve from *Catéchisme positiviste* (Paris, 1852).
—, *A discourse on the Positive spirit* (London, 1903), trans. E.S. Beesly from *Discours sur l'esprit positif* (Paris, 1844).

Congreve, R., *Essays, political, social and religious* (London, 1874–1900, 3 vols).
Congreve, R. (ed.), *International policy: essays on the foreign relations of England* (London, 1866).
Congreve, R., et al *Papers on the war between France and Germany* (London, 1870).
Cooke, A.B., and Malcomson, A.P.W. (eds), *The Ashbourne papers* (Belfast, 1974).
Cooke, A.B., and Vincent, J., *The governing passion: cabinet government and party politics in Britain, 1885–6* (Hassocks, 1974).
Cooke, A.B., and Vincent, J., (eds), *Lord Carlingford's journal: reflections of a cabinet minister, 1885* (Oxford, 1971).
Cosgrove, A., and McCartney, D., (eds), *Studies in Irish history* (Dublin, 1979).
Cosgrove, R., *The rule of law: Albert Venn Dicey, Victorian jurist* (London, 1980).
Cotton, H., *India and home memories* (London, 1911).
Coupland, R., *The Empire in these days: an interpretation* (London, 1935).
Cowling, M., 1867: *Disraeli, Gladstone and revolution: the passing of the second Reform Bill* (Cambridge, 1967).
— , *The impact of Labour, 1920–1924: the beginning of modern British politics* (Cambridge 1971).
—, *The impact of Hitler: British politics and British policy, 1933–1940* (Cambridge, 1975).
—, *Mill and Liberalism* (Cambridge, 2nd ed, 1990, first published 1963).
Crankshaw, E., *The foresaken idea: a study of Viscount Milner* (London, 1952).
Crompton, H., *Letters on social and political subjects* (London, 1870).
—, *The Irish state trial* (London, 1881).
Crone, J.S., *A concise dictionary of Irish biography* (Dublin, 1937).
Cross, C., *The Liberals in power (1905–1914)* (London, 1963).
Crossman, V., *Politics, law and order in nineteenth-century Ireland* (Dublin, 1996).
Cubitt, G. (ed.), *Imagining nations* (Manchester, 1998).
Cunningham, M., *British government policy in Northern Ireland, 1969–1989: its nature and execution* (Manchester, 1991).
Curran, J.M., *The birth of the Irish Free State, 1921–1923* (Alabama, 1981).
Curtis, L.G., *With Milner in South Africa* (Oxford, 1951).
Curtis, L.G., (ed.), *The commonwealth of nations, part 1* (London, 1916).
—, *The problem of the commonwealth* (London, 1916).
[Curtis, L.G., (ed.)], *A practical enquiry into the nature of citizenship in the British Empire and into the relations of its several communities to each other* (London, 1914).
Curtis, L.P., Jr., *Coercion and conciliation in Ireland, 1880–92: a study in constructive Unionism* (Princeton, 1963).
— , *Anglo-Saxons and Celts: a study of anti-Irish prejudice in Victorian England* (Bridgeport, Connecticut, 1968).
Dahrendorf, R., *LSE: a history of the London School of Economics and Political Science* (Oxford, 1995).
Dangerfield, G., *The damnable question: a study in Anglo-Irish relations* (London, 1977).
—, *The strange death of liberal England* (New York, 1980, first published 1935).
Davies, A.J., *We, the nation: the Conservative party and the pursuit of power* (London, 1995).

Davies, J.T., *The Prime Minister's secretariat, 1916–1920* (Newport, 1951).
Dicey, A.V. *England's case against home rule* (London, 3rd ed, 1887, first published 1886).
—, *Letters on Unionist delusions* (London, 1887).
—, *The verdict: a tract on the political significance of the Parnell Commission* (London, 1890).
—, *A leap in the dark: a criticism of the principles of home rule as illustrated by the Bill of 1893* (London, 1893).
—, *A fool's paradise: being a constitutionalist's criticism on the Home Rule Bill of 1912* (London, 1913).
—, *Lectures on the relation between law and public opinion in England during the nineteenth century* (London, 2nd ed, 1914, first published 1905).
Dickinson, G.L., *After the war* (London, 1915).
Digby, M., *Horace Plunkett: An Anglo-American Irishman* (Oxford, 1949).
Dilks, D., (ed.), *Retreat from power: studies in Britain's foreign policy of the twentieth century* (London, 1981, 2 vols), vol. I.
Douglas, R., *The history of the Liberal party, 1895–1970* (London, 1971).
Dunn, W.H., *James Anthony Froude: a biography* (Oxford, 1961–3, 2 vols).
Dunphy, R., *The making of Fianna Fáil power in Ireland, 1923–1948* (Oxford, 1995).
Dutton, D., *'His Majesty's loyal opposition': the Unionist party in opposition, 1905–1915* (Liverpool, 1992).
—, *Simon: A political biography of Sir John Simon* (London, 1992).
Eagleton, T., (ed.), *Ideology* (Oxford, 1994).
Eddy, J., and Schreuder, D., (eds), *The rise of colonial nationalism* (Sydney, 1988).
Eldridge, C.C., *England's mission: the imperial idea in the age of Gladstone and Disraeli, 1868–1880* (London, 1973).
—, *Victorian imperialism* (London, 1978).
Eldridge, C.C., (ed.), *British imperialism in the nineteenth century* (London, 1984).
Ellis, E.L., *T.J.: a life of Dr Thomas Jones, C.H.* (Cardiff, 1992).
Ellis, H., *What Positivism means: a brief summary of its doctrines and aims* (London, 1887).
Elton, O., *C.E. Montague: a memoir* (London, 1929).
Emy, H.V., *Liberals, radicals and social politics, 1892–1914* (Cambridge, 1973).
English, R., *Radicals and the Republic: socialist republicanism in the Irish Free State, 1925–1937* (Oxford, 1994).
English, R., and Walker, G., (eds), *Unionism in modern Britain: new perspectives on politics and culture* (Basingstoke, 1996).
Ensor, R.C.K., *England, 1870–1914* (Oxford, 1936).
Essays in honour of Gilbert Murray (London, 1936).
Essays in Liberalism, by six Oxford men (London, 1897).
Evans, B., and Taylor, A., *From Salisbury to Major: continuity and change in Conservative politics* (Manchester, 1996).
Evans-Pritchard, E.E., *The sociology of Comte: an appreciation* (Manchester, 1970).
Everett, E.M., *The party of humanity: the 'Fortnightly Review' and its contributors, 1865–1874* (New York, 1939).
Eyck, F., *G.P. Gooch: a study in history and politics* (London, 1982).

Fair, J.D., *British interparty conferences: a study of the procedure of conciliation in British politics, 1867–1921* (New York, 1980).
Falkiner, C.L., *Memoir of John Kells Ingram* (Dublin, 1907).
Farrell, M., *Northern Ireland: the Orange State* (London, 1976).
Fforde, M., *Conservatism and collectivism, 1886–1914* (Edinburgh, 1990).
Fisher, H.A.L., *James Bryce* (New York, 1927, 2 vols).
Flint, J., and Williams, G., (eds), *Perspectives of empire* (London, 1970).
Follis, B., *A state under siege: the establishment of Northern Ireland, 1920–1925* (Oxford, 1995).
Foster, R.F., *Modern Ireland, 1600–1972* (London, 1985).
—, *Paddy and Mr Punch: connections in Irish and English history* (London, 1993).
—, *W.B. Yeats: a life. I: the apprentice mage, 1865–1914* (Oxford, 1997).
Francis, M., and Zweiniger-Bargielowska, I., (eds), *The Conservatives and British society, 1880–1990* (Cardiff, 1996).
Fraser, P., *Joseph Chamberlain: radicalism and empire, 1868–1914* (London, 1966).
Freeden, M., *The new Liberalism: an ideology of social reform* (Oxford, 1978).
—, *Liberalism divided: a study in British political thought, 1914–1939* (Oxford, 1986).
—, *Ideologies and political theory: a conceptual approach* (Oxford, 1996).
Freeden, M., (ed.), *J.A. Hobson: a reader* (London, 1988).
—, (ed.), *Minutes of the Rainbow Circle, 1894–1924* (London, 1989).
Froude, J.A., *The English in Ireland in the eighteenth century* (London, 1881, 3 vols, first published 1872–4).
—, *Oceana, or England and her colonies* (London, 1886).
—, *Short studies on great subjects* (London, new ed, 1892–3, 4 vols).
Froude, J.A., et al, *Lights on home rule: reprinted from the 'National Observer'* (Westminister, 1893).
Gailey, A., *Ireland and the death of kindness: the experience of constructive Unionism, 1890–1905* (Cork, 1987).
Gallagher, F., *The Anglo-Irish Treaty* (London, 1965).
Gardiner, A.G., *Prophets, priests and kings* (London, 1908).
—, *The life of George Cadbury* (London, 1923).
—, *The life of Sir William Harcourt* (London, 1923, 2 vols).
Garvin, J.L., *The economic foundations of peace: or, world-partnership as the truer basis of the League of Nations* (London, 1919).
—, *The life of Joseph Chamberlain* (London, 1932–4, 3 vols).
Garvin, K., *J.L. Garvin: a memoir* (London, 1948).
Garvin, T., *Nationalist revolutionaries in Ireland, 1858–1928* (Oxford, 1987).
Gellner, E., *Nations and nationalism* (Oxford, 1983).
George, W., *The making of Lloyd George* (London, 1972).
Gibbon, P., *The origins of Ulster Unionism: the formation of popular Protestant politics and ideology in nineteenth-century Ireland* (Manchester, 1975).
Gilbert, B.B., *The evolution of national insurance in Great Britain: the origins of the welfare state* (London, 1966).
Gilbert, M., *Churchill: a life* (London, 1991).
Girvin, B., *Between two worlds: politics and economy in independent Ireland* (Dublin, 1989).

Viscount Gladstone, *After thirty years* (London, 1928).
Gladstone, W.E., *The Irish question* (London, 1886).
—, *Special aspects of the Irish question* (London, 1892).
Godkin, E.L., *Reflections and comments, 1865–1895* (Westminster, 1896).
Gollin, A.M., *The 'Observer' and J.L. Garvin, 1908–1914: a study in great editorship* (London, 1960).
—, *Proconsul in politics: a study of Lord Milner in opposition and in power* (Letchworth 1960).
Gooch, G.P., *History of our times, 1885–1911* (London 1911).
—, *The life of Lord Courtney* (London, 1920).
—, *Nationalism* (London, 1920).
Good, J.W., *Ulster and Ireland* (Dublin, 1919).
Gordon, P., (ed.), *The red Earl: the papers of the fifth Earl of Spencer* (Northampton, 1981, 2 vols).
Gould, F.J., *Whither British? A brief survey of the social and political situation* (London, 1913).
—, *The life-story of a humanist* (London, 1923).
Grant, A.J., et al, *An introduction to the study of international relations* (London, 1916).
Grant, M., *Propaganda and the role of the State in inter-war Britain* (Oxford, 1994).
Green, A.S., *Ourselves alone in Ulster* (London, 1918).
Green, E.H.H., *The crisis of Conservatism: the politics, economics and ideology of the British Conservative party, 1880–1914* (London, 1995).
Grigg, J., *Lloyd George, the people's champion, 1902–1911* (London, 1978).
—, *Lloyd George: from peace to war, 1912–1916* (London, 1985).
Guderzo, G., (ed.), *Lord Lothian: una vita per la pace* (Florence, 1986).
Gupta, P.S., *Imperialism and the labour movement, 1914–1964* (London, 1975).
Gwynn, D., *The life of John Redmond* (London, 1932).
Gwynn, S.L., *Experiences of a literary man* (London, 1926).
Gwynn, S.L., (ed.), *The anvil of war: letters between F.S. Oliver and his brother, 1914–1918* (London, 1936).
Halfpenny, P., *Positivism and sociology: explaining social life* (London, 1982).
Halperin, V., *Lord Milner and the Empire: the evolution of British imperialism* (London, 1952).
Hamer, D., *John Morley: liberal intellectual in politics* (Oxford, 1968).
—, *Liberal politics in the age of Gladstone and Rosebery: a study in leadership and policy* (Oxford, 1972).
Hammond, J.L., *The terror in action* (London, 1921).
—, *C.P. Scott of the 'Manchester Guardian'* (London, 1934).
—, *Gladstone and the Irish nation* (London, 1938).
Hammond, J.L., and Foot, M., *Gladstone and Liberalism* (London, 2nd ed, 1967, first published 1952).
Hammond, J.L., and Hammond, B., *The village labourer, 1760–1832* (London, 1911).
—, *The town labourer, 1760–1832* (London, 1917).
—, *The skilled labourer, 1760–1832* (London, 1919).

—, *The age of the Chartists, 1832–1854: a study of discontent* (London, 1930).
—, *James Stansfeld: a Victorian champion of sex equality* (London, 1932).
Hammond, J.L., et al. *Towards a social policy: or, suggestions for constructive reform* (London, 1905).
Hancock, W.K., *Smuts* (Cambridge, 1962–8, 2 vols).
Hand, J.E., (ed.), *Good citizenship* (London, 1899).
Harbinson, J.F., *The Ulster Unionist party, 1882–1973* (Belfast, 1977).
Harkness, D., *The restless Dominion: the Irish Free State and the British Commonwealth of Nations, 1921–31* (London, 1969).
Harlow, V., *The character of British imperialism* (London, 1939).
Harris, J., *Private lives and public spirit: a social history of Britain, 1870–1914* (Oxford, 1993).
Harrison, A., *Frederic Harrison, thoughts and memories* (London, 1926).
Harrison, F., *Martial law: six letters to the 'Daily News'* (London, 1867).
—, *Order and progress* (London, 1875).
—, *The present and the future: a Positivist address* (London, 1880).
—, *Mr Gladstone – or anarchy!* (London, 1886).
—, *New Year's address, 1888* (London, 1888).
—, *Oliver Cromwell* (London, 1888).
—, *Memories and thoughts* (London, 1906).
—, *The creed of a layman: apologia pro fide mea* (London, 1907).
—, *National and social problems* (London, 1908).
—, *Realities and ideals: social, political, literary and artistic* (London, 1908).
—, *A real upper house* (London, 1910).
—, *Autobiographic memoirs* (London, 1911, 2 vols).
—, *The Positive evolution of religion: its moral and social reaction* (London, 1913).
—, *The German peril* (London, 1915).
—, *On society* (London, 1918).
—, *Novissima verba: last words* (London, 1920).
—, *De senectute: more last words* (London, 1923).
Harrison, F., Swinny, S.H., and Marvin, F.S., (eds), *The new calendar of great men* (London, new ed, 1920, first published 1892).
Harrison R., *Before the socialists: studies in labour and politics, 1861–1881* (Aldershot, 1994, first published 1965).
Harrison, R., (ed.), *The English defence of the commune, 1871* (London, 1971).
Hart, P., *The IRA and its enemies: violence and community in Cork, 1916–1923* (Oxford, 1998).
Hartley, S., *The Irish question as a problem in British foreign policy, 1914–18* (Basingstoke, 1987).
Harvie, C., *The lights of liberalism: university liberals and the challenge of democracy, 1860–1886* (Oxford, 1976).
Haultain, A., (ed.), *A selection from Goldwin Smith's correspondence* (London, 1913).
Havighurst, A.F., *Radical journalist: H.W. Massingham (1860–1924)* (Cambridge, 1974).
Hayes, R.J., (ed.), *Manuscript sources for the history of Irish civilisation, with supplement* (Boston, 1965 and 1979).

Hayward, F.H., and White, E.M., *The last years of a great educationist: the work and thought of F.J. Gould from 1923 to 1938* (Bungay, n.d.).
Headlem, C., (ed.), *The Milner papers* (South Africa) (London, 1931–3, 2 vols).
Hechter, M., *Internal colonialism: the Celtic fringe in British national development* (London, 1975).
Hewins, W.A.S., *Tariff reform and home rule* (London, 1912).
—, *Trade in the balance* (London, 1924).
—, *Empire restored* (London, 1927).
—, *The apologia of an Imperialist: forty years of empire policy* (London, 1929, 2 vols).
Heyck, T.W., *The dimensions of British radicalism: the case of Ireland, 1874–1895* (Urbana, Illinois, 1974).
—, *The transformation of intellectual life in Victorian England* (London, 1982).
Hill, F.H., et al, *Questions for a reformed parliament* (London, 1867).
Hillmer, N., and Wrigley, P., (eds), *The first British Commonwealth* (London, 1980).
Hirst, F.W., *Early life and letters of John Morley* (London, 1927, 2 vols).
—, *In the golden days* (London, 1947).
Hirst, F.W., Murray, G.G.A., and Hammond, J.L., *Liberalism and the Empire: three essays* (London, 1900).
The history of the 'Times': the 150th anniversary and beyond, 1912–48, vol.IV (London, 1952), parts I–II.
Hobhouse, L.T., *The labour movement* (London, 1893).
—, *Mind in evolution* (London, 1901).
—, *Democracy and reaction* (London, 1904).
—, *Social evolution and political theory* (Washington, 1911).
—, *The world in conflict* (London, 1915).
—, *Questions of war and peace* (London, 1916).
—, *The metaphysical theory of the state* (London, 1918).
—, *The elements of social justice* (London, 1922).
—, *Morals in evolution: a study in comparative ethics* (London, 1951, first published 1906).
—, *Liberalism* (New York, 1964, first published 1911).
—, *Social development: its nature and conditions* (London, 1966, first published 1924).
—, *Sociology and philosophy* (London, 1966).
Hobsbawm, E., and Ranger, T., (eds), *The invention of tradition* (Cambridge, 1983).
Hobson, J.A., *The social problem: life and work* (London, 1902).
—, *The German panic* (London, 1913).
—, *Towards international government* (London, 1915).
—, *Democracy after the war* (London, 1917).
—, *Richard Cobden: the international man* (London, 1919).
—, *Problems of a new world* (London, 1921).
—, *Free-thought in the social sciences* (London, 1926).
—, *The crisis of Liberalism: new issues of democracy* (Hassocks, 1974, first published 1909).
—, *Confessions of an economic heretic* (Hassocks, 1976, first published 1938).

—, *Imperialism: a study* (London, 3rd ed, 1988, first published 1902).
Hobson, J.A., and Ginsberg, M., *L.T. Hobhouse: his life and work* (London, 1931).
Home rule: a reprint from the 'Times' of recent articles and letters (London, 1886, 2 vols).
Hoppen, K.T., *Ireland since 1800: conflict and conformity* (London, 2nd ed, 1999, first published, 1989).
Horgan, J.J., *Parnell to Pearse: some recollections and reflections* (Dublin, 1948).
[Horgan, J.J.], *The complete grammar of anarchy* (Dublin, 1920).
Howe, S., *Anticolonialism in British politics: the left and the end of empire, 1918–1964* (Oxford, 1993).
Hurst, M., *Joseph Chamberlain and Liberal reunion: the round table conference of 1887* (London, 1967).
Hutton, H.D., *History, principle and fact in relation to the Irish question* (London, 1870).
—, *Comte, the man and the founder: personal recollections* (London, 1891).
—, *Comte's life and work: exceptional, but finally normal: an address* (London, 1892).
Hutton, H.D., et al, *Proposals for the gradual creation of a farmer-proprietary in Ireland* (Dublin, 1868).
Hyam, R., and Martin, G., *Reappraisals in British imperial history* (London, 1975).
Hyde, H. Montgomery, *Carson* (London, 1953).
Hyde, H. Montgomery (ed.), *A Victorian historian: private letters of W.E.H. Lecky, 1859–1878* (London, 1947).
Viscount Hythe, *The case for devolution and a settlement of the home rule question by consent* (London, 1913).
—, *The need for the immediate appointment of a commission to devise a scheme of devolution for the United Kingdom as a whole* (Westminster, 1914).
Inglis, B., *Roger Casement* (London, 1973).
Ingram, J.K., *Work and the workman* (Dublin, 1880).
—, *A history of political economy* (Edinburgh, 1888).
—, *Outlines of the history of religion* (London, 1900).
—, *Sonnets and other poems* (London, 1900).
—, *Human nature and morals according to Auguste Comte* (London, 1901).
—, *Practical morals: a treatise on universal education* (London, 1904).
—, *The final transition: a sociological study* (London, 1905).
Ingram, T.D., *A history of the legislative Union of Great Britain and Ireland* (London, 1887).
Irish home rule: a speech delivered by the Rt. Hon. Winston Churchill, MP (London, 1912).
Jackson, A., *The Ulster party: Irish Unionists in the House of Commons, 1884–1911* (Oxford, 1989).
Jalland, P., *The Liberals and Ireland: the Ulster question in British politics to 1914* (Aldershot, 1993, first published 1980).
James, R. Rhodes, *Rosebery* (London, 1963).
—, *The British revolution: British politics, 1880–1939* (London, 1978).
'Janitor', *The feet of young men: some candid comments on the rising generation* (London, 1920).

'Jason' [pseud. J.L.Hammond], *Past and future* (London, 1918).
Jay, P., *Joseph Chamberlain: a political study* (Oxford, 1981).
Jenkins, R., *Mr Balfour's poodle: an account of the struggle between the House of Lords and the government of Mr Asquith* (London, 1954).
Jenkins, T.A., *Gladstone, whiggery and the Liberal party, 1874–1886* (Oxford, 1988).
John, A.V., and Eustance, C., (eds), *The men's share: masculinities, male support and women's suffrage, 1890–1920* (London, 1997).
Johnston J., *Civil war in Ulster: its objects and probable results* (Dublin, 1914).
Jones, G., *Social Darwinism and English thought: the interaction between biological and social theory* (Brighton, 1980).
Jones, G.A., *The politics of reform, 1884* (Cambridge, 1972).
Jones, G. Stedman, *Languages of class: studies in English working-class history, 1832–1982* (Cambridge, 1983).
Jones, H.S. (ed.), *Auguste Comte: early political writings* (Cambridge, 1998).
Jones, R.A., *Arthur Ponsonby: the politics of life* (London, 1989).
Jones, T., *Lloyd George* (London, 1951).
—, *Whitehall diary*, ed. K. Middlemas (London, 1969, 3 vols).
Judd, D., *Empire: the British imperial experience from 1765 to the present* (London, 1996).
Kedourie, E., *Nationalism* (Oxford, 4th expanded ed, 1993, first published 1960).
Kendle, J.M., *The Round Table movement and imperial union* (Toronto, 1977).
—, *Ireland and the federal solution: the debate over the United Kingdom Constitution, 1870–1921* (Kingston, 1989).
—, *Walter Long, Ireland and the Union, 1905–1920* (Montreal, 1992).
—, *Federal Britain: a history* (London, 1997).
Kennedy, D., *The widening gulf: Northern attitudes to the independent Irish State, 1919–49* (Belfast, 1988).
Kennedy, P., *The rise of Anglo-German antagonism, 1860–1914* (London, 1980).
—, *Strategy and diplomacy, 1870–1945: eight studies* (London, 1983).
Kent, C., *Brains and numbers: Elitism, Comtism and democracy in mid-Victorian England* (Toronto, 1978).
Kenyon, J., *The history men: the historical profession in England since the Renaissance* (London, 1983).
Keogh, D., *The Vatican, the bishops and Irish politics, 1919–39* (Cambridge, 1986).
Kerr, P., and Curtis, L., *The prevention of war* (New Haven, 1923).
Kinzer, B., (ed.), *The Gladstonian turn of mind* (Toronto, 1985)
Kinzer, B., Robson, A.P., and Robson, J.M., *A moralist in and out of parliament: John Stuart Mill at Westminster, 1865–1868* (Toronto, 1992).
Knights, B., *The idea of a clerisy in the nineteenth century* (Cambridge, 1978).
Koebner, R., and Schmidt, H.D., *Imperialism: the story and significance of a political word, 1840–1960* (Cambridge, 1964).
Koss, S., *John Morley at the India office, 1905–1910* (New Haven, 1969).
—, *Lord Haldane: scapegoat for Liberalism* (New York, 1969).
—, *Sir John Brunner: radical plutocrat, 1842–1919* (Cambridge, 1970).
—, *Fleet Street radical: A.G. Gardiner and the 'Daily News'* (London, 1973).
—, *Asquith* (London, 1976).
—, *The rise and fall of the political press in Britain* (London, 1981–4, 2 vols).

Koss, S., (ed.), *The pro-Boers: the anatomy of an anti-war movement* (Chicago, 1973).

Laffan, M., *The partition of Ireland, 1911–1925* (Dundalk, 1983).

Lavin, D., *From empire to international commonwealth: a biography of Lionel Curtis* (Oxford, 1995).

Lawlor, S., *Britain and Ireland, 1914–1923* (Dublin, 1983).

Lecky, E., *A memoir of the Rt. Hon. William Edward Hartpole Lecky* (London, 1909).

Lecky, W.E.H., *The leaders of public opinion in Ireland* (London, 1871, first published 1861).

—, *A history of Ireland in the eighteenth century* (London, new ed, 1892, 5 vols).

—, *Democracy and liberty* (London, 1899, 2 vols, first published 1896).

—, *The leaders of public opinion in Ireland* (London, new ed, 1903, 2 vols).

—, *Historical and political essays* (London, 1908).

—, *History of the rise and influence of the spirit of rationalism in Europe* (London, 1910, 2 vols in 1, first published 1865).

—, *Clerical influences: an essay in Irish sectarianism and English government*, ed. W. Lloyd and F. Cruise O'Brien (Dublin, 1911).

—, *A history of European morals: from Augustus to Charlemagne* (London, 1911, first published 1869).

Lee, A.J., *The origins of the popular press, 1855–1914* (London, 1976).

Lenzer, G. (ed.), *Auguste Comte and positivism: the essential writings* (New Brunswick, 1998).

Lettres d'Auguste Comte à Henry Dix Hutton (Dublin, 1890).

Leventhal, F.M., *The last dissenter: H.N. Brailsford and his world* (Oxford, 1985).

Liberal Unionist Association, *The case for the Union* (London, 1888, 3 vols).

Liveing, S.H., *A nineteenth-century teacher: John Henry Bridges* (London, 1926).

Loughlin, J.L., *Gladstone, home rule and the Ulster question, 1882–93* (Dublin, 1986).

—, *Ulster Unionism and British national identity since 1885* (London, 1995).

Louis, W.R., *In the name of God, go! Leo Amery and the British Empire in the age of Churchill* (London, 1992).

Lubenow, W.C., *Parliamentary politics and the home rule crisis: the British House of Commons in 1886* (Oxford, 1988).

—, *The Cambridge Apostles, 1820–1914: liberalism, imagination and friendship in British intellectual and professional life* (Cambridge, 1998).

Lynd, R., *Ireland a nation* (London, 1919).

—, *'Y.Y.': an anthology of essays* (London, 1933).

—, *Galway of the races: selected essays*, ed. S. McMahon (Dublin, 1990).

Lyons, F.S.L., *The Irish parliamentary party, 1890–1910* (London, 1950).

—, *The fall of Parnell, 1890–91* (London, 1960).

—, *Internationalism in Europe, 1815–1914* (Leyden, 1963).

—, *John Dillon: a biography* (London, 1968).

—, *Ireland since the famine* (London, 1971).

—, *Culture and anarchy in Ireland, 1890–1939* (Oxford, 1979).

Lyons, F.S.L., and Hawkins, R.A.J., (eds), *Ireland under the Union* (Oxford, 1980).

MacColl, M., *Reasons for home rule* (London, 4th ed., 1886).

MacCoole, S., *Hazel: a life of Lady Lavery* (Dublin, 1996).

MacDonagh, O., *States of mind: a study of Anglo-Irish conflict, 1780–1980* (London, 1983).
MacDonald, J.A. Murray, *Notes on the constitutional reconstruction of the Empire* (Westminster, 1917).
—, *The Case for federal devolution* (London, 1920).
MacGee, J., *A crusade for humanity: the history of organised Positivism in England* (London, 1931).
MacKenzie, J.M., *Propaganda and empire: the manipulation of British public opinion, 1880–1960* (Manchester, 1984).
Madden, F., and Fieldhouse, D.K., (eds), *Oxford and the idea of commonwealth* (London, 1982).
Maine, H., *Popular government: four essays* (London, new ed, 1890, first published 1885).
Mangan, J.A., (ed.), *Making imperial mentalities: socialisation and British imperialism* (Manchester, 1990).
Mansergh, N., *The Irish question, 1840–1921: a commentary on Anglo-Irish relations and on social and political forces in Ireland in the age of reform and revolution* (London, 1965, first published in 1940 as *Ireland in the age of reform and revolution*).
— , *The Commonwealth experience* (London, 2nd ed, 1982, 2 vols first published 1969), vol.I.
— , *The unresolved question: the Anglo-Irish settlement and its undoing, 1912–1972* (London, 1991).
Marjoribanks, E., and Colvin, I., *The life of Lord Carson* (London, 1932–6, 3 vols), vols II–III.
Marlow, J., *Milner, apostle of empire* (London, 1976).
Martin, H., *Ireland in insurrection: an Englishman's record of fact* (London, 1921).
— , *Battle: the life story of the Rt. Hon. Winston S. Churchill* (London, 1932).
Martineau, H., (ed.) *The Positive philosophy of Auguste Comte* (London, 1896, 3 vols, first published 1853 in 2 vols), based on A. Comte, *Cours de philosophie positive* (Paris, 1830–42, 6 vols).
Marvin, F.S., *The century of hope: a sketch of western progress from 1815 to the Great war* (Oxford, 1919).
— , *Comte: the founder of sociology* (New York, 1965, first published 1936).
Marvin, F.S., (ed.), *Progress and history* (London, 1916).
— , (ed.), *The unity of western civilisation* (London, 2nd ed, 1922, first published 1915).
— , (ed.), *Western races and the world* (London, 1922).
— , (ed.), *England and the world* (London, 1925).
Massingham, H.J., *Remembrance: an autobiography* (London, 1942).
Massingham, H.J., (ed.), *H.W.M.: a selection from the writings of H.W. Massingham* (London, 1925).
Massingham, H.W., *The Gweedore hunt: a story of English justice in Ireland* (London, 1890).
Massingham H.W., (ed.), *Labour and protection: a series of studies* (London, 1903).
Masterman, C.F.G., *The condition of England* (London, 1909).
— , *The new Liberalism* (London, 1920).

Masterman, C.F.G., (ed.), *The heart of the empire: discussions of the problem of city life in England with an essay on imperialism* (London, 1901).
Masterman, L.B., *C.F.G. Masterman: a biography* (London, 1939).
Matthew, H.C.G., *The Liberal imperialists: the ideas and politics of a post-Gladstonian élite* (London, 1973).
—, *Gladstone* (Oxford, 1986–95, 2 vols).
McBriar, A.M., *Fabian socialism and English politics, 1884–1918* (Cambridge, 1962).
—, *An Edwardian mixed doubles: the Bosanquet versus the Webbs: a study in British social policy 1890–1929* (Oxford, 1987).
McCartney, D., *W.E.H. Lecky: historian and politician, 1838–1903* (Dublin, 1994).
McDowell, R., *Alice Stopford Green: a passionate historian* (Dublin, 1967).
—, *The Irish Convention, 1917–18* (London, 1970).
McKibbin, R., *The evolution of the Labour party, 1910–24* (Oxford, 1991, first published 1974).
McLeod, H., *Religion and society in England, 1850–1914* (Basingstoke, 1996).
McMahon, D., *Republicans and imperialists: Anglo-Irish relations in the 1930s* (New Haven, 1984).
McNeill, R., *Ulster's stand for union* (London, 1922).
Meller, H., *Patrick Geddes: social evolutionist and city planner* (London, 1990).
Messinger, G.S., *British propaganda and the state in the First World War* (Manchester, 1992).
Mill, J.S., *Collected works of John Stuart Mill*, eds J.M. Robson et al (Toronto, 1963–88), vols I, VI–VIII, X and XVIII.
Mills, W. Haslam, *The 'Manchester Guardian': a century of history* (London, 1921).
Milner, A., *The Nation and the Empire: speeches and addresses* (London, 1913).
—, *The British Commonwealth* (London, 1919).
—, *Questions of the hour* (London, 1923).
Mitchell, A., *Labour in Irish politics, 1890–1930: the Irish labour movement in an age of revolution* (Dublin, 1972).
—, *Revolutionary government in Ireland: Dáil Éireann, 1919–21* (Dublin, 1995).
Monypenny, W.F., *The two Irish nations: an essay on home rule* (London, 1913).
Moody, T.W., and Hawkins, R., (eds), *Florence Arnold-Forster's Irish journal* (Oxford, 1988).
Moore, J., *The life and letters of Edward Thomas* (London, 1939).
Morgan, A., *Labour and partition: the Belfast working class, 1905–23* (London, 1991).
Morgan, D., *Suffragists and Liberals: the politics of women's suffrage in England* (Oxford, 1975).
Morgan, J.H., *John, Viscount Morley: an appreciation and some reminiscences* (London, 1924).
Morgan, J.H., (ed.), *The New Irish Constitution: an exposition and some arguments* (London, 1912).
Morgan, K., *Consensus and disunity: the Lloyd George coalition government, 1918–1922* (Oxford, 1979).
Morison, J.C., *Irish grievances shortly stated* (London, 1868).

Morley, J., *The life of William Ewart Gladstone* (London, 1908, 2 vols, first published 1903 in 3 vols).
—, *Recollections* (London, 1917, 2 vols).
—, *On compromise* (London, 1923, first published 1874).
Morris, A.J.A., *Radicalism against war, 1906–14* (London, 1972).
—, *The scaremongers: the advocacy of war and rearmament, 1896–1914* (London, 1984).
Morris, A.J.A., (ed.), *Edwardian radicalism, 1900–1914: some aspects of British radicalism* (London, 1974).
Motion, A., *The poetry of Edward Thomas* (London, 1991, first published 1980).
Mueller, I.W., *John Stuart Mill and French thought* (Urbana, Illinois, 1956).
Muenger, E.A., *The British military dilemma in Ireland: occupation politics, 1886–1914* (Kansas, 1991).
Murray, A.E., *A history of the commercial relations between England and Ireland from the period of the Restoration* (London, 1903).
Murray, B.K., *The People's Budget, 1909–10: Lloyd George and Liberal politics* (Oxford, 1980).
Murray, G.G.A., *The foreign policy of Sir Edward Grey, 1906–1915* (London, 1915).
—, *Faith, war and policy: lectures and essays* (Boston, 1918).
—, *Essays and addresses* (London, 1921).
Nash, D., *Secularism, art and freedom* (Leicester, 1992).
Nevinson, H.W., *Essays in freedom and rebellion* (New Haven, 1921).
—, *Changes and chances* (London, 1923).
—, *More changes and more chances* (London, 1925).
—, *Last changes, last chances* (London, 1928).
—, *Running accompaniments* (London, 1936).
—, *Visions and memories* (London, 1944).
Nevinson, H.W., (ed.), *England's voice of freedom: an anthology of liberty* (London, 1929).
Nevinson, M.W., *Life's fitful fever: a volume of memories* (London, 1926).
Ní Dhonchaddha, M., and Dorgan, T., (eds), *Revising the Rising* (Derry, 1991).
Nimocks, W., *Milner's young men: the Kindergarten in Edwardian imperial affairs* (London, 1970, first published 1968).
Nisbett, R., and Ross, L., *Human inference: strategies and shortcomings of social judgement* (Englewood Cliffs, 1980).
Norman, E.R., *Anti-Catholicism in Victorian England* (London, 1968).
O'Brien, C.C., *Parnell and his party, 1880–90* (Oxford, 1957).
O'Brien, J.V., *William O'Brien and the course of Irish politics, 1881–1918* (London, 1976).
—, *'Dear, dirty Dublin': a city in distress, 1899–1916* (Berkeley, 1982).
O'Brien, R.B., *Irish wrongs and English remedies, with other essays* (London, 1887).
—, *The home rulers' manual* (London, 1890).
O'Brien, T.H., *Milner: Viscount Milner of St James and Cape Town, 1854–1925* (London, 1979).
O'Brien, W., *The responsibility for partition, considered with an eye to Ireland's future* (Dublin, 1921).
—, *The Irish revolution and how it came about* (London, 1923).

O'Broin, L., *Protestant nationalists in revolutionary Ireland: the Stopford connection* (Dublin, 1985).
O'Callaghan, M.M., *British high politics and a nationalist Ireland: criminality, land and the law under Forster and Balfour* (Cork, 1994).
O'Day, A., *The English face of Irish Nationalism: Parnellite involvement in British politics, 1880–6* (Toronto, 1977).
—, *Parnell and the first home rule episode, 1884–7* (Dublin, 1986).
O'Day, A., et al, *Reactions to Irish nationalism* (London, 1987).
O'Donnell, C.J., and Clifford, B., *Ireland in the Great War: the Irish insurrection of 1916 set in the context of the World War* (Belfast, 1992).
O'Farrell, P., *England and Ireland since 1800* (London, 1975).
O'Halpin, E., *The decline of the Union: British government in Ireland, 1892–1920* (Dublin, 1987).
O'Hegarty, P.S., *Sinn Féin: an illumination* (Dublin, 1919).
Oldmeadow, E., *Francis Cardinal Bourne* (London, 1940, 2 vols).
O'Leary, B., and McGarry, J., *The politics of antagonism: understanding Northern Ireland* (London, 1993).
Oliver, F.S., *Alexander Hamilton: an essay on American union* (London, 1906).
—, *The alternatives to civil war* (London, 1913).
—, *What federalism is not* (London, 1914).
—, *Ordeal by battle* (London, 1915).
—, *Ireland and the Imperial Conference: is there a way to settlement?* (London, 1917).
—, *Ulster and a federal settlement* (London, 1918).
—, *The endless adventure* (London, 1930–5, 3 vols).
—, *Politics and politicians* (London, 1934).
Owen, J.E., *L.T. Hobhouse: sociologist* (London, 1974).
Page, M., *Britain's unknown genius: an introduction to the life-work of John MacKinnon Robertson* (London, 1984).
Pakenham, F., *Peace by ordeal: an account from first-hand sources of the negotiation and signature of the Anglo-Irish Treaty, 1921* (London, 1935).
Parker, P.L., (ed.), *Character and life: a symposium* (London, 1912).
Parry, J.P., *Democracy and religion: Gladstone and the Liberal party, 1867–75* (Cambridge, 1986).
—, *The rise and fall of Liberal government in Victorian Britain* (New Haven, 1993).
Paul, H., *The life of Froude* (London, 1905).
Pedersen, S., and Mandler, P., (eds), *After the Victorians: private conscience and public duty in modern Britain* (London, 1994).
Peele, G., and Cook, C., (eds), *The politics of reappraisal, 1918–1939* (London, 1975).
Pelling, H., *Popular politics and society in late Victorian Britain* (London, 1968).
— , *A history of British trade unionism* (Harmondsworth, 4th ed, 1987, first published 1963).
Perkin, H., *The origins of modern English society, 1780–1880* (London, 1969).
Phillips, W. Alison, *The revolution in Ireland, 1906–1923* (London, 1923).
Phoenix, E., *Northern nationalism: nationalist politics, partition and the Catholic minority in Northern Ireland, 1890–1940* (Belfast, 1994).

Pickering, M., *Auguste Comte: an intellectual biography Vol.1* (Cambridge, 1993).
Pinder, J., and Bosco, A., (eds), *Pacifism is not enough: collected lectures and speeches of Lord Lothian (Philip Kerr)* (London, 1990).
Pittock, M., *Inventing and resisting Britain: cultural identities in Britain and Ireland, 1685–1789* (Basingstoke, 1997).
Plunkett, H., *Ireland in the new century* (London, 1904).
Porter, B., *Critics of empire: British radical attitudes to colonialism in Africa* (London, 1968).
Porter, R., (ed.), *Myths of the English* (Cambridge, 1992).
Positivist comments on public affairs: occasional papers issued by the London Positivist Society, 1878–1892 (London, 1896).
Pound, R., and Harmsworth, G., *Northcliffe* (London, 1959).
Price, R., *An imperial war and the British working class: working-class attitudes and reactions to the Boer War, 1899–1902* (London, 1972).
Prill, F., *Ireland, Britain and Germany, 1871–1914: problems of integration in nineteenth-century Europe* (Dublin, 1975).
Professor Hewins, MP, on the Home Rule Bill (Irish Unionist Alliance pamphlet, no.209) (Dublin, 1913).
Pugh, M., *The Tories and the people, 1880–1935* (Oxford, 1985).
Quin, M., *The problem of human peace: studied from the standpoint of a scientific catholicism* (London, 1916).
—, *The politics of the proletariat: a contribution to the science of citizenship based chiefly on the sociology of Auguste Comte* (London, 1919).
—, *Memoirs of a Positivist* (London, 1924).
Rafferty, O.P., *Catholicism in Ulster, 1603–1983: an interpretative history* (London, 1994).
Rait, R.S., *Memorials of A.V. Dicey* (London, 1925).
Ramsden, J., *The age of Balfour and Baldwin, 1902–1940* (London, 1978).
Ramsden, J., (ed.), *Real old tory politics: the political diaries of Sir Robert Sanders, Lord Bayford, 1910–35* (London, 1984).
Ratcliffe, S.K., *The story of South Place* (London, 1955).
Raymund, E.T. [pseud. E.R. Thompson], *All and sundry* (London, 1919).
—, *Portraits of the new century (the first ten years)* (Edinburgh, 1928).
Read, D., *England, 1868–1914: the age of urban democracy* (London, 1979).
Report of the Irish Boundary Commission, 1925 (Dublin, 1969).
Reprints from the 'Cork Free Press': 1910–1916: an account of Ireland's only democratic anti-partition movement (Belfast, 1984).
Richter, M., *The politics of conscience: T.H. Green and his age* (London, 1964).
Ring, J., *Erskine Childers* (London, 1996).
Robbins, K., *The abolition of war: the 'peace movement' in Britain, 1914–1919* (Cardiff, 1976).
—, *John Bright* (London, 1979).
—, *The eclipse of a great power: modern Britain, 1870–1975* (London, 1983).
—, *Great Britain: identities, institutions and the idea of Britishness* (London, 1997).
Robertson, J.M., *The saxon and the celt* (London, 1897).
—, *The common sense of home rule: a reply to Lord Hugh Cecil* (London, 1911).

—, *The meaning of liberalism* (London, 1912).
—, *The evolution of states: an introduction to English politics* (London, 1912).
Robinson, R., Gallagher, J., and Denny, A., *Africa and the Victorians: the official mind of imperialism* (Cambridge, 1961).
'Roland' [pseud. J.M. Robertson], *The future of militarism: an examination of F. Scott Oliver's 'Ordeal by battle'* (London, 1916)
Rosenbaum, S., (ed.), *Against home rule: the case for the Union* (London, 1912)
Roskill, S., *Hankey, man of secrets* (London, 1970–4, 3 vols), vol.II.
'The Round Table', *The Irish question* (London, 1914).
Round Table studies (London, 1910–15, two series, 7 vols).
Rowland, P., *The last Liberal governments: the promised land, 1905–1910* (London, 1968).
—, *The last Liberal governments: unfinished business, 1911–1914* (London, 1971).
Rowse, A.L., *All Souls and appeasement: a contribution to contemporary history* (London, 1960).
Royle, E., *Radicals, secularists and republicans: popular freethought in Britain, 1866–1915* (Manchester, 1980).
Russell, A.K., *Liberal landslide: the General Election of 1906* (Newton Abbot, 1973).
Ryan, A.P., *Lord Northcliffe* (London, 1953).
—, *Mutiny at the Curragh* (London, 1956).
Ryan, D., *James Connolly: his life-work and writings* (Dublin, 1924).
Saab, A.P., *Reluctant icon: Gladstone, Bulgaria and the working class, 1856–1878* (Cambridge, Mass., 1991).
Samuel, R., (ed.), *Patriotism: the making and unmaking of British national identity* (London, 1989, 3 vols), vol.1.
Sandars, M.L., and Taylor, P.M., *British propaganda in the First World War, 1914–18* (London, 1982).
Saunderson, H., *The Saundersons of Castle Saunderson* (London, 1936).
Scally, R.J., *The origins of the Lloyd George coalition: the politics of social imperialism, 1900–1918* (Princeton, 1975).
Seaman, L.C.B., *Victorian England: aspects of English and imperial history, 1837–1901* (London, 1973).
Searle, G., *The quest for national efficiency* (Oxford, 1971).
—, *The Liberal party: triumph and disintegration, 1886–1929* (Basingstoke, 1992).
—, *Country before party: coalition and the idea of 'national government' in modern Britain, 1885–1987* (London, 1995).
Seddon, A., and Ball S., (eds), *Conservative century: the Conservative party since 1900* (Oxford, 1994).
Lord Selborne and Oliver, F.S., *A method of constitutional co-operation: suggestions for the better government of the United Kingdom* (London, 1918).
Semmel, B., *Imperialism and social reform: English social-imperialist thought, 1895–1914* (London, 1960).
—, *The Governor Eyre controversy* (London, 1962).
—, *The liberal idea and the demons of empire: theories of imperialism from Adam Smith to Lenin* (Baltimore, 1993).
Shannon, C.B., *Arthur J. Balfour and Ireland, 1874–1922* (Washington, 1988).

Shannon, R.T., *Gladstone and the Bulgarian agitation* (Hassocks, 1975).
—, *Gladstone: heroic minister, 1865–1898* (London, 1999).
Sharp, E., *Unfinished adventure: selected reminiscences from an Englishwoman's life* (London, 1933).
Shaw, G.B., *John Bull's other island* (London, 1957, first published 1907).
—, *Fabianism and empire: a manifesto* (London, 1900).
Shirlow, P., and McGovern, M. (eds), *Who are 'the people'? Unionism, Protestantism and Loyalism in Northern Ireland* (London, 1997).
Sidgwick, A., and E.M., *Henry Sidgwick: a memoir* (London, 1906).
Simon, W., *European Positivism in the nineteenth century: an essay in intellectual history* (Ithaca, New York, 1963).
Sked, A., and Cook, C., (eds), *Crisis and controversy* (London, 1976).
Skorupski, J., *John Stuart Mill* (London, 1989).
Smith, A.D.S., *Nationalism in the twentieth century* (Oxford, 1979).
Smith, G., *Irish history and Irish character* (Oxford, 1861).
—, *The Irish question: three letters to the editor of the 'Daily News'* (London, 1868).
—, *Dismemberment no remedy* (London, 1886).
—, *Irish history and the Irish question* (Toronto, 1905).
—, *Reminiscences*, ed. A. Haultain (New York, 1910).
Smith, J., and Toynbee, A., (eds), *Gilbert Murray: an unfinished autobiography* (London, 1960).
Smith, M.L.R., *Fighting for Ireland? the military strategy of the Irish republican movement* (London, 1995).
The sociological society (London, 1904).
Soffer, R.N., *Ethics and society in England: the revolution in the social science* (Berkeley, 1978).
Southgate, D., *The passing of the whigs* (London, 1962).
Spiller, G., *The ethical movement in Great Britain: a documentary history* (London, 1934).
Spinner, T., Jr., *George Joachim Goschen: the transformation of a Victorian liberal* (Cambridge, 1973).
Steele, E.D., *Irish land and British politics: tenant-right and nationality, 1865–1870* (Cambridge, 1974).
Stewart, A.T.Q., *The Ulster crisis* (London, 1967).
—, *Edward Carson* (Dublin, 1981).
Stocks, M., *Ernest Simon of Manchester* (Manchester, 1963).
Strauss, E., *Irish nationalism and British democracy* (Westport, Connecticut, 1951).
Stuchtey, B., *W.E.H. Lecky (1838–1903): historisches Denken und politisches Urteilen eines anglo-irischen Gelehrten* (Göttingen, 1997).
Sturgis, J.L., *John Bright and the Empire* (London, 1969).
Style, S., *In memoriam: Albert Crompton* (Liverpool, 1908).
Swartz, M., *The Union of Democratic Control in British politics during the First World War* (Oxford, 1971).
Swinny, S.H., *The history of Ireland: three lectures given in Newton Hall* (London, 1890).
Sykes, A., *Tariff reform in British politics, 1903–1913* (Oxford, 1979).

Symonds, R., *Oxford and empire: the last lost cause?* (Basingstoke, 1986).
Tanner, D., *Political change and the Labour party, 1900–1918* (Cambridge, 1990).
Taylor, A.J.P., *The trouble makers: dissent over foreign policy, 1792–1939* (London, 1957).
Thomas, R.G., *Edward Thomas: a portrait* (Oxford, 1985).
Thompson, K., (ed.), *Auguste Comte* (London, 1976).
Thompson, P., *Socialists, Liberals and Labour: the struggle for London, 1885–1914* (London, 1964).
Thornley, D., *Isaac Butt and home rule* (London, 1964).
Thornton, A.P., *The imperial idea and its enemies: a study in British power* (London, 1959).
Torlesse, F., *Some account of John Henry Bridges and his family* (London, 1912).
Torrance, D.E., *The strange death of the liberal empire: Lord Selborne in South Africa* (Liverpool, 1996).
Townshend, C., *The British campaign in Ireland, 1919–1921: the development of political and military policies* (Oxford, 1975).
—, *Political violence in Ireland: government and resistance since 1848* (Oxford, 1983).
Toynbee, A.J., *Acquaintances* (London, 1967).
Trevelyan, G.M., *The life of John Bright* (London, 1913).
Tulloch, H., *James Bryce's 'American commonwealth': the Anglo-American background* (Cambridge, 1988).
Turner, F.M., *Between science and religion: the reaction to scientific naturalism in late Victorian England* (New Haven, 1979).
Turner, J., *Lloyd George's secretariat* (Cambridge, 1980).
—, *British politics and the Great War: coalition and conflict, 1915–1918* (New Haven, 1992).
Turner, J., (ed.), *The larger idea: Lord Lothian and the problem of national sovereignty* (London, 1988).
Vincent, A., and Plant, R., *Philosophy, politics and citizenship: the life and thought of the British Idealists* (Oxford, 1984).
Vincent, J., *The formation of the Liberal party, 1857–1868* (London, 1966).
Vogeler, M.S., *Frederic Harrison: the vocations of a Positivist* (Oxford, 1984).
Von Arx, J.P., *Progress and pessimism: religion, politics and history in late nineteenth-century Britain* (New Haven, 1985).
Walker, B.M., *Ulster politics: the formative years, 1868–1886* (Belfast, 1989).
Wallace, E., *Goldwin Smith: Victorian liberal* (Toronto, 1957).
Wallace, S., *War and the image of Germany: British academics, 1914–1918* (Edinburgh, 1988).
Waller, B.C., *Hibernia, or the future of Ireland* (London, 1928).
Walling, R.A.J., (ed.), *The diaries of John Bright* (London, 1930).
Ward, A.J., *Ireland and Anglo-American relations, 1899–1921* (London, 1969).
—, *The Irish constitutional tradition: responsible government and modern Ireland, 1782–1992* (Blackrock, 1994).
Ward, J.C., *British economists and the Empire* (London, 1974).
Ward, M., *Hanna Sheehy-Skeffington: a life* (Cork, 1997).
Ward, M.E., and Montague, C.E., *William Thomas Arnold* (Manchester, 1907).

Wason, J. Cathcart, *Home rule all round versus fiscal independence, separation and tariff reform* (Westminster, 1912).
Wasserstein, R., *Herbert Samuel: a political life* (Oxford, 1992).
Weaver, S. A., *The Hammonds: a marriage in history* (Stanford, 1997).
Webb, B., *My apprenticeship* (London, 1926).
—, *Our partnership*, ed. B. Drake and M.I. Cole (London, 1948).
—, *Beatrice Webb's diaries, 1912–1924*, ed. M.I. Cole (London, 1952).
Webb, D.A., and McDowell, R.B., *Trinity College Dublin, 1592–1992: an academic history* (Cambridge, 1982).
Webb, S. and B., *The history of trade unionism* (London, new ed., 1902, first published 1894).
Weiler, P., *The new Liberalism: Liberal social theory in Great Britain, 1889–1914* (New York, 1982).
Wells, G.A., (ed.), *J.M. Robertson (1856–1933), Liberal, rationalist and scholar: an assessment by several hands* (London, 1987).
Wells, H.G., *The new Machiavelli* (London, 1994, first published 1911).
West, F., *Gilbert Murray: a life* (London, 1984).
West, T., *Horace Plunkett: co-operation and politics, an Irish biography* (Gerrards Cross, 1986).
Williams, B., *Cecil Rhodes* (London, 1921).
—, *Botha, Smuts and South Africa* (London, 1946).
Williams B., (ed.), *Home rule problems* (London, 1911).
Wilson, D., *Gilbert Murray O.M., 1866–1957* (Oxford, 1987).
Wilson, T., *The downfall of the Liberal party, 1914–1935* (London, 1966).
Wilson, T., (ed.), *The political diaries of C.P. Scott, 1911–1928* (London, 1970).
Winkler, H.R., *The League of Nations movement in Great Britain, 1914–1919* (New Brunswick, 1952).
Winter, J.M., *The Great War and the British people* (Basingstoke, 1985).
Winter, J.M., and Baggett, B., *1914–1918: the Great War and the shaping of the twentieth century* (London, 1996).
Wolff, S. (ed.), *Nationalism in Europe, 1815 to the present: a reader* (London, 1996).
Wrench, J., *Geoffrey Dawson and our times* (London, 1955).
—, *Alfred Lord Milner: the man of no illusions, 1854–1925* (London, 1958).
Wright, P., *On living in an old country: the national past in contemporary Britain* (London, 1985).
Wright, T.R., *The religion of humanity: the impact of Comtean Positivism on Victorian Britain* (Cambridge, 1986).
Wrigley, C., *Lloyd George and the challenge of Labour: the post-war coalition, 1918–1922* (New York, 1990).
Zimmern, A.E., *Henry Grattan* (London, 1902).
—, *Nationality and government, with other essays* (London, 1918).
—, *The League of Nations and the rule of law, 1918–1935* (London, 1936).

ELECTRONIC RESOURCES

Société Positiviste Internationale, *Auguste Comte (1798–1857) et le Positivisme*
Site hosted by Multimania
< http://www.multimania.com/clotilde/ >
Last accessed 20 July 2000.

ARTICLES

Acton, H.B., 'Comte's Positivism and the science of society', *Philosophy*, xxvi (1951), 291–310.

Anderson, P., 'Components of the national culture', *New Left Review*, no.50 (1967), 3–58.

Annan, N., 'The intellectual aristocracy', in J.H. Plumb (ed.), *Studies in social history* (London, 1955), pp.241–87.

Armytage, W.H.G., 'The railway rates question and the end of the third Gladstone ministry', *Eng.Hist.Rev.*, lxv (1950), 18–51.

Arnstien, W.L., 'Victorian prejudice reconsidered', *Vict.Stud.*, xii (1968–9), 452–7.

Arthur, P., 'Time, territory, tradition and the Anglo-Irish peace process', *Government and Opposition*, xxxi (1996), 426–40.

Auld, J.W., 'The Liberal pro-Boers', *Journ.Brit.Stud.*, xiv (1974–5), 78–101.

Bentley. M., 'Liberal politics and the Grey conspiracy of 1921', *Hist.Journ.*, xx (1977), 461–78.

Bernstein, G.L., 'Liberalism and the progressive alliance in the constituencies, 1900–1914 – three case studies', *Hist.Journ.*, xxvi (1983), 617–40.

—, 'Yorkshire Liberalism during the First World War', *Hist.Journ.*, xxxii (1989), 107–29.

Bittner, E., 'Radicalism and the organisation of radical movements', *American Sociological Review*, xxviii (1963), 928–40.

Blewett, N., 'Free Fooders, Balfourites, Whole Hoggers: factionalism within the Unionist party, 1906–10', *Hist.Journ.*, xi (1968), 95–124.

Bowen, D., 'Ireland's two nations', *Journ.Imp. & Comm.Hist.*, i (1973), 385–90.

Boyce, D.G., 'British Conservative opinion, the Ulster question and the partition of Ireland', *Ir.Hist.Stud.*, xvii (1970–1), 90–112.

—, 'British opinion, Ireland and the war', *Hist.Journ.*, xvii (1974), 575–93.

Boyce, D.G., and Hazlehurst, C., 'The unknown Chief Secretary: H.E. Duke and Ireland, 1916–1918', *Ir.Hist.Stud.*, xx (1976–7), 286–311.

Boyce, D.G., and Stubbs, J., 'F.S. Oliver, Lord Selborne and federalism', *Journ.Imp. & Comm.Hist.*, v (1976–7), 53–81.

Boyle, J.W., 'Ireland and the first International', *Journ.Brit.Stud.*, xi (1971–2), 44–62.

Boyle, T., 'The Liberal Imperialists, 1892–1906', *Bull.Instit.Hist.Research*, lii (1979), 48–82.

Buckland, P., 'The unity of Ulster Unionism, 1880–1939', *History*, lix (1973), 211–23.

Bull, P., 'The United Irish League and the reunion of the Irish parliamentary party, 1898–1900', *Ir.Hist.Stud.*, xxvi (1988–9), 51–78.

— , 'The significance of the Nationalist response to the Land Act of 1903', *Ir.Hist.Stud.*, xxviii (1992–3), 283–305.

Cain, P., 'J.A. Hobson, Cobdenism and the radical theory of economic imperialism, 1898–1914', *Ec.Hist.Rev.*, 2nd ser., xxxi (1978), 565–84.

— , 'Hobson's developing theory of imperialism', *Ec.Hist.Rev.*, 2nd ser., xxxiv (1981), 313–16.

— , 'J.A. Hobson, financial capitalism and imperialism in late Victorian and Edwardian England', *Journ.Imp. & Comm.Hist.*, xiii (1985), 1–27.

Clarke, P.F., 'The progressive movement in England', *Trans.Royal Hist.Soc.*, 5th ser., xxiv (1974), 159–81.

— , 'Liberals, Labour and the franchise', *Eng.Hist.Rev.*, xcii (1977), 582–9.

— , 'Hobson, free trade and imperialism', *Ec.Hist.Rev.*, 2nd ser., xxxiv (1981), 308–12.

Clune, M.J., 'Horace Plunkett's resignation from the Irish Department of Agriculture and Technical Instruction, 1906–1907', *Éire-Ireland*, xvii (1982), no.1, 57–73.

Collini, S., 'Political theory and the "science of society" in Victorian Britain', *Hist.Journ.*, xxiii (1980), 203–31.

— , 'Hobhouse, Bosanquet and the State: philosophical Idealism and political argument in England, 1880–1918', *Past & Present*, no.72 (1976), 86–111.

Cooke, A.B., and Vincent, J., 'Ireland in party politics, 1885–7: An unpublished Conservative memoir', *Ir.Hist.Stud.*, xvi (1968–9), 154–72, 321–38, 444–71.

— , 'Herbert Gladstone, Forster and Ireland, 1881–2', *Ir.Hist.Stud.*, xvii (1970–1), 521–48: xviii (1972–3), 74–89.

Cosgrove, R.A., 'The relevance of Irish history: the Gladstone-Dicey debate about home rule, 1886–7', *Éire-Ireland*, xiii (1978), no.4, 6–21.

Cromwell, V., 'The losing of the initiative by the House of Commons, 1780–1914', *Trans.Royal Hist.Soc.*, 5th ser., xviii (1969), 1–24.

David, E., 'The Liberal party divided, 1916–8', *Hist.Journ.*, xiii (1970), 509–33.

Davis, H.B., 'Hobson and human welfare', *Science and Society*, xxi (1957), 291–318.

Davis, P., 'The Liberal Unionist party and the Irish policy of Lord Salisbury's government, 1886–92', *Hist.Journ.*, xviii (1975), 85–104.

De Roux, P.L., 'The "Curragh mutiny" and the House of Lords', *Éire-Ireland*, xvii (1983), no.2, 104–20.

Dewey, C.H., 'Celtic agrarian legislation and the Celtic revival: historicist implications of Gladstone's Irish and Scottish Land Acts, 1870–1886', *Past & Present*, no.64 (1974), 30–70.

Donnelly, M.S., 'J.W. Dafoe and Lionel Curtis: two concepts of commonwealth', *Political Studies*, viii (1960), 170–82.

Dunne. T., '*La traihson des clercs*: British intellectuals and the first home rule crisis', *Ir.Hist.Stud.*, xxiii (1982–3), 134–73.

— , 'Responses to Gladstonian home rule and land reform', *Ir.Hist.Stud.*, xxv (1986–7), 432–8.

Eisen, S., 'Huxley and the Positivists', *Vict.Stud.*, viii (1964–5), 337–58.

—, 'Herbert Spencer and the spectre of Comte', *Journ.Brit.Stud.*, vii (1967–8), 48–67.

—, 'Frederic Harrison and the religion of humanity', *South Atlantic Quarterly*, lxvi (1967), 574–90.

—, 'Frederic Harrison and Herbert Spencer: embattled unbelievers', *Vict.Stud.*, xii (1968–9), 33–56.

Ellinwood, D.C. Jr., 'The Round Table movement and India, 1909–20', *Journ. of Commonwealth Political Stud.*, ix (1971), 183–209.

Ensor, R.C.K., 'Some political and economic interactions in later Victorian England', *Trans.Royal Hist.Soc.*, 4th ser., xxxi (1949), 17–28.

Evans, S., 'The Conservatives and the redefinition of Unionism, 1912–21', *Twentieth-Century British History*, ix (1998), 1–27.

Fair, J.D., 'The King, the Constitution and Ulster: interparty negotiations of 1913 and 1914', *Éire-Ireland*, vi (1971), no.1, 35–52.

— , 'The Anglo-Irish Treaty of 1921: Unionist aspects of the peace', *Journ.Brit.Stud.*, xii (1972–3), 132–49.

Fanning, J.R., 'The Unionist party and Ireland, 1906–10', *Ir.Hist.Stud.*, xv (1966–7), 147–71.

Fieldhouse, D.K., ' "Imperialism": an historiographical revision', *Ec.Hist.Rev.*, 2nd ser., xiv (1961), 187–209.

Fitzpatrick, D., 'The geography of Irish nationalism, 1910–21', *Past & Present*, no.78 (1978), 113–44.

Ford, T.H., 'Dicey as a political journalist', *Political Studies*, xviii (1970), 220–35.

—, 'Dicey's conversion to Unionism', *Ir.Hist.Stud.*, xviii (1972–3), 552–82.

—, 'The remaking of a Unionist', *Éire-Ireland*, xvii (1983), no.1, 107–36.

Foster, R.F., 'History and the Irish question', *Trans.Royal Hist.Soc.*, 5th ser., xxxiii (1983), 169–92.

Freeden, M., 'J.A. Hobson as new Liberal theorist: some aspects of his social thought until 1914', *Journ.Hist.Ideas*, xxxiv (1973), no.3, 421–43.

—, 'Biological and evolutionary roots of new Liberalism in England', *Political Theory*, iv (1976), 471–90.

Gailey, A., 'Unionist rhetoric and local government reform', *Ir.Hist.Stud.*, xxiv (1984–5), 52–68.

— , 'King Carson: an essay in the invention of leadership', *Ir.Hist.Stud.*, xxx (1996–7), 66–87.

Galbraith, J.S., 'Cecil Rhodes and his "ccosmic dreams"', *Journ.Imp. & Comm.Hist.*, i (1973), 173–90.

Garvin, J.L., 'History of our own times', in F.H. Hooper (ed.), *These eventful years: the twentieth century in the making, as told by many of its makers: being the dramatic story of all that has happened throughout the world during the most momentous period in all history* (London, 1924, 2 vols.), i.1–194.

Garvin, T., 'Priests and patriots: Irish separatism and the fear of the modern, 1890–1914', *Ir.Hist.Stud.*, xxv (1986–7), 67–86.

Gilbert, B., 'David Lloyd George: land, the Budget, and social reform', *Amer.Hist.Rev.*, lxxxi (1976), 1058–66.

Gilley, S., 'English attitudes to the Irish in England, 1780–1900', in C. Holmes (ed.), *Immigrants and minorities in British society* (London, 1978), pp.81–110.

Goldman, L., 'The origins of British "social science": political economy, natural science and statistics, 1830–1835', *Hist.Journ.*, xxvi (1983), 587–616.

— , 'The Social Science Association, 1857–1886: a context for mid-Victorian Liberalism', *Eng.Hist.Rev.*, ci (1986), 95–134.

— , 'A peculiarity of the English? The Social Science Association and the absence of sociology in nineteenth-century Britain', *Past & Present*, no.114 (1987), 133–72.

Goodlad, G.D., 'The Liberal party and Gladstone's Land Purchase Bill of 1886', *Hist.Journ.*, xxxii (1989), 627–41.

Goodman, G.L., 'Liberal Unionism: the revolt of the Whigs', *Vict.Stud.*, ii (1958–9), 173–89.

Hamer, D.A., 'The Irish question and Liberal politics, 1886–94', *Hist.Journ.*, xii (1969), 511–32.

Harker, D., 'May Cecil Sharp be praised?', *History Workshop*, xiv (1982), 44–62.

Harrison, B., 'Mrs Thatcher and the intellectuals', *Twentieth-Century British History*, v (1994), 206–45.

Harrison, R., 'E.S. Beesly and Karl Marx', *International Review of Social History*, iv (1959), 22–58, 208–38.

Harvie, C, 'Ideology and home rule: James Bryce, A.V. Dicey and Ireland, 1880–7', *Eng.Hist.Rev.*, xci (1976), 298–314.

— , 'Ireland and the intellectuals, 1848–1922', *New Edinburgh Review*, nos. xxxviii–xxxix (1977), 35–42.

— , 'Anglo-Saxons into Celts: the Scottish intellectuals, 1760–1930', in T. Brown (ed.), *Celticism* (Amsterdam, 1996), pp.231–56.

Hawking, F.M.A., 'Defence and the role of Erskine Childers in the Treaty negotiations of 1921', *Ir.Hist.Stud.*, xxii (1980–1), 251–70.

Heim, J.C., 'Liberalism and the establishment of collective security in British foreign policy', *Trans.Royal Hist.Soc.*, 6th ser., v (1995), 91–110.

Helfhand, M., 'T.H. Huxley's *Evolution and ethics*: the politics of evolution and the evolution of politics', *Vict.Stud.*, xx (1976–7), 159–78.

Herrick, F.W., 'Gladstone and the concept of the "English-speaking Peoples"', *Journ.Brit.Stud.*, xii (1972–3), 150–6.

Hopkinson, M., 'The Craig-Collins pacts of 1922: two attempted reforms of the Northern Ireland government', *Ir.Hist.Stud.*, xxvii (1990–1), 145–58.

Howe, J., 'Liberalism, Lib-Labs and independent Labour in North Gloucestershire, 1890–1914', *Midland History*, xi (1986), 117–37.

Jackson, A., 'Irish Unionism and the Russellite threat', *Ir.Hist.Stud.*, xxv (1986–7), 376–404.

— , 'The failure of Unionism in Dublin, 1900', *Ir.Hist.Stud.*, xxvi (1988–9), 377–95.

— , 'Unionist politics and Protestant society in Edwardian Ireland', *Hist.Journ.*, xxxiii (1990), 839–66.

— , 'Unionist myths, 1912–85', *Past & Present*, no.136 (1992), 164–85.

— , 'British Ireland: what if home rule had been enacted in 1912?', in N. Ferguson (ed.), *Virtual history: alternatives and counterfactuals* (London, 1997), pp.175–227.

Jacobsen, P.D., 'Rosebery and Liberal Imperialism, 1899–1903', *Journ.Brit.Stud.*, xiii (1973–4), 83–103.

Jalland, P., 'United Kingdom devolution, 1910–14: political panacea or tactical diversion?', *Eng.Hist.Rev.*, xciv (1979), 757–83.

Jalland, P., and Stubbs, J.O., 'The Irish question after the outbreak of war in 1914: some unfinished party business', *Eng.Hist.Rev.*, xcvi (1981), 778–807.

Jenkins, T.A., 'Hartington, Chamberlain and the Unionist alliance, 1886–1895', *Parliamentary History*, xi (1992), 108–38.

Joll, J., 'Politicians and the freedom to choose: the case of July 1914', in A.P. Ryan (ed.), *The idea of freedom* (Oxford, 1979), pp.99–114.

Jones, G.A., 'Where "governing is the use of words"', *Hist.Journ.*, xix (1976), 251–6.

Kelleher, J.V., 'Matthew Arnold and the Celtic revival', in H. Levin (ed.), *Perspectives in criticism* (Cambridge, Mass., 1950), pp.197–222.

Kendle, J., 'The Round Table movement and home rule all round', *Hist.Journ.*, xi (1968), 332–53.

—, 'Federalism and the Irish problem in 1918', *History*, lvi (1971), 207–30.

Kinzer, B.L., 'J.S. Mill and Irish land: a reassessment', *Hist.Journ.*, xxvii (1984), 111–27.

Lavin, D., 'History, morals and the politics of empire: Lionel Curtis and the Round Table', in J. Bossy and P. Judd (eds), *Essays presented to Michael Roberts* (Belfast, 1976), pp.117–32.

Lawlor, S.M., 'Ireland from truce to Treaty: war or peace? July to October 1921', *Ir.Hist.Stud.*, xxii (1980–1), 49–64.

Lebow, N., 'British historians and Irish history', *Éire-Ireland*, viii (1973), no.4, 3–38.

Lloyd, T., 'Africa and Hobson's *Imperialism*', *Past & Present*, no.55 (1972), 130–53.

'Lord Oranmore's Journal, 1913–27', *Ir.Hist.Stud.*, xxix (1994–5), 553–93.

Loughlin, J.L., 'The Irish Protestant Home Rule Association and nationalist politics', *Ir.Hist.Stud.*, xxiv (1984–5), 341–60.

—, 'Joseph Chamberlain, English nationality and the Ulster question', *History*, lxxvii (1992), 202–19.

Lubenow, W.C., 'Irish home rule and the social basis of the great separation in the Liberal party in 1886', *Hist.Journ.*, xxviii (1985), 125–42.

—, 'Liberals and the national question', *Parliamentary History*, xiii (1994), 119–42.

Lyons, F.S.L., 'The Irish Unionist party and the devolution crisis of 1904–5', *Ir.Hist.Stud.*, vi (1948–9), 1–22.

—, The political ideas of Parnell', *Hist.Journ.*, xvi (1973), 749–75.

—, 'Parnellism and crime', *Trans.Royal Hist.Soc.*, 5th ser., xxiv (1974), 123–41.

Mason, T.W., 'Nineteenth-century Cromwell', *Past & Present*, no.40 (1968), 187–91.

Matthew, H.C.G., McKibbin, R.I., and Kay, J.A., 'The franchise factor in the rise of the Labour party', *Eng.Hist.Rev.*, xci (1976), 723–52.

McCartney, D., 'Lecky's *Leaders of public opinion in Ireland*', *Ir.Hist.Stud.*, xiv (1964–5), 119–41.

McClean, D., 'English radicals and the fate of Persia, 1907–13', *Eng.Hist.Rev.*, xciii (1978), 338–53.

McColgan, J., 'Implementing the 1921 Treaty: Lionel Curtis and constitutional procedure', *Ir.Hist.Stud.*, xx (1976–7), 310–33.

McCready, H.W., 'British labour and the Royal Commission on trade unions, 1867–9', *University of Toronto Quarterly*, xxiv (1953–4), 390–409.

—, 'Home rule and the Liberal party, 1899–1906', *Ir.Hist.Stud.*, xiii (1962–3), 316–48.

—, 'Sir Alfred Milner, the Liberal Party, and the Boer War', *Canadian Journ. of Hist.*, ii (1967), 13–44.

McDowell, R.B., 'Henry Dix Hutton – Positivists and cataloguer', *Friends of the Library of Trinity College Dublin Annual Bulletin*, (1952), 6–7.

McEwan, J.M., 'The Liberal party and the Irish question during the First World War', *Journ.Brit.Stud.*, xii (1972–3), 109–31.

Mitchell, H., 'Hobson revisited', *Journ.Hist.Ideas*, xxvi (1965), 397–416.

Moody, T.W., 'The *Times* versus Parnell and co., 1887–90', *Historical Studies*, vi (1968), 147–82.

Mulvely, H., 'The historian Lecky, opponent of Irish home rule', *Vict.Stud.*, i (1957–8), 337–51.

Murphy, R., 'Faction in the Conservative party and the home rule crisis', *History*, lxxi (1986), 222–34.

—, 'Walter Long and the making of the Government of Ireland Act, 1919–20', *Ir.Hist.Stud.*, xxv (1986–7), 82–96.

Nash, D., 'F.J. Gould and the Leicester Secular Society: a Positivist commonwealth in Edwardian politics', *Midland History*, xvi (1991), 126–40.

O'Callaghan, M., 'Language, nationality and cultural identity in the Free State, 1922–7: the *Irish Statesman* and the *Catholic Bulletin* reappraised', *Ir.Hist.Stud.*, xxiv (1984–5), 226–45.

—, 'Irish history, 1780–1980', *Hist.Journ.*, xxix (1986), 481–95.

O'Day, A., 'The Irish problem', in T.R. Gourish and A. O'Day (eds), *Later Victorian Britain, 1867–1900* (Basingstoke, 1988), pp.229–49.

O'Donovan, T., 'Ulster and home rule for Ireland to 1914', *Éire-Ireland*, xviii (1983), no.3, 6–22.

O'Halpin, E., 'H.E. Duke and the Irish administration, 1916–19', *Ir.Hist.Stud.*, xxii (1980–1), 362–76.

Orwell, G., 'Notes on nationalism', in *Decline of the English murder and other essays* (London, 1965), pp.155–75.

O'Tuathaigh, G., 'The Irish in nineteenth-century Britain: problems of integration', *Trans.Royal Hist.Soc.*, 5th ser., xxxi (1981), 149–73.

Packer, I., 'The Liberal cave and the 1914 Budget', *Eng.Hist.Rev.*, cxi (1996), 620–35.

Parker, C.J.W., 'The failure of liberal racialism: the racial ideas of E.A. Freeman', *Hist.Journ.*, xxiv (1981), 825–46.

Parry, J.R., 'Religion and the collapse of Gladstone's first government, 1870–4', *Hist.Journ.*, xxv (1982), 71–101.

—, 'High and low politics in modern Britain', *Hist.Journ.*, xxix (1986), 753–70.

Peatling, G.K., 'Who fears to speak of politics? John Kells Ingram and hypothetical nationalism', *Ir.Hist.Stud.*, xxxi (1998–9), 202–21.

—, 'New Liberalism, J.L. Hammond and the Irish question, 1897–1949', *Historical Research*, lxxiii (2000), 48–65.
Perkin, H., 'Individualism versus collectivism in nineteenth-century Britain: a false antithesis', *Journ.Brit.Stud.*, xvii (1977–8), 105–18.
Phillips, G.D., 'Lord Willoughby de Broke and the politics of radical toryism, 1909–1914', *Journ.Brit.Stud.*, xx (1980–1), 205–24.
—, 'The Whig Lords and Liberalism, 1886–93', *Hist.Journ.*, xxiv (1981), 167–73.
Pilling, N., 'Lecky and Dicey: English and Irish histories', *Éire-Ireland*, xvi (1981), no.3, 43–57.
Powell, D., 'The new Liberalism and the rise of Labour', *Hist.Journ.*, xxix (1986), 369–93.
Pugh, M.D., 'Asquith, Bonar Law and the first coalition', *Hist.Journ.*, xvii (1974), 813–36.
—, ' "Yorkshire and the new Liberalism"?', *Journ.Mod.Hist.*, l (1978), no.3, on demand supplement, D1139–D1155.
Ram, A., 'The parliamentary context of cabinet government, 1868–1874', *Eng.Hist.Rev.*, xcix (1984), 739–69.
Ramsey, A.D., 'Who were the Auxillaries?', *Hist.Journ.*, xxxv (1992), 665–9.
Roach, J.P., 'Liberalism and the Victorian intelligentsia', *Cambridge Historical Journal*, xiii (1957), 71–88.
Robinson, R., and Gallagher, J., 'The imperialism of free trade', *Ec.Hist.Rev.*, 2nd ser., vi (1953), 1–15.
Rodner, W., 'Leaguers, Covenanters, moderates: British support for Ulster, 1913–4', *Éire-Ireland*, xvii (1982), no.3, 68–85.
Savage, D.W., 'The attempted home rule settlement of 1916', *Éire-Ireland*, ii (1967), no.3, 132–45.
—, ' "The Parnell of Wales has become the Chamberlain of England": Lloyd George and the Irish question', *Journ.Brit.Stud.*, xii (1972–3), 86–108.
Schroeder, P.W., 'Munich and the British tradition', *Hist.Journ.*, xix (1976), 223–43.
Schuhard, R., ' "An attendant Lord": H.W. Nevinson's friendship with W.B. Yeats', in W. Gould (ed.), *Yeats Annual*, no.7 (Basingstoke, 1990), 90–130.
Searle, G.R., 'The Edwardian Liberal party and business', *Eng.Hist.Rev.*, xcviii (1983), 28–60.
Shannon, C.B., 'The Ulster Liberal Unionists and local government reform, 1885–98', *Ir.Hist.Stud.*, xviii (1972–3), 407–23.
Simon, W.M., 'Auguste Comte's English disciples', *Vict.Stud.*, vii (1963–4), 161–72.
Skinner, Q., 'Meaning and understanding in the history of ideas', *History and Theory*, viii (1963), 3–53.
Smith, J., 'Bluff, Bluster and Brinkmanship: Andrew Bonar Law and the Third Home Rule Bill', *Hist.Journ.*, xxxvi (1993), 161–78.
Smith, P., 'Liberalism as authority and discipline', *Hist.Journ.*, xxxii (1989), 723–37.
Soffer, R.N., 'Why do disciplines fail? The strange case of British sociology', *Eng.Hist.Rev.*, xcvii (1982), 767–802.
Steele, E.D., 'Ireland and the Empire in the 1860s: imperial precedents for Gladstone's first Irish Land Act', *Hist.Journ.*, xi (1968), 64–83.

—, 'J.S. Mill and the Irish question: the principles of political economy, 1848–1865', *Hist.Journ.*, xiii (1970), 216–36.

—, 'J.S. Mill and the Irish question: reform and the integrity of the Empire, 1865–1870', *Hist.Journ.*, xiii (1970), 419–50.

—, 'Gladstone and Ireland', *Ir.Hist.Stud.*, xvii (1970–1), 58–88.

Stokes, E., 'Milnerism', *Hist.Journ.*, v (1962), 47–60.

Stubbs, J.O., 'The Unionists and Ireland, 1916–1918', *Hist.Journ.*, xxxiii (1990), 867–94.

Stuchtey, B., 'Literature, liberty and life of the nation: British historiography from Macaulay to Trevelyan', in S. Berger, M. Donovan and K. Passmore (eds), *Writing national histories: Western Europe since 1800* (London, 1999), pp.30–46.

Studdert-Kennedy, G.S., 'Political science and political theology: Lionel Curtis, federalism and India', *Journ.Imp.& Comm.Hist.*, xxiv (1996), 197–217.

Tanner, D., 'The strange death of Liberal England', *Hist.Journ.*, xxxvii (1994), 971–9.

Tawney, R., 'J.L. Hammond, 1872–1949', *Proc.Brit.Acad.*, lxvi (1960), 267–94.

Taylor, A.J.P., 'Politics and the First World War', *Proc.Brit.Acad.*, lxv (1959), 67–95.

Taylor, G.P., 'Cecil Rhodes and the second Home Rule Bill', *Hist.Journ.*, xiv (1971), 771–81.

Thompson, P., 'Liberals, radical and labour in London, 1880–1900', *Past & Present*, no.27 (1964), 73–101.

Towey, T.F., 'The reaction of the British government to the 1922 Collins-de Valera pact', *Ir.Hist.Stud.*, xxii (1980–1), 65–78.

Trentmann, F., 'Wealth versus welfare: the British Left between free trade and national political economy before the First World War', *Historical Research*, lxx (1997), 71–98.

Tulloch, H., 'A.V. Dicey and the Irish question, 1870–1922', *The Irish Jurist*, new series, xv (1980), 825–40.

Turner, J., 'The formation of Lloyd George's "garden suburb": "Fabian-like Milnerite penetration"?', *Hist.Journ.*, xx (1977), 165–84.

Walker, B., 'The Irish electorate, 1868–1915', *Ir.Hist.Stud.*, xviii (1972–3), 359–406.

Ward, A., 'Frewen's Anglo-American campaign for federalism, 1910–1921', *Ir.Hist.Stud.*, xv (1966–7), 256–75.

—, 'Lloyd George and the 1918 Irish conscription crisis', Hist.Journ., xvii (1974), 107–29.

Warren, A.L., 'Gladstone, land and social construction in Ireland', *Parliamentary History*, ii (1983), 153–73.

Weiler, P., 'The new Liberalism of L.T. Hobhouse', *Vict.Stud.*, xvi (1972–3), 141–61.

Weinroth, H.S., 'The British radicals and the balance of power, 1902–1914', *Hist.Journ.*, xiii (1970), 653–82.

Wyatt, A., 'Froude, Lecky and the humblest Irishman', *Ir.Hist.Stud.*, xix (1974–5), 261–85.

Yearwood, P., '"On the safe and right line": the Lloyd George Government and the origins of the League of Nations, 1916–1918', *Hist.Journ.*, xxxii (1989), 131–55.

Zastoupil, L., 'Moral government: J.S. Mill on Ireland', *Hist.Journ.*, xxvi (1983), 707–17.

Biographical Notes

Amery, Leopold Charles Maurice Stennett (1873–1955) Politician. Born in India, the son of a civil servant. Educated at Harrow, Oxford and the Inner Temple. MP for South Birmingham from 1911. Acted as Milner's secretary from 1916–21. Parliamentary Secretary to the Admiralty from 1921–2, promoted to First Lord of the Admiralty, 1922. Secretary of State for the Colonies from 1924–9 and also Secretary of State for Dominion Affairs from 1925–9. Secretary of State for India from 1940–5.

Astor, Waldorf (Second Viscount Astor) (1879–1952) Public servant. Effective proprietor of the *Observer* after its purchase in 1911 by his father the first Viscount Astor. Unionist MP for Plymouth from 1910 until 1919 (when he was succeeded by his wife Nancy, the first woman to take a seat in the House of Commons), and associate of the Round Table.

Beesly, Edward Spencer (1831–1915) Historian and writer, one-quarter Irish on his mother's side. Educated at Wadham College, Oxford. Professor of Modern History at University College, London, 1860–93. Chaired the first meeting of the International Working Men's Association in 1864. President of the LPS, 1878–1901. Editor of the *Positivist Review*, 1893–1901.

Bentinck, Lord Henry Cavendish (1863–1931) Politician. Unionist (and later a Conservative) MP 1886–1892, 1895–1906 and 1910–1929. Served in the Boer and the Great Wars.

Berkeley, George Fitz-Hardinge (1870–?) Historian. Member of the Liberal home rule committee in 1911. Saw active service during the Great War. Founded the Peace with Ireland Council in 1920. His most notable historical work was *Italy in the making* (1932–40).

Bourne, Francis Alphonsus (1861–1935) Cardinal. Born Clapham, one-quarter Irish on his mother's side. Educated at theological colleges in England and France. Appointed Bishop of Epiphania in 1896, Bishop of Southwark in 1897 and Archbishop of Westminster in 1903. Appointed Cardinal Priest in 1911.

Brailsford, Henry Noel (1873–1958) Writer. Contributed to the radical and labour press throughout his life and wrote a number of influential books on socialism and on international relations. Joined the Independent Labour party in 1907 and edited the *New Leader* from 1922–6.

Brand, Robert Henry (Baron Brand) (1878–1963) Banker and administrator. Permanent secretary of the Intercolonial Council of the Transvaal and the Orange River Colony from 1904, and secretary of the Transvaal delegation to the South African constitutional conventions of 1908–9. Contributor to, and member of the editorial board of, the *Round Table* after 1910.

Bridges, John Henry (1832–1906) Health inspector, physician and writer. Educated at Wadham College, Oxford. Health inspector for the local government board, 1869–91. First President of the EPC in 1878–9. Author of books on a range of subjects, including public health, Positivism and French history.

Bright, John (1811–1889) Statesman. Prominent popular leader and Liberal MP from the 1840s to the 1880s. His staunch opposition to imperialism inspired him to resign from Gladstone's second government in 1882. Although an advocate of reform in Ireland, his opposition to home rule in 1886 was an important factor in the defeat of the first Home Rule Bill.

Bryce, James (Viscount Bryce of Dechmont) (1838–1922) Jurist, historian, and politician. Born Belfast, of Protestant descent. Regius Professor of Civil Law at Oxford, 1870–93. Under-Secretary of State for Foreign Affairs in 1886. Chancellor of the Duchy of Lancaster from 1892–4. President of the Board of Trade from 1894–5. Chief Secretary for Ireland, 1905–6. British Ambassador to the United States of America, 1907–13.

Cadbury, George (1839–1922) Businessman. Prominent member of the Quaker Cadbury dynasty, the founders of the cocoa and chocolate manufacturing company Cadbury Brothers. Founder of the Bournville Village Trust and proprietor of the *Daily News* from 1901.

Campbell, George Douglas (Eight Duke of Argyll) (1823–1900) Whig statesman. A minister in every Whig or Liberal government from 1853 until he resigned in protest at Gladstone's 1881 Irish Land Bill. Also a critic of Gladstone's home rule policy.

Casement, Roger David (1864–1916) Civil servant and Irish nationalist. Knighted in 1912 for his distinguished career as a consular official in Africa and South America. In 1914 he opposed the Redmondite Nationalists' support of the imperial war effort. With a measure of support from the German authorities, he helped to organise a wartime insurrection against British rule in Ireland, but his attempted landing in April 1916 failed and he was executed.

Childers, Robert Erskine (1870–1922) Author and politician. Born London of part Irish background. Author of the popular novel *The riddle of the sands* (1903).

Married the Bostonian Mary Alden Osgood in 1904. Assisted the illegal importation of arms for the National Volunteers at Howth in July 1914. Served with distinction in the imperial forces during the Great War, but thereafter joined Sinn Féin. Appointed Minister of Propaganda by the self-constituted Dáil Éireann in May 1921. Arrested and shot by the Free State authorities in November 1922 after opposing the Anglo-Irish Treaty.

Congreve, Richard (1818–99) English Positivist leader. Educated Wadham College, Oxford where he also taught for a decade. Took holy orders in 1842, but returned his letters of ordination in 1857 after meeting Comte. Founded the London Positivist Society in 1867, and what ultimately became the Church of Humanity in Chapel Street, London, in 1870. Published many books, sermons and translations of Comte's writings.

Coupland, Sir Reginald (1884–1952) Historian. Elected Fellow and Lecturer in ancient history at Trinity College, Oxford in 1907. Beit Lecturer in Colonial History from 1913–20 and Beit Professor of Colonial History from 1920–48 at Oxford.

Courtney, Leonard Henry, (Baron Courtney of Penwith) (1832–1918) Statesman. Occupied three minor posts in Gladstone's second ministry, but opposed Gladstone's Home Rule Bills. A persistent critic of imperialism.

Craik, Sir George Lille (1874–1929) Administrator and senior police officer. Educated New College, Oxford. Served in the Boer War and as a legal advisor in the Transvaal thereafter. Chief Constable of the Metropolitan Police from 1910–4. Served with distinction during the Great War.

Crompton, Albert (1843–1908) Born Liverpool, brother of Henry. Educated Trinity College, Cambridge. Trained as a barrister. Joined the Liverpool shipping firm Holt's in 1872. Effective director of Liverpool Positivism, 1890–1908.

Crompton, Henry (1836–1904) Born Liverpool, educated in London and Cambridge. Clerk of assize on the Chester-North Wales circuit, 1858–1903. Served on the Jamaica Committee (which attempted the prosecution of Governor Eyre of Jamaica) with Harrison and Beesly in 1867. Leader of the Church of Humanity, Chapel Street, 1898–1902.

Curtis, Lionel George (1872–1955) Writer and public servant. Educated New College, Oxford. Fought with the City Imperial Volunteers during the Boer War, and served in South Africa in an administrative capacity after that war. Closely involved in the Round Table movement for most of his life, and wrote several books and articles on imperial affairs. Part of the British delegations to the Paris Peace Conference of 1919 and the Anglo-Irish Treaty negotiations of 1921.

Devlin, Joseph (1871–1934) Irish Nationalist politician. An Ulster Roman Catholic, he was elected to Parliament in 1902. President of the Ancient Order of

Hibernians, 1905–1918. Elected to the Northern Ireland Parliament in 1921, though he did not initially take his seat.

Dicey, Albert Venn (1835–1922) Jurist. Vinerian Professor of English Law at Oxford, 1882–1909. Author of a number of highly influential books, including critiques of Gladstonian home rule.

Dove, John, (1872–1934) Journalist. Worked with the Kindergarten in South Africa after the Boer War, and in the Intelligence Department of the War Office during the Great War. Editor of the *Round Table,* 1920–1934.

Feetham, Richard (1874–1965) Judge. Member of the Legislative Council of the Transvaal, 1907–10, and of the South African Legislative Assembly, 1915–23. Served as a judge on the South African Supreme Court, 1923–44. Chancellor of the University of the Witwatersrand from 1949–61.

Fisher, Herbert Albert Laurens (1865–1940) Historian and statesman. Liberal MP, 1916–1926. President of the Board of Education from 1916–22, the most important measure during his time in office being the 1918 Education Act. Warden of New College, Oxford from 1926.

Gardiner, Alfred George (1865–1946) Author and journalist. Editor of the *Daily News*, from 1902 to 1919. Continued to write independently thereafter and published several collections of essays.

Garvin, James Louis (1868–1947) Journalist. The younger son of an Irish immigrant who was lost at sea when Garvin was two, Garvin was brought up as a Roman Catholic. Editor of the *Observer*, 1908–42. One of Britain's most prolific and widely-read early twentieth-century journalists.

Gooch, George Peabody (1873–1968) Historian. Editor of the *Contemporary Review* from 1911 to 1960. Liberal MP for Bath, 1906–10.

Green (née Stopford), Alice Sophia Amelia (also known as Alice Stopford Green) (1847–1929) Historian. Daughter of the Archdeacon of Meath. Wrote several books on Irish history after her husband J. R. Green's death in 1883. Appointed a senator in the Irish Free State, 1922.

Grigg, Edward William Macleay (Baron Altrincham) (1879–1955) Administrator and politician. Educated New College, Oxford. After working on the *Times* and the *Outlook*, in 1913 he became joint editor of the *Round Table*. Saw distinguished active service in the Great War. Private Secretary to Lloyd George 1921–2. Governor of Kenya from 1925–30. Joint Parliamentary Under-Secretary at the War Office during the Second World War.

Gwynn, Stephen Lucius (1864–1950) Author and Irish nationalist politician. A Protestant and the grandson of William Smith O'Brien, the Irish rebel of 1848. Redmondite Nationalist MP for Galway City, 1906–1918. Served in the Connaught Rangers during the Great War. Member of the Irish Convention in 1917.

Hammond, John Lawrence Le Breton (1872–1949) Journalist and Historian. Educated St John's College, Oxford. Writer of several books on eighteenth- and nineteenth-century social and political history, especially with his wife Lucy Barbara Hammond (née Bradby). A contributor to the Liberal press throughout his life.

Hammond (née Bradby), Lucy Barbara (1873–1961) Historian. Educated Lady Margaret Hall, Oxford. Married Lawrence Hammond in 1901. Author of several works in social and political eighteenth- and nineteenth-century history along with her husband.

Harmsworth, Alfred Charles William (Viscount Northcliffe) (1865–1922) Journalist and newspaper proprietor. Born near Dublin. Started his own publishing business in London in 1887. Founded the *Daily Mail* in 1896. Proprietor of the *Observer* from 1905–11, and of the *Times* from 1908–22.

Harrison, Frederic (1831–1923) Writer and barrister. One-quarter Irish by descent. Educated at Wadham College, Oxford. Author of the Minority Report of the Royal Commission on Trade Unions in 1867–9. President of the English Positivist Committee, 1879–1904. London County Councillor from 1889–93. A prolific writer on a remarkable range of subjects.

Hewins, William Albert Samuel (1865–1931) Economist. Educated at Pembroke College, Oxford. Director of London School of Economics from 1895–1903. Secretary of the Tariff Commission from 1903–1917. MP for Hereford City from 1912–8 and Under-Secretary of State for the Colonies from 1917–8.

Hobhouse, Leonard Trelawny (1864–1929) Philosopher and writer. Educated Corpus Christi College, Oxford. London University's joint first Professor of Sociology, 1907–29. Frequent contributor to the *Manchester Guardian* and the author of many books and articles on philosophy, sociology and politics.

Hobson, John Atkinson (1858–1940) Economist and writer. Educated Lincoln College, Oxford. Author of several books, mostly on economic subjects, the best known of which is perhaps *Imperialism: a study* (1902). Also helped to found the Union of Democratic Control during the Great War.

Hutton, Henry Dix (1825–1908) Barrister and writer. Educated in London, Dublin and Leipzig. He met Comte in 1854 and became a disciple. Worked as a catalogue editor at Trinity College Dublin Library, 1872–87. A contributor to the

Fortnightly Review and to *International policy*, he also published a number of pamphlets and books on Positivism and on the Irish land issue.

Ingram, John Kells (1823–1907) Economist, poet and academic. Educated Trinity College Dublin, where he occupied a series of posts from 1846 to 1899. Published *A history of political economy* (1888), and a number of books on Positivism in the final years of his life. Gave two important addresses, one as president of the economic science and statistics section of the British Association for the Advancement of Science in 1878, and one to the Trades Union Congress in Dublin in 1880.

Kerr, Philip Henry (Eleventh Marquess of Lothian) (1882–1940) Statesman. A member of one of Britain's most prominent Roman Catholic families, though he became a believer in Christian Science. Educated at the Oratory School, Edgbaston and at New College, Oxford. Occupied a series of administrative posts in South Africa from 1904. Edited the *Round Table* from 1910–11. Private secretary to Lloyd George from 1916–21. Chancellor of the Duchy of Lancaster in 1931 and Under-Secretary of State for India from 1931–2. British Ambassador to the United States from 1939–40.

Lecky, William Edward Hartpole (1838–1903) Political historian and historian of ideas. Born Dublin. Educated Trinity College Dublin. The most eminent historian in Ireland of his day. Unionist MP for Dublin University from 1895–1902.

Lynd, Robert Wilson (1879–1949) Journalist and writer. Born and educated in Belfast, the son of a Presbyterian minister. Moved to England in 1901 and from 1908 until his death he was a frequent contributor to the *Daily News*, the *Nation* and the *New Statesman*.

MacSwiney, Terence Joseph (1879–1920) Irish nationalist politician. Implicated in the Easter Rising and imprisoned from 1916–17. Elected to the Dáil in 1919. Lord Mayor of Cork from March 1920. Arrested in August 1920 and died after seventy-three days on hunger strike.

Martin, Hugh (1881–?) Journalist. Born in Sussex. Worked for the *Daily News* from 1907. He acted as a special correspondent from a variety of locations during the Great War and frequently wrote on Irish politics after 1916. Also wrote an entertaining biography of Winston Churchill, *Battle* (1932).

Marvin, Francis Sydney (1863–1942) Educationalist and writer. Educated at St John's College, Oxford. Worked as a school inspector for the Board of Education (as did his wife, Edith Deverell). Author and editor of several historical works, including the 'Unity History' series from 1915.

Massingham, Henry William (1860–1924) Journalist. Born in Norwich, the son of a Methodist preacher. After working on the *Star* (as editor from 1890), he edited the *Labour World* and, from 1895, the *Daily Chronicle*, resigning at the start of the Boer War. Edited the *Nation* from 1907.

Masterman, Charles Frederick Gurney (1873–1927) Politician, author, and journalist. Educated at Christ's College, Cambridge. Elected Liberal MP for West Ham (North) in 1906 and occupied a series of minor posts in the pre-war Liberal government. Wrote a series of books on social conditions and politics, and contributed frequently to the Liberal press.

Mill, John Stuart (1806–1873) Philosopher. Educated by his father the Utilitarian James Mill. Author of several widely-read books on philosophy, religion, politics and economics, and a respected commentator on political and social affairs. Prominent advocate of female emancipation. Liberal MP for Westminster, 1865–8.

Milner, Alfred (Viscount Milner) (1854–1925) Statesman. Educated in Tübingen, London and Oxford. Chairman of the Board of Inland Revenue from 1892–1897. Member of Lloyd George's War Cabinet from 1916–18. Secretary of State for War, 1918. Secretary of State for the Colonies from 1918–21.

Montague, Charles Edward (1867–1928) Journalist and writer. The son of an Irish priest who recanted and settled in England. Joined the *Guardian* in 1890 and returned to the paper in 1918 after seeing active service during the Great War. Also published several books on that war.

Monypenny, William Flavelle (1866–1912) Journalist and writer. Joined the *Times* in 1893. His work at the paper was interrupted only by his active service in the Boer War, and by his editing the Johannesburg *Star* from 1899–1903.

Morgan, John Hartman (1876–1955) Lawyer and writer. Twice stood unsuccessfully as a Liberal candidate in the 1910 Elections. Professor of Constitutional Law at University College, London from 1915–41, and, in 1916, counsel for the defence for Roger Casement.

Morison, James Augustus Cotter (1832–1888) Historian and writer. Educated Lincoln College, Oxford, where he taught in the 1850s and 1860s, numbering John Morley among his pupils. Heavily influenced by French culture, especially Comte. Contributed to the *Saturday Review* and the *Fortnightly Review*, and wrote several books, including *The service of man* (1887).

Morley, John (Viscount Morley of Blackburn) (1838–1923) Statesman and writer. Educated Lincoln College, Oxford. Editor of the *Fortnightly Review*, 1867–82, and of the *Pall Mall Gazette* in the 1880s. Chief Secretary for Ireland, 1886 and 1892–5. Secretary of State for India from 1905–11. Lord President of the Council, 1911–14. Author of books on a wide range of subjects, including French thought.

Murray, George Gilbert Aimé (1866–1957) Classical scholar. Born in Sydney of Irish descent. Professor of Greek at Glasgow, 1889–1899. Regius Professor of Greek at Oxford, 1908–36. Extremely active between the wars in the League of Nations Union, and, after 1939, in the United Nations Association.

Nevinson, Henry Woodd (1856–1941) Journalist, author and political campaigner. Educated Christ Church, Oxford. Frequently acted as a correspondent in the Liberal press on wars and revolutions. Also an accomplished writer of prose. Nevinson married twice, to Margaret Wynne in 1884, and, after her death, to Evelyn Sharp in 1933.

O'Brien, William (1852–1928) Irish nationalist politician. Prominent in the Parnellite land agitation and thrice imprisoned by the authorities. Founded the United Irish League in 1898, and, after a rift with the 'official' Nationalist leadership, the 'All for Ireland' League in 1910. After 1918, his Independent Nationalist party withdrew from contesting elections to leave the path clear for Sinn Féin.

O'Connor, Thomas Power (1848–1929) Irish Nationalist politician. Elected Parnellite MP for Galway in 1880. In 1885 he was elected to a parliamentary seat in Liverpool, assisted by the votes of many Irish immigrants, which he held until his death.

Oliver, Frederick Scott (1864–1934) Businessman and publicist. Born in Edinburgh and educated in Edinburgh, Cambridge and London. Joined Debenham and Freebody in 1892. Wrote articles and pamphlets on many political topics, including federalism and the Irish question, and also the influential *Alexander Hamilton* (1906).

Palmer, William Waldergrave, Second Earl of Selborne (1859–1942) Statesman. Under-Secretary of State for the Colonies from 1895–1900. First Lord of the Admiralty from 1900–1905. High Commissioner for South Africa from 1905–1910. President of the Board of Agriculture and Fisheries from 1915–16, resigning in protest at home rule. Married Lady Beatrix Maud Cecil, daughter of the third Marquess of Salisbury (the Unionist Prime Minister).

Phillips, Walter Alison (1864–1950) Historian and contributor to the *Encyclopaedia Britannica* and the *Times*. Lecky Professor of Modern History at Trinity College Dublin from 1914–39.

Plunkett, Sir Horace Curzon (1854–1932) Statesman and founder of the Irish cooperative movement. Son of Lord Dunsany. Unionist MP for South County Dublin, 1892–1900. President of the Irish Agricultural Organisation Society from 1894–9 and after 1907. Founded the Irish Dominion League in 1919. Appointed a senator in the Irish Free State, 1922.

Quin, Malcolm (1854–1946) Positivist and political activist. Son of an Irish Protestant civil servant and an English mother. Quin came to Positivism through the Leicester Secular Society and established a Positivist church in Newcastle in 1882. This closed in 1910 and Quin subsequently became a Catholic lay worshipper sympathetic to the Labour movement.

Robinson, George Geoffrey (1874–1944) Editor. Educated Eton and Magdalen College, Oxford. Edited the Johannesburg *Star* from 1905. Editor of the London *Times* for two periods (1912–19, 1922–41), and also twice editor of the *Round Table* (in 1920 and 1941–4). Changed his surname to Dawson in 1917.

Russell, George William, better known as Æ (1867–1935) Poet and writer. Born in Armagh. Joined the Irish Agricultural Organisation Society in 1897. Edited the *Irish Homestead,* 1906–1923 and the *Irish Statesman,* 1923–1930. Member of the Irish Convention in 1917. Published collections of poetry and books on economics and religion.

Scott, Charles Prestwich (1846–1932) Editor. Educated Corpus Christi College, Oxford. Editor of the *Manchester Guardian* until 1929 when succeeded by his son Ted. Also became proprietor of the paper from 1905 after the death of his cousin the then proprietor John Edward Taylor. Liberal MP for Leigh, 1895–1905.

Sharp, Evelyn (1869–1955) Writer and suffragist, twice imprisoned for her political activities before the Great War. After the war she joined the Labour party and wrote for the *Daily Herald* and the *Manchester Guardian*, notably on Germany, Russia and Ireland.

Shaw, George Bernard (1856–1950) Playwright and Fabian socialist. Born in Dublin. Joined the Fabian Society in 1884 and edited *Fabian Essays* in 1889. His most famous plays include *Saint Joan*, *John Bull's Other Island* and *Pygmalion*. Awarded the Nobel prize for literature in 1925.

Sheehy-Skeffington, Francis (1878–1916) and Sheehy-Skeffington, Hanna (1877–1946) Women's rights activists, married in 1903. Co-founders of the Irish Women's Franchise League in 1908. After Francis's death, Hanna was Director of Organisation for Sinn Féin during the truce of 1921, and a member of the Fianna Fáil executive from 1926–7.

Smith, Goldwin (1823–1910) Historian and writer. Regius Professor of Modern History at Oxford, 1858–1866. Moved to America (and ultimately to Canada) in 1868, occupying a series of posts at Cornell University. An outspoken critic of imperialism, clericalism and Irish home rule.

Swinny, Shapland Hugh (1857–1923) Barrister and writer, born in Dublin. Educated St John's College, Cambridge. Joined the LPS in 1885, President in

1901–23. EPC President, 1904–23. Chairman of the Council of the Sociological Society, 1907–9. Secretary of the South Africa Conciliation Committee, 1900–2.

Waller, Rev. Bolton Charles (1890–1936) Protestant churchman. Served in the Great War. Secretary of the Peace with Ireland Council from 1921–1922. On the North-Eastern Boundary Bureau of the Free State Government from 1923–4. Secretary of the League of Nations Society of Ireland from 1927–1930.

Williams, (Arthur Frederick) Basil (1867–1950) Historian. Twice stood unsuccessfully as a Liberal candidate in the 1910 elections. Kingsford Professor of History at McGill University (1921–5), and Professor of History at Edinburgh University thereafter.

Zimmern, Sir Alfred Eckhard (1879–1957) Scholar and historian. Born in Surbiton of German and Jewish descent. Wilson Professor of International Politics at the University of Aberystwyth from 1919–21. Montague Burton Professor of International Relations at Oxford from 1930–44.

Index

(NB: Page references in *italics* indicate definitions or explanations of concepts or events, or biographical notes about individuals.)